U.S.S.R. LABOR CAMPS

HEARINGS

BEFORE THE

SUBCOMMITTEE TO INVESTIGATE THE ADMINISTRATION OF THE INTERNAL SECURITY ACT AND OTHER INTERNAL SECURITY LAWS

OF THE

COMMITTEE ON THE JUDICIARY
UNITED STATES SENATE
NINETY-THIRD CONGRESS

FEBRUARY 1, 1973

Printed for the use of the Committee on the Judiciary

U.S.S.R. LABOR CAMPS

ISBN 0-88264-159-x

Copyright © 1987 By Living Sacrifice Book Co.
Printed in U.S.A.

COMMITTEE ON THE JUDICIARY

JAMES O. EASTLAND, Mississippi, *Chairman*

JOHN L. McCLELLAN, Arkansas
SAM J. ERVIN, Jr., North Carolina
PHILIP A. HART, Michigan
EDWARD M. KENNEDY, Massachusetts
BIRCH BAYH, Indiana
QUENTIN N. BURDICK, North Dakota
ROBERT C. BYRD, West Virginia
JOHN V. TUNNEY, California

ROMAN L. HRUSKA, Nebraska
HIRAM L. FONG, Hawaii
HUGH SCOTT, Pennsylvania
STROM THURMOND, South Carolina
MARLOW W. COOK, Kentucky
CHARLES McC. MATHIAS, Jr., Maryland
EDWARD J. GURNEY, Florida

SUBCOMMITTEE TO INVESTIGATE THE ADMINISTRATION OF THE INTERNAL SECURITY ACT AND OTHER INTERNAL SECURITY LAWS

JAMES O. EASTLAND, Mississippi, *Chairman*

JOHN L. McCLELLAN, Arkansas
SAM J. ERVIN, Jr., North Carolina
BIRCH BAYH, Indiana

HUGH SCOTT, Pennsylvania
STROM THURMOND, South Carolina
MARLOW W. COOK, Kentucky
EDWARD J. GURNEY, Florida

J. G. SOURWINE, *Chief Counsel*
SAMUEL J. SCOTT, *Associate Counsel*
WARREN LITTMAN, *Associate Counsel*
JOHN R. NORPEL, *Director of Research*
ALFONSO L. TARABOCHIA, *Chief Investigator*

(II)

NOTES ON TESTIMONY OF AVRAHAM SHIFRIN

[During the course of the hearing of February 2, 1973, Counsel for the subcommittee recommended that "in the interest of continuity and clarity," and for the purpose of completing the record, the entire text of the staff summaries prepared in advance of the hearing be incorporated into the hearing record. The Chairman ordered this done. It was decided to print the staff summaries preceding the record of the hearing proper because it was felt that this would facilitate the reading of the hearing record.]

BASIC CONTENT OF TESTIMONY

According to Shifrin, the concentration camps house far fewer people than they did during the peak years of Stalin's terror. But the sad fact is that there are millions of political prisoners in the concentration camps and prisons of the Soviet Union today; that the camps, far from having disappeared, number into the thousands; and that the conditions are just as bestial as they were in the days of Stalin.

That conditions in Soviet concentration camps have changed little since the times of Stalin is evidenced by numerous letters received by Alexander Solzhenitsyn after the publication of his novel *One Day In The Life of Ivan Denisovich*. Excerpts from these letters were released by Solzhenitsyn and published in the collection of his works (v. 5, *Possev*, West Germany, 1969). In general, these letters said that conditions were very much the same, or that they were even worse than those described by Solzhenitsyn.

A group of prisoners of the Ust-Nera camp, for example, wrote: "Our conditions now are much worse (worse than those described in your novel). We are not being beaten, but soldiers say that we should all be done away with. Where does such hatred come from in boys 18–20 years old? They are obviously being incited . . . In December 1962 [when the novel was published] out of a total of 300 prisoners in our zone, 190 of us were suffering from scurvy."

Thousands and thousands of men and women languish in concentration camps because of their faith in God. The Communists want to destroy all confessional groups, all religions. The believers cannot pray, they are denied the opportunity to observe religious holidays. The guards deride them, molest them, and throw them into punitive cells whenever they catch them praying.

This is a situation, says Shifrin, that should be of profound concern to the entire free world. It should be of concern, first, on moral and humanitarian grounds. But beyond this, the existence of this massive concentration camp system poses a serious danger to the security of the Free World. To the extent that the men in the Kremlin are able to repress all dissident opinion and all restraining voices, they are freer to engage in subversion and blackmail and expansion abroad.

USSR
CONCENTRATION
CAMPS 1972

Shifrin feels it to be his moral duty to tell about the new wave of arrests in the Soviet Union, about starvation in concentration camps and prisons, about the mortal danger to which sick prisoners—like Silva Zalmanson, Eduard Kuznetsov, and Anatoli Altman—are exposed there. Shifrin recalls the conditions under which Yuri Galanskov died only a few weeks ago. His friends had appealed to the free world time and again. They warned how gravely ill Galanskov was, but nobody seemed to have listened to them. (A pathetic appeal from Galanskov, written shortly before his death, is reprinted in the Appendix to part 2 on page 120.)

The concentration camp map of the Soviet Union which Shifrin prepared (see opposite page) presents only a small part of the total picture—"there would not have been enough room on the map to stick in a flag for every single camp." Each red flag on his map may stand for several camps in the vicinity of a single city. (In the reproduction of the map on the opposite page, the red flags show up as gray shaded triangular flags.) Each rectangular black flag in the middle of a shaded area stands for a concentration camp complex—which may contain a hundred or more camps and several hundred thousand prisoners.

Shifrin is also submitting for the record a blown up map showing the camps along the private KGB railroad which runs from Potma to Barashevo—a very tiny segment of the camp of the Soviet Union (see page 43.)

THE SOURCES FOR SHIFRIN'S MAPS

Shifrin's maps are based on the following sources:

(1) Shifrin's personal experience in the camps until 1963, and his systematic collection of information until he left the Soviet Union in 1970;

(2) Numerous letters from people in the camps and their families;

(3) Supplementary information smuggled out of the Soviet Union;

(4) The systematic debriefing of emigrants from the Soviet Union who recently emerged from the camps.

(5) Shifrin's experience in the transportation camps:

Shifrin's personal experience in the camps was not limited to what he saw with his own eyes, but included numerous eye-witness accounts he received from other prisoners, especially during his sojourn in the transportation camps. Prisoners were constantly on the move. They rarely remained in any one camp for more than six months or a year. The probable reason for this was certainly not economic; Shifrin's best guess is that this was a strategy for preventing the formation of an *esprit de corps* and reducing possibility of organized opposition, revolt, and escape. The prisoners would come to the transportation camps from many different camps, and were again dispersed to many differ-

---

OPPOSITE PAGE: CONCENTRATION CAMPS IN THE SOVIET UNION
(Map prepared by Avraham Shifrin)

The red flags (dark gray triangular in the photograph) mark single camps or small groups of camps. The black rectangular flags in shaded areas mark major camp complexes, the largest of which may contain hundreds of camps and many hundreds of thousands of prisoners.

The solid black line depicts the concentration camp travels of Avraham Shifrin from 1953 to 1963. The broken black line depicts his travels through the Soviet Union in 1966 and 1967.

ent camps. They remained in the transportation camps for varying periods of time, ranging from 3–5 days to 3–4 weeks. During their stay in the transportation camps, prisoners had many opportunities to swap experiences with prisoners who had been in other camps.

The transportation camps, as Shifrin puts it, were "universities" where a man with an active mind could study in depth the entire concentration camp system in the Soviet Union.

There are no accurate statistics on the number of people in Soviet concentration camps in Stalin's day, or in the post-Stalin era. But rough estimates are possible on the basis of information compiled from the sources described above.

Shifrin points out that Robert Conquest, in his definitive work "The Great Terror," estimated that the number of prisoners in the camps during the peak years may have approximated 20 million. This figure did not include foreign prisoners of war—Germans, Italians, Japanese, etc.—who probably totaled 4–5 million. This would make an aggregate figure of close to 25 million for the peak years. Shifrin says he is prepared to accept this as a working figure, although he is inclined to believe that the real figure was substantially higher than this.

How large is the camp population today? While there is a lot of information available, it is nowhere near as voluminous as the massive body of information about the Soviet concentration camp system under Stalin which was compiled after World War II. The range of estimates is, for this reason, somewhat broader. On the basis of all the information which he has accumulated, Shifrin is convinced that there are at least several million prisoners in the camps today and that the real figure may surpass the 5 million mark.

Shifrin's Travels After Release from Camps

After Shifrin's release in 1963, he first went to Moscow without permission (he was supposed to go directly to Kazakhstan). He remained there for a month—constantly tailed by four KGB men. He thought they would arrest him, but for some reason they didn't. From Moscow Shifrin went first to Odessa and then to Karaganda, in Kazakhstan. Here he got a position, first as legal adviser to the Karaganda Building Trust, and then as legal adviser to the Kazakhstan Coal Mining Ministry.

Shifrin explains that recent prisoners had no difficulty in getting jobs in Kazakhstan because Kazakhstan was a *land of ex-prisoners in exile*. Fully 70 percent of the population in Karaganda. he said. had come from the camps. He even had one friend who, while legally in exile, rose to the rank of the Director of the Industrial Construction Trust for Kazakhstan.

In 1966, with his exile approaching termination, Shifrin decided to do some extensive traveling around the Soviet Union (a) to see some of the many friends, Jewish and non-Jewish, he had made in the camps who were now in exile in various parts of the country; (b) to see the country; (c) to arrange a communication code with his friends; (d) to learn as much as he could from the outside about the camp system. He was able to get permission to make this trip because he was on very good personal terms with his chief. But the KGB tailed him all the way on his trip—never interfering with his travels, because they probably wanted to see where he would go and whom he would visit. Over a two month period, he traveled over 10,000 miles. He noted the camps wherever he went—and while he could not enter the camps, he was always able to get information from ex-inmates of the camps who were then living in exile in the nearby towns and villages.

In the Urals he visited Sverdlovsk, Chelyabinsk, Magnitogorsk, Perm, Verchneuralsk. In Siberia he visited Krasnoyarsk, Novosibirsk, Tomsk, Irkutsk, Tayshet, and Chita.

In Central Asia, he traveled from Alma Alta to the Caspian Sea. Then he traveled through the Caucasus and the Black Sea area, the Ukraine, and then back to Moscow.

THE SHIFRIN STORY

Born October 8, 1923, in Minsk, Belorussia; moved to Moscow at age one and lived in Moscow subsequently; educated in Moscow for 10 years; completed high school; in Moscow Law University for one year before war.

In 1938 his father was arrested on a charge of anti-Soviet propaganda (Article 58/10) and sentenced to 10 years hard labor in Siberia. When his father was arrested, the KGB tried to press his mother to become a secret agent by telling her that, if she provided information about neighbors, his father would be sent to a "good" concentration camp. His mother refused. His father was sent to the Kolyma complex, where he died after ten years. He was rehabilitated posthumously in 1958.

To this day, KGB puts pressure on relatives of political prisoners to become agents—using provocateurs to test the reliability of those who are foolish enough to consent, but who do so in the hope that they will not really have to inform on innocent people.

WORLD WAR II

When he was conscripted in 1941, he was sent immediately to a penal battalion because his father was an "enemy of the people." There were 500 men in Shifrin's battalion. Penal battalions were used in front line positions—with machine guns behind them. For the 500 men, they had 100 old rifles. Their officers told them: "Your weapons are in the hands of the Nazis. Go get them."

When Shifrin asked why he was being sent to a penal battalion—pointing out that "it is written in the Soviet constitution that a son may not be punished for the sins of his father"—the officer in charge replied to him: "You are not being punished for the sins of your father. If you were, you, too, would be sent to a concentration camp."

Officers told all members of the penal battalion: "If you are wounded or decorated you may be transferred to the regular army unit." Shifrin was wounded on the West Moscow front, near Kaluga, on January 1, 1942 in the early morning. But after hospitalization they returned him to the penal battalion instead of transferring him to the regular army. He was wounded a second time—this time in the legs—near Lake Ilmen, on June 16, 1942. On the way to the hospital he decided he would not return to the penal battalion; he would change his identity. He changed his date of birth to 1920, and his first name to Ibrahim.

The change was simply a matter of giving this information when he was being registered as a patient. Penal battalion members had no papers because internal passports had been taken from them.

When discharged from the hospital, Shifrin was sent to a regular Red army unit. In his first battle his unit officer was killed and he was given a battlefield promotion to First Lieutenant. By the end of the war he had risen to the rank of Major. He fought in a motorized unit, all the way to Königsberg (East Prussia). He was demobilized in September 1945.

POST WORLD WAR II

After demobilization, Shifrin was employed by the Department to Combat Banditry and was sent as an investigator to the Krasnodar region to help suppress widespread post-war banditry. He soon became chief of the investigative unit. In 1946 he was transferred to headquarters of the Department in Moscow. While serving in this position he took a correspondence course in Law. In 1947 he was sent as a Chief Investigator to Tula, 180 km. from Moscow. In Tula he became Chief Legal Adviser in secret War Plant No. 535. This plant made automatic guns for fighter aircraft, AA guns for Navy and mine launchers. Shifrin served there from '48 to '52. In '52, he moved to Moscow where he became Chief Legal Adviser in the Contract Division of the Ministry of Defense. He got his law diploma in 1953.

DISGUISED DEFENSE PLANTS

As a result of his personal experience, largely in the Ministry of Defense, Shifrin knows of a number of defense plants which are disguised as Light Machinery Industry plants, and receive their funds from the Ministry for the Light Machinery Industry.

The weapons plant at Tula, for example, had one shop (out of 42) that produced stockings—this justified listing it as light machinery industry.

In Tula also there was a plant that made shells and cartridges, but one shop in this plant made Samovars—the entire plant therefore was listed as local industry, and the official name of the plant was "Samovar Factory."

At Chelyabinsk, a plant which made barrels for guns and rifles was listed as a "pipe plant."

Shifrin knows of this situation personally because as Chief Legal Adviser of the Contract Division of the Ministry of Defense he worked on drawing up contracts between these plants and the Ministry of Defense.

In Izhevsk, in the Urals, there is a large plant which produces motorcycles for civilian use and which comes under the Light Machinery Ministry. But most of the plant's efforts go into producing tracked vehicles, armed with guns and rockets, motorcycles equipped with machine-guns, and tanks.

The Ministry of Medium Machinery has constructed and controls all atomic plants, both peaceful and military, and all atomic research facilities.

When Shifrin returned to Moscow from Siberia in 1967, his old friends in the Defense Ministry confirmed to him that this practice, as well as other old practices, was still adhered to.

ARREST

The year 1953 was the peak year of anti-Jewish terror (Doctor's Plot). There were slogans on the fences: "Kill the Jews." During the first days of June, 1953 the KGB tried to arrest Shifrin's boss, Alexander Lieberman, who was in charge of the entire legal division of the Defense Ministry. Lieberman committed suicide by jumping from a 6th story window. (Lieberman's secretary recounted the incident to Shifrin.) Two days later—on June 6—Shifrin was arrested in the street. (Stalin had died in March 1953—but the anti-Jewish terror continued, by inertia, for some time after his death.)

He was first sent to Lubyanka, the central Moscow prison for political prisoners, on Dzerzhinsky Place. It is a 6 or 8 story building with a large underground adjunct under Dzerzhinsky Place, with hundreds of meters of cells and corridors.

During the investigative period, prisoners are kept in small cells barely large enough to accommodate their bunks. They are taken for walks on the roof, surrounded by high fences with armed guards posted at intervals.

In Lubyanka, Shifrin was put in a cell for half a day with scenario writer Maklyarsky, who specialized in scripts glorifying the KGB and had won the Stalin prize three times. Maklyarsky was a personal friend of Stalin. He was in prison because he had written a pro-Zionist poem for a little paper in Odessa in 1921 or '22.

During the six or seven hours in the cell with Maklyarsky, Maklyarsky cried and told Shifrin the story of how, in the three years since his arrest, the KGB had tried to break him. They had broken his limbs, broken his teeth, etc. Shifrin understood that this conversation was intended to weaken him psychologically.

Shifrin was interrogated for 23–25 days nonstop. Some six interrogators participated in this relay. They threw water on him when he collapsed. He was kept standing for the first several days. After this he was permitted to sit. KGB interrogators said they knew he was a spy, and asked for a complete statement. Shifrin replied over and over again that he had nothing to tell them. Then he was returned to his cell and permitted to sleep. Then there was a series of meetings with several high KGB officials: Colonel-General Kabulov (adviser to Beria), and Vladimirsky (Chief of Investigation Department). Colonel Medvedev (aide to Kabulov), and Colonel-General Mirkulov (adviser to Beria). During these interrogations Shifrin was kept in a normal cell. In the final meeting with Kabulov, Kabulov told him that they knew about his father and his false documents and that they were now certain that he was a spy, and they demanded a full statement from him about his spying activities on behalf of Israel and America. Kabulov told Medvedev to bring Shifrin to a place where he would be encouraged to ask to see Kabulov again.

Lefortovo Prison

The KGB took him to Lefortovo prison and put him in a basement cell approximately 4–5 feet square. Cells all had about five inches of mud and water on the floor, and there was no bunk or chair. Shifrin was held there for 28 days. He kept his back to the door so as to face away from the spy hole in the door through which a guard's eye constantly peered. In this position he faced a blank wall covered with green mold. He kept record of the days by making vertical lines in the mold when they brought him his daily bread ration. After a number of days he began to see patterns in the mold. Then he imagined he saw entire scenes, with bloody bodies, etc. He thought he was going mad. Then he began to suspect that the scenes were being projected from a small aperture in the vicinity of the light bulb. He threw his shirt up in the air in front of the bulb—and the scenes were interrupted. At this point he told the guard to tell his idiot commander that he didn't need television for entertainment. The projections stopped.

Shifrin learned that three of the doctors arrested in the "Doctor's Plot" had died in cells similar to the one in which he was confined. At the time of the doctors' arrest, several hundred doctors were arrested in Moscow—almost all Jewish.

During this period Shifrin was taken twice to see Colonel Medvedev. When he said he had no information to give, Medvedev on both occasions ordered him immediately returned to his cold cell.

During all this time, Shifrin had not been served with a warrant for his arrest, although he repeatedly demanded to see the warrant under which he was arrested.

Butyrki Prison; Court Martial; and Death of Beria

Shifrin says that no physical torture was used on him during the investigation. The investigation was continued by minor functionaries—captains, majors, etc.

In October the KGB put him in Butyrki Prison in the special political section, in isolation. In early December 1953 he was brought before the Moscow Military District Court Martial. The court consisted of a Colonel and two officers. Asked if he was a spy, Shifrin said no. The Court said they had enough evidence to prove that he was a spy. He asked what evidence it was. The Court told him that it was "none of his business." He asked whether they had not been told that he had consistently denied spying in his numerous interrogations by Kabulov, Mirkulov, Vladimirsky and Medvedev. The Court replied: "You must not mention the names of these enemies of the people!"

Shifrin asked: "What, have they been shot?" They answered: "That's none of your business either." Before he left the room a KGB guard whispered to Shifrin: "Don't you know that they've shot Beria and all of his aides?" Shifrin replied—with scarcely disguised glee: "What—Beria too?" (Beria was arrested and shot in July 1953.) Shifrin is convinced that the death of Kabulov and company saved him from death.

The Court Martial read the sentence to him, which said: "Sentenced to be shot—as the highest measure of protection of our society." Shifrin was put in a cell for people sentenced to death in Butyrska prison. There were 20 cells, 2 people in each cell.

Prisoners had to go to sleep at 10. The guard came at 11 p.m. to fetch those to be shot—there was one almost every night. The corridor had doors at both ends and was used as a short cut through the building. Tension was high every time the door opened, and there was great relief when the guards passed their doors and went to other doors. Prisoners who were led to execution had a large pear-shaped rubber object stuffed in their mouths. Sometimes the prisoners heard the last cry from fellow-prisoners before their mouths were stuffed; sometimes they heard only a choking sound. The prisoners would get hysterical and pound the doors and call the guards vile names. The guards would sometimes respond by hosing them down with fire hose through apertures used for passing food into the cells.

After about ten days in this cell, Shifrin was approached by a prison officer who told him that his sentence had been commuted to 25 years in strict labor camps—plus 5 years of exile, plus 5 years deprivation of rights.

After being sentenced, Shifrin was transferred to another special section in Butyrki Prison, for people about to be deported. Cell No. 58—one of ten identical cells in the corridor—was meant to accommodate 25 prisoners, and had twenty-five steel bunks that folded against the wall in the daytime, but the cells contained 60 to 65 prisoners (the number varied from one day to another). All the prisoners in these cells had been sentenced to 25 years hard labor—which was the maximum under law. Prisoners told Shifrin that almost everyone was getting 25 year sentences. One day a new prisoner came to the cell and fainted after being pushed inside. When he came to, the prisoners asked him why he had fainted. He said he had just been sentenced to 15 years hard labor—and what a bleak outlook! The other prisoners laughed uproariously—because to them it was funny that a man who had been sentenced to only 15 years should lament his fate!

Some of the People in Butyrki

Shifrin met some highly interesting prisoners in Burtyrki, and he heard about some other interesting cases from fellow prisoners.

(1) There were many officers and soldiers of the Vlassov army who were in transit to other camps—all with 25 year sentences. There were also some former Soviet POWs who had served several years in the camps after their release, and had now been rearrested and sentenced to 25 years.

(2) *Prince Konojo.* Shifrin couldn't converse with him. Other prisoners told him that Konojo was a member of Hirohito's family and had been a General in the Japanese Kwantung army.

(3) *Lev Bernstein*, a Jewish engineer, the inventor of system for harnessing tidal power and converting it to electricity. He had begun work on an experimental station near Murmansk before World War II. He was arrested as a spy after accidentally meeting an American engineer who told him he had heard about his work. They had exchanged addresses and agreed to communicate. Bernstein was sentenced to 25 years because the American engineer's address was found on him. He was first sent to a camp at Norilsk in the Arctic Sea. He was sentenced to a second 25 years on the charge that he had sought to escape to the West on an ice floe—because a magnetic needle had been found in his possession! Bernstein was first released in 1959—and then on his way out of the camp, the authorities discovered the record of his second 25 year sentence and told him he couldn't be released. He served another 6 months before they permitted him to go. He went back to work on the Murmansk tidal power station—which he had abandoned in 1940.

(4) There was a simple man who had shared a large cooperative apartment dwelling with several other families. Once he had a dream and he related to his frends in the morning that he had dreamed Stalin

had been assassinated. He was sentenced to 25 years as a "potential terrorist."

(5) *West German Featherweight Boxer, Branislaw* . . . (Shifrin cannot recall last name). Branislaw was arrested as a spy while visiting his mother in Latvia. He was repeatedly beaten, but refused to confess. After several months he decided to confess in order to live. He confessed that he was a spy, but said that he would have to eat and sleep before he gave them a detailed statement. He was given a good bed and wonderful food. After two days he began to make a detailed statement. He gave the names and addresses of German and European boxers whom he knew, because he didn't want to risk forgetting fabricated names. He received good treatment for two months, while he was giving detailed accounts of "spying." Meanwhile, his story was being checked out by KGB agents in West Germany. One day KGB officers came to his cell, accused him of lying, and beat him mercilessly for 24 hours. He was sentenced to 25 years as a spy. But as he said, he had eaten well for two months!

(6) There was *an engineer from Moscow named Krasnilikov* who had been sentenced as a spy from Guatemala. He had agreed to confess to spying after being repeatedly beaten. When he signed the paper that was put in front of him, the KGB asked him to name the country for which he had been spying. He said, "Put down any country you want to—it's O.K. with me." They insisted that *he* name the country. Afraid of damaging his own position if he named a big Western country, he said that he had spied for Guatemala. He was, accordingly, sentenced to 25 years as a spy for Guatemala!

(7) There was a *Dr. Kogan* who was arrested at the time of the Doctors' Plot. He had been a Professor at Botkinskaya hospital, which services the Kremlin. Kogan told Shifrin about hundreds of other Moscow doctors who had been arrested as a result of the "Doctors' Plot" hysteria. Kogan said that to his knowledge the KGB had released only 6 to 9 arrested medical academicians (three of these died, or were killed in prison while under investigation).

(8) There was a Ukrainian boy of 20–21, *Pyotr Pavluk*, sentenced to 25 years as a guerrilla. He told Shifrin he had not been a guerrilla—but his family had given a guerrilla shelter without knowing his identity. When they were arrested and confronted with captured guerrillas, they admitted that they had given overnight shelter to one of them as an act of hospitality to a traveler. The young man and his mother and sister had all been arrested and sentenced to 25 years as "guerrillas."

(9) There were *three Chukchi hunters* (the Chukchis are a tribe related to the Eskimos) from the horn at the North of the Bering Strait. The hunters had attacked a Russian submarine with harpoons, thinking it was a whale. As they told the other prisoners, "the 'whale' had surfaced and swallowed them." They were sentenced to 25 years hard labor as "diversionists."

(10) Another man with 25 year term, *Dykereff*, was sentenced because he had produced an anti-Beria typewritten tract, which he had sent to a few friends. This was before the downfall of Beria. When his trial took place, Beria had already been shot. He said to the court: "Look, Beria has just been shot as an enemy of the people. Are you going to prosecute me because I was opposed to an enemy of the

people?" The court answered: "You were not only against Beria. You were deriding a member of the Government."

(11) Another young man who was facing a 25 year sentence was a *young Ukrainian*, sentenced for nationalist activity. In prison in the town of Mukachev he was beaten repeatedly by investigator during his interrogation. He said to the investigator: "Why do you beat me when I am only under investigation and have not been found guilty of anything? Maybe I'll be found innocent!" In reply, the guard grabbed him by the scruff of the neck, dragged him to the window, and pointed to throngs of people in the Mukachev market place. "*Those* people," he said, "are under investigation. *You* are here because you are already condemned."

(12) There was also *Grigory Artiomovich Tsaturov*, former First Secretary of the Central Committee of the Communist Party of Armenia, a close friend of Stalin's and Beria's. He was personally the spitting image of Stalin. He was arrested by Beria in '38 because, in a drunken state, he told Mikoyan that he knew the details of Beria's criminal past. He was in camps in Siberia until 1953. He was brought to Moscow to give testimony against Beria at the time of his downfall. He was told that he would be released afterwards. Instead, the KGB sent him to Butyrki to await transportation back to camps. He was— understandably—very angry, and talked freely during his first days in Butyrki. He also claimed to be familiar with Stalin's criminal record—including how Stalin sold pornographic pictures in Tbilisi, Tsaturov died in the camps in '58 or '59.

(13) *General Mikhail Gurevich*, of the Soviet Air Force, a "hero of the Soviet Union," was also serving 25 years. He was in Butryki, in transit to another camp. Before World War II, he had served as a Soviet air specialist in Spain. After World War II, he was in charge of all arms development programs for the Air Force. At the end of the War, Gurevich went to Bulganin and urged an all-out effort to produce a supersonic plane, because of Western efforts in this field. Bulganin said, "no," because Soviet scientists had told him it was impossible to fly at supersonic speed. Then Gurevich went to Stalin and got approval for several hundred millions in foreign currency in order to establish and equip a supersonic development and research institute.

In 1949, in reply to Stalin's question: "What about our supersonic aircraft program?" Bulganin replied that Gurevich had been wasting money and had not achieved any results with his work. Stalin asked: "And he's still in charge of Air Force arms program?" The conversation immediately changed—but Gurevich was arrested a few hours later. He was charged with economic subversion and with having squandered funds on the instruction of American intelligence.

Gurevich accompanied Shifrin to Tayshet camp and was with him there until he died in 1956. Gurevich had three heart attacks. After his last attack, he was paralyzed. There was no doctor in the camp. He lay in his barrack bunk, without care, urinating and defecating in bed. The prisoners demanded that he be removed from the cell because the odor was unbearable. He was moved to the morgue (autopsy room) and laid on straw on the floor. He lay there for seven or eight days and then died. Shifrin and other prisoners brought him food in the evening and tried to look after him. When he died, his body was stripped, as was customary, a small wooden tag was attached to his ankle, and he was brought to the gate—where the guard pierced his body with a hot iron (a ritual to make certain that the dead were really dead), and then they pulled his body into the forest and left it in the snow, for the animals to eat.

Thus died a "hero of the Soviet Union."

One month later, a delegation of Generals came from Moscow to bring Gurevich back and rehabilitate him. They brought Gurevich's uniform with them—not knowing he was dead.

DEPORTATION

Towards the end of December, Shifrin was deported. He was brought together with some 40–50 other prisoners in a special cell— a very crowded cell—where they were kept briefly. They were then called out one at a time, for baggage and body searches—including all the body cavities. Then they were led down to a waiting van and loaded aboard, compressed like sardines. The last two or three prisoners could not be forced into the van, so the guards hoisted them up on the shoulders of the jam-packed prisoners. The van was disguised ingeniously: each side bore the words "Ice Cream" in large black letters, and a drawing of a bear lapping up ice cream.

They were taken to a small street near the railroad station, but they did not board the train at the station. Instead, they were ushered between waiting rows of guards, through a hole in the fence, aboard the train.

The special cars for prisoners had prison-like interiors. The compartments—which were made for eight people—were surrounded by wire cages. The corridor through the car, too, had wire its full length.

Although compartments were intended for eight people, there were 18 people in Shifrin's compartment, together with their luggage. People were also jammed into luggage areas. The prisoners ate bread and herring and some sugar—which was poured on the bread by the guards.

They traveled for three days. They were allowed to go to the lavatory twice a day. People sometimes shouted and screamed for permission to go—but to no avail. One man who urinated through the wire of his cell compartment into the corridor was taken out and beaten mercilessly by the guards.

Political prisoners were mixed with criminals. The criminals forced the political prisoners to surrender their better items of clothing— which they then gave to the guards in exchange for permission to go to the lavatory, or for bottles of vodka.

Conversation between a guard and a prisoner through the wire mesh:

Guard: "How long are they sending you up for?" Prisoner: "25 years." Guard: "Why did they sentence you?" Prisoner: "Really for nothing." Guard: "You're a liar. For nothing they only give you 10 years!" This was said in a completely serious and indignant tone— and at this, all the other prisoners burst out laughing.

After three days they came to Chelyabinsk. There was a second search after arriving. They were transported from the station in a van which bore the caption "MEAT" instead of "Ice Cream." They were brought to a deportation prison—which was separate from the prison.

Here there was a third search of the prisoners, after which they were sent to cold showers. They were then divided into groups and sent to the cells. Shifrin was placed in the same cell as Tsaturov (former First Secretary, Central Committee, Communist Party of Armenia). This was a large cell—roughly 7 by 10 meters—but crowded with 150 inmates, with two tiers of bunks along two walls.

Some of the criminals were under 200–250 year sentences, made up of consecutive 25 year terms for separate crimes.

After two or three days at Chelyabinsk, Shifrin was moved by train to Novosibirsk. The reception room at Novosibirsk was covered with handwriting—desperate notes from prisoners to loved ones, denunciation of informers, etc. The latrine barrack had long boards with 100–150 holes. It also had hordes of giant tawny rats, 12–18 inches long, which frequently attacked the prisoners. Shifrin subsequently encountered very similar giant rats in all the other camps in which he stayed. He jocularly suggests that the Soviet regime may have cultivated a special giant breed of concentration camp rats as part of their planning effort over a 50 year period.

In Novosibirsk Shifrin had first experience with "normal incarceration." Shifrin had pushed aside a guard who was beating elderly prisoners. He was seized and put in chains, and confined, with a bread and water diet, in a well-like concrete cell, deep down in a dungeon.

OMSK: After 5–6 days in Novosibirsk, Shifrin was placed in another train and taken to Omsk—to Kamyshlag concentration camp complex, containing 100,000–150,000 people. He arrived there early January 1954. The prisoners had been brought there to build an industrial complex. Shifrin was confined in Camp No. 3, which had 5–6,000 people, in starved condition. A medical commission, with physicians in KGB uniform, examined the prisoners twice a year. Shifrin arrived at the time of the New Year medical commission inspection. The examination was conducted by feeling buttocks. If the buttocks had meat on them, prisoners were sent to work brigades. If their buttocks had only loose skin and prominent coccyx (or tail bone) they were sent to nonworking brigades until their condition improved. The daily diet contained 1,290 calories for working prisoners, but only 716 calories for those who were incarcerated.

All prisoners had numbers on clothes—one over the heart, one on the leg, one one on the back, and one on the cap. Shifrin was given number S–720. Each letter of the alphabet stood for 1,000 prisoners—so S–720 stood for 17,720. The complex at Omsk had been established roughly a year before Shifrin's arrival. In a year's time, 17,720 prisoners had passed through this camp complex—but only 5,000 were in the camp at the time he arrived. Where had the others gone? They were either dead, or had been transferred to other camps.

The death rate was staggering at Omsk. Every day some 30 to 40 naked corpses were loaded aboard horse-drawn sleds and taken out into the woods and left in the snow. Most had died of disease or starvation, but a substantial percentage had been killed during the night. Prisoners killed those whom they believed to be informers. KGB circulated rumors about people they wanted to get rid of. They also used killings to incite prisoners of one nationality against prisoners of another nationality, operating on the rule that divided subjects are easier to govern.

Divide and Rule

Shortly after Shifrin arrived in Omsk, there was a major battle resulting from KGB provocations designed to set Russian and Ukrainian prisoners against each other. There were in the camp about 2,000 Russians, about 2,000 Ukrainians, about 1,000 of other nationalities. Ukrainian KGB officers told the Ukrainians that the Russians were making knives to attack them—and they wanted to warn them because, even though they were KGB, they were also Ukrainian. Russian KGB officers told similar story about Ukrainians to Russian prisoners. Both sides started making knives. The situation became tense. All that was needed was a small incident.

One day, Shifrin was standing in line at the gate. In exiting from the barrack area to work, prisoners were first herded into barbed wire corridor about 10′ wide and 150′ long, with the camp gate and guard towers at one end. While waiting for the gate to open Shifrin suddenly felt pushing, heard shouting, and was thrown to ground and trampled. A general melee ensued, with prisoners slashing at each other with knives and other crude weapons. Guards opened fire, and surrounded prisoners. They shouted over the loudspeaker system for the prisoners to lie down. Then they ordered them to stand up with hands behind their heads. Hundreds of bodies lay on the ground. Shifrin heard later that more than 300 had been killed.

The KGB executed 30 prisoners who had been closest to the gate, on the charge of political terrorism.

Over the next ten years, Shifrin was a witness to three such incidents, each involving a hundred or more victims. He was also told by an Italian prisoner who had been confined in a camp close by the town of Angarsk, near Irkutsk, that 1,600 people had been killed in a 2–3 day battle between Russians on the one hand, and Georgians and Chechens on the other.

Shifrin remained in the Kamyshlag concentration camp until June, 1954. He tried to escape from it but he was captured.

SEMIPALATINSK; UST-KAMENOGORSK; TAYSHET

From Kamyshlag, Shifrin was sent to a penal prison in Semipalatinsk in Kazakhstan. This was the prison in which Dostoyesky had been confined, and the street on which it was situated was called Dostoyevsky Street. Whereas the cells had held two men in Dostoyesky's days, they now held twelve. The cots had been removed and had been replaced with two tiers of metal bunks, made of metal rods, laid lengthwise at two inch intervals.

From this cell he was transferred after one month to another cell, slightly bigger, which also contained 12 prisoners. The prisoners were given heavy mattresses filled with coarse scraps of leather—waste from a local leather factory. The mattresses sank between the steel rods at night—so again they were sleeping on steel.

There were many women in separate cells in the same corridor. The guards accompanied them to toilet and watched them—in clear violation of the law.

Prisoners from many other camps arrived, bringing news of widespread revolts.

Also. Shifrin met Alexander Shornik, a former American officer, who had come to Russia in 1948-49 to try to get his father out. He had tried to smuggle him out through underground channels—Ukrainian nationalist guerrillas. All were arrested and sentenced to ten years. In 1955, Shifrin was moved from Semipalatinsk to a little prison in Ust-Kamenogorsk. This was also a Dostoyevsky prison. Prisoners were sometimes put in chains and placed in punitive cells to intimidate them. The prison had a special building for juveniles, from the age of 12 to 16 or 17.

Shifrin remained in Ust-Kamenogorsk until November–December 1955, and then he was sent to Tayshet. On the way, he stopped over at Novosibirsk transit camp.

THE GREAT CONCENTRATION CAMP UPRISING OF 1953–54

In Novosibirsk, Shifrin met people who had come from Kingir where there had been a major camp uprising. Tanks had crushed 500 women who had tried to protect their men by standing in front of them. (The fences separating women from men had been broken down.) In Novosibirsk, he also met people who had taken part in major uprisings in the Vorkuta complex, where prisoners held out for months before they were crushed, and in similar uprisings, in Norilsk, in Tayshet and in the Kolyma, and Barnaul complexes. All of these uprisings took place in the last part of 1953 and the first part of 1954. The prisoners said that all coal mining and gold mining and other labor had come to a complete stop in these camps and the prisoners had taken complete control of the camps. In some places the guards remained on the towers, but they did not dare come inside. In other places, the guards were disarmed. Members of the Government—Mikoyan, Khrushchev, Voroshilov, Budenny, Molotov—came to see them and told them they must stop their strike in the national interest. They replied that they wanted freedom because they were innocent. Then the Government sent troops and tanks and planes and artillery, and many thousands were killed in the suppression of these uprisings. (The Appendices to Volume III will contain a number of eyewitness accounts of the great concentration camp uprisings of 1953–54.)

The Soviet Government and the KGB made important concessions to terminate the uprisings. They agreed to permit prisoners to remove the numbers from their clothing. They increased letters from one a year to any number (written and received). They increased packages from one a year to unlimited numbers. And they promised pay for work. Salaries were in fact paid—but the authorities made deductions for food, clothing, housing, guards, food for dogs, transportation, etc. The result was that the prisoners were left with 3–5 rubles per month. This arrangement continues to this day.

These concessions remained in force until 1957–58—but after that they were progressively whittled away. Now there is one letter per month, and one parcel per year—and these can be denied for very minor infractions, like failing to doff one's hat to a guard. There are so many minor infractions today that, in practice, only informers and a few rare prisoners actually receive their one parcel a year.

From Novosibirsk they brought Shifrin to the railway concentration camp complex Tayshet-Bodaybo, where he was confined until

1961. The first stop in Tayshet was transportation camp No. 025, right alongside the main Moscow-Vladivostok line. There was a very high fence around the camp, so that the camp could not be seen from the railroad. The fence was higher at the corner to conceal the guard-towers.

THE INCIDENT OF THE RUSSIAN REPATRIATES FROM CHINA

In November '55, several days after Shifrin's arrival at Tayshet, there was a tragic incident involving repatriates from China. Shortly after the end of World War II the Soviets had launched a big campaign to entice White Russians who had fled to China and other countries after the Revolution to return to their motherland. Many White Russians in China were taken in by the lies and blandishments, and agreed to return with their children. The husbands were told that they would have to go first in order to get jobs and prepare homes for their families. Their wives and children would follow later. The husbands were sent to concentration camps instead.

On the day of the incident, some prisoners, including White Russians from China, were standing on the roofs of barracks in an effort to get a look at people in passing trains. A train stopped outside the camp and women and children got off. Some of the White Russians on the roof recognized their wives. They shouted to each other. The husbands asked their wives what they were doing there, at a concentration camp. "What do you mean, concentration camp?" the women shouted back. "The big sign on the fence says 'Petroleum Storage Depot.' "

The guards broke up the exchange by pulling the men from the roofs and pushing the women back aboard the train. Shifrin does not know what happened to the women afterwards. But before the exchange was broken up by the guards the women told the men that they had been informed that their husbands wanted them to join them.

SOME PEOPLE IN TAYSHET

Among the people Shifrin met in Tayshet were:

Aaron Yarkho, a Jewish general, who had been Chief of Chemical warfare troops. Assigned to occupation duty in Germany, he decided to defect and go to Israel. He was kidnapped from Milan in 1950 while on his way to Israel.

Siegfried Oelsner, a Wehrmacht captain, captured in World War II. He told Shifrin that Tayshet had housed at least 500,000 POWs at the end of the war. Now there were no more than 10,000. All the rest had died.

Oelsner told Shifrin that they had been sent into the forests with guards, had cut trees, built barracks and towers and fences. Then they made log roads from one camp to another, and from Tayshet to the Bodaybo gold mines. All the time, more and more prisoners—hundreds of thousands of Japanese, etc.—arrived in the camps. Then there came prisoners from all over the USSR. Oelsner said the death rate at times was almost ten per 1,000 per day.

Baron DeSainteur, a Frenchman, who said that he had been kidnapped from his office in Paris.

Henri Hevyurts, a French officer, who told Shifrin that he had been a French major in Vienna, and had been kidnapped in 1949.

There were also many Soviet Jewish intellectuals who had been arrested after Stalin's death. The Jewish poet Grisha Bieryoskin said that he had been with a large group of Jewish writers arrested in 1947 and afterwards, and that most of them had been shot—including Markish, Bergelson, and approximately 30 other writers.

From the transportation camp, Shifrin was sent to penal concentration camp No. 306, approximately 300 km. from Tayshet. Along the entire route on both sides of the railway he saw an unbroken stretch of concentration camps. Sometimes they were interrupted for a mile or two, sometimes only a few hundred meters between camps. Each camp had its own cemetery nearby.

CRIME, PUNISHMENT AND REHABILITATION IN THE U.S.S.R.

Shifrin makes the interesting observation that mass political arrests in the U.S.S.R. occur with remarkable regularity at ten year intervals—1918, 1928, 1938, 1948, 1958, 1969–72.

Shifrin believes that the phenomenon of the ten year intervals and the fact that a great majority of the prisoners served a minimum of ten years is due to the fact that in most cases men are incapable of more than ten years hard labor in the camps, and the camp population had to be periodically replenished.

Prisoner labor on a mass scale was necessary for the Soviet regime because, in the absence of enormous economic incentives, no workers would normally go to God-forsaken places like Vorkuta, Karaganda, Norilsk, and Wrangel Island.

Shifrin was told by a Government friend that prisoners account for 30% of labor force.

The severity of the sentences handed down for political crimes, varied from one period to another. Thus, in the 1930s political prisoners were frequently sentenced to five years in the camps, while in 1951 the twenty-five year sentence became an almost universal rule—whether the prisoner in question had committed espionage, or had simply told a joke about the regime. Roughly 1958 there was a formal moderation in severity of sentence, when the theoretical maximum was set at 15 years.

Like so many other Soviet reforms, this limited concession to humanitarianism turned out to be fraudulent. Many criminal elements who had originally been sentenced to 25 years and had served more than 15 years were, in fact, released. But the same clemency was not extended to political prisoners, who continued to serve their full 25 year term. Among those released in 1972 after serving 25 years were Vladimir Gorbovoy, Ekaterina Zaritzkaya and Vasili Pirus, while Mikhail Soroka died after twenty-four years in prison. There were many others.

Legal maximums and the length of sentence handed down meant very little even in legal terms, because there were several legal devices for getting around the limitation.

Prisoners who were originally sentenced to three to five years were frequently resentenced in the camps to another three to five years. Shifrin met a Jewish Trotskyist by the name of Goldberg (or Goldbart) in camp No. 04 in Tayshet in 1955 who told him that he had been arrested as a Trotskyist in 1934 and he was then serving his fifth consecutive five year sentence. He died in the camp shortly after Shifrin met him.

Then there are the prisoners who are sentenced to indefinite terms, without being charged with any specific crime, as "Members of Families of Enemies of the People" (Ch S V N). To identify their crime, the letters Ch S V N were stamped on their dossiers. Among those thus sentenced were Pyotr Yakir, son of a Russian-Jewish General who had been executed, and Yuri Shukhevich, son of a Ukrainian insurgent general. Both Yakir and Shukhevich were arrested at the age of 14 years and sent to camps. Both were released after serving twenty years. Both were rearrested in 1972, only several years after their release, and both are now back in the camps. Also among those sentenced as "Member of Families of Enemies of the People" were members of the families of Marshal Tukhachevsky, Yagoda, Beria, Yezhov, Bukharin, etc.

After the Khrushchev speech on the secret crimes of Stalin, Khrushchev embarked on an apparent "liberalization." In May of 1956 special rehabilitation commissions visited all the camps. These Commissions interviewed the prisoners for only five or six minutes, and asked them simple questions like name, birth date, and the article under which they were imprisoned, and then informed them that they were rehabilitated. In a period of about three months, millions upon millions of prisoners were released, and most of the camps were half-empty. (Shifrin at the time was in Camp No. 019 at Chuna, near Tayshet.)

Two years later, however, the camps were full again. The clampdown began immediately following the suppression of the Hungarian uprising in November, 1956. The camps soon filled up again as a result of the new stream of prisoners, which included many students, and soldiers and officers who had served with the Red Army in Hungary.

It was during this period that Shifrin made the acquaintance in the camps of some of the youthful Soviet dissidents whose names have since become widely known—among them were Vladimir Bukovsky, Vladimir Telnikov, Eduard Kutznetzov, Yuri Osipov, Ilya Bokshtein.

TAYSHET: KGB DISCIPLINE, WORKING CONDITIONS, PRISONER SELF-MUTILATION

From Camp No. 025, Shifrin was taken to Camp No. 307, 300 Km. from Tayshet. Here there were approxmiately 2,000 prisoners in a camp set in the forest near the Angara river.

The prisoners worked on the construction of a power station and on cutting lumber in the forest. In building the dam for the power station, giant rocks would be pulled to the site by companies of 100 to 150 prisoners hauling on ropes—in the manner of the ancient Egyptians building pyramids.

The camp contained all nationalities. Most of the prisoners were Russians, Ukrainians and Balts. There were also quite a few foreigners, including Japanese POWs, Germans and Austrians, and Polish Jews. The Austrians, for the most part, had been arrested or kidnapped by the Soviet authorities after occupation.

Polish-Jewish prisoners told Shifrin that when Soviet troops moved into Polish towns, the KGB came immediately to their flats with prepared lists of names, clearly drawn up in advance of Soviet invasion. People were arrested on the basis of these lists, and without trial, sent to the camps as "Anti-Soviet elements." Among the Polish Jews, Shifrin recalls particularly the names of Professor Griff, Professor Geffen, and the artist Weinbaum. They were in sad shape when Shifrin arrived, reduced to skin and bones, and they died shortly after his arrival.

Prisoners worked ten hours a day—seven days a week until 1956, and six days a week after that. The KGB guards were brutal and merciless. When they shot prisoners who attempted escape at any distance from the camp, corpses were not brought back to camp but were left in the forest. They brought back only index fingers for the purpose of fingerprint identification. If escaping prisoners were shot down close to the camp, however, the bodies were put near the gate for three to five days for the purpose of terrorizing other prisoners.

Prisoners were required to work in the forest unless, the temperature fell below −40–45 degrees Fahrenheit. How did they know it was −40°? (1) There was a thermometer at the gate as they went out; and (2) if you spat and the spit turned to ice by the time it hit the ground—it was 40° below! Their clothing was completely inadequate. They had thin cotton underwear, and quilted cotton outer jackets. Their faces they covered—all but their eyes—with any cloth they could find. Their feet they wrapped in the foot cloths which were issued in lieu of socks—and then, if it was real cold, they would wrap them further with strips of heavy paper from cement bags. Fortunate prisoners, especially in the later years, were issued heavy felt boots when they worked in the forests. But most prisoners had very crude rubber boots which shoemaker-prisoners fashioned from old truck tires—first dividing segments of the tire casing into five or six layers, and then shaping rough boots from them. These boots were *not* warm!

Prisoners frequently had frozen hands and legs and ears. Shifrin had frozen legs 4 or 5 times—this certainly had something to do with the impaired circulation which made his leg amputation necessary in 1968. There were quite a few cases, too, where prisoners froze their male organs—and went through the most excruciating agonies when they thawed out. To protect their mid-sections, prisoners frequently stuffed paper concrete bags into their trousers.

Prisoners were prohibited from wearing any clothes which they brought with them or any clothes which they received from home.

When prisoners left the camps to go to work, guards—dressed in fur hats and fur coats!—checked them out at the gate in groups of five. As each group of five came forward, they were required to open up their tunics or sometimes take them off, drop their trousers and pull out their pockets. If the guards were suspicious that a prisoner was concealing something, prisoners had to strip to underwear and take off their footcloths, while the guards went through their clothing carefully. Sometimes the guards would also examine body cavities. If the guards were kind, they might permit the prisoners, during such examinations to stand on a board to keep their feet "warm."

As incentive to the guards to be merciless with escapees, guards were given fifteen days leave and the right to visit relatives whenever they shot down escapees.

Guards sometimes arranged provocations so that they could shoot down prisoners who were *not* attempting escape, and thus earn their fifteen day leave. When working in the forest, guards placed flags to mark off the work area, and any prisoner crossing the flag line was presumed to be an escapee and fair game for shooting. In one incident Shifrin witnessed a guard calling to a prisoner to come to him—and when the prisoner crossed the flag line he shot him down.

Brutal punishment would be meted out for minor infractions. One prisoner who had cursed a guard was tied naked to a forest tree at a time of year when the forest was infested with swarms of poisonous gnats (Moshka); prisoners had to cover their heads with nets while working in the forest. The naked prisoner screamed and shouted for the first several hours—and then he became quiet. In the evening they brought his terribly swollen corpse to the camp. (Shifrin witnessed one other such incident.)

Prisoners who died during the winter were not buried because the ground was too hard. Bodies were dragged naked into the forest and left in the snow—this was the winter "cemetery!" Almost invariably when they hauled out the next batch of dead prisoners the following day, the corpses which had been deposited the previous day had disappeared. They had been eaten during the night by the black foxes and other forest animals.

The water given to the prisoners was brackish—and most unpleasant to drink. 400–500 prisoners were housed in a single large wooden barrack. But while conditions remained generally grim, there was one small but important improvement. Khrushchev had just made his famous secret speech denouncing the crimes of the Stalin era—and now the prisoners were permitted to take off the numbers which they had worn on their hats and backs and breasts. In this way was the regime humanized!

Shifrin met with many good people in this camp whom he remembers vividly; the engineer, *Arkadi Suchodolsky;* the students, *David Mazur* and *Genadi Cherepov;* the Ukrainian underground army officer, *Ivan Dolishy.* They had all been working on the Volga-Don canal—an enormous construction project on which—according to these prisoner-laborers—almost 1,000,000 men had been working.

There Shifrin also met for the first time *Yuri Shukhevich*, son of the executed Ukrainian General, *Roman Shukhevich.* Yuri had been sent to a special camp for juveniles at age 14. He told Shifrin that there were many thousands of juveniles in these camps, where the working conditions were almost as arduous as they were in the camps for adults. (A new book has just been published in the Russian language, *Concentration Camp Childhood*, written by Pyotr Yakir during his brief emergence from the camps.)

The camp hospitals

In 1957, Shifrin became very ill. He had lost a tremendous amount of weight and his legs were badly swollen. He was brought in a semi-conscious condition to the camp hospital at Vikhorevka. Vikhorevka housed prisoners who had been brought from many camps over roughly a 600 km. radius. It was directed by a KGB officer. It had no medicine for TB or other serious diseases.

Criminal prisoners were brought together with political prisoners. Prisoner-doctors did their best under the circumstances to look after their fellow-prisoners—but the pay they were supposed to get went to the wives of the KGB officers. When the KGB did not like a prisoner-doctor for any reason, they would send him to hard labor. This was the case with a very good surgeon by the name of Konsky, who was sent to hard labor. His place was filled by a dentist (an informer)—many prisoners died under his surgery.

One of the officers' wives who was being paid as a doctor—a woman called "Domino" by the prisoners—was one day playing "doctor" with the surgeon in charge of the hospital barrack. She came to a prisoner who was suffering from a very nasty "mastirka," or self-inflicted wound, on his leg. His leg showed the beginnings of gangrene, and the real doctor emphasized this to her. But she said, "We must wait until morning." By morning, the gangrene had spread so widely in the prisoner's body that he died shortly afterwards.

The new wave of prisoners

In 1957 and 1958, in the wake of the suppression of the Hungarian revolution, a new wave of prisoners came to the camps. They were for the most part young people, caught up in the epidemic of dissent which wracked the entire Communist world in the wake of Hungary. The Kremlin was obviously afraid of these young students, whom it accused of being "revisionists." But for the most part the students who came to the camps still considered themselves Marxists ideologically; they were just dissatisfied with the Soviet regime. From its own standpoint, the Soviet Government made a big mistake, says Shifrin, because these young students emerged from the camps completely anti-Soviet, and they now play a prominent role in the ranks of the dissidents.

Pimps for Beria and Stalin

In the camp, Shifrin also met a number of former KGB officers who had served under Beria. They had been arrested at the time of Beria's downfall in 1953, but at that time they were sent to special camps where they lived under relatively good conditions. In 1958, however, Khrushchev decided to transfer them to ordinary concentration camps. Among the former KGB officers were one Lt.-General and two Colonels from Georgia. The two Georgian Colonels were once called before a special commission which was visiting the camps for the purpose of reviewing sentences. When they were asked what they had been charged with, they replied that they had been charged with providing women for Beria. The Commissioners were indignant at this, and one of them said, "It's a shame; you did very dirty work!" To which the Colonels replied, "We were only officers, and we did what Beria told us to do—and the women we brought to Beria always came home alive. But ask the officers who brought girls to Stalin—none of them ever came home alive!"

Shifrin witnessed this personally, because prisoners were permitted to attend these hearings.

The massacre of the Yiddish writers

During the last years of the Stalin regime many hundreds of Jewish intellectuals were murdered or executed—among them some of the best known writers in the Yiddish language and key figures in the famed Yiddish theatre in Moscow. One of the most celebrated cases involved

Peoples Artist of the USSS, Samuil Michoels. The story put out by the regime at the time was that Michoels had been the victim of a hit-and-run driver—his body had been found on the sidewalk in Minsk.

In Tayshet, Shifrin got a first-hand account of the murder of Michoels from a fellow prisoner, Lev Sheinin, a top ranking official of the Moscow Procuratura who had been sent to Minsk to report on the death of Michoels. When Sheinin returned and submitted his report (which was never published), he was arrested as a "spy of the USA." He told Shifrin that in Minsk the head of the KGB had refused to speak to him, but that when he examined the body of Michoels, there were many signs of beating and torture. There were numerous perforations made by some sharp instrument like a pen—and his entire body was purple from beating. He was convinced the KGB had done it. When he came back to Moscow and submitted his report to the office of the Procurator-General (his chief), the KGB arrested him shortly afterwards, beat him, and said, "You dirty Jew! Are you trying to swim against us?"

Prisoner self-mutilation

Sometimes prisoners engaged in unbelievable acts of self-mutilation, either out of hopelessness and absolute desperation or because they had come to the end of their physical energies and found the ten hour workday intolerable. Some prisoners sought escape from work by producing artificial infections or "mastirki" on their bodies. This they frequently did by pulling a thread through the plaque between their teeth, then running the thread through a few inches of flesh with a needle, and leaving it there for twenty minutes to half an hour. The result was an almost immediate massive infection—which gave them hospitalization. Sometimes the prisoners swallowed pens or forks, or spoons to get themselves hospitalized. On one occasion a prisoner made a small anchor from heavy iron wire, tied a fine flexible wire to the end of the anchor and swallowed it—with the end of the fine wire protruding from his mouth. He told Shifrin that he had done this because he was seriously ill and had to get to the hospital immediately, but had so far been refused hospitalization.

Shifrin saw other prisoners who cut their stomachs or their veins, or cut off their toes or fingers because, as they told Shifrin, they could no longer bear the arduous daily labor which they felt would shortly destroy them—and they preferred to live without fingers or hands, but to live. Shifrin recalls one prisoner who cut off his hand with an ax and asked another prisoner to put the hand inside the lumber which had been loaded for shipment. When Shifrin asked him why he had done this, he answered that this lumber would go to other countries, and the hand might help people there to understand the conditions under which the lumber was cut.

Shifrin recalls another incident which took place in Camp No. 20 of the Potma complex in 1962. The 22nd Party Congress was about to take place. The official Communist newspapers (which prisoners were permitted to read) were full of "letters to the 22nd Congress" from workers leaders, promising to "fulfill and overfulfill" their production quotas as a "present to the Congress." A 20–21 year old prisoner named Nikolai Scherbakov had a fellow prisoner tatoo on his ears "Present to the 22nd Congress"—and then cut off his ears. In the exercise area in the presence of other prisoners he threw them in the face of a KGB guard. An investigative commission came to the camp a few days later and took photographs of Scherbakov, his head swathed in bandages and his ears on the table in front of him. When Shifrin asked Scherbakov why he had done this, Scherbakov replied that, had he not done this, people would never believe his account of life in the camps. Now, when he was a free man, at least he would be believed.

Shifrin underscores the point that prisoners who engaged in such self-mutilation were not insane but simply absolutely desperate. His accounts of self-mutilation are confirmed in statements by other concentration camp prisoners—e.g., in the book *My Testimony* by Anatoli Marchenko.

Camp No. 019—DOK

Shifrin remained in Camp No. 307 for approximately one year. Then he was brought, first, to camp 308 and then to camp 019–DOK, 019 was a large camp housing some 7–8,000 prisoners. Prisoners worked for the government's structural lumber combine (*combinat*) or DOK, which prepared prefab structural units for houses, etc. which were sent by trains to other parts of the country.

THE "SPECIALLY STRICT" PUNITIVE PRISON AT VIKHOREVKA

In the Fall of 1960, after his 7th attempt to escape, Shifrin was sent to the "Specially Strict" punitive concentration camp prison at Vikhorevka near Bratsk (Prison No. 410). There were only 250 people there—but they came from all the concentration camps of the USSR. It was a prison for really "bad" prisoners. The great majority of the prisoners who were brought to Vikhorevka never emerged from it. Many of them died within the first few years. Shifrin considers himself fortunate to have been sent to Potma at the end of six months. Some prisoners had been there 2 or 3 years when he arrived.

The main prison building was a rectangular block of reinforced concrete. When the first prisoners had built it, they had used railway rails instead of steel rods to reinforce the concrete, because rails were available while rods were not. There were two rows of 10–12 cells, each approximately 12′ by 16′, on either side of a center corridor, each cell housing twelve prisoners. They slept on common two-tier bunks against the window side of the cell. The free space in the cells had a common pot ("parasha,") in one corner, a small crude table, and two small benches in the other corner. There was one heating stove for each two cells, fed with logs from the corridor side. Each stove was fed with only two logs a day, so that the cells were bitterly cold. Frost several centimeters thick covered the inside of the outer wall and the window. The ceiling, where the air was warmest, was covered with condensation from the prisoner's breathing. When water ran down the walls to the floor (where the air was coldest) it froze— so that when Shifrin arrived in his first cell he noted that the floor was "like a skating rink."

Prisoners were given one blanket for each man. They had thin cotton underwear—"like handkerchiefs." Diet consisted of 500 gms (1¼ lbs.) of hard black bread ("like clay"), a bowl of soup made with rotten cabbage and frozen potatoes, and a small piece of fish.

Adjoining the cell block was a small exercise area, roughly 10m by 15m, where prisoners—with just over a square meter of space per prisoner—were permitted to "exercise" for half an hour a day, in two batches.

The prison area was surrounded by a high wooden fence and barbed wire, the area consisting of—from inside to outside: (1) coils of barbed wire; (2) a barbed wire fence about 9' high; (3) a ploughed earth strip about 3 meters wide; (4) a wooden fence about 12' high with 3' of barbed wire on top; (5) more ploughed earth; (6) another 9' high barbed wire fence; (7) more coils of barbed wire. At each corner and in the center of each fence were watch towers.

Prisoners had no work or occupation of any kind—they simply sat in their cells all day. Initially they had no reading material. But after a little revolt, they permitted prisoners a handful of books and one letter per month. Prisoners sought to keep up their morale and entertain themselves in various ways. One man who knew English conducted classes in English. A professor of physics conducted classes in cybernetics and nuclear physics, etc. Cardinal Slipy, who was in Shifrin's cell, gave lectures on religious philosophy.

The KGB director of the camp was a coarse, squat man, with a sadistic face. The prisoners had nicknamed him "Hitler."

At one end of the cell block were two "punitive cells," very narrow and without windows, heat, or furniture. Prisoners who were sent to punitive cells were reduced to 300 grams (¾ pound) black bread per day as their total diet, were stripped to their cotton underwear, and denied blankets. On the second or third day of their confinement in punitive cells prisoners invariably received a visit from "Hitler," who beat them mercilessly with a long stick.

Sick prisoners and mad prisoners were confined with those still healthy. In Shifrin's cell, one prisoner, Baranov, was suffering from advanced TB and coughed and spat blood constantly. Prisoners received occasional visits from medical orderlies and rare visits from a doctor. When a woman inspector from the Procurator's Office once visited the cell and saw Baranov spitting blood, she asked him if he was ill. In reply, Baranov spat some blood into his cupped hands, and showed it to her. The woman inspector said to "Hitler": "Have you had this man X-rayed for TB?"

"Yes, we had him X-rayed," said Hitler, "and he does have TB."

When the inspector remarked that this was not a good place for a man with TB, "Hitler" replied: "I am not a doctor—I am the director of a prison." Nothing was done to help Baranov or to hospitalize him, even though there was a hospital only a few miles away.

At one point in his incarceration, Shifrin's legs (both legs had been wounded in the war) became terribly swollen and painful from lack of nourishment and cold. He could barely walk. A KGB doctor whom he had previously met in the camps came to his cell with "Hitler." Shifrin asked the doctor if he could have hot water bottles twice a day. When the doctor suggested to "Hitler" that this would be a good idea, he replied, "I'm not running a resort here—I'm running a prison. When he's finished serving his time, then he can go to a resort and get himself some hot water."

In several cells there were prisoners who went insane after their arrival. They made life virtually impossible for their cellmates—frequently talking to themselves and screaming, sometimes defecating and urinating on the floor. But there was no way of getting them isolated.

It was in Prison No. 410 that Shifrin witnessed one of the most sickening incidents involving the abuse of women by the KGB guards. It was Sunday. The women were being escorted through the gate from the women's prison to the washroom to take showers. A group of nuns pleaded to be permitted to take their showers the following day because they did not want to violate their Sabbath or interrupt their prayer meeting. In reply, the guards pulled their clothes from the nuns (in freezing weather) and dragged them, naked, by their heels through the snow to the washroom. Shifrin and one other prisoner were able to see all this because they were in the exercise court at the time, cutting logs. The KGB officer responsible for this atrocity was "Hitler's" Deputy, Buriak.

Men who had been in Prison No. 410 for long periods of time frequently sought to kill themselves by slitting their veins with pieces of glass or sharpened stones, or even by cutting open their own bellies in hara kiri fashion. There were also the most gruesome incidents of self-mutilation. One prisoner, for example, pulled a few nails from the ceiling of the log washroom, and, using a rock as a hammer, drove one nail through his scrotum into the bench, another nail through the flesh of his hand into the bench and another nail through the flesh between his toes.

In April 1961, in one of their many inexplicable transportation operations, the KGB moved all of the political prisoners of the Tayshet "Ozerlag," including the prisoners in Prison 410, to the Potma complex, which bore the name "Dubravlag."

Shifrin has recent information that the "Specially Strict" camp prison No. 410 is still in operation today.

The trip from camp No. 410 to Potma

The anouncement in April 1961 that prisoners in Camp No. 410 were to be moved to another camp came out of the blue. The prisoners could hardly believe their luck because there had been no previous instance of large scale transfers out of Camp No. 410.

The morning after they were told of their impending move, the prisoners were taken to the railroad track and placed in cattle cars. There were 70 prisoners to a car, but there was sitting room for only 40 on the benches—so thirty had to sit on the floor between the benches. Armed soldiers, assisted by dogs, stood by while the prisoners were loaded aboard the train. In small towers above the train were guards armed with machine guns. Because there had been a number of instances where prisoners in transport had cut holes in the floors of the cars and dropped through to the track bed, the bottom of the end car was equipped with a giant steel rake, whose teeth reached within a few inches of the track bed.

The train traveled for six days and six nights. The prisoners received each day a meager ration of bread and salt fish, and a cup of water twice a day. They were not permitted to leave the car to tend to their needs—the latrine was inside the car.

When they emerged from the cars at Potma it was a warm sunny day (when they had left Vikhorevka, Camp No. 410, it was 25–30° below zero). All told, some 2,000 prisoners emerged from the train, which apparently brought prisoners from many camps in the Tayshet complex.

While the sun was warm, the view around them was grim. On both sides of the railroad track were the fences of concentration camps—old, grey fences topped with barb wire, with corner watchtowers manned by armed soldiers. The fences and watchtowers succeeded each other without interruption as far as the eye could see.

While the Tayshet prisoners were standing there, surrounded by armed guards, the camp gates across from them swung open—and out came 200–250 women carrying little children in their arms, surrounded by soldiers with rifles and dogs. The camp guards immediately realized that they had made a mistake in permitting the women and children to be seen by the two thousand prisoners from Tayshet—and they began to herd the women back through the gate, using their rifle butts liberally. The women were crying, the children were crying, soldiers were cursing, and the dogs were barking.

Unable to contain their indignation at the treatment of the women and children, many of the Tayshet prisoners shouted their protests to the guards, calling them "Fascists!" The guards shouted back at the prisoners—then fired their weapons in the air and shouted to the prisoners to lie down.

At this very moment the camp loud speaker came on with "the glorious news that the Soviet astronaut Gagarin is now in orbit in his rocket!" This, said the commentator demonstrated the superiority of Soviet society over capitalistic society.

Shifrin had heard of special camps for women before but this was the first time he had seen one. In the Soviet Union there are not only special camps for women, but special camps for women with children, and special camps for children.

After the incident with the women, the prisoners who had been unloaded from the train were placed in a transportation camp near the railway. In this camp there were prisoners not only from the Tayshet complex, but also from Vorkuta, from Inta, from Igarka and from Kolyma. The prisoners remained in the transportation camp for 10–15 days, during which there was ample time to swap experiences.

Some of the prisoners told stories which even Shifrin, with his experiences, found particularly horrifying.

He learned that in some camps guards could wantonly kill prisoners—and frequently did—without investigation or punishment of any kind.

He was told by prisoners from Vorkuta that once in 1961, the Vorkuta guards had made an "example" of one prisoner by pouring water over him in 30° below zero—converting him into an ice-statue in a few minutes time.

The prisoners from Vorkuta said that their guards and officers had behaved like sadists in dealing with the relatives who came to see the prisoners—often traveling thousands of miles from Moscow by train. They tried to obtain bribes from the relatives—and frequently, in return for their "favors," they demanded that prisoners' wives sleep with them.

Shifrin recalls a particularly tragic case in 1969 involving a Belorussian engineer by the name of Evgeny Rusinovich. When Rusinovich's wife came to see him, the officer in charge refused to permit a meeting, even though his wife had traveled 3,000 km. for the meeting and she had every right to visit him under Soviet law. When she left the camp commander's office, crying, some indignant prisoners who worked with the guards showed her the building where her husband worked in the daytime, and showed her a place where she could hide away overnight. When Rusinovich came to work in the morning he met his wife—but someone passed the information on to the guards, and the commanding officer came and took the wife to the gates of the camp where he beat her fiercely before the eyes of her husband, and then, for good measure, beat her husband before her eyes. Then he had the guard cut off the wife's hair and hang it on the barbed-wire fence.

Rusinovich went mad with the desire for vengeance. When the incident was over, he went and found himself an ax and with this he killed an officer and a soldier. Taking the soldier's automatic rifle, he then shot down more officers and more guards. Commandeering a vehicle by shooting the guards, he drove like a madman from camp to camp in the complex. Aided by the element of surprise and by the cowardice of the guards, he shot down, according to reports, scores of officers and guards in a number of camps before he was finally cornered and encircled by a small army towards the end of the day. At this point, he killed himself. The "victorious" guards stomped his body and set their dogs upon it.

The Old Believers

During their stay in the transportation camp the prisoners were sent every day to cut lumber. One day Shifrin was sick and unable to work, and they put him in a punishment cell. There he met a group of strange people with long beards and handmade clothes and boots.

The strange people were "Old Believers," religious fundamentalists who recognized only the authority of God. They told Shifrin that their village had originally been in the Southern Urals, but that in 1919, in order to get away from the endless war, they had moved their entire village a distance of almost 1,500 km to a site in the virgin forests of the Northern Urals, far removed from any other community. There they had been able to live until 1959 without any contact with the Communist government or, for that matter, with the outside world. In 1959, however, their community had been "discovered" by a KGB helicopter. The KGB promptly paid a visit to the village. On their heels, came Red Army officers to conscript the young men of the village into the Red Army. But, as absolute pacifists, the Old Believers refused to serve. All of the men in the village had been arrested and sent to concentration camps, while the women had been distributed to different kolkhozes.

From the punitive cells the guards brought them the following morning to one of the barracks. Standing on a table to greet them, dressed in a fur coat with a riding whip in his hand, was Major Ribakov, the camp commander. Ribakov immediately started cursing the prisoners demanding to know why they were not at work. "You are sick?" he asked one prisoner. "Yes," answered the prisoner. "Then get to work immediately!" said Ribakov. "It's the best medicine we have in the camp!"

Then the guards brought in the Old Believers. Ribakov shouted, "Why aren't they in camp clothes? Why aren't they at work?" To this the Old Believers answered, "We do not wish to work for anti-Christ." Ribakov exploded and shouted, "Put them in the punitive cells for six months."

The Old Believers, prodded by the guards, moved toward the door. At the door they stopped and turned in the direction of Ribakov and each of them made the sign of the cross directly toward Ribakov and said. "Be gone, Satan!"

During his ten years in the camps Shifrin saw many thousands of believers of all faiths—orthodox Catholics, Baptists, Jehovah's Witnesses, Muslims, and Jews. Prisoners were not permitted to have Bibles in the camp because the Bible was considered anti-Soviet literature; nor were they permitted to pray or to observe their holy days. On one occasion they attempted to shave the beards off the Old Believers, and when the Old Believers resisted, they chained their hands so tightly that some of them fainted.

"Specially Strict" camp No. 10

From the transportation camp near Potma, they brought the prisoners to "Specially Strict" camp No. 10 near Udarnol. Here there were roughly 250 prisoners in the cell block, with seven men squeezed into a ten foot by nine foot cell. There was one common bunk across the wall barely wide enough for all the prisoners to lie on their sides. The rest of the cell consisted of an "exercise space," 9 feet long by 30 inches wide. The 9 foot length in practice was closer to 6½ feet because there was the common pot at one end of the exercise space and a small table at the other end. During the day time, when all seven prisoners were in the cell, they would take turns, two at a time, in walking around the exercise space. While the two men exercised, the other five were confined to the common bunk. In the summer and fall the prisoners worked six days a week, making bricks by hand. During this period even the one day a week of rest was an agony because on that day they were confined to the cell. But the real agony was the winter and spring when the temperature made it impossible to make bricks and they were confined to their cell for weeks on end.

Once they asked the prison commander, Major Likin, for permission to make a flower garden in the prison grounds. They told him that his superiors would be impressed by the fact that he had been able to get his prisoners to do this with voluntary labor. When Likin gave permission, the prisoners were glad because this would give them an opportunity to get out of their cells and get some fresh air in the springtime. But when they began to dig, the prisoners were astonished to find almost everywhere in their plot human bones and hair at a depth of six to eight inches. They later learned that the authorities had built prison Camp No. 10 on the site of a forest cemetery for camp prisoners.

The cell block, which was made of brick, was relatively warm compared to other prisons in which Shifrin spent time. But there was no way of opening the windows, and with seven men in a cell it would become unbearably stuffy. With Shifrin as the principal instigator, the prisoners broke the window to let in air. Major Likin was beside himself with anger when he came in to view the damage—but Shifrin was able to escape punishment for his role in this incident, first, because Likin was not the worst of camp commanders, and second, because both Likin and Shifrin had fought in the Königsberg campaign and Likin respected him because of this.

There were in Camp No. 10 a new population of dissidents of all kinds—Russians, Ukrainians, Jews, Balts, Tartars, Georgians, etc. They had been swept up in the new drive against intellectual dissidents and minority nationalism.

In this camp, Shifrin met some men who had been in the Zionist movement in the USSR from the beginning. Among them were David Havkin, Podolski, whose entire family—father, mother, and son—have been arrested at the same time, and many others whose only crime was that they had wanted to go to Israel.

There were many other Jews who had been arrested primarily because of the role they had played in the general dissident movement—for example, I. Bokshtein, who, together with Eduard Kutznetsov, had made an anti-Soviet speech in Mayakowski Square.

There were some other Jewish prisoners—actors and writers from Minsk—who had been arrested because they belonged to the group of people who each day had brought flowers faithfully to the place where the body of the famous Jewish actor, Michoels, had been found in the street. The KGB had said it was a hit and run accident. But everyone knew it was a KGB murder.

There were also in the camp many religious believers—among them Boris Zdorevich, a Baptist leader from Kharkov, who told Shifrin that the KGB was attempting to arrest all those Baptists who refused cooperation with the special priests whom the KGB had placed at the head of the Russian Baptist Church. There was also one of the leaders of the Seventh Day Adventists in the USSS—Vladimir Shelkov—who was serving his third term in the camps, where he had already passed 21 years. There was the Baptist, Saveli Solodiankin, 81 years old, who was serving his third consecutive ten year term in the camps.

There were many religious prisoners whose faiths required that they eat special types of food or food specially prepared. They asked the camp officials for food which they could cook themselves. In reply, the authorities prohibited them from receiving parcels of food from their families. In 1963, in another camp, Shifrin saw the KGB destroy a little vegetable garden which religious believers had created with much labor and sacrifice. Denied foods prepared according to the requirements of their religion, many of the religious believers subsisted on black bread and 14 grams of sugar a day. Recently there arrived in Israel Machmum Kaganov, who was with Shifrin in Potma, and who ate only bread every day for seven years.

Sadistic Treament of Relatives

Many of the officers and guards were real sadists who enjoyed particularly tormenting the prisoners' relatives.

Shifrin's mother was very ill and broken after suffering through ten years of his father's imprisonment and eight years of Shifrin's. The adviser to the Commander ofi Camp No. 10 once said to Shifrin, "I know from your mother's letter how sad she is and how ill. I will permit you to write to your mother so that she can send you a food package." Shifrin wrote to his mother. A month later the officer asked him to his office, gave him a letter from his mother, and said, "Read."

His mother's letter said, "Dear son: Where are you? I was so astonished whén the parcel I sent you came back marked: 'Addressee not here.' Are you alive? I cannot sleep or eat.... Write me!"

The officer sat and watched Shifrin read this with a smirk on his face. He had contrived the entire situation for the satisfaction he derived from watching Shifrin's torment!

A few months later, the sadistic captain permitted Shifrin's mother to visit him—the first visit she had been permitted in eight years. When she came to Potma, the captain harangued her for several hours, telling her that her son was a criminal, that he had been a principal instigator of prison riots and uprisings, and that he would remain in prison until the end of his life. After this lengthy cheerful preface, he permitted Shifrin's mother to meet with him for four hours.

When Shifrin finally saw his mother, she was so upset and broken that virtually the entire four hours she begged him to be good and not to get into trouble. Shifrin tried to explain to his mother that the captain was a sadist who enjoyed tormenting people. But she was too frightened to listen. When she returned to Moscow she had a stroke, was in a coma for several months, and then died.

Concentration Camp No. 7

In February 1963, Shifrin was moved from prison Camp No. 10 to Camp No. 7, which was also in the Potma "Dubravlag," or complex, at a distance of 20 to 25 kms. from No. 10.

Concentration Camp No. 7 had a very strict regime, but here people lived in barracks rather than in cells. Shifrin was initially placed in an invalid barrack, which housed about 400 prisoners. The prisoners in this camp worked in a plant where they made furniture, including cabinets for TV and radio.

In this, Shifrin's last year in the camps, the camp regime became stricter from day to day. The rules governing meetings with relatives became constantly more arduous. There were frequent searches—body searches and barracks searches. When the guards went through the barracks, the prisoners were required to stand outside, sometimes for hours on end.

Returnees to the Soviet Union

In Camp No. 7 Shifrin met a number of one-time refugees from Communism, who had lived in France and Germany and other countries, and who had been foolish enough to believe the propaganda campaign which the Soviet regime had addressed to expatriates all over the world. When the expatriates returned to their "motherland," the press made a tremendous noise about them. But they carried the virus of foreign exposure, and, not very surprisingly, some months after their return quite a number of them found themselves sentenced to 10 years in the concentration camps. In this category, Shifrin recalls the names of Golub and Ponomarenko.

The Translation of Exodus

It was during his stay in Camp No. 7 that Shifrin translated Leon Uris' book, *Exodus* into Russian—a version which was subsequently widely circulated in the Soviet Union via numerous handtyped *Samizdat* copies. A paperback copy of *Exodus* had been smuggled into the camp. As he read it, Shifrin would translate portions of it aloud to groups of Jewish prisoners. One day he decided to make a written translation. This was an enormously complicated and risky operation. Simply to get the paper on which to write, he had to enlist the aid of all the Jewish prisoners, and many nonJewish prisoners. They brought him sheets of paper, one at a time, or two at a time. Although they all knew that Shifrin was working on something big, no one betrayed him. When the translation was completed, Shifrin decided to make one copy in a hurry—so that there would be a backup copy if anything happened to the original. He divided the translation between 30 prisoners, 20-30 pages per prisoner, and, working together, they completed the second copy in very short order. Again, no one betrayed him.

When Shifrin was released on June 6, 1963 (he was informed shortly before his release that his sentence had been reduced from 25 years to 10 years) he was able to smuggle one of the two copies of the translation out of the camp in his baggage. A typewritten copy was subsequently made by a sympathetic non-Jewish girl in Odessa—and this became the beginning of the round-robin *Samizdat* copying operation on a national scale.

Among the signed statements which Shifrin has submitted for the record is one from a fellow-veteran of Camp No. 7 who worked on the translation of *Exodus* with Shifrin. (See Appendix to Part 2, P. 111.)

FOREIGN POWS IN SOVIET CONCENTRATION CAMPS

From '53 to '56 Shifrin met many thousands of POWs of all nationalities—Germans, Italians, Frenchmen, Spaniards, etc.—scattered through most of the camps in which he was detained. In '55, *10 years after the war* ended, there began large-scale repatriation of POWs—or at least of those who had survived. By the end of 1956 the process of repatriation appeared to have been completed, or almost completed. Shifrin no longer met POWs in the long list of camps through which he moved. However, in 1962, *17 years after the war ended*, he did encounter a group of some dozen Belgian officer POWs who, he believes, were finally released as a result of the intervention of the Belgian queen on visit to Moscow.

Some weeks before Shifrin's release in June of 1963, some new prisoners arrived in Camp No. 7 who told Shifrin that they had come there from a camp on Wrangel Island—one of the northernmost and bleakest outposts of Soviet territory. Shifrin was surprised at this, because he had not previously heard of a camp as far north as Wrangel Island. The prisoners said that they had served for five years on Wrangel Island, in a special detachment which brought food to three concentration camps in which lived only "fascist generals" and other high-ranking foreign officers. When Shifrin said that all POWs had been repatriated in 1956, they persisted in their statement that high-ranking foreign officers, POWs from 1945, were still on Wrangel Island.

Shifrin was not disposed to believe this at the time, but recently he has had confirmation from another source. He has received a statement from a recent immigrant to Israel, a former concentration camp inmate, who reported that he was interned on Wrangel Island until 1962; that there he met many former POWs, Italian, German, Spanish; that there he also met R. Trushnovich, the NTS leader [NTS is a Russian anti-communist organization] who was kidnapped from West Germany in 1951, and Raoul Wallenberg, the Swedish diplomat who was credited with saving many thousands of Hungarian Jews from deportation by the Nazis, and who disappeared when the Red Army entered Budapest. (The Swedish Government addressed a whole series of inquiries to the Soviet Government *re* the fate of Wallenberg, but the Soviet Government always took the stand that it knew absolutely nothing about what happened to Wallenberg—this, in the face of eye-witness reports that Wallenberg was last seen being marched off under Red Army escort.)

Both the Israeli resident and the prisoners whom Shifrin met in Camp No. 7 before his release, told him that the POW's on Wrangel Island were used for medical experiments, some involving the effects of radiation on the human body, others involving the effects of prolonged submersion at great depths. (NOTE: A translation of this statement appears in the Appendix to Part 2, P. 127. The Israeli citizen who submitted it asks that his name not be made public because he still has family in the Soviet Union. His real name has been given in confidence to the subcommittee.)

Stalin's plan for the liquidation of the Jews

From prisoners whom he met in the Tayshet complex, Shifrin heard a bizarre story about Stalin's plan to liquidate the Jews. The prisoners told him that in 1952 (a time which coincides with the peak of the anti-Jewish terror) they had been sent to the Lake Baikal area to help construct a railroad spur. The spur ran from the main line of the TransSiberian railroad for a distance of two or three kilometers to the shore of the lake—to be more exact, to the edge of a vertical cliff several hundred feet high that overlooked the lake.

The prisoners worked overtime every day, seven days a week, on the project—and as a bonus for their special efforts they were told that each day of their labor would be counted as ten days of their term. For the three months that they worked on the railroad, therefore, they were credited with having served thirty months of their terms.

Because the railroad had no conceivable justification, the prisoners asked the officers in charge why they were building a railroad that led to the edge of a cliff. The officers explained to them that Stalin wanted the railroad completed in a hurry because he planned to announce the forcible deportation of all Soviet Jews to the already aborted "Jewish Soviet Republic" of Birobidjan. But, under the Stalin plan the Jews would never get as far as Birobidjan. The railway spur to the cliff overlooking Lake Baikal was being built so that the Jews could be liquidated without the trouble of building crematoria. (Lake Baikal at that point was many thousands of feet deep).

Shifrin was skeptical about the story at the time. But in the course of his travels around the Soviet Union in 1966–67 he made it a point to visit the point south of Lake Baikal which the prisoners had described; and, sure enough, the railroad spur was there terminating on the top of a cliff several hundred feet high. Everything was as the prisoners had described it, except that the roadbed was now overgrown with weeds and the rails were badly rusted.

Political, religious, and national resistance in the Soviet Union.

Numerous underground groups and movements are springing up all over the Soviet Union. Many hundreds of freedom fighters have been arrested, and sent to jails and concentration camps for up to 15 years.

The civil rights movement in the Soviet Union goes back to before the Hungarian revolution of 1956. Among the early heroes of this resistance, Shifrin notes particularly the names of Eduard Kuznetsov, Ilya Bokshtein, Igor Avdeev, Viktor Khaustov, and Yuri Osipov. They began their resistance with the public readings of poetry in Mayakovsky Square. First they read the poems of Mayakowsky. Then they began to read some of their own poetry that contained criticisms of the Soviet regime. Then Bokshtein one day climbed up on the statute of Mayakowsky and delivered a passionate oration against Soviet tyranny. A battle ensued with the secret police, and scores of those who took part in the demonstration were arrested and imprisoned.

Since that time there have been many similar public protests in the Soviet Union—some of them inspired by the suppression of the Hungarian Revolution, some of them inspired by the desire for more freedom and hatred of the regime of oppression, some of them inspired at least in part by the recurring food shortages. In every case the answer of the regime has been more arrests and more repression. Over the past 16 or 17 years in the Soviet Union there have been riots and even major clashes in a whole series of Soviet cities, including Ryazan, Timyr Tau, Krasnodar, Vladivostok, and Novocherkask. Only half a year ago there was a major riot in which many people were killed in the city of Dnieprodzerzhinsk, on the river Dnieper.

Intellectuals like Galanskov and Ginzburg tried during this period to publish an underground magazine. The *Samizdat* movement became nationwide—thousands of people participating in the laborious copying of documents of opposition. The *Chronicle of Current Events*, chief of the *Samizdat* publications, began to come out on a regular basis—and despite frantic efforts on the part of the regime it continues to come out until this day. A Jewish underground chronicle, *Exodus*, also begin to appear on a regular basis. Entire books, like Marchenko's "My Testimony," were circulated in *Samizdat* form.

There were many casualties in this unrelenting battle for freedom—men and women whose names are justly honored throughout the world. Among the best known of these martyrs for freedom were Sinyavsky and Daniel, Pavl Litvinov, General Grigorenko, Anatoli Marchenko, Victor Krasin and Victor Feinberg. All of these men are still in prison.

One of the principal heroes of the Soviet resistance to whom Shifrin wants to call attention is Vladimir Bukovsky, with whom he spent some time in prison.

Bukovsky was one of the initiators of the Russian democratic opposition. Out of 30 years of his life, 9 were spent in psychiatric prisons and concentration camps. In January 1972 he was sentenced to a total of 12 years for having sent to the West a collection of documents concerning the confinement of healthy dissenters to special psychiatric instiutions. [These documents together with other materials were released by this subcommittee on December 4, 1972.]

Igor Ogurtsov, Mikhail Sado, Yevgeni Vagin, and Boris Averochkin, leaders of the *All-Russian Social-Christian Union for the Liberation of the People*, and some sixty of their followers were arrested in Leningrad, Tomsk, Irkutsk, Petrozavodsk, and other cities, because their patriotic appeal for the revival of Russia's spiritual and religious values did not fit into the pattern of the Communist-sponsored policy of "Russification."

Also arrested during '71 and '72 were Vyacheslav Chornovil, Valentin Moroz, Ivan Dzyuba, Svyatoslav Karavansky and scores of other Ukrainian nationalists who resisted the ruthless "Russification" campaign unleashed by the Kremlin leaders, who want to divide and rule. When riots broke out in Novocherkask and Dnieprodzerinsk, the Communists suppressed them with the hands of the Uzbeks—but in Tashkent they used Ukrainians to crush the rioting Uzbeks.

Freedom fighters in the Baltic countries have also paid a heavy price for their continuing resistance.

Victor Kalninsh, Juozas Zdebkis, Willi Saarte, and many other Latvian, Lithuanian, and Estonian patriots strove for the independence of their nations. Shifrin also calls attention to the plight of Rollan Kadyev, Reshat Bairamov and other Crimean Tartars who demanded the right for their people to return to their native land. (More than 500,000 Crimean Tartars were deported to Siberia at Stalin's orders and are still denied the right to return home by the present government.)

Navy Captain Gennady Gavrilov and scores of his friends were arrested in Leningrad, Moscow, Talin, Riga, Baku, Perm, and Khabarovsk in connection with "the conspiracy of the Baltic Fleet officers." These are just a few of the examples Shifrin will present.

Despite numerous arrests the unbroken spirit of the Jewish resistance manifests itself in many ways. In November 1972, Grisha Berman went to the draft board in Odessa and declared that he refused to serve in the Red Army because in his heart he felt himself a citizen of Israel. He got a three year sentence. A three year sentence was also imposed on Vladimir Markman just for a few telephone conversations with friends in Israel. Eduard Kuznetsov, Silva Zalmanson, Anatoli Altman, and their friends tried to fly secretly to Israel because the government stubbornly refused to permit them to emigrate legally. Today they languish in the Potma concentration camp No. 10—the most horrible of all in the Soviet Union—locked up for 15 years.

Shifrin's warning to the free world

Shifrin has prepared an opening statement for his own guidance—which he will not read but paraphrase extemporaneously. The final paragraphs of this statement are worth quoting.

"And now let me voice a note of warning. The cancer of Communism has now spread over half of Europe, China, Cuba, and parts of Africa. The Communists try to destroy your society with the help of all those radical groups. They deceive your youth with propaganda; they try to demoralize you so that they can seize power in your country. And don't think that I am spreading panic. Remember that there was a time when there was no Communism in Eastern Europe or in Cuba, and the red flags were not exposed so boldly in France and Italy. In the Soviet Union, Communists try to eradicate all dissidents, all democratic elements. They lock people up only because they dare to think. All this spells danger to you: The more they consolidate their power internally, the greater is the threat to the free countries.

"That is the reason why I am here today. I want to remind you of our responsibility to those who are oppressed. They need our help. How can we help them? We can help them in two ways: first, by exposing the facts; and second, by voicing our indignation.

"In helping them we shall also be helping ourselves."

*   *   *   *   *

[Commenting on Mr. Shifrin's closing warning to the Free World, Senator Gurney, who chaired the hearing, made this concluding statement:

"I share your same fear about the ultimate goal of Communism. I think many of our people, not only in this country but also in the free world are not aware of the fact that concentration camps, political prisoners, slave camps, are pretty much the same in the Soviet Union as they ever were, and that is why I think this testimony is so important.

"It is hard to believe that over a century or more after most civilized countries have done away with slavery, that we have slavery in one of the most powerful nations in the world and on a scale such as never existed before at any time in the history of the world."]

AVRAHAM SHIFRIN: CHRONOLOGY OF IMPRISONMENT

June 6, 1953: Arrested.

Until December 1953: Lefortovo, Lubyanka, and Butirskaya prisons.

December 1953: Deportation—Sverdlovsk, Cheliabinsk, Novosibirsk prisons.

January–June 1954: Omsk—"Kamyshlag."

June 1954 to July 1955: Smipalatinsk and Ust Kamenogorsk prisons—in "Peschlag."

July 1955: Deportation to Tayshet "Ozerlag" (on the way in prisons Rubtsovsk, Barnaul, Novosibirsk).

July 1955 to April 1961: Tayshet (concentration camps)—Nos. 025, 0625, 04, 019, 014, 042, 038, 016, 307, 308, 420, 02, 410, and hospital—camp in Vikhorevka.

April 1961 to June 1963: Potma—"Dubravlag":

    (a) April 1961—Strict Camp No. 10 (prison) until May 1962.

    (b) May 1962 to June 1963—No. 7.

June 1963 to May 1967: Exiled to Karaganda (on the way, in Moscow, Kharkov, Vinnitza, Odessa, Petropavlovsk, Tselinograd, Kustanai).

U.S.S.R. LABOR CAMPS

THURSDAY, FEBRUARY 1, 1973

U.S. Senate,
Subcommittee To Investigate the
Administration of the Internal Security Act
and Other Internal Security Laws
of the Committee on the Judiciary,
Washington, D.C.

The subcommittee met, pursuant to notice, at 9:30 a.m., in room 2228, Dirksen Senate Office Building, Senator Edward J. Gurney presiding.

Also present: J. G. Sourwine, chief counsel; Samuel J. Scott, associate counsel; A. L. Tarabochia, chief investigator; and David Martin, senior analyst.

Senator GURNEY. The subcommittee will come to order.

The hearings today, I think, are very important. There is a feeling of euphoria in the United States among Americans, and also in the Western democracies, about communism in general, and Russian communism in particular. This is neither the time nor the place for a detailed history of why this is so. However, I think it is well to mention a few of the more recent reasons—the easing of the cold war tensions, especially in Europe; the German agreements of 2 years ago; the agreements more recently over West Berlin; the SALT talks that have been going on for some period of time; the discussions of a reduction in force between NATO and the Warsaw Pact nations; and especially, President Nixon's historic trip to Moscow and the agreements signed there last year—the anti-ballistic-missile treaty, the interim agreement on nuclear weapons, the wheat sale, the trade agreements, the space agreement. All this has brought about a feeling of a sense of euphoria about the nature of Soviet communism. The U.S. people believe or think that the Russian attitudes are changing, that they are maturing, that they want to be part of the rest of the world. There is even the suggestion that the Soviets are becoming more like the Western democracies and we are becoming more like Russians, especially in their social programs.

Again, the purpose of these hearings is not to explore that vast and complicated subject. The purpose of these hearings is to shed some light on one aspect of Russian Soviet society which is totally repugnant, repulsive, barbaric and unacceptable to the United States and Western democratic societies, and that is the continuous existence of Russian concentration camps.

No one thing could better point up the inappropriateness of that sense of euphoria that I mentioned than this aspect of Soviet life, these concentration camps. There was a time when much was written in this country about the brutal treatment of the Russian people by the masters in the Kremlin. We knew and wrote and talked about and condemned the murder of millions of Russians by Stalin and his mass liquidator, Nikita Khrushchev, who succeeded him as the Russian Premier. We knew and wrote and talked about the arrest and conviction and imprisonment without fair trial of millions of Russians in concentration camps.

There was a time when the word Siberia had no other meaning here in the United States, and around the world for that matter, than one vast prison camp for political prisoners of the Russian Communists. But in recent years, most of that has been forgotten. World War II and the horror of the concentration camps of Hitler's Third Reich diverted our attention and focused it upon the crimes of the Nazis perpetrated on their political opposition and especially upon the German Jews. We forgot and overlooked that Hitler merely stole a page from the Communist way of life and that while concentration camps were eliminated in Germany by World War II and many of the Nazis' concentration camp people were tried and convicted for their crimes against humanity, the same brutal barbaric treatment of Soviet citizens and concentration camp imprisonment continues to flourish today.

This morning, we are fortunate to have as our witness a former Russian citizen who spent some 10 years in various concentration camps in Russia. It is our privilege to hear his testimony about his experience in these concentration camps and his opinion as to whether this kind of treatment of Soviet citizens continues today and on what scale.

Now, as is customary in these hearings, the witnesses are sworn before the testimony is taken. We have the principal witness who is Avraham Shifrin. We also have an interpreter in case we have problems with understanding some of the testimony, Mr. Boldyreff—is that how you pronounce that?

Mr. BOLDYREFF. Yes.

Senator GURNEY. What is your first name, Mr. Boldyreff?

Mr. BOLDYREFF. Constantin.

Senator GURNEY. You two gentlemen will please stand, first, Mr. Boldyreff, will you raise your right hand?

Do you solemnly swear that you will faithfully and truly interpret the questions to the witness and his answers?

Mr. BOLDYREFF. I do.

Senator GURNEY. And Avraham Shifrin, do you solemnly swear that the testimony you are about to give will be the truth, the whole truth, and nothing but the truth, so help you God?

Mr. SHIFRIN. I do.

TESTIMONY OF AVRAHAM SHIFRIN, ACCOMPANIED BY CONSTANTIN BOLDYREFF, INTERPRETER

Mr. Sourwine. Mr. Shifrin, where were you born?

Mr. Shifrin. May I be seated?

Mr. Sourwine. Oh, yes.

Mr. Shifrin. I was born in 1923 in Minsk, Belorussia.

Mr. Sourwine. Tell us briefly what your education was?

Mr. Shifrin. When I was only a little child, my parents brought me to Moscow and all my life, from 1 year old, I was in Moscow and then I finished school—in Union Soviet Socialist Republics, there is no college. It is 10 years schools. Then I became a student in a law institute. Then it was war, and I finished this institute only after Second World War.

Mr. Sourwine. You have spent years in labor camps in the U.S.S.R.?

Mr. Shifrin. Yes.

Mr. Sourwine. You have studied the labor camp system in the U.S.S.R.?

Mr. Shifrin. Yes; from 1953, June 6, to 1963, June 6, I was in concentration camps and then they sent me to exile to Kazakhstan.

Mr. Sourwine. Do you want to tell us, just as an overview and in general words, what the purport of your testimony will be today with regard to the extent of the camps, the number of prisoners, and perhaps the proportion of these prisoners who are Jews or other minorities? Then we can go into details.

Mr. Shifrin. Yes. Thank you.

First I must ask you to excuse my English, because I cannot speak like you. I learned my English in concentration camps and first my teachers were kidnaped American officers.

I also want to tell you that I am very glad to be here, and I must tell you that it is big pride for me to give testimony in Senate of United States about these questions. Also, I must tell to my friends in concentration camps from this room they must excuse me, because I cannot mention all these hundreds, hundreds, and hundreds of names which I know sit now in the prisons.

Now, I will tell you from which source I have information, to tell you not only about my own experience from 1953 to 1963——

Senator Gurney. This is the period of time that you were prisoner?

Mr. Shifrin. Yes; these 10 years I was personally in prisons. I was in this 10 years, in Omsk, in Kazakhstan, Semipalatinsk—I was in Tayshet, a district near Baikal; and I was also in this district, Dubrovlag. That is my own experience.

Senator Gurney. These prison camps were both in what we call European Russia as well as Siberia?

Mr. Shifrin. Yes; Potma, that is in the U.S.S.R., in central Russia—European. (Points to map, which is reproduced on p. 2.)

This district is the district of Kazakhstan, north Kazakhstan, I was here in two different prisons, in Semipalatinsk—here—and here; and Tayshet, that is a district with 600 kilometers railway with only concentration camps on both sides of this railway. How many concentration camps we have there, I do not know.

Also, in this big black line, you see my way to prison in prison car. With this line, you can see that I came to one, two, three, four, five, six prisons on the way—transportation prisons—because they have prisons like you have here motels on the way. And I was there, and I was inside these prisons in Kuybischev, in Sakhalinsk, in Sverdlovsk, in Kavaya, and I have seen what it is in this prison. I have seen this way, not one time—I was here three times—because I was first in Omsk, then I was in this district, Semipalatinsk, then I was in Orsha, and always I was in these concentration camps and prisons. That is why, this way, I have seen minimum three times inside these prisons and concentration camps on the way.

Now, when I finished those 10 years, I came to this district for exile in Kazakhstan.

Senator GURNEY. How many prison camps were you in altogether?

Mr. SHIFRIN. Oh, I am not statistician; I did not make this count. But I think that maybe 30, 30–35, not more. And maybe five or six prisons.

Also, I was in Moscow. In Moscow I was in three prisons—in the prison Lefortovo, Lubyanka, and I was in the prison Butirskaia. This is a map of Moscow. (Points to map.) I cannot show you all the prisons in U.S.S.R. and Moscow. Once we make this count with my friends which know other prisons and we make count of 27 prisons in Moscow. I put here only 14. Butirskaia—that is a prison in which you can see maybe 10–12 buildings with prisoners. That is a little city inside the city of Moscow.

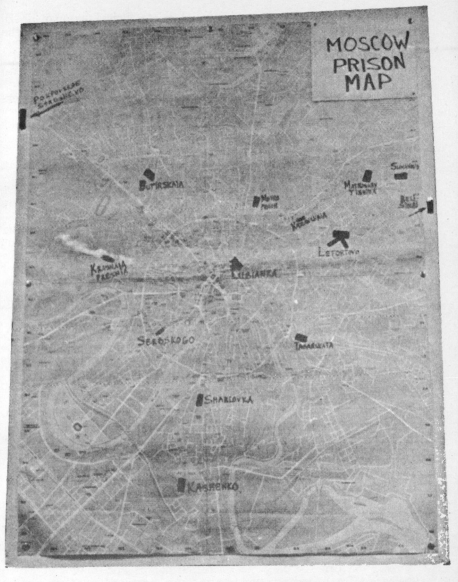

Moscow Prison Map Prepared by Avraham Shifrin.—The map above shows 14 of the major prisons in the Moscow area. The population of these prisons is heavily political. The largest of them, Lubyanka, Butirskaia and Lefortovo, are reputed to have 10,000 or more prisoners each. The Serbskogo institution is the best know of the psychiatric prisons, and through it have passed most of the well known intellectual dissidents who have fraudulently been confirmed as insane by the KGB psychiatrists.

Here is the Lefortovo prison—special strict political prison of KGB. Lefortovo prison has such special shape; I was here also in the months of investigation.

Senator GURNEY. How many prisoners were there?

Mr. SHIFRIN. Here is big building and here are two wings, two buildings. All this is only one building.

I cannot count prisoners in five stories prison. Each cell two meters wide and five meters long, in a five-story building. This building is very big and these two wings also. I think that may be 10,000 people they can hold in this building. How many is there now, I do not know.

Senator GURNEY. What year was this?

Mr. SHIFRIN. 1953. In the center of this prison, you can see big round room. In this room stays the officers and two soldiers and they see when soldiers bring prisoners from these cells in wings, they have flags in their hands and they show way to prisoners because prisoners must not meet each other. It is a very big prison with big "traffic."

And this prison, Lubyanka, in which I was is only 2 or 3 hundred meters from Kremlin. I was not in Kremlin—but I was in this prison, Lubyanka. This prison is KGB office building in the center of Moscow and inside this building there is big eight-story prison. And another big prison—you can see this is round on the map, underground prison, under Dzerzhinsky Square of the city. I was there also.

Here you can see on the map big prison—transportation prison— "Krasnaia Presnya." All Moscow people know this.

In this other prison, "Matrosskaya Tishina" was my father. My father was 10 years in the prison camps, and died there: 1938 to 1948. I am second political prisoner in family. And I remember this prison because I was in the lines in the nights to give to father bread, because people in concentration camps and prisons always are in starvation.

I think that is enough now about this. If you would be interested, I will tell again about it.

Senator GURNEY. You mentioned KGB. Does that term refer to the Soviet Secret Police?

Mr. SHIFRIN. KGB, the Secret Service of the U.S.S.R., political secret service.

Now, you see, on the map I was here in Potma, only 500 kilometers from Moscow. If you would look on all the maps of the U.S.S.R., you cannot find a railway in this place. But you can find on my map this railway which goes in reality from Potma and Zubova Polyana, north to Barashevo. This rail is the railway of the KGB only: the secret service is the owner of this railway. In both sides, in the wild forest, you can see only concentration camps and plants in which prisoners from concentration camps work. I can tell you that because I was in these concentration camps. These stars on the map—they are concentration camps. These rounds on the map, those are prisons, because they have their special prisons also, not only concentration camps. And also I was here in concentration camp which only have name.

I will show you later a plan of the cell in which I was there. It is a prison with the name "Camp", it is a "special strict concentration camp." That is a prison like all the prisons, with bars and cells, and people work there in the brick plant near this prison.

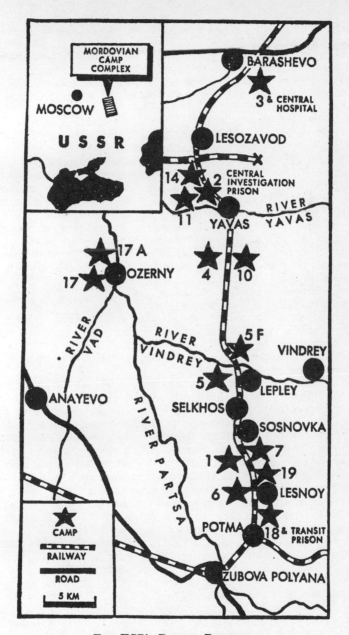

THE KGB's PRIVATE RAILROAD

The railroad running from Potma to Barashevo which is depicted on the above map (a small segment of the concentration camp map of the Soviet Union) does not appear on any official map of the Soviet Union. It is a railroad run by the KGB for the purpose of servicing the numerous concentration camps on both sides of the track. It runs north from Potma, on the Moscow-Saransk-Kuybishev line, or a distance of some 60 kms.

I was in Potma in all these concentration camps. For example, in Concentration Camp 7, you can see one of the biggest in the U.S.S.R., DOK, in which they make furniture for people, and also cabinets for television and radio sets.

Also, the same you can see in Camp 19, and also in Camps 17 and 11, big plants for furniture.

Here in Potma you can see an investigation prison. And in Barashevo, there is special concentration camps for women and concentration camp-hospital No. 3.

I know all this part of the U.S.S.R. very well. I have seen it with two guards in my back and with dogs, but I have seen it very well because I was here two years in this district.

Senator GURNEY. I understand that is a map that shows a railroad operated by the KGB servicing these concentration camps?

Mr. SHIFRIN. Only concentration camps, and also we have here 1971 testimony of Alexander Krimgold. He is a free man who was there to see prisoners, relatives.

Senator GURNEY. And your testimony is that this railroad does not show on any official map that describes Soviet railroads?

Mr. SHIFRIN. Yes. And also, he said that when they came to see relatives, they permitted them to go with special train which goes twice a day on this railway, to go to the prison camps in which they have relatives.

Senator GURNEY. How long is this railroad?

Mr. SHIFRIN. Sixty kilometers to Barashevo. From Potma to Barashevo, it is a very little district of concentration camps. I was there and I can show you this.

Senator GURNEY. How many concentration camps are on this railroad line?

Mr. SHIFRIN. I do not know, because you see, maybe here I was in 10 or 15. But they have another here and also, I explained when we spoke before testimony that here we have in the side, in the wild forest, we have one place about which no one except KGB in the U.S.S.R. can tell anything. We know that there is a big concentration camp with the name Sarovo. In this concentration camp, they have not only fences and earth and guards and so on, they have a special highway around this concentration camp, with more secret police which see that no one would come to this district. Because they have this concentration camp so secret that no one knows what it is in there. They bring cars with the prisoners only in the night and a special guard takes them from Barashevo to this site.

But you see, that is a very little district of concentration camps.

Now, I would show you another concentration camp district. That is Lake Baikal. This is a railway which goes from Moscow to Vladivostok. From a little station on this railway, Tayshet, trains go to Bratsk. Six hundred kilometers to Ust Kut, 300 kilometers to Bratsk. I was not in Ust Kut. I cannot show concentration camps in another part of this 600 kilometer railway. I can show you concentration camps in which I personally was in this part of country, you see on the map, here.

They brought me to this transportation camp 625. Then I was in 025. That is another transportation camp.

Senator GURNEY. What is a transportation camp?

Mr. SHIFRIN. That is a simple concentration camp, with fences, with barracks, with guard, with towers on the corners of the fence, with very bad food and with very strict regimes, but people do not live there permanently. They live there 10 days, 15 days, 20 days, waiting for documents which they would prepare for you, and for train, with which they would send you to your permanent place.

Senator GURNEY. The word "transportation camp," then, would mean——

Mr. SHIFRIN. It is a transit camp.

Mr. SOURWINE. Would it be fair to say that the transportation camps you are describing are the waiting rooms on the Soviet forced labor railway?

Mr. SHIFRIN. Oh, yes, and also "post offices" in concentration camps. I can tell you that when I first came to the big room in such concentration camp and prison on the way from Moscow, I was astonished. It was a room maybe like this room, not so high ceiling, and it had white walls, and on these walls was, in handwriting, scratched with pencil, with nails—"Mama, they killed father"; "Kostia they sentenced me with 25 years"; "Vera, I go to exile"; "Sergei, they sent my friend Victor to the death." That is a "post office" on the route. All the walls, and sometimes on the ceilings, you can see such writings.

When I came to this room, and I have seen this "post office," I said to my friends: "We should send one picture of this wall to the New York Times."

Senator GURNEY. These were messages that prisoners have left hoping that they will get to relatives?

Mr. SHIFRIN. Yes, they know that maybe relatives or friends will go this way, because they have railway to the east to concentration camps and maybe relatives would see.

I was in these concentration camps of Ozerlag. I cannot show you all concentration camps, because in all the wild forest here, they were a distance from one to the other—a kilometer, half kilometer, two kilometers—in all these forests around this railway, maybe thousand of concentration camps. Today they destroyed the concentration camp in Bratsk. Maybe a half million prisoners built here a big power station on the Angara River. We built this power station for 5 years with our bare hands, without any machinery. We pulled stones big like this door, giant stones, on these slides, with the bare hands—200 prisoners. In this way we built this dam and when we finished the dam, they announced in all the newspapers that it would be "Komsomol power station" which was built by Komsomol (Young Communist League) and they destroyed our concentration camps. No, they don't really destroy concentration camps; they only take out fences and they bring to the barracks youth from all the country to finish this power station, to finish the mechanisms, turbines and so on. I cannot tell you how many prisoners died here.

Senator GURNEY. But you say that approximately a half million prisoners worked on this?

Mr. SHIFRIN. Was there in my days, yes.

Senator GURNEY. For about 5 years. And all these many camps— perhaps a thousand, I think you testified——

Mr. Shifrin. No, at other places in forests were also labor concentration camps. Prisoners cut lumber in the forest, they make bricks, they work in the special wood plants after they finished dam. It was here, the circle of camps around Bratsk. And in Bratsk they put free people in these barracks. They moved me from Bratsk to concentration camps 37 and 38—I was here 2 years. And we cut lumber in the place in which now you can see big lake because we made this dam and now there is a lake on Angara.

Mr. Boldyreff. They flooded the area.

Senator Gurney. I understand.

Mr. Shifrin. And also prisoners were here before me. I came here in 1964 and prisoners explained to me that they brought them in 1945 in hundreds of thousands to Tayshet, and from Tayshet they brought prisoners to the wild forest. It was not here a railway; it was not here also a highway. It was here only wild forests. And they put these prisoners in the wild forest and in this wild forest they built at first a highway and they built this railway. All this is the work of prisoners.

Senator Gurney. How long is that highway?

Mr. Shifrin. To Ust Kut, 600 kilometers and to Bratsk, 300 kilometers.

Senator Gurney. Is that from the bottom of the map?

Mr. Shifrin. I was in this 300 kilometers strip. I was not in another part of concentration camps. I will tell you what I have seen now before all, because I want to explain to you from which source is my information. Maybe it would be better not to go into details now.

Also, when I was released, and came to exile I was in district of Kharaganda; and here they have coal mines, and in these coal mines were only prisoners and people which came from the prisons and lived there in exile. That is "Prisoners Land" in U.S.S.R., people said. I was here in exile 4 years and I was in all these districts and I have seen all these districts with my own eyes.

I cannot show you exactly this concentration camp here but I know this concentration camp in Dolinka, I know this concentration camp in Kazakhstan. I know also these concentration camps in Kiev, and in Latvia. I have seen them. I have seen hundreds of concentration camps near the railway in all the plants, in all the coal mines. You can see them today.

Why I tell? Why I say today? I told you that I was here in 1967 only. But my friends live now there, and I have letters from my friends, and I asked them to write to me in the special language we use about concentration camps, and in these letters they wrote to me many times now, in 1971 and 1972. They said to me in these letters, "Everything in these places in the old conditions when you were here." And that is why I know that these concentration camps stay today.

Senator Gurney. In other words, your testimony is that even up through last year, 1972, you received letters from friends of yours who have been in concentration camps?

Mr. Shifrin. Oh, yes.

Senator Gurney. Your friends say the concentration camps are still there, in approximately the same number and same condition that they were when you were there?

Mr. SHIFRIN. I can tell you that sometimes they destroy some concentration camps, because now I have letters that in this railroad, Tayshet to Bratsk, they destroy concentration camps. Not really destroy, they only take out fences and put in barracks for free workers because foreigners came to see this Bratsk and they don't want that foreigners will see from the car, from railway, these concentration camps. These concentration camps in that railway they destroyed.

And some of the concentration camps they disguised. I can tell you, this concentration camp 025 in Tayshet remains only 10 meters or 15 meters from the railroad that goes from Moscow to Vladivostok. And I can tell you, in one case I would tell you in my testimony, wife of prisoner have seen prisoner on the roof on the concentration camp building and asked him how to come to him, and he answered, you cannot come to me, I am in concentration camp.

This woman answered, why? On the fence, in one-meter-big letters, they wrote "neftebaza"—"petroleum depot.

Senator GURNEY. When was this?

Mr. SHIFRIN. It was in 1955. They don't want that free people would see concentration camps near the railway, and in the places in which in the fence you can see the tower, they make the fence higher. And that is why it says "petroleum depot" when people go near and can't understand what is it.

Senator GURNEY. Well, if we can go back now to those last three areas that you pointed out. Your testimony, as I understand it, was that you have received letters from people who are in those concentration camps within the past 2 years. Is that correct?

Mr. SHIFRIN. Yes, I will show you now real letters.

Senator GURNEY. And the testimony or the communications in the letters from your friends was to the effect that the concentration camps are still there and pretty much the way they were when you knew them?

Mr. SHIFRIN. Yes, they tell me in letters, I have also letters from people which came from the prisons only now in September, October, November, and December 1972. Alexander Voloshin they released in October of 1972, Galperin in December 1972; Reyza Palatnik they released in December 1972, and I have these letters from them.

Senator GURNEY. As we get into the more specific questions, we will get into the letters and you can put them into the record.

Mr. SHIFRIN. Yes, I ask you very much, I gather letters, photographs, I gather real testimony from concentration camps, which was there many years. I have all these documents here in these files and I ask you very much to see them and to put them in the record.

Senator GURNEY. We will.

Now, let me ask you another question about those three areas you mentioned. I think you used the words "when I was in exile."

Mr. SHIFRIN. Yes.

Senator GURNEY. What do you mean by that? Is this after the 10-year prison period?

Mr. SHIFRIN. Yes—after this 10 years, yes.

Senator GURNEY. Yes.

Mr. SHIFRIN. They sent me as a free man to live in Kazakhstan and I was there free. But I can go about without guard, but I must come each month to the KGB. I must each month come to KGB to make signature and I cannot go to another place. But I was in a little special position, because I said that it was "prisoner land." In Karaganda it was maybe a million people living, and 800,000 former prisoners. And that is why they permit a prisoner sometimes to be in a high position. After prison I was their chief legal adviser in the industry of coal mining. And that is why they permitted me to go to another part of the country when I must go with my business, with my work. That is why I was not there only in one place.

Mr. SOURWINE. Mr. Shifrin, just one question. You say you went down there in Kazakhstan and you were free. You were free to go wherever you wanted to go, if you did not leave your cage. That is right, is it not?

Mr. SHIFRIN. No, I was not absolutely free. All former prisoners in exile, they are not free. They must live in one place, or one village.

Mr. SOURWINE. That is what I wanted to get clear.

Mr. SHIFRIN. But I was a little more free because of my position. I also was not free because when I made a special trip to another part of the country, always two KGB came to me in my back, secret service. They came with me.

Senator GURNEY. And you were not free to do what you wanted to, you had to do the work that they assigned to you?

Mr. SHIFRIN. Yes, but they gave me good work in my education. It was very good for me.

Senator GURNEY. And you could only move around at their orders to perform your particular position?

Mr. SHIFRIN. Yes.

Now maybe you would hear these parts of the letters—not all the letters, but parts of the letters, because I cannot tell only my words. You can hear these words of prisoners also. Permit me, please, to have Mr. Boldyreff read them for me.

Mr. BOLDYREFF. Here is a statement of Alexander Krimgold, who now resides in Israel.

In July 1971, I had occasion to visit Potma while escorting Nina Krasnova, the wife of Anatoli Altman, who had been sentenced in prison during the first Leningrad trial. A narrow gauge railroad, on both sides of which like so many boils lie scattered the terrible labor camps of Mordovia. This railroad runs deep into the forest from the main junction. Potma is a fearful place which readily evokes Nazi concentration camps—barbed-wire fences, watch towers, dogs set in pursuit of people. These camps are the worthy heirs of Hitler's and Stalin's work.

Senator GURNEY. What date is that?

Mr. BOLDYREFF. This is July 1971. He describes the condition when he says about these boils, describing Potma, the area that Mr. Shifrin has shown first.

Senator GURNEY. If you will just excuse me for a moment, for the purposes of the record, all letters will be received in evidence, but the chairman will make a determination later what letters will be printed in the written record.

(The letters referred to may be found in the appendix, Part 2, p. 107.)

Senator GURNEY. Also for the purposes of the record, all of the maps that have been referred to so far this morning will also be received in evidence and will be printed in the record.

Mr. SOURWINE. May I make a suggestion, Mr. Chairman. It might be, since these maps are being printed in color, that the maps should be reduced to line drawings in black and white for printing in the record. I also note that the witness has submitted a list of Soviet concentration camps. I wish to suggest that this list be printed in the record.

Senator GURNEY. Yes, that may be done.

(The prison map of Moscow is on p. 41. The other maps referred to may be found on pp. 2 and 3. The list of Soviet concentration camps will be found in the appendix Part 2, p. 105.)

Mr. SHIFRIN. Now another letter.

Mr. BOLDYREFF. This is a letter of December 1972 from Reyza Palat·nik. She arrived on the 21st of December 1972 to Israel. She gives her deposition. She said, "This is a womens' camp. The camps were located in a swamp, indicative of special care and concern for women."

She got out herself on December 1, 1972.

A continuously semicold and hungry existence. No medical service. Grippe and quinsy were not considered illness. One had to lose consciousness to be allowed off for a day. Only the prison uniform was allowed—in summer a cotton dress, in winter the same dress and a padded jacket which provided no warmth. The camp had approximately 1,100 persons despite the fact that it was designed for only 700. The result, terribly crowded conditions. I was intentionally placed in the veneral disease ward. Hot water for laundry and bathing was available only once in 10 days. The food—garbage. Pigs are fed better by good masters.

Now, there is a third testimony here. The writer of the following statement could not sign his real name because he still has close relatives in Russia. However, Shifrin knows him and could supply his name confidentially to the subcommittee. Now, he writes here: He was arrested and located in Wrangel Island. This is the little island there at the very top, over in the Arctic.

I was arrested again in 1958, thrown into prison, and without any trial, sent to autonomous republic, and from there to the Island of Wrangel, where I remained until 1962. At the camp I made the acquaintance of a former physician, Vasiliy Ivanovich Polakov, Colonel, of Vlassov Army, a larger number of SS and Gestapo Germans and many Italians, who had long been declared dead but who are actually still living on Wrangel in the Belopolyar'ye.

There follows a list of 17 German and Italian names.

Now I quote further:

The camp of Wrangel Island was an experimental camp where experiments were conducted on living people. The experiments were in the form of injections, diets, oxygen tests on people who were long declared dead but were alive at that time—1962—and were working very hard in the camp. There was also Raoul Wallenberg who was [Swedish] consul in Budapest during the War and who under the German occupation, aided by money, helped Jews escape from Hungary through Switzerland into other countries. When the Soviets entered Budapest, Raoul Wallenberg was immediately arrested at the order of the Commandant of Budapest and sent by special train to Moscow. He was then 27 years old and was a handsome, educated young man.

I think that is enough.

Mr. SHIFRIN. Can I continue?

Senator GURNEY. Yes.

Mr. SHIFRIN. Also my experience about these concentration camps in the U.S.S.R. I can prove with my other trip. After exile, I made a trip in this line. You can see this trip on the map of U.S.S.R. which I made—you see this line to Chita. I made this trip because I was too long in one place and also because I want to see my friends. I have thousands of friends all over the world from concentration camps. I have also many in Hawaii and I have in Japan also, and here also in the

United States. In the U.S.S.R., it was my friends and I want to see them and to make this big trip. And on my trip, I was astonished at the places with concentration camps.

Senator GURNEY. When was this?

Mr. SHIFRIN. It was in 1967 and you see once in this place, near a lake Isik Kue, I was in a little town, Narin. I never had heard that they have a concentration camp. When I came in the night, I have seen this big, big concentration camp. You can see immediately in the night lights and fences and barracks. I asked this chauffeur, what is it? He said, "oh, you don't know? Concentration camps here."

Also, I can tell you that in all the country, in big towns—I was here many times around these central towns, like Kharkov, Kiev, Odessa, Leningrad, Moscow, Rovno, Riga—in the central part of the country, near each town, you can see four or five concentration camps, near each big town.

I can tell you a real example with a little town, Orsha. It is a little town, not a big town. But we have now in this Orsha six concentration camps. I have their numbers, their addresses. I can give you these addresses, I would give you these.

Senator GURNEY. In what part of Russia is this town?

Mr. SHIFRIN. Orsha is here in Belorussia.

Senator GURNEY. That is up in the——

Mr. SHIFRIN. In Belorussia. It is near Mogilev, 50, 60 kilometers from Mogilev.

Senator GURNEY. In other words, your testimony is that there are concentration camps all over Russia?

Mr. SHIFRIN. All over Russia.

Senator GURNEY. All over European Russia as well as in Siberia?

Mr. SHIFRIN. All over Russia. Because I can tell you that once we tried to count what part of industry they build with concentration camps' prisoners hands. In the days of Stalin, it was a bigger part, I think, but I am sure, with my friends who talk about this, 20 to 25 percent of the heavy labor is the work of the prisoners.

You see, all this gold mining in Kolyma, only prisoners.

All this coal mining in Vorkuta, Pechora, Inta, only prisoners.

All this coal mining in Kazakhstan, prisoners.

All this mining with molybdenum in Norilsk, prisoners.

Kamerevo—mining nickel, molybdenum, chrome, and cutting lumber—prisoners.

Senator GURNEY. In other words, at mines or other installations where you need manual labor, you always find big concentration camps?

Mr. SHIFRIN. Yes. They build these concentration camps in the places in which people do not want to work themselves. You see, who would want to go to this place at the polar circle in which you can find in the winter 40, 50 degrees below zero Centigrade to work? No one wants to go. They send prisoners. That is why in my testimony, I tell not about past times, not about the time in 1953, 1963 and 1967 when I was in the prisons and in exile, but I tell of 1972, December—because the last letter which I got from Reyza Palatnik, that was December 1972 when she was released from a womens' concentration camp.

Senator GURNEY. I wonder, Mr. Shifrin, if we can go back now to this 1967 trip you are telling us about?

Mr. SHIFRIN. Yes.

Senator GURNEY. Tell us where you started and where you went.

Mr. SHIFRIN. When I was on this trip?

Senator GURNEY. That is right.

Mr. SHIFRIN. Please.

I came from Kharaganda to Frunze. That is a like Isik Kue in the big, big mountains.

From Isik Kue, I came to this Narin about which I explained to you about these concentration camps and I have seen near Frunze and this other town these concentration camps.

Then from Osh I came to Samarkand and I have seen concentration camps around this big town, Bokhara.

I have heard that they have also camps in Tambul, but I was not there.

Now, in this way, from Ashkhabad I came to Caspian and I have seen these concentration camps on the way in these town—Ashkhabad, Krasnovodsk and so on. Then I crossed with the ship the Caspian Sea. When I crossed the Caspian Sea, I was in Derbent and I have seen there my friends who live there also. Then I was in Batumi and all the Caucasus. Then by ship I came to Odessa. From Odessa I was in all the east and west Ukraine and I have seen these concentration camps in Kishinev, Rovno, Kiev, Kharkov, and also in Crimea. And also Byelorussia, from where I came to Moscow.

In another trip—I made two trips, not one——

Senator GURNEY. Before we get on that, now, this trip was made by automobile?

Mr. SHIFRIN. No. I made it with trains, with ships, with hitchhiking on the highways, with planes. I have not automobile in the U.S.S.R. I made it myself.

Senator GURNEY. Different kinds of transportation?

Mr. SHIFRIN. With all the kinds of transportation.

Senator GURNEY. Did you talk to people in each of these places?

Mr. SHIFRIN. Oh, yes. In each town, I stayed 2 or 3 days to see my friends and to ask about the situation here.

Senator GURNEY. Now, were these friends in these concentration camps?

Mr. SHIFRIN. Pardon?

Senator GURNEY. Were your friends that you talked to in concentration camps?

Mr. SHIFRIN. No; they were free, but they live near concentration camp complexes in which they was before. They put people in exile sometimes in another part of the country but in many cases, they put them in exile near concentration camp in which they was.

Senator GURNEY. Can you give some general description of how large these concentration camps were in these various places where you went?

Mr. SHIFRIN. Most little concentration camp in which I was, it was 250 people—the smallest. It was strict "concentration camp-prison," 250 prisoners. I have not seen smaller camp. Most big in which I was, in Omsk, in Tayshet, was 8, 9, 10,000 people in one concentration camp. They have many different concentration camps.

Senator GURNEY. They vary in size, then, from 250 which was the smallest, to as much as 10,000 for the largest?

Mr. SHIFRIN. Yes. In Bratsk, it was a concentration camp from 5,000 to 10,000 people in one concentration camp.

Senator GURNEY. How long did your trip take?

Mr. SHIFRIN. Oh, this trip, it was 2 months, 2½, maybe. It was a big trip.

And also, I wanted to see these places in which I was in the prisons, but not as a prisoner. And I came to Tayshet.

Senator GURNEY. This is after you left Moscow?

Mr. SHIFRIN. Yes.

Senator GURNEY. This was still in 1967?

Mr. SHIFRIN. Yes—no, it was 1966 and 1967, two trips.

When I came to Tayshet, I was before only in transit prisons and concentration camps. In this time, I have seen all these from the outside.

When I was here, I have seen one place about which I must tell you one interesting thing. When I was in Tayshet—that is not far from Lake Baykal—it was there prisoners told me about the plan of Stalin in 1952, 1953, the plan of deportation of all the Jews to Birobidjan, on the China border. It was a real plan of Stalin, a plan of deportation, like the deportation of Tartars from Crimea, and many other nations.

These prisoners in Tayshet, they told me a very interesting story. In 1951–52, near Lake Baykal in this place, where the railway goes only two or three kilometers from Lake Baykal, they were sent to this place with special guards in the summer and they built in only 2 or 3 months a little railroad from the main railroad to the cliff to the shore of Baykal. But it was not a shore, it was a cliff, 150 meters high in this place. And they have seen absolutely no reason to build this railway and they asked officers and guards, why do we build in such speed this railway? They gave to them credit in building this railway for 1 day in labor 10 days.

Mr. BOLDYREFF. They gave them credit for 1 days' work, they counted as if they worked 10 days. So their term of service was reduced. That was a premium that they were getting.

Mr. SHIFRIN. In these 3 months, they have credit 30 months, these prisoners. They asked, what is the work, why, without any reason to lay it to a cliff? And the officers explained to them: we make it so big and high because our great leader, Stalin, wants to throw these Jews, on the way to Birobidjan, from this cliff into Lake Baykal, from this 150 meters cliff. They wanted to kill these millions of Jews without extermination camps like Auschwitz.

Senator GURNEY. In other words, this was a short spur of a railroad that came off the main track?

Mr. SHIFRIN. Yes.

Senator GURNEY. And went to Lake Baykal, a distance of about 2 or 3 kilometers?

Mr. SHIFRIN. Yes.

Senator GURNEY. And your friends testified that there was nothing on the railroad at all?

Mr. SHIFRIN. I was there and I have seen with my own eyes.

Senator Gurney. It just went to a high cliff that overlooked the lake?

Mr. Shifrin. Yes, I was there. This railroad stays now there without any use, with grass and with corrosion—all rusted—stay this railway, without nothing. Now in 1973 they have again this plan of deportation of Jews to Birobidjan. They now make again these lists and now they build there barracks in Birobidjan. We know this from letters and from eyewitnesses who came from there to Israel.

Permit me please to make a little summary about this situation in concentration camps and about this situation with new arrests. I want to tell you that I am Zionist and all my life I was a Zionist and I am proud that I was a Zionist. I was in this work from 1948 and that is why I was in the prisons. But I believe that nationalists must love all the nations. That is why I would testify not only about Jews, I would tell you about all the nationalities in U.S.S.R. which sit in the prisons and in exile. I must tell you that only one place in the U.S.S.R. you can find without discrimination of nations—concentration camps and prisons. In all other places, discrimination.

Senator Gurney. Before we get into that, the Chair will call a short recess.

(A short recess was taken.)

Senator Gurney. Mr. Shifrin, would you describe the circumstances of your arrest, why you were arrested and the kind of trial you received?

Mr. Shifrin. It is very simple to describe, because there was a big wave of arrests in these days in the U.S.S.R. There was a big wave because Stalin died, but his work did not die. The day after the death of Stalin, work was like in the days of Stalin. They arrested me on the 6th of June 1953. They brought me to Lubyanka prison, to this prison you see on this map, and they told to me that I am an Israeli-American spy.

Senator Gurney. Who arrested you?

Mr. Shifrin. KGB.

Senator Gurney. How many?

Mr. Shifrin. Two colonels. In the street they arrested me in the street Solyanka in Moscow. They came to me in two cars when I came from the home and they sprung from the cars with pistols. Because they want to show to the people in Moscow that they work and all the people who have seen this will tell to the relatives: "I have seen KGB arrest a spy in the street."

Senator Gurney. They arrested you at pistol point and threw you into the car, is that right?

Mr. Shifrin. It was two cars, it was two colonels, but they were in civilian clothes. Only in the car, they told me their names and rank. I asked them.

They brought me with these cars—it was not only two colonels—it was maybe three or four other people—I did not know how many of them—it was not time to count them.

Senator Gurney. And what did they say to you when they arrested you?

Mr. Shifrin. They put on me pistols, and told me: "Get in the car, in the car, in the car." And I came to the car. What can I do?

Senator Gurney. Go on.

Mr. SHIFRIN. And you see, in the U.S.S.R., if you would come without a pistol to the simple man in the street and would say, "You are arrested," he would go with you to all the places, because people are used to this. My chief in the Ministry of Defense, 3 or 4 days before my arrest, when they came to arrest him, sprang from the window from the sixth story to the courtyard, committed suicide. People know what it is to be arrested in the U.S.S.R.

They brought me to Lubyanka prison and I was the first days in Lubyanka. Then I was in Lefortovo prison, then I was in Butirskaya prison. To make it more understandable for you what it is to be spy in U.S.S.R., I must tell you not about myself, because it is not good to tell only for myself. Sergei Krasilnikov——.

Senator GURNEY. But let's get the details of this, because this is interesting. After they took you to the car, they took you to their barracks or station or office? Where did they take you?

Mr. SHIFRIN. They brought me to big prison—Lubyanka prison.

Senator GURNEY. They took you right to a prison?

Mr. SHIFRIN. Yes, KGB office building.

Senator GURNEY. Then what happened?

Mr. SHIFRIN. This KGB office building in Lubyanka has inside the building a big prison. You see in Lubyanka prison, they have KGB building. All your tourists from the United States can have this map and go to see these prisons. When they would be in the Square Dzerzhinskaya, under their feet, it would be prisoners and in this building, it would be prison. When I way brought to this prison, they made a search, they took off all my clothes, made a big search. They looked into all the openings of the human body. Big search. Yes. And this search make colonels. Very good work for a colonel, yes?

And when they finished this search, they brought me to the prison, to the cell, and I was there only some days, because I would not tell them that I am a spy. And they put me in another prison.

Senator GURNEY. During this time, did they interrogate you?

Mr. SHIFRIN. Pardon?

Senator GURNEY. Did they question you?

Mr. SHIFRIN. Oh, yes. They did not show me any order for arrest. They did not show me any document. But they asked me, what is the connection you have had with Israel and American diplomats? What documents of our Defense Ministry did you give them? What are the secrets you gave to them?

And I answered that I am not a spy and I do not know nothing about this. And I have seen in these few days such people like Generals Kabulov, Mirkulov, that were advisers of Beria. And once in the investigation, in the interrogation room of Kabulov, first adviser of Beria, when I answered that I do not know nothing, he told his adviser, Colonel Medvedev to bring me to the special Lefortovo prison.

Senator GURNEY. How long did this interrogation go on?

Mr. SHIFRIN. I was in interrogation half a year.

Senator GURNEY. No. I mean here.

Mr. SHIFRIN. I do not remember. Month and 10 days, maybe I was in the prison at Lubyanka.

Senator GURNEY. Can you describe in more detail how the investigation was carried out?

Mr. SHIFRIN. Oh, yes.

Senator GURNEY. One person, two persons? How long?

Mr. SHIFRIN. They made interrogation in many ways. Once they tried to speak with me in interrogation without stopping 23 or 25 days. It was six, seven, eight, interrogators and they changed and I cannot change.

Senator GURNEY. Do you know their names?

Mr. SHIFRIN. One name I know, this Colonel Medvedev. Others I never have heard their names. And I remember this Lieutenant General Mirkulov and Lieutenant General Vladimirsky. These people I remember.

When I fell from my chair, from my little chair—I fall always because you cannot be without sleep so long—without sleep, without interruptions they make it—in Russian language, they call this method of interrogation "melnica," which means "the mill."

Senator GURNEY. If I understand your testimony, they interrogated you around the clock, 24 hours a day?

Mr. SHIFRIN. Yes, and 23 or 25 days—I cannot tell exactly because only after this I tried to make count. They tried to press me, to push me to tell them that I am a spy.

Senator GURNEY. And this continued for how many days?

Mr. SHIFRIN. Twenty-five, I think, approximately.

Senator GURNEY. Were you in one room all the time?

Mr. SHIFRIN. I was always in one room. I was unconscious many times. I many times was on the floor and would feel on my body water; and they put me again on the chair and again questioned me—and I sleep, I fall unconscious. And when they have seen that I do not want to say that I am spy, they put me in the cell and they permit me a week of rest.

Senator GURNEY. This is after the 25 days?

Mr. SHIFRIN. Yes. And then they brought me to this Kabulov, Lieutenant General Kabulov.

Senator GURNEY. During this 25-day interrogation, if you would fall asleep and fall off the chair, they would put you back up on it?

Mr. SHIFRIN. Yes. Always, they put me on the chair—always.

Senator GURNEY. And continue the interrogation?

Mr. SHIFRIN. Oh, yes. But they never beat me. They never touched me with their hands. Only once Kabulov shouted, "I will beat you now!" But they never beat me.

Senator GURNEY. Did they give you any food or drink?

Mr. SHIFRIN. Yes, they give me water and they give me food. I do not remember now what food it was, but they gave me. And they permitted me to go to W.C.

Senator GURNEY. How long would each interrogator interrogate?

Mr. SHIFRIN. They changed interrogators after 4 hours.

Senator GURNEY. And six people did it altogether?

Mr. SHIFRIN. Six or eight.

Senator GURNEY. Six or eight?

Mr. SHIFRIN. I do not remember. Always new faces; always new faces. They only have one task, one goal: do not permit me to sleep. It was simple interrogators, not big—simple lieutenants. And only sometimes came General Vladimirsky or Kabulov who asked: "He speaks—or not?" and went out.

Senator GURNEY. These were the two generals?

Mr. SHIFRIN. Yes. And when I rest in this cell after this interrogation, also they brought me to Kabulov, Lieutenant General Kabulov, first adviser of Beria, and he told me:

You see, I permit to you rest because I see that you are not a person which we can push to something with this way. I permit you to rest. Now speak with me openly, because I have in my arsenal such things that you cannot know about. You will talk. Now, it is the best way to tell you, because if another way, you would see what it would mean.

And I answered: "I have nothing to tell." And it was at night, 4 o'clock in the night—they always interrogate in the nights—and he shouted, "Bring him to special cell!" and they put me in Lefortovo in underground cell. It was—I do not remember now how many steps it was, but it was very many staircases underground. And It was a corridor with only nine cells. And in this corridor, I was put in the cell with the No. 3. It was a high cell, but only maybe a meter and half wide, in a square.

Senator GURNEY. Was this in the same prison?

Mr. SHIFRIN. Yes, in Lefortovo prison.

Senator GURNEY. This was after you were transferred——

Mr. SHIFRIN. Yes, from Lubyanka to Lefortovo.

Senator GURNEY. All right.

Mr. SHIFRIN. And when I came to the cell, I was astonished because I stepped in mud, watery mud. It was not deep, maybe 15 centimeters deep only, 10 or 15, but you stay in the mud, in water. And all their walls were moldy, and you cannot lie in this cell. You have not bunk, you have not chair. And I was there 28 days in standing position.

Senator GURNEY. There was nothing in the cell at all except you?

Mr. SHIFRIN. Nothing absolutely. After 12—maybe 12, maybe 14 days—I sat in this mud, because it was impossible. My legs was like lumbers.

Senator GURNEY. They were all swollen?

Mr. SHIFRIN. Yes, because it is impossible to stand. And all the day, I asked the chief of the prison to come to me. Why I know exactly 28? Because I make stripes on this green mold. When they give me this piece of bread and glass of water, it is one day for me, because once in the day, such a piece of bread and one glass of water in the morning and in the evening. And that was my calendar on the wall, and with bread.

When the chief came to me and asked me why I asked him to see him, I asked only one question; where is the order of my arrest? And he answered me: I will tell it to the investigators; and he went out.

It was 28 days. Then they released me from this cell and put me in the simple cell in the same Lefortovo prison. And only after 6 months, after a court-martial when they sentenced me to death, I have known that in this day, when they permit me to go to the ordinary cell from this mud, they arrested Beria, Kabulov, Vladimirsky and the other. All these generals were arrested together with Beria.

Senator GURNEY. These are the ones that interrogated you?

Mr. SHIFRIN. Yes, they were arrested and killed.

Senator GURNEY. Why was that?

Mr. SHIFRIN. Why? Ask the Soviet Government. They always kill all these interrogators. Always, they change them. They shot Beria with thousands of interrogators; they shot Yezhov and Yagoda—they were ministers of the KGB.

Senator GURNEY. This was the purge after Stalin's death?

Mr. SHIFRIN. Yagoda and Yezhov were before Stalin's death, but Communists can't change. They was in the days of Stalin this way, they are now this way. And they shot Beria because they knew that in another situation, Beria would shoot all government. It is only battle inside government. You have here elections; they have the KGB. That is the difference.

Senator GURNEY. You mean they purge their ranks periodically?

Mr. SHIFRIN. Yes, if they want change, they send to KGB not with elections, but with arrests. It is another way of democracy—"Communist democracy."

Mr. SOURWINE. Who shot Beria, if you know?

Mr. SHIFRIN. I do not know this secret, who shot Beria. The Communist government shot Beria and all these generals of Beria. Now we have other killers in the head of this KGB and they put in the prisons other millions of people.

I have here only a little part of prisoners photos. Those are people which are now in the prisons which were arrested in 1969, 1970, 1971, and 1972, and some of them died in the prisons.

Galanskov, Talantov——

Senator GURNEY. These are pictures of whom?

Mr. SHIFRIN. These are new prisoners; I show you new photos.

This woman, Ekaterina Zaritzkaya—they released this woman after 25 years' imprisonment. Her husband, Mikhail Soroka, was with me. He died in prison after 23 years and she was released in December of 1972, after 25 years imprisonment.

This man, Galanskov, died in December 1972 in concentration camp in Potma.

Senator GURNEY. Are these pictures of new political prisoners in the last few years?

Mr. SHIFRIN. Yes. This is photo of man who on the island of Wrangel met Dr. Trushnovich, one of leaders of Russian underground NTS.

This man, Talantov, died in prison now, he was theologian, a Christian theologian.

That is General Grigorenko. Now he is in a mental prison asylum, because he is dissident.

And that is only a little part of photographs. This is Anatoli Marchenko. Maybe you know his book about prisons and concentration camps.

Senator GURNEY. Are these important people in government?

Mr. SHIFRIN. Some of them. Some of them like General Grigorenko, he was very important. He was a head of cybernetics department in the War Academy of Officers in the U.S.S.R. in Moscow.

Senator GURNEY. How do you know about the imprisonment of these particular people?

Mr. SHIFRIN. Because all these people are my friends. I know them personally.

Senator GURNEY. You know each one of them?

Mr. SHIFRIN. I know each one of them personally. I can tell their biographies to you, I met them many times.

Senator Gurney. How did you hear about their imprisonment?

Mr. Shifrin. Some of them were arrested when I was in the U.S.S.R. About some of the arrests I know from your newspapers; and also, we call to Moscow and to Leninigrad, to other cities, each week to the U.S.S.R., and their friends tell us about these new arrests.

And only 2 weeks ago, they arrested Irina Belogorodskaia a second time. I know her. They now arrested my friend Viktor Khaustov, also a second time.

Yuri Shukhevich here, he was 20 years in the prisons in the days of Stalin and now he is again in the prison since 1971.

Or this man you see here, Pyotr Yakir—also he was in the prison. He was 20 years in the prisons. I must tell you about these two fates.

Senator Gurney. What are the reasons for the new arrests of these people?

Mr. Shifrin. I will tell you. Now they want to finish the political dissidents in the U.S.S.R. They make one big wave of arrests in 1958, and 1960, when they sent thousands and thousands of students and professors and soldiers and officers to concentration camps. And they thought in this time, 1958 to 1960, that they finished with dissidents. But these dissidents came again and again from people, ordinary people, some of them very ordinary people.

All the world, now have heard name of Anatoli Marchenko. After 10 years in the prisons—I was with him—he wrote a book about prisons, concentration camps, in the U.S.S.R., and they sent him after this again to the prison. He is a simple worker.

Senator Gurney. Approximately how many people were arrested during this period of 1958?

Mr. Shifrin. From 1958 to these days or in 1958?

Senator Gurney. No, in that era of 1958.

Mr. Shifrin. In 1958, I have seen in my own opinion, I have seen thousands, because I was in these years in many concentration camps, and in each concentration camp, I have seen hundreds, hundreds, and hundreds of newcomers.

Senator Gurney. Many thousands of people were arrested?

Mr. Shifrin. Many thousands I have seen. I do not know the figure. How can you know this figure?

Senator Gurney. Well, I am saying approximately. Of course you can't know exactly.

Mr. Shifrin. I cannot tell figures because it is a big secret. I have seen thousands and I am sure that now, in these concentration camps, you can find millions of prisoners, because thousands of concentration camps and that is why millions of prisoners.

Senator Gurney. Now, as I understand it, there were a great many arrests around the 1958 period. Then is it my understanding that there were new waves of arrests 10 years later?

Mr. Shifrin. Yes, I can tell you that we have seen in concentration camps a very interesting thing. From 1918 to 1972, you can see each 10 years a new wave of arrests. In 1918, 1928, 1938, 1948, 1958, 1969. And now from 1969 without interruption to 1972.

Senator Gurney. In other words, your testimony is that approximately every 10 years there are new waves of political arrests?

Mr. Shifrin. Every 10 years you can see a big new wave of arrests.

Senator Gurney. Now, if we can, let's get back to you own experience. Let's go back to Lefortovo. They transferred you out of the underground cell to another cell. Let's pick up the story from there, if you can.

Incidentally, you mentioned a court-martial. What do you mean by that?

Mr. SHIFRIN. After 6 months, they gave me documents to read, in which was an accusation, charge, and it said there that they in these months decided that I am an Israeli-American spy and that is why they would send me to court-martial.

Senator GURNEY. This is 6 months after your initial arrest?

Mr. SHIFRIN. Yes.

Senator GURNEY. All right, go on.

Mr. SHIFRIN. Then they brought me to the court-martial of Moscow garrison of troops. In this court-martial was three officers. I do not remember their names. One was a colonel or under colonel; and two were lieutenants or captains. And it was so short a procedure. They read this document, they showed me a big file with 500 pages, my investigation protocol. I asked them what is the approval they have that—the proof they have that I am a spy?

They answered, we know that you are spy. Then it was an interruption. They go in another room.

Senator GURNEY. Were you permitted to read the dossier of 500 pages?

Mr. SHIFRIN. Oh, yes, I have seen all 500 pages, It was only protocols of my interrogations, only what they wrote about, what I said to them about all my life, my wartime—all about my life.

Senator GURNEY. This was the transcription of your interrogation in the prison?

Mr. SHIFRIN. Yes.

Senator GURNEY. Did they have any witnesses?

Mr. SHIFRIN. No, was not one witness.

Senator GURNEY. Did you have any counsel, any lawyer?

Mr. SHIFRIN. No.

Senator GURNEY. Did they have a counsel to present the case or the court-martial board?

Mr. SHIFRIN. No, there was only inside the room the court-martial and I and four or six soldiers with the tommy guns. That is all.

After 10 minutes, they came from another room to this room. It was not so big a room. It was maybe one-sixth this room. They came and this colonel read to me that they sentenced me, as an Israeli-American spy, to death. And after this sentence, they brought me, not to Lefortovo prison, but to this prison, Butirskaya, in which you can see, maybe 40 buildings with prisoners and big courtyard, like a city.

Senator GURNEY. There was no appeal from this court? That is the last you were to have of any trial?

Mr. SHIFRIN. No, I did not make any appeal. They brought me to this cell to a special part of this prison in which sit only people which are sentenced to the death. And I was 2 weeks in the death cell. And I have heard each night when they came to take people to their death— to their execution. Because always, when they came, they came in the night. All the people don't sleep in the night because they await these steps. And when they try to take a man, they put inside his mouth a rubber ball, because they do not want him to scream. And when they try to put this ball inside the mouth, all these men shout something. Then all the prisoners in this corridor—in all the cells—shout and beat on the doors. They were not good nights. Then the guards open little doors inside the big door, and with the water hoses, they quiet people inside the cell.

After 14 days, came an officer and they opened the little door in my cell and he read to me that they changed my sentence to 25 years in the concentration camps, 5 years in exile, and 5 years of deprivation of rights of a citizen. And in the same minute, they brought me from this death cell to another cell, cell number 58. I remember this because I was sentenced under article 58 in Code and I came to cell 58.

In this cell was—it was a transit cell—sometimes 60, sometimes 75 people together. All of them have a 25-year sentence. And it was corridor with cells and each cell with prisoners with 25-year sentence. In this cell, I first met some American officers which were kidnapped from the border and also Japanese Prince Konoye.

Senator GURNEY. Kidnapped from where?

Mr. SHIFRIN. From Osterreich, from Vienna. And I would give you their photographs and names. I have all this.

Senator GURNEY. What were their names, the American officers?

Mr. SHIFRIN. It was one of them, Alexander Shornik, one of your officers. He was not kidnapped. They arrested him when he came to visit father in U.S.S.R.

Senator GURNEY. How do you spell that last name?

Mr. SHIFRIN. Shornik.

Senator GURNEY. S-h-a-w-n-i-k?

Mr. SHIFRIN. No.

Mr. BOLDYREFF. S-h-o-r-n-i-k.

Mr. SHIFRIN. Another officer with the name Stanley was kidnapped from Vienna.

Senator GURNEY. That is the one they kidnapped?

Mr. SHIFRIN. Yes.

Senator GURNEY. Stanley who?

Mr. SHIFRIN. I have a little problem with this officer, because his second name is a little secret here. Maybe I will tell you privately about this? It was important American officer which they kidnapped from Vienna. He was one of my first teachers of the English language.

There was there a Russian general, Mikhail Gurevich, which died after some years on my hands in a concentration camp. He was a Jew which was in the head of all the Department of Weapons in the Russian Air Force—a very big man. It was there a Japanese, Prince Konoje, which was arrested with Kwantung Army. It was there many interesting and not interesting people.

I was in this cell maybe 1 month, maybe a little less, and then, they sent me to this—my first trip—to Omsk, and then to another concentration camp.

Senator GURNEY. Could you tell us a little more about your accommodations in that prison where you spent the month?

Mr. SHIFRIN. Yes; but I think it is not very interesting because in all these prisons, you have an equalization. If it is a transit camp or transit prison, it is a big cell for 70, 80, 90, a hundred people together and they lie in the common bunk in two tiers. Inside the cell, you can see a latrine which prisoners have, "parasha" in the Russian language. Once in a day, they permit you to go to the courtyard for "exercise"; to stay in the open place half an hour.

Senator GURNEY. What was the size of the cell?

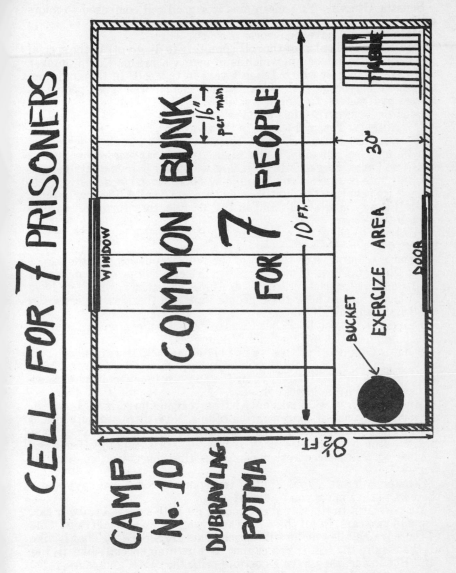

CELL FOR 7 PRISONERS

CAMP No. 10 DUBRAVLAG POTMA

COMMON BUNK FOR 7 PEOPLE

16" per man

WINDOW

10 FT.

30"

EXERCIZE AREA

DOOR

BUCKET

TABLE

18 ½ FT.

Mr. SHIFRIN. It was a big cell. I think if you cut your room in this place to this wall; maybe 50 square meters.

Senator GURNEY. From this wall back to where you were?

Mr. SHIFRIN. Yes; like so big a cell.

Senator GURNEY. And about 70 people were in that cell?

Mr. SHIFRIN. 60 to 70. It was changed every day.

Senator GURNEY. In other words, they were herded together like cattle?

Mr. SHIFRIN. Oh, yes, but this was good in the U.S.S.R.

Senator Gurney. You mean this is a good cell compared to many others?

Mr. Shifrin. I have seen worse prisons.

You can see this plan of the cell (pointing to diagram) in the special strict concentration camp, which is in reality a prison. Camp number 10 in Dubrovlag in which I was 1 year in this cell. In this building, they have maybe 50 such cells. In each cell, it was seven people—3 meters by 3 meters. In feet, it was about 8½ by 10 feet.

Senator Gurney. 8½ feet on one side?

Mr. Shifrin. Yes, and 10 feet in the width.

We was here seven prisoners. It was a common bunk in which we can lie only on our side in the night. In the daytime, we have this "exercise" area. It was only 30 inches wide, and here is a latrine, you see, and here is a little table. And it was here seven steps—seven little steps. Two people in the daytime stay here and "walk" like a pendulum, in such a way. They walk and in this middle, they turn face to face to pass each other.

We tried to show the people in the Senate office how it is. It was impossible.

Senator Gurney. And the rest of the people would stay on the bunk?

Mr. Shifrin. Yes, if two people walk here, five people can lay on their bunk and speak and read something, and that is why they have this place. Half an hour these people walk and then two others walk. Walkers changing all the time.

I was in such a cell here; but I was in more strict concentration camp prison, number 410, in Siberia, in Vikhorevka.

Senator Gurney. Perhaps we had better go back, if we can keep this in order, to the prison you were in before and then proceed from there. Let's go back to the Butirskaya prison and continue from there, so we can keep it in chronological order.

Mr. Shifrin. First, I was only half a year in Omsk, here. It was in my days a district of concentration camps. Now there are only 1, 2, 3 concentration camps here. In this concentration camp, I was in concentration camp No. 4 in this place. It was 5,000 prisoners together when I came to this concentration camp. In this concentration camp, it was——

Senator Gurney. What kind of transportation did you have to get there? Did they move you by train?

Mr. Shifrin. In the way they brought me with a special railway car. I was in two cars. In all these 10 years I was in two special trains. One of these trains, they make with special cars from outside. That is, like all the cars in the train; you cannot see anything special: like all the cars. But inside, they have a corridor with the cages, and cages, cells. In each cell, they have place for eight people, but in reality, they put all of us—always 15, 20 people—together in one cell.

Senator Gurney. That was an accommodation for eight?

Mr. Shifrin. Yes. Not eight, but 15 or 20.

Once it was 22 and all the prisoners shout, it is not good, 22, because it was against the rule. Always 15 or 20. That is like a rule.

And they give to the people in this way salt fish and black bread and two times in the day a flask of water and two times in the day, they permit to go to the WC—to the toilet. People sit in this compartment, not like herrings in the barrel, but in worse condition. It was impossible to be there. People fall unconscious there. You cannot breathe and you cannot have any medical help, any physician there, and guards don't want to speak with you. If you fall unconscious, they can give you water on the head only.

They moved prisoners from prison to prison; I told you about transit prisons on the way. That is why I have seen many prisons on my way—Kuybishev, and many others. It is rotten cabbage in the prison when you stay there 2, 3, 5, 7, 10 days. Rotten cabbage, rotten potatoes, and rotten salt fish is the only food.

In this Omsk, when I came to Omsk, it was 5,000 prisoners in my concentration camp No. 4, but it was a group of concentration camps in so big a half circle, because we built there many, many special buildings, apartment buildings, and we built there a big oil plant and big streetcars and UP plants.

Senator GURNEY. You say there were a hundred concentration camps there?

Mr. SHIFRIN. Yes.

Senator GURNEY. Can you describe generally what a concentration camp would consist of?

Mr. SHIFRIN. In our concentration camp, No. 4, in which I was?

Senator GURNEY. This would be typical of the others?

Mr. SHIFRIN. Yes, it is typical, really typical. In our concentration camp was 25, 27 big long barracks. In some barracks, 300 people, in some barracks 200 people, I was in a barrack with 500 people together, in common bunks in two tiers.

Senator GURNEY. This is one big long room?

Mr. SHIFRIN. Yes; it is a barrack, a long barrack, 50 meters, 75-meter barrack, and on both sides of the barrack they have two tiers common bunks and people sleep there in the night.

They have a little room in this barrack to dry your boots in the night and your clothes, because it is all watery and dirty in the day work. We built a big oil plant, a very big oil plant, maybe a kilometer long oil plant, in Omsk.

Senator GURNEY. Is this an oil refinery?

Mr. SHIFRIN. Refinery, yes. A big plant.

I was there maybe 5 months only because I tried to make escape from this camp.

Senator GURNEY. Now, if we can go back just to complete the picture of a concentration camp, you described the barrack. How many people were in these barracks?

Mr. SHIFRIN. From 200 to 500 people in each barrack.

Senator GURNEY. And how many barracks in your concentration camp?

Mr. SHIFRIN. Twenty-five—26 barracks it was in this concentration camp.

Senator GURNEY. So there were approximately how many prisoners?

Mr. SHIFRIN. In our concentration camp, it was 5,000 prisoners. When I came to this concentration camp, they quote to me a number. All the prisoners in a concentration camp have numbers—you have not your name.

Senator GURNEY. And you say there are about 100 similar camps in this complex?

Mr. SHIFRIN. Yes.

Senator GURNEY. And they would contain about the same number of people, 5,000?

Mr. SHIFRIN. Yes, average of 4,000–5,000 in each concentration camp. I have seen people from other concentration camp in the daytime.

Senator GURNEY. In this particular area, in the day, then, there would have been imprisoned in these concentration camps somewhere between 400,000 and 500,000 people; is that right?

Mr. SHIFRIN. Yes, because it was a big construction project. Today you cannot see there so many prisoners. Now I was in Omsk in this place. Only three or four concentration camps remain there, because they finished this work.

Senator GURNEY. Now, describe your work here. What kind of work did you do?

Mr. SHIFRIN. Yes. In 6 o'clock, you must be near the gates. Before this, you must go to a special barrack, kitchen barrack. You can have 500 grams of water which they tell to you is "soup," from rotten cabbage and rotten potatoes, and 600 grams of bread for all the day.

Senator GURNEY. This was a ration that you drew in the morning after you got up?

Mr. SHIFRIN. Yes, before work.

Now, bread for all the day. In the middle of the day and in the evening, they would give you another food. I will tell you now.

This water with the name "soup," they give you in the morning and they give you 600 grams of bread in the morning for all the day. Then with this bread, you must come to the gate. Near the gate stay guards and after the gate also stay guards, with the dogs, machineguns, and bayonets. This guard inside came, put us in the line with five people together in the row. Then they began a search. Before work, they search all the prisoners. In the winter, in the summer.

Stay at gate five soldiers. Came five prisoners and you must show to them your body. Sometimes they permit you to show only that you wear nothing here, only your prisoner clothes. Sometimes, if they suspect something, they told you, take off all the clothes—and you take off your clothes and stay naked in the snow when they search your clothes.

They permit to you only prisoner clothes. That is very cold clothes and many prisoners wore before these clothes. When they died, they give these clothes to other prisoners.

Senator GURNEY. Of what did that clothing consist?

Mr. SHIFRIN. Trousers, boots, a shirt, and in the winter, a padded jacket. And these boots, they are made of tires, of old tires. They tore tires to pieces and from these, they made these boots.

When they finished this search, with the groups of two kinds of prisoners in each part—around your group, dogs, soldiers, machineguns—you go to your place of work. In this place, you work 10 hours each day. In these 10 hours, you have 1-hour interval for food and rest. In day meal, they would give you again this soup, this water with some pieces of rotten cabbage or rotten potatoes. Always black potatoes. I never have seen white potatoes in these 10 years.

Senator GURNEY. This would be a noontime meal?

Mr. SHIFRIN. Yes, noontime.

Senator GURNEY. How far would the work be away from the prison camp?

Mr. SHIFRIN. In this Omsk, it was approximately 4 kilometers. In his plain, we would go 4 kilometers.

Senator GURNEY. You would walk the 4 kilometers?

Mr. SHIFRIN. Yes.

Senator GURNEY. And then you would work the 10 hours after that?

Mr. SHIFRIN. Yes, after that.

Then they would give you gruel, watery gruel, and I have never seen in Europe such grain—gray, half black, without any taste. You can put salt, without any taste. It sounds impossible. Prisoners explain to me that they have this grain from China. I do not know. Like artificial, this grain.

Then again, you work, and in the evening, another search in the work. Then back to the prison. Then another search in the gates.

Senator GURNEY. A search at the place of work before you started?

Mr. SHIFRIN. Yes, because they do not want that you take something from the work. And then another search in the gates of the concentration camps. And then you came to the concentration camp. All like in books of Solzhenitsyn.

Senator GURNEY. What kind of work did you do here?

Mr. SHIFRIN. Myself?

Senator GURNEY. Yes.

Mr. SHIFRIN. Metallic construction in the high. I was not an invalid in this time.

Senator GURNEY. This would be a steelworker's kind of work?

Mr. SHIFRIN. Steelwork, yes, on big buildings. I was in a very "high position."

Senator GURNEY. High up, at least.

Mr. SHIFRIN. Yes.

After 6 months, in 1954—in the summer of 1954—I tried to make an escape from this concentration camp and they caught two of us. Eight people were successful and two, my friend and I, were not. And they sent us to a special political "closed" prison. In Russia, if you think that they have open prisons, you are mistaken.

A closed prison in city Semipalatinsk, this place you see on the map. There I was a year. And after this, I was in another district prison in Ust-Kamenogorsk.

Senator GURNEY. Was this prison any different from the other one?

Mr. SHIFRIN. Yes, in this prison you can see a really big difference from concentration camp. In my cell, it was 12 people. In cells 4 meters to 6 meters. A very big cell for a prison. We were very lucky in these days. It was the prison in which was writer Dostoyevsky in the days of Czarism. When I asked the chief of the prison, where is the cell of Dostoyevsky, he asked me: "From which concentration camp came this Dostoyevsky?" He thought that I was talking about one of our prisoners.

It was a prison with cells, with a concrete floor, with brick walls. It was very good, because with concrete walls, you live worse. I was also—after this, I will tell you—in concrete prisons. It was a little window in this cell. It was a common bunk, but not from wood, from iron. And it was made from strips of iron. And they gave to us mattresses. Inside the mattresses was not straw or cotton, but it was inside the mattresses little scraps of hard leather. Because in Semipalatinsk, they have a big slaughter house and it was pieces of this leather, very hard. And this mattress, when you put it on this part of this iron strips, in the nighttime, this leather came through these parts and you lie on this iron in the night. It was not good, believe me.

Senator GURNEY. I can believe it.

Mr. SHIFRIN. It was food worse than in the concentration camp, because you have only 500 grams of bread and you have half a portion of food, of this rotten food. But you do not work there. You only sit in the cell for 24 hours from day to day. Half an hour they permit you to go to a little courtyard in which you can only stand and you see the sky. But I will tell you about another prison in which I was and you would understand that this was a resort for us.

Senator GURNEY. How long did you stay in this prison?

Mr. SHIFRIN. One year. One year with my friends.

Senator GURNEY. Is there anything else you want to tell us about that prison?

Mr. SHIFRIN. What can I tell you? It was maybe 400 prisoners there, political prisoners, and maybe 100 women was there. They also sit in these conditions. It was political women prisoners. Most of them were nuns which they arrest mercilessly in the U.S.S.R.

Senator GURNEY. And you stayed—the rations were cut in half, no work, you could not do anything, you had to stay in the cell except for a small exercise period?

Mr. SHIFRIN. Yes, only. Without any work.

Senator GURNEY. And you stayed there a year?

Mr. SHIFRIN. A year, yes.

Senator GURNEY. Did they do anything else like interrogate you or beat you or anything of that nature?

Mr. SHIFRIN. No, nothing. They try sometimes if you do not make something like they want, they put you in more strict cell, underground, with cold and with only 200 grams of bread and two glasses of water in the 24 hours.

Senator GURNEY. Cut in half again?

Mr. SHIFRIN. And without a bunk, on concrete you must sleep. That is a special strict cell—*Kartser*, as they call it.

Senator GURNEY. Did you spend any time there?

Mr. SHIFRIN. In this prison, I was not there. My friends was there, but I was not there. I was in another prison. so I will tell you about it also.

Senator GURNEY. All right, now, what was the next prison?

Mr. SHIFRIN. The next prison was Ust-Kamenogorsk.

Senator GURNEY. Where is this?

Mr. SHIFRIN. Also here, 300 kilometers to the east.

Senator GURNEY. What period of time?

Mr. SHIFRIN. 1955.

Senator GURNEY. When did you go there—in 1954?

Mr. SHIFRIN. In 1954, I came. I was there and——

Senator GURNEY. What month?

Mr. SHIFRIN. It was—I came there in July of 1954.

Senator GURNEY. And you stayed until——

Mr. SHIFRIN. Until July of 1955.

Senator GURNEY. All right, go on.

Mr. SHIFRIN. Then I was 3 or 4 months in another prison.

Senator GURNEY. Will you describe that prison now?

Mr. SHIFRIN. Another prison?

Senator GURNEY. The one where you stayed a year, from June until July?

Mr. SHIFRIN. What can I tell about this prison also?

Senator GURNEY. Why did they transfer you?

Mr. SHIFRIN. Again, we tried to make an escape from this prison, from Semipalatinsk.

Senator GURNEY. From the other prison?

Mr. SHIFRIN. They was very frightened and they sent us to a more strict prison in Ust-Kamenogorsk, also a prison which held Dostoyevsky about which he wrote in his books. It was a big difference in the days of Dostoyevsky and in our days.

Senator GURNEY. Go on.

Mr. SHIFRIN. In Ust-Kamenogorsk, I was only 3 or 4 months. It was a very strict prison. It was there maybe 600 or 700 prisoners in this prison. The prison was from the days of Stalinism, also. It is a very big prison and it was a very strict regime there. Overseers, they beat people mercilessly, without any reason sometimes, only if you speak loudly in the cell or if you curse a soldier or something like this, they tear a prisoner from the cell, put them in this room and beat them mercilessly. It was there once a hunger strike and a little riot when I was there, because it was impossible to live there.

Senator GURNEY. How would they beat them?

Mr. SHIFRIN. How would they beat them? With their fists.

Senator GURNEY. Kick them?

Mr. SHIFRIN. Yes, with their fists, they beat them. They put chains on your hands and you cannot do nothing, then they beat you. That is all. People returning to their cells, all black and violet from these beatings. I have seen this many times.

Also, in this prison, it was inside the courtyard a little prison for children. In the U.S.S.R., they have special concentration camps and special prisons for children to the age of 18. If they arrest a child of 14 or 15, they send them to this special concentration camp.

Senator GURNEY. What crimes would they be charged with?

Mr. SHIFRIN. Some of them are criminals, some of them children of political prisoners. I have seen many of them. I was in a concentration camp with Yuri Shukhevich—he was arrested at age 14 years.

Senator GURNEY. You mean because they arrested the father or the mother, they threw the children in prison, too?

Mr. SHIFRIN. Yes. I was very lucky. When they arrested my father, I was 14 years old. They did not send me to the prison because my father was not an important man. If they arrest people more important, like they arrested the father of Pyotr Yakir—his father was a general of Red Army, this Jewish General Yakir—then they sent Pyotr Yakir, his son, at age 14, to the concentration camp for children. And Pyotr Yakir was in the prisons and concentration camps without any crime 20 years.

Senator GURNEY. How long?

Mr. SHIFRIN. Twenty years.

Senator GURNEY. Twenty years?

Mr. SHIFRIN. From 1936 to 1956. He was in these concentration camps to 1956. Then they released him. And now he is again in concentration camp.

This man, the son of a Ukrainian, Shukhevich—this Shukhevich's father was killed by Stalin. The father of Pyotr Yakir was also killed by Stalin. The father of this young man was killed by Stalin and he was in a concentration camp also from the age of 14 years, and also 20 years.

Shukhevich is also my friend. I was with him also. He was released like Pyotr Yakir was released, but he was released only in 1968, because his father was arrested after Yakir.

Senator GURNEY. Why were these children not permitted to stay with relatives rather than being thrown in prison?

Mr. SHIFRIN. No, they have special concentration camps also for relatives. They are very "human."

Senator GURNEY. You mean they have concentration camps for everybody?

Mr. SHIFRIN. Yes, I have seen these people. For you it is a good joke. For them, it is not a good joke. These people were not in prison under articles of code. They have only letters, Ch. S.V.N.—"Member of Family of Enemy of People." That is the "Article" written on the file. Absolutely without any law! And they were sent to concentration camp without any crime and without sentences to 5 or 10 years. They sent them to their death. Some of them were 5 years, some 10, some 20, some died in concentration camps.

These people, Yuri Shukhevich and Pyotr Yakir were 20 years in concentration camps. First years in the children concentration camps and prisons, and then with us together.

Permit me to finish fate of these two people. They was in the freedom, one of them, 5 years, another 7 years. Now, both of them, Pyotr Yakir and Yuri Shukhevich are now again in the prison. A 10-year sentence again, without any crime.

Senator GURNEY. When were they thrown in prison again?

Mr. SHIFRIN. Yuri Shukhevich a year ago, a little less than a year, and Pyotr Yakir only 4 months ago. Equal fate of these two people——

I told you, they have no discrimination of nations in concentration camps.

Senator GURNEY. Now, let's go back to the relatives, if we can. If important political prisoners were sent to a concentration camp, how many relatives would also be sent?

Mr. SHIFRIN. I did not understand.

Senator GURNEY. If an important political prisoner were arrested, like this man here, and sent to a concentration camp, how many relatives would also be sent to concentration camps?

Mr. SHIFRIN. You see, it depends on the importance of this prisoner.

Senator GURNEY. I understand.

Mr. SHIFRIN. From the family of Stalin, 20 relatives of Stalin were in concentration camps. The wife of the first advisor of Stalin, Molotov, was in a concentration camp. She was there. It was there big people, like ministers, admirals, generals, heroes of the U.S.S.R.

Senator GURNEY. In other words, if the political prisoner was important, then quite a few relatives probably would be sent to concentration camp?

Mr. SHIFRIN. Yes. Sometimes only wife, sometimes wife and children, sometimes all the relatives.

Senator GURNEY. I understand. Go on.

Mr. SHIFRIN. It depends on the importance and on the KGB. What they want, they do.

Now, sometimes, they put in the prison, they are so human that they send to the prison not only the son or father or mother, they do not want to "divide" families and that is why they arrest all the family. I was in concentration camp with the Jewish family Podolsky. Father and son were with me and the wife, mother was in another concentration camp near us. They like "order." They have many sorts of concentration camps: for grown people, for children, for relatives.

Now, they have special concentration camps for women, and others for women with children. Once I have seen such a case. When they brought us—excuse me, I do not go in order. When they brought us from the district of Tayshet, from this district on the map, to Potma, 6,000 kilometers away, it was in 1960, in the spring, in April. They brought us with another sort of train, "prisoner train"—cattle cars. In each cattle car, 70 prisoners, 50 cars together. They sent this big train from Tayshet because they organized in this time, in this Mordovia, special prisoner district for special political prisoners, dangerous prisoners. They sent us to this place. It was sunshine and melting snow when we came from these cars and have seen—such things I have seen first in my life! We stayed in the corridor of the fences of concentration camps to the horizon.

In this place—that is this place on the map, Potma, it was in this place which stayed our train. And in this place, you can see all the concentration camps without interruption—only fences and towers near a railway, to the horizon. There goes in the wild forest this railway with concentration camps.

And we told each other, what is it? What is the district? To the horizon, concentration camps. In Tayshet, it was little intervals between concentration camps. And in this time, they opened the gate of one of the concentration camps. It was maybe 50 meters from the place where I was and from these gates came 200, maybe 250 women, and each woman had a baby on her hands, 5- or 6-month-old baby, and around these women, soldiers with the machine guns, dogs barking, soldiers cursing; before deportation, they always searched women, like all prisoners. That is why the babies were crying. Women crying, with tears. Really, the first time in my life I have seen it, the first in my 10 years—because I only have heard about these concentration camps for women with children. And when this group, this big group of women, came, we were astonished for a second—and then all our 2,000 prisoners, with numbers, with stripes on their clothes—yes, yes, now, also in 1972, people prisoners, political prisoners, go with numbers like in concentration camps in the Hitler time. My number was S720. We shouted, "Murderers, fascists!" And they were so frightened that they began to shoot in the air. And then they shouted to us, "lie down on the earth, with the face to the earth!" And they shouted and they put us on the earth with this shouting and shooting. And then with the butts, they put these women again into the concentration camp.

Try to believe me, that is not a scenario for a film. It was something I have eyewitnessed, my friends. In this same second, a loudspeaker on the fence of the concentration camp said with a loud voice: "Citizens of U.S.S.R., I must tell you big news. Our rocket is in the space with a man, Gagarin is in the space"—it was at the moment when they put Gagarin in the sky. It is not a scenario. It was in reality.

Now I will try again to go in the order.

Senator GURNEY. I wonder if this would not be a good time to break. We will recess until 2 o'clock this afternoon.

(Whereupon at 12:10 p.m., the subcommittee recessed to reconvene at 2 p.m., the same day.)

U.S.S.R. LABOR CAMPS

THURSDAY, FEBRUARY 1, 1973

U.S. SENATE,
SUBCOMMITTEE TO INVESTIGATE THE
ADMINISTRATION OF THE INTERNAL SECURITY ACT
AND OTHER INTERNAL SECURITY LAWS
OF THE COMMITTEE ON THE JUDICIARY,
Washington, D.C.

The subcommittee met, pursuant to notice, at 2 p.m., in room 2228, Dirksen Senate Office Building, Senator Edward J. Gurney, presiding.

Also present: J. G. Sourwine, chief counsel; Samuel J. Scott, associate counsel; A. L. Tarabochia, chief investigator; and David Martin, senior analyst.

AFTERNOON SESSION

Senator GURNEY. The subcommittee will come to order.

Mr. Sourwine?

Mr. SOURWINE. Mr. Shifrin, what can you tell us about the great concentration camp uprising of 1953–54?

TESTIMONY OF AVRAHAM SHIFRIN—Resumed

Mr. SHIFRIN. In 1953, 1954, it was awful conditions in concentration camps. It is hard to explain how bad it was. It was a time when people worked without holidays or any days when they can rest—10, 12, sometimes 15 hours in a day, with one letter to their relatives in the year. One to the year. And without meeting relatives, without any salary, with such bad food that when I came to the concentration camp, I have seen prisoners which have only bones and skin. Each day in our concentration camp, I do not remember a day when it was less than 30, 35 people—less than 35—which died from starvation. People died from scurvy, from pellagra also, a sort of scurvy, and from other diseases, because the body can't work in these conditions when men are so hungry. And that is why people was in such a condition that one day, in Vorkuta, in this district, which you can see on this map up near the polar circle—it was in these days, maybe some millions prisoners in this district—spontaneously, they began to strike. Then they asked some prisoners to speak with the guards, with officers. And they stopped the work in all the coal mines.

Mr. SOURWINE. Please do not be upset by the buzzers. They represent the bells which tell Senators what the conditions are on the floor of the Senate. Go right ahead.

Mr. SHIFRIN. Okay.

They stopped work in the coal mines. This coal mining, it is very important in the U.S.S.R. because industry works on this coal. That is why came to them Khrushchev, Bulganin, Voroshilov, many members of the government, the General Procurator of the U.S.S.R., with members of the Supreme Court, with members of the Supreme Soviet of Ministers. They came to these concentration camps and spoke with these prisoners, but the prisoners answered, "We would work in these coal mines if you would take away these numbers and you would permit us first to live like people; and then you would examine our files again, because we are innocent." And they refused to do this. And these conversations was maybe 20, 25, 30 days in some concentration camps.

Then the government sent bombers and then they sent tanks. They sent troops, and they drowned this uprising in the blood. Thousands and thousands of prisoners was killed.

But in the same time, they caught people from these camps and sent them to other concentration camps. It was a big mistake of this government, because when these people came to these transit camps and prisons, this news came to every part, to all the concentration camps. After 2 months began a strike in Kolyma gold mine; in Norilsk, where there were molybdenum and other mines; in the district of Kemerovo, coal and molybdenum mines; and in Kazakhstan and Dzheskazgan.

What can I tell you? In this place, in Dzheskazgan, it was a complex of concentration camps. A very impressive complex. They have concentration camps in many places, with interval 1 kilometer, 2 kilometers. In Dzheskazgan, they built really a city of prisoners, maybe 10 kilometers long and 5 wide, and inside these square walls, it was also walls which divided this "city" into concentration camps. From concentration camp to concentration camp, it was gates and corridors for guards and prisoners. Prisoners seized all this "city" in their hands during uprising. It was there big concentration camp for women and most of these women was from the Ukraine and there were also nuns, religious believers. And when they have in their hands all this Dzheskazgan, there also came to them members of government from Moscow, because here in this place, in Dzheskazgan, they have copper mining, biggest in U.S.S.R. They came to them and spoke with them and they answered, "We want freedom; we are innocent." It was there special committee of prisoners led the strike.

Approximately 2 months were conversations. They tried to stop it. Then Communists sent tanks against these prisoners and they crushed these walls and came with the tanks against the prisoners.

Mr. SOURWINE. Tanks against the prisoners?

Mr. SHIFRIN. Yes, and it was a big mass, thousands, maybe hundred thousand people in this camps. And the women tried to protect these men prisoners, and they stayed in the line in front of the prisoners, a line of women. Five hundred women were crushed with these tanks. We have here an eyewitness letter from people which were there in Dzheskazgan in these days. I personally have spoken with them.

Mr. SOURWINE. Mr. Chairman, we do have for proposed insertion in the record a number of eyewitness accounts of these concentration camp uprisings. I would respectfully suggest that they be ordered into the record subject to the same caveat that the Chair made this morning, that the actual printing in the record of the appendix is to be determined by the chairman.

Senator GURNEY. They will be so ordered.

Mr. SOURWINE. Go ahead, sir.

Have there been any similar uprisings in concentration camps?

Mr. SHIFRIN. There was in Norilsk. In Norilsk, there was big uprising. In Norilsk is big mining for molybdenum and uranium and they need uranium in industry. That is why in Norilsk, they tried to speak for weeks; and then these killers sent big guns and tanks and they crushed these people. Thousands of prisoners were killed in Norilsk.

Norilsk is a place in which, before there came prisoners to Norilsk, it was mountains and plain with snow. You could not find there any buildings. Then prisoners build the city for 300,000 or 400,000 people. Now it is a big city. And all this city was built by prisoners.

Senator GURNEY. This was all done by concentration camp labor?

Mr. SHIFRIN. Only. You see, in all the country, if you hear they built some big plant or they began to build some dam, believe me, you can find there prison camps.

Building Volga-Don Canal, it was a half million prisoners in the center of the U.S.S.R. Here it was. [pointing to map reproduced on p. 2 of Part 1] Yes, it was a half million prisoners in this Volga-Don Canal.

Belomorsky Canal here [pointing to map]—also prisoners.

I talked to you about this Omsk refinery [pointing to map]—also built by prisoners. I talked to you about this biggest power station, Bratsk—also prisoners. I can show you here it was in Angarsk [pointing to map] they brought from Germany one of the biggest in Germany refinery, artificial gasoline. And it was here—I have had many friends here—100,000 people for 5 years, they build this synthetic refinery.

They built all the Kolyma gold mines with the hands of prisoners.

You can see on all these places from which they think to send to the United States these rockets, all these missile bases and airfields—all build by prisoners. All the railways in the country—only prisoners. Highways—all prisoners. All lumber cutting—only prisoners. Today, in 1973.

I have seen many times—I have heard, excuse me, please—I have seen twice myself and I have heard many times when prisoners cut their own hands and put them in the cars with lumber. They said to me, "We want that people in the freedom in the West will know who cut this lumber." You know—this lumber goes to free world. When I came to the West and I asked some people which make trade with the U.S.S.R. in this lumber, I asked these people: "It was such cases when came lumber with cut hands?" They answered me, "Yes; it was."

I ask, why you did not tell to the press or to the radio about this? They answered: "It is impossible. Then we must stop our trade with the U.S.S.R."

In all the U.S.S.R., these slaves work without salary, only because prisoners want to live. They work in this industry, in this lumber cutting, in all this country.

Mr. SOURWINE. You gave us a figure earlier of 20 to 25 percent of all industrial production in the U.S.S.R., and I understood you to say it was done with slave labor.

Mr. SHIFRIN. Yes; it is true—with mining, lumbering, and construction.

Mr. SOURWINE. Do you think that figure holds true today?

Mr. SHIFRIN. No, I said that now 20–25 percent and before, in the days of Stalin, it came in some, in coal mining, in molybdenum, in cutting lumber, to 80 percent.

Mr. SOURWINE. How many slave laborers do you estimate that there are in the U.S.S.R. today?

Mr. SHIFRIN. You see, it is impossible to tell how many concentration camps and prisoners they have. I am sure only that you cannot have so many concentration camps without millions of prisoners. If you would try to make this in a mathematic way, we would come to this figure. You see, here in my days, it was maybe 5 million in Vorkuta-Pechora. Here, it was maybe 7 millions in Kolyma.

Senator GURNEY. In those areas?

Mr. SHIFRIN. In these two only places.

Senator GURNEY. Twelve million in just two areas?

Mr. SHIFRIN. Yes; maybe more; these figures came from prisoners which were in these places in camps.

And in Karaganda, it was also maybe 2 millions, and 2 million in Kemerovo. But then in 1956, they released, I think, 50–60 percent of prisoners. It was days when they tried to cheat all the free world in this way. At first, they did not need in these days so many workers and that is why they released these slave laborers from concentration camps. And in all newspapers in the West, Khrushchev made announcement: "We are finished with concentration camps!" And really, millions—maybe 10 million—came home, and all the West was cheated in this way. Because millions stay in concentration camps.

Senator GURNEY. What year was this?

Mr. SHIFRIN. It was 1956. They released part of the prisoners. It is very characteristic for the U.S.S.R. They sent for many years before 1956 people without any trial to concentration camps. You know that they have had special three men "Troikas" which send people to the prisons without trial. They have special three-man courts—and they only have files of these people, and a special secretary explains them: "These men have spoken an anti-Soviet anecdote". Without presence of these men, without eye witnesses, without nothing. In such a way, they sent millions to the prisons.

That is why, when they came in 1956, also came these three-man "Troikas" to concentration camps and they released 50, sometimes 60 percent of prisoners from concentration camps.

Senator GURNEY. Fifty or sixty percent?

Mr. SHIFRIN. Yes. And they release them without seeing their files, you see; only when they see that these men or women were sentenced by Troikas, they release these people, without anything. They know that these people are innocent.

Senator GURNEY. They knew they were political prisoners and were really innocent?

Mr. SHIFRIN. Yes.

Senator GURNEY. Now, why did they release them in that year, in 1956?

Mr. SHIFRIN. I think it was several reasons. First, Khrushchev wanted to look good in your eyes, in the eyes of all mankind.

Second, in these days, they did not build all this big industry in the country, and that is why they do not need so many millions. And also, a third reason, Khrushchev wanted to kill again Stalin and to talk to all the world about the crimes of Stalin. And also millions of prisoners were in bad conditions they could not work—it was better to send them home to families.

Senator GURNEY. He, Khrushchev, was a good man?

Mr. SHIFRIN. Yes. Good killer.

Senator GURNFY. Compared to Stalin?

Mr. SHIFRIN. Telling the world that he released these millions of people, Khrushchev cheated free world. It looks good, but not to Khrushchev, because he did not make it with good heart—I am sure, because he was a killer like all these government killers.

Senator GURNEY. Of course, this was before you ever went there yourself?

Mr. SHIFRIN. No; it was in my time.

Senator GURNEY. Oh, that is right, it was. It was when you were in the prison camps?

Mr. SHIFRIN. I have seen all this, yes. And after he released these prisoners, at this time, I was once in train and Khrushchev was here in the United States, and I was in a special car for prisoners, with guards, with soldiers, and so on. And Khrushchev here in the U.N. made this speech, "I have finished with all the concentration camps in the U.S.S.R.; now we have no prisoners in the U.S.S.R.; we are finished with all the crimes of Stalin." And in a corridor in another stage of this cage stayed an officer. He smoked, smiled, and said to us: "When we come to the station, I will release you because you are not here."

You see, in the U.S.S.R., no one believes the government, because they lie in the eyes of people. People in U.S.S.R. used to all this. I know—I am sure that my father was innocent. I was sure of this when he was arrested. He never was an anti-Soviet man. He was a simple civil engineer. And then came this great purge. He was sent to the prison and died after 10 years. And in 1958, they sent to my mother so little letter, "Your husband, Shifrin, Itzak, was innocent and today he is rehabilitated after death."

Sad. You enjoy here your rights. We also have rights in U.S.S.R. And one of our rights is "after death rehabilitation;" such sad joke in U.S.S.R. you can hear.

Once in such a prisoner railway car, a soldier asked a prisoner, "Why do you sit here in the prison?" And the prisoner answered "I am innocent; for nothing."

"And how many years they gave you?"

The prisoner answered "25 years."

And the soldier said to the prisoner, "Ah, you liar! If men are innocent, they always give only 10 years!"

You understood me?

Senator GURNEY. I am not sure.

Mr. BOLDYREFF. Well, the sense is this. The prisoner, answering the soldier's question about the length of his sentence, said 25 years—but then said he was innocent. And the soldier indignantly said, no, those who are innocent get only 10 years—and you got 25.

Senator GURNEY. I see.

Mr. SHIFRIN. Excuse, please, my English. When I came to the free world, I was really astonished because I know how big propaganda makes this Communist regime in the U.S.A. and in all the world. When I came, I have seen it with my own eyes and I have seen that people here do not know truth about U.S.S.R. They think that we have not in the U.S.S.R. concentration camps. Well, here it was this case 2 days ago, some idiots shot your Senator [Stennis]. Some people here in the Senate said to me with envy: "And you in the U.S.S.R., you are lucky, you have not criminals there."

"We have not criminals?" I said, "We have criminals 10 times more than here."

"No," answered me this man, "we never have seen that in your newspapers."

It is for us like a joke. In the U.S.S.R., they never print in the newspaper nothing about criminals. You cannot find there no one story with man that shot other man, or suicide or something like this. Nothing about criminals in papers; but all prisons now are full with criminals like killers and robbers—I do not know what to tell you. You cannot go in the suburbs, but only in the center of the city you can go in the evening. In all the streets are robbery, killing of the people. And here people do not know nothing.

Why? Because your foreigners come to the U.S.S.R., live in special hotels for foreigners, two or three KGB go in the back of all the foreigners. All the bandits know that the KGB goes with the foreigners and they never will come to the foreigners or to the hotel. That is why your foreigners never meet with an accident and robbery in the U.S.S.R. And all the KGB work in these hotels and that is why you cannot see these thieves. No one thief would go to this hotel for foreigners. He knows that would be prison for him.

But ordinary people know in the U.S.S.R.—know everything. Ordinary people know very well about all this situation with concentration camps. Here in this room now my friend, from U.S.S.R. with two little daughters. These girls smile when I speak about all this, and ask me: why do you speak about things which all people know? They cannot understand that you do not know about these concentration camps.

What to tell you? How to explain to you? In Odessa, you see this town, Odessa on the map—excuse me, please, I forgot to put here a flag. In Odessa, a city on the Black Sea, a resort city—ask your people, many American people was there—foreigners come with beautiful ships with planes. They see the shore with palms and with all these beautiful restaurants. But only 2 kilometers from shops in the center of the city, you can find big prisons, six-story prisons, and near these prisons, you can find a big concentration camp—in the center of the city—with barbed wire, towers. Openly. They never permit foreigners to go inside city. And it is in the center of the country, in the resort, they have a concentration camp.

I can tell you address of these concentration camps—Odessa; Chernamoskaya Doroga, 75 or 78, something like this, this big concentration camp, with two-story barracks. You can see from the street all these barracks. They make it very open. They do not permit the foreigner to go free to many cities and that is why it is very open.

Excuse me, please, that I am so long in my answers.

Mr. Sourwine. Sir, you said you could not estimate the total number of slave laborers in the Soviet Union, but you did say that they did 20 to 25 percent of all the industrial production. Must they not constitute at least 20 to 25 percent of all the industrial workers in the U.S.S.R.?

Mr. Shifrin. I cannot answer to this, because it would not be good. I am not statistician.

Mr. Sourwine. Does the slave laborer produce more than the free laborer in the U.S.S.R.?

Mr. Shifrin. In some branches of industry, they make more with free people—with food, yes, with cars, with clothes, Yes. But with coal mining, with big buildings, with this gold—all the gold is only prisoners. You cannot find many free people in the gold mines or in the coal mines in the north.

Senator Gurney. I think you mentioned one figure in one of the mining areas.

Mr. Shifrin. Yes, here in Vorkuta-Pechora maybe 5 million.

Senator Gurney. How many?

Mr. Shifrin. Maybe 5 million.

Senator Gurney. How did you arrive at that figure, Mr. Shifrin?

Mr. Shifrin. You see, when I came to Potma, to this place, from Vorkuta and Pechora-Inta, came many thousand political prisoners. Among them, I have many friends and we tried to count this. They told me this figure.

Also, when I was here in Tayshet, many people came from Magadan and that is why I know about this from them. They know all the concentration camps in this district and they try to count figures.

Senator Gurney. I understand. In other words, you had a fairly accurate count on the number of individual camps and you knew approximately how many slave laborers there were in each camp and from those two figures you approximated your 5 million?

Mr. Shifrin. Yes, approximately, we have these figures. You cannot know real figures.

For example, when I came to concentration camp, Omsk 4, it was there approximately 5,000 prisoners I told you. They gave me a number with which I was identified, number S. 720. Each letter in the alphabet, mean a thousand people in this concentration camp. That is why letter "S" mean 17,000, because the letter "S", that is 17 in the Russian alphabet. That's why I was prisoner 17,720. But it was there only 5,000 prisoners. From this you can understand how many people died in this concentration camp. Some of them they sent to other camps, but most of them died in this camp.

Once when I was in Tayshet, they brought me to the train to send to another concentration camp. They sent me to strict concentration camp. That is why I was alone with four guards and two dogs. And when we came to the station, we lost the train. It was only 30 or 40 kilometers to another camp and they asked a horse with a cart and we came with the cart these 40 kilometers. Believe me, all the 40 kilometers in this forest we go through a big cemetery—cemetery, cemetery, cemetery without end.

Senator Gurney. Cemetery?

Mr. Shifrin. Yes. It was biggest cemetery in my life which I have seen, because it was 40 kilometers. And after that friends-prisoners said : you can see cemetery in all 600 kilometers. I have one photograph from this place. I would show you. It is only little mounds on the graves and sometimes a stick with the wood and numbers of prisoners on this piece of wood, without names, only numbers.

And I thought, that is graves for prisoners which died in the summer, because in the winter, they never put prisoners in the graves. In the winter—I made it many times when they sent me to make it—

these corpses we bring to the gate. And then always was such procedure with dead prisoners.

Near the gate, we must put them on the earth, these corpses. Then came soldier. In some cases, he came with big hammer on a big handle, and he crushed the skulls of the corpses to see, maybe they live—naked corpses in 40° below zero in centigrade! Maybe they want to make an escape, these naked people.

In other cases, this soldier—in all the concentration camps they have their own rules—this soldier came with a stick of iron and this iron always they have in the stove and that is why the third part is red, and he put this red-hot iron in the body, in the corpses, to see also maybe they live.

When this procedure is finished, we can take these corpses on the sleds, like firewood we put them together, and we bring them to this wild forest. And you cannot make a grave in such frost. That is why, we put them in standing position, these corpses, or we lay them on the snow. And if you would come tomorrow with other corpses, you cannot find these corpses from yesterday. They disappeared. Wild beasts like bears, black foxes, sables—they are there in thousands—they ate these corpses in the night. Maybe some bones you can see in the place.

And these soldiers which stay around concentration camps, they put near this "cemetery," they put traps and they catch these black foxes and sables. Then they sell them to other countries. And that is why you have here so beautiful shops with Russian furs, in New York and Washington and London and in Paris. I have seen them in all cities of the free world.

This cemetery I have seen that is 40 kilometers, they are people that have died in the summer.

Senator GURNEY. This area, or this distance between the two camps, 40 kilometers, as I understand your testimony, was just one vast grave from one camp to the other?

Mr. SHIFRIN. Yes. You see, in this district, I came from one camp to another, but in this district was tens and tens of concentration camps—and they bring these people to these graves. They send me to a special concentration camp, but on this road, there were many concentration camps on the south side of railway.

Senator GURNEY. How far back from the road could you see?

Mr. SHIFRIN. This would go maybe only a hundred meters from the road. Sometimes it goes near the railroad. And always, I have seen these cemeteries.

Senator GURNEY. You mentioned in your testimony the numbers in in those two mining areas Your estimates were 7 million or 10 million. Now this was, I take it, in the period that you also were a prisoner, in 1953–63?

Mr. SHIFRIN. You see, Khrushchev, when he said about crimes of Stalin, he mentioned this figure 15 millions of prisoners, political prisoners. He mentioned only this, 15 million political prisoners. He did not tell about criminals. And in the U.S.S.R. was twice as many criminals than political prisoners. Now try to imagine this figure. Among prisoners, I have heard many times that in the days of Stalin, in concentration camps was approximately 40 million prisoners, criminals and politicals altogether.

Senator GURNEY. But my question is, again, in these two mining areas, these very large concentration camps where there were figures of 5 and 7 million.—that was during your time?

Mr. SHIFRIN. Yes, when I came in 1954 to 1956, it was. I think that now they have there less prisoners.

Senator GURNEY. That was going to be my next question. Are there still prisoners in those areas?

Mr. SHIFRIN. Yes, in these areas there is still concentration camps.

Senator GURNEY. Still using slave labor to work these mines?

Mr. SHIFRIN. Yes. But you see, why I tell that now it is less number of prisoners, when they finished to build in Norilsk a big city, they sent to work here free people. Many people which finished prison stayed there in exile and live now like free people.

Also in Kolyma, they have now many people which finished sentences in the prisons and stayed there. Former prisoners afraid to live in the center of U.S.S.R., because some of them were arrested the second and third time. I told you that here live many people which was before in the prisons and concentration camps.

Also, some of these camps they now obliterate, for example in Norilsk you cannot see how many camps. You cannot see now many camps near Karaganda, they sent free people to work on those places. Now I am sure they have not 40 millions in concentration camps today. I do not know this figure, maybe it is 5 millions, maybe it is 10 millions, in all the U.S.S.R. But I am sure that it is millions.

You see, I mentioned here about 1956, when they permit 50 percent of prisoners to go home. But in the same year, it was a Hungarian riot and it was many riots and strikes inside the U.S.S.R. It was riot in Timyr Tau, in Kazakhstan, in Odessa, in Novocherkask in Ryazan, in Krasnodar, in Vladivostok. And also after the Hungarian uprising it was many strikes of students. And the government was so frightened with all this that they began in 1957–58 a new wave of arrests. They released people in 1956—and 2 or 3 years after, all the concentration camps in which I was there again full. Also in 2 or 3 years, they returned many former prisoners to concentration camps. That is why they have now millions prisoners there again.

Senator GURNEY. Your testimony, then, is that Khrushchev released about 50 percent of the political prisoners, but after the Hungarian uprisings they rearrested a whole lot and filled the prisons once more?

Mr. SHIFRIN. Yes, it was a new stream. It was a stream of students, of workers, of soldiers, of young professors, of officers. You see, it was one of the biggest mistakes of the U.S.S.R. Government. It is my opinion that they make two or three mistakes with which they killed themselves. It is an irreversible process.

What did they make? In the U.S.S.R. these students and professors and soldiers and workers was, inside, Communists or Socialists. They was rosy, or red, inside. But they want to make communism with a human face in the U.S.S.R. Government was so frightened in these days after the Hungarian uprising that they sent these friends of the Soviet Government to our concentration camps. And from concentration camps, these people returned as real anti-Soviet fighters. Because they lost this red and rosy skin in concentration camps. They now are anti-Soviet fighters. They came to the freedom—this Bukovsky, Telnikov, Bokshtein, Dunayevsky in hundreds and thousands. Government released them after 5, 6, 7 years. Because in 1958, they gave people not 25 years like in my days, they gave 5 or 7 years only. That is why these people, when they were released, they came to the freedom and they openly told to the people about this situation, about this hypocrisy of this government. These people built this democratic movement in the U.S.S.R. which you know now, and the power of this movement is ordinary people which live there. Now they have many real anti-Soviet organizations. Now you can see people like Sado and many others which make Russian Christian organizations in all the country. They are now in the prison.

In Leningrad-Riga, officers of the fleet make big underground organization of officers to throw out the government. Now, students and all these people which came from the prisons organized many groups from the right to the left wing. But all of them are enemy of this government.

Second mistake. Another mistake they make is with the Jews. In 1948, when Israel was established, my friends and also I, we tried only to understand what is it Israel. Because in the U.S.S.R., it was obliterated absolutely Jewish culture. You cannot find in the U.S.S.R. any newspaper, Jewish newspaper, any theater, you cannot find any library, you cannot find any magazine. Yon can see in all the U.S.S.R. with 3 million Jews, four synagogues in all the country. In these synagogues, they implant KGB informers, and that is why people are frightened to go there. They try that Jewish boys and girls know only Russian history but no Jewish history.

That is why they made a very big mistake when they send us to prisons. When we tried to understand something about Israel, we were not dangerous for this government. But they arrested all the people which tried to know and understand something about Israel. In concentration camps, these dilettantes became real Zionists—and we came from concentration camps also as fighters and we organized our Samizdat, and democratic movements organized their Samizdat. From these two sources came two big, strong movements, anti-Soviet movements, in U.S.S.R.

Third mistake. In West Ukraine of the U.S.S.R.—before 1939 it was Poland—and in Baltic, people never have heard about communism. They seize Ukraine and Baltic countries in the day of nazism. Communists made an agreement with Hitler, and they seized this Latvia, Lithuania, Estonia, and part of Poland. These people struggled 7, 8 years, against Communist troops. And the Communists sent—maybe, I am not sure, but I think they sent half of the adult population of the west Ukraine and Baltic to concentration camps. In concentration camps, it was hundreds and hundreds of thousands of Ukrainian and Baltic people. And these people got education in concentration camps, because it was many professors, it was many educated people, and people tried to make lectures there also, in this "dog's life". Dogs in United States of America must excuse me. Your dogs live much better than people in U.S.S.R.—I would like to live like your pets!

These Ukrainians, when they finished this sentence in the prisons, they never permitted these Ukrainians to go to the west Ukraine. They sent them to exile in Kazakhstan or they sent them to the east part of the Ukraine. And these former prisoners made propaganda, in this part of the Ukraine also. And now they have maybe—I do not know—

but maybe the biggest movement in the U.S.S.R., Ukrainian nationalist movement, in the Ukraine.

Because in all the U.S.S.R., you can see a democratic movement. There is a Russian movement. In the Ukraine, it is a Ukrainian movement. Now, in the Baltic, they have also movement—you remember this riot in Kaunas only some months ago. It was a riot and they killed the people with the troops.

Now Communists have on their neck these three or four big movements inside the country. And what did they try to do? They know very well this proverb of reigning: "Divide and rule." They try to divide these nations and rule the people in this way.

How do these professional Communist killers do it?

There was a riot in Lithuania. They sent troops, Kazakhs and Uzbeks. You know that is an absolutely different nation. They are all citizens of the U.S.S.R.; but these Kazakhs and Uzbeks are like Chinese people and they do not know nothing about these Europeans, and they hate them. Why? Because in their opinion, European Russians bring to them all this dog's life. And they sent these Asiatic troops, and these troops shot and drowned in the blood this riot in Lithuania. Now Lithuanians hate Kazakhs.

Then there was a riot in Tashkent, in Uzbekistan, because they also live very bad. They sent Ukrainian troops, because for Ukrainians that is another nation. And these Ukrainians shot these Asiatics. Now Asiatics hate Europeans twice as much.

When there was a riot in Ryazan, they sent also Tadzhiks and Uzbeks. They always send another nation's troops to kill these people in another part of the country. That is why they have this hate among the nations, and can rule them.

And all these nations they try to throw against Jews, because that always was the "scape goat" in the U.S.S.R. The life of Jews in the U.S.S.R. is very hard to explain, because for Jews impossible to go to good work, Jews cannot go to the many institutes. They discriminate against you in every way. And now last news from the U.S.S.R.: You can see now in the streets special KGB provocators which go like drunken people and shout, "We must kill these Jews because the Jews make here in the U.S.S.R. starvation." They have starvation now, big starvation. But Brezhnev made this starvation, not the Jews. And now they try to throw people against the Jews. You know—that is not first case. And in Ukraine, you can hear from Ukrainian people, the government of Communists try to make Russification of the Ukraine. Yes, they tried to do it. It is a real fact. But at the same time, they send Ukrainian engineers and directors of the plants to work in Kazakhstan, in Baltic countries, in Urals, in all the U.S.S.R. in the Russian part of the U.S.S.R. And now in the Russian part of the U.S.S.R., you can hear people shout: "What is it? Ukrainianization of Russia?" They try to have people hate each other. In this way, they try to rule these people.

Senator GURNEY. Sort of divide and conquer.

Mr. SHIFRIN. Yes; divide and rule. They remember this.

I am sure that Stalin was biggest student of Machiavelli, because Machiavelli's teaching you can see in the U.S.S.R.

Senator GURNEY. Do you think this freedom movement is going to get anywhere?

82

Mr. Shifrin. I said to the committee that I am sure that this process is an irreversible process. One French philosopher, Montesquieu, said that the "Last stage of slavery is when slaves do not understand that they are slaves." You understood me, yes?

Mr. Boldyreff. The terminal stage of being a slave is when the slave no longer understands that he is a slave.

Senator Gurney. I understand.

Mr. Shifrin. And now in the U.S.S.R., you can see that these slaves understand that they are not slaves. That is why it is a irreversible process with which communism cannot deal. But I have too short a beard to be a prophet. I cannot tell in which year it would be. I can tell nothing; only what I know, that people, Jews and non-Jews, go with open breasts against these rifles.

What to tell you? I have seen many people which was in the prisons years—and not years but tens of years—and which was released unbroken. I have seen in the prison many political prisoners which was unbroken in such a situation. For example, Rabbi Kaganov, Nachim Kaganov. KGB do not permit this rabbi to pray in the prison. They do not permit him to go with yarmulke on the head. They do not permit him to observe Jewish holy days. They cut off his beard. They put him in the chains to do this. He fell unconscious because they put these chains very tight and struck with iron rod between his hands, and he became unconscious. They did not permit him to have kosher food. And this rabbi, 10 years in the prison, ate only bread and drank water—10 years. And he came unbroken from concentration camp. I know this man. Thanks to God, he is now in Israel.

I have seen there many Christian people, believers, which was there not only 10 years, but some of them 15 and 20 years. Such people like Shelkov, a Russian man who in U.S.S.R. is a believer of Seventh Day Adventism. I have seen many Russians and Ukrainian religious believers, and also not religious—political prisoners—which came out after 15, 20, and 25 years unbroken. Only now they released one of my friends, Volodymyr Horbovyi, Ukrainian leader. He was 25 years in the prisons. Each year, this government brought him to Kiev, showed him city from the car, these people on the streets, and said to him: "Only that statement, only your signature that you are not now a nationalist, that you were on the wrong way—and you can go home with your family." Twenty-five years they did it—killers! After 25 years, they released him now in November of 1972, an old man. But he is unbroken.

Another Ukrainian man, Michael Soroka, after 23 years, he died in the prison. But he was unbroken.

Now died in the prison a Christian theologian, Talantov. He died, but he was unbroken.

Died in the prison some of my friends, Tartars and Latvians. Died many of my friends—Jews: Gurevich, Melamed, Epshtein—how can I tell all this catalog of matters without end? And some of my friends came from the prison to freedom and they now work against this government. That is why I think this process in the U.S.S.R. is irreversible.

Now you have another trend in the U.S.S.R. among Jews. Jews do not want to serve in the Russian Red Army. Yes. That is big crime in the U.S.S.R. They came to the War Department and said: "I am a Jew.

Inside my heart, I am an Israeli citizen. That is why I cannot go to the Russian Army because you struggle against my Israel."

Now they sent only in November 1972 some of these young boys to concentration camps. Among them Grigoriy Berman from Odessa. I have his photo. I will give you his biography, his photo, because I have got it now.

Senator GURNEY. That will be received in evidence.

(The above material will be found in the Appendix, p. 122.)

Senator GURNEY. Do you have other photos?

Mr. SHIFRIN. Yes, I have it. I have photographs also for other prisoners. Here we have this face of Ekaterina Zaritskaya, a woman. She was a Ukrainian woman. She was 18 years in solitary confinement and 25 years in the prisons and concentration camps. They put her 20 years old in the prison and now she is 45.

Senator GURNEY. Thirty-eight years in prison?

Mr. SHIFRIN. Twenty-five years, from 20 to 45.

Mr. BOLDYREFF. She was 20 years of age when she was imprisoned.

Mr. SHIFRIN. She was age 20 when they arrested her and now she is 45. And I know not only one Ekaterina—I know many of these women which were there 25 years: Galina Didik and Kersnovskya, for example.

Mr. SOURWINE. Mr. Shifrin, you have given in staff interviews the names of a great many individuals whom you met in the earliest prison camps.

Mr. SHIFRIN. Yes.

Mr. SOURWINE. And with your help, the staff has prepared brief paragraphs to explain who these people are, where that is necessary. I am going to ask, in the interest of saving time, that the Chair instruct that between now and tomorrow, you have an opportunity to look once more at these lists to be sure that they are accurate and that we then be permitted to offer them as lists for insertion in the record in the morning; that we prepare copies for the press and save the time of asking you about it, name by name.

(The above material will be found in the Appendix to Part 3.)

Mr. SHIFRIN. Wonderful.

Senator GURNEY. We will have the list tomorrow.

Mr. SHIFRIN. You see, I know all these people and facts—it is not from the school. All these prisoners are my friends. I would see again and I would give to you their biographies in English. You would see them. You would see their faces. Some of them now are in prisons. Yakir is second time in the prison. Bukovsky, third time in the prison, Eduard Kuznetsov, second time in the prison—15 years imprisonment again. I know them, they are my friends. I cannot make mistakes.

Also, what I want to tell you in the end of this statement about these prisoners old and new. I am sure—it is my opinion, but I am sure—that now in the U.S.S.R., they tried to kill these dissidents because they need a free hand against another part of the world, against you. They want to have free hands, without opposition in the U.S.S.R., to be more powerful against you. I am sure of this. Now we see that all the free world permits to kill these people in the concentration camps, prisons and mental asylums in the U.S.S.R.—and I am sure it is the biggest mistake of the free world, because when these people will be killed, the Soviet Communists will try to kill you.

Remember, please, that when they came to Latvia, Lithuania, Estonia, the east part of Poland, when they came to Czechoslovakia, Bulgaria, Rumania, Yugoslavia, East Germany, to all these countries, they have with the troops, special groups of KGB and these groups came immediately in Warsaw, in Bucharest, in Belostok, in Riga, in Kaunas, in Prague, they came immediately with addresses, to people's homes and flats, because they made these lists many years before of this. And I am sure that here, diplomats of the U.S.S.R. have these lists with your names. They only wait this day when they can kill the free world. That is why it is the biggest danger for the free world that they kill now these dissidents.

Senator GURNEY. Your testimony is that where they moved into countries in Eastern Europe, they had already decided, of the government leaders and establishment leaders, whom to liquidate so they could get rid of the countries' leaders?

Mr. SHIFRIN. Yes, you are right. That is what I want to tell you.

Senator GURNEY. Well, we can do that. Let's adjourn now until tomorrow morning at 10 o'clock. I have people coming into my office now and we can go into that tomorrow morning at 10 o'clock.

So the subcommittee will stand in recess until tomorrow morning at 10.

(Whereupon at 3:35 p.m., the subcommittee recessed to reconvene at 10 a.m., Friday, February 2, 1973.)

U.S.S.R. LABOR CAMPS

FRIDAY, FEBRUARY 2, 1973

U.S. SENATE,
SUBCOMMITTEE TO INVESTIGATE THE
ADMINISTRATION OF THE INTERNAL SECURITY ACT
AND OTHER INTERNAL SECURITY LAWS
OF THE COMMITTEE ON THE JUDICIARY,
Washington, D.C.

The subcommittee met, pursuant to notice, at 11:10 a.m., in room 2228, Dirksen Senate Office Building, Senator Edward J. Gurney, presiding.

Also present: J. G. Sourwine, chief counsel; Samuel J. Scott, associate counsel; A. L. Tarabochia, chief investigator; David Martin, senior analyst.

Senator GURNEY. The subcommittee will come to order.

STATEMENT OF AVRAHAM SHIFRIN, ACCOMPANIED BY CONSTANTIN BOLDYREFF—Continued

Senator GURNEY. Yesterday we spent some time talking about the general subject of concentration camps in the Soviet Union, the numbers involved, the number of people who are in these slave camps, their operation, the kind of treatment their prisoners received. And now I think in the second part of the hearing, today, we ought to get into more the specifics. I wish, Mr. Shifrin, that you would go into more details as to some of the political reasons why people are arrested and imprisoned and placed in Soviet slave camps. I would like you to address yourself particularly to the persecution of Jews in Russia, a matter with which, of course, you are familiar since that is one of the reasons why you were arrested and thrown in these camps. Could we go into these areas this morning, the political reasons why people have been thrown into these prison camps?

Mr. SHIFRIN. Yes, Senator. I understand.

But, maybe you would permit me in the beginning of the day to speak about some of the figures about which we have spoken yesterday. Yesterday you asked me how many prisoners it was in prisons and concentration camps, and how many prisoners we have now, and I have thought in this night about this question again, and I have seen some documents, because not only I was in the prisons, millions were there, and many of them are alive today. Also we have the figure of the former Russian Premier, Khrushchev. He said when he spoke about Stalin, that in the days of Stalin it was 15 million prisoners, but he

(85)

mentioned only about political prisoners because his whole goal was to
speak about political prisoners. And I told you also that in 1956, he
released approximately 10 million prisoners in 2 or 3 months. And
that is why Khrushchev mentioned this figure, 15 million. Maybe they
released 15 million. I don't know. But from what I saw and heard in
the camps, I thought that approximately half of the prisoners in
1956 was not released.

Now, we have this big book, "The Great Terror of Stalin." Mr.
Conquest wrote this book, and he mentioned also prisoners in the
U.S.S.R. in the days of Stalin up to 20 million, and also that is ap-
proximate, because no one, no one can say for sure. Maybe only the
KGB Minister knows this real figure. And Mr. Conquest didn't mention about maybe 5 million prisoners of war, and that is why we have
the total figure for people in camps of approximately 25 million. And
Khrushchev made this figure smaller. But I think that figure 25 million also is enough, 25 million is also such an astonishing figure, that
maybe it is enough for us. And that is why again I must tell you, I
am not a statistical man. I am not a man which made these statistics.
I was in concentration camps. I have seen that it is really millions—but
who can count them?

Senator GURNEY. I understand.

Mr. SHIFRIN. Now, I understand that you want to hear about real
prisoners?

Senator GURNEY. Yes.

Mr. SHIFRIN. And real life in the prisons. What to tell you?

Mr. SOURWINE. Would you permit me, sir? The chairman asked if
you would discuss the reasons primarily, the political reasons people
are imprisoned in concentration camps in the U.S.S.R.

Mr. SHIFRIN. Yes. Again I must tell you that in the days of Stalin,
I mentioned this 10-year interval of millions of prisoners which came
to the camps in the days of Stalin. I was sure, and I am sure, that in
these days a real goal of arrests was only one: to have slaves in concentration camps to do heavy labor and build all this industry.

Senator GURNEY. The prime reason was to have a slave work force?

Mr. SHIFRIN. Yes. Yes—10,000 times yes. After 1958, 1959. I have
seen another sort of prisoners. From 1958 they arrest mostly not only
for reason of slave labor, but for the reason to stop dissident movement in the U.S.S.R. And that is why now the "color" of these concentration camps changed. In 1958–59, we were astonished when there
came to us thousands and thousands of students, simple workers,
officers. Why they brought them to these camps I will tell. Before
1958, I have seen such cases that really I will tell you now, two or
three examples, and you will see that really it was only draft of slaves
to concentration camps.

One man—a real example—I have spoken with this man, and he
told me: "I came in the morning in the kitchen." In the U.S.S.R.
they have kitchens, one kitchen for 10, 15 families, because such flats
they build there. "I came to the kitchen and I said to my neighbor:
'I had a bad dream in the night.' 'What is the dream?' 'I have seen
that someone killed Stalin.'" He got 25 years for "terrorism."

Senator GURNEY. You mean he was thrown in prison for 25 years?

Mr. SHIFRIN. He was sent to the prison and sentenced to 25 years as potential terrorist.

Senator GURNEY. Because he had a dream?

Mr. SHIFRIN. Yes. You see, I am a lawyer, and I was in the U.S.S.R. astonished with this practice. They have article called analogy in the criminal code. And under analogy they can put anything what you want.

I have seen once there came four or five Chukchi's, people who live near Alaska. Here they live, you see on this map—not far from Moscow—only 20,000 kilometers. They live in snow homes, they eat seals, they have reindeers, and they absolutely are uncivilized people. Once when they hunt they have seen in the sea a big whale. And with their harpoons they try to kill this whale. This whale, they explain to us, swallow them. It was a Russian submarine. They never have seen before a submarine.

What do you want from them? They came to the concentration camp, the barracks, was for them like for me your skyscrapers and maybe more. They got sentence under article called diversion by analogy—diversionistic attack with harpoons against submarines.

I have seen cases about which it is really impossible to tell. There came to us once a man who was deaf and dumb. And we asked: Why they send you to the concentration camp? He answered, for anti-Soviet propaganda. How is it possible? You are deaf and dumb. And this man explained that is was an announcement on all of the walls of Moscow that the Government made the prices of the food double. It was such a day in U.S.S.R.—double in 1 day. And he came to this announcement with his friend, also deaf and dumb, and there was many people there, and he read this announcement, and made such a sweet gesture [indicating spitting]. It was enough. Twenty-five years imprisonment for anti-Soviet propaganda.

Senator GURNEY. What was the announcement about?

Mr. SHIFRIN. An announcement that prices of food would double.

Mr. BOLDYREFF. The rise in prices was announced in 1 day.

Mr. SHIFRIN. Why they gave to him 25 years, because they explained to him "You made your propaganda in the presence of many people, and it could lead to an uprising." You see, from these examples that they were really unconscious, from legal point of view. But they were really very conscious what they do; they gave to some districts the figures of prisoners that they must arrest in this district.

Senator GURNEY. Now, you mentioned that many students were arrested.

Mr. SHIFRIN. No, no. I will come to this. Excuse me, please.

Senator GURNEY. You are still in Stalin's time?

Mr. SHIFRIN. In Stalin's time, and these years were before 1956, 1958. It was to 1958 in the same wave of arrests. After 1958 it changed.

Also, I have seen some cases when really I was astonished because they work against themselves, these Communists. I met in the prison when I came to the prison a Jewish general, from Russian Army. He was the head of all of the weapons for the air forces. His name, Mikhail Gurevich.

Senator GURNEY. You mean in charge of research and development?

Mr. SHIFRIN. Not research.

Mr. BOLDYREFF. Production of weapons.

Mr. SHIFRIN. Yes; for air force.

Senator GURNEY. In the Russian Air Force?

Mr. SHIFRIN. In all the Russian Air Force. He was the first man in the Air Force weapons. When I came to the prison, I had known about his arrest before my arrest. He was arrested in 1948—1949, maybe—and with him they arrested 39, 40 officers, some of them colonels, and also generals. And in our Ministry of Defense it was rumored that KGB in this case really charged this man with espionage. Yes, you have many spies there. But you don't know about this one. Gurevich and his officers were sentenced to death as American spies. When I came to the prison, I met with General Gurevich. In Ministry of Defense, I have seen him before. He never has seen me. I was too little for him. I was only legal adviser then.

I came to him in concentration camp and talked to him and told him the news from the Ministry of Defense, and he was very moved. We had very close relations in the concentration camp, and he gave me to read his complaint to the court about his sentence. I have seen it with my own eyes.

Senator GURNEY. These were the charges filed against him?

Mr. BOLDYREFF. No, he was writing a complaint against the charges.

Mr. SHIFRIN. Against the charges.

Senator GURNEY. I see.

Mr. SHIFRIN. And what it was in this complaint? He told in 1946–47 to Stalin personally, that in the United States you make American research in supersonic aviation—the Air Force. And he suggested to Stalin to begin also this investigations in institute of aerodynamics with a big tunnel.

Mr. BOLDYREFF. A wind tunnel.

Mr. SHIFRIN. With wind tunnel to make this research. And Stalin permitted him, and gave him the budget, $400 or $500 millions for this research work.

But, General Gurevich was in very bad relations with adviser of Stalin—Bulganin—he was first adviser of Stalin in all of the field of weapons. And once, after 2 years, when Gurevich was not in the meeting with Stalin—it was a meeting in the Kremlin—and Bulganin was there. It was in 1949, it was in the beginning of the big wave of anti-Semitism, and Stalin asked Bulganin: "How is it going with this supersonic aviation?" and Bulganin answered: "Nothing. This Gurevich has thrown this money out for nothing—to the wind. He wasted it, and we have no supersonic aviation: Gurevich wasted more money than you gave, and that is not good." And Stalin asked Bulganin: "And Gurevich is in charge now?" and immediately interrupted the conversation and began to speak with another minister. This was enough. After some hours Gurevich was arrested. With him was arrested all of the staff of the supersonic aviation. KGB charged them as American spies which throw to the wind money, gold of the U.S.S.R., with special goal to make the U.S.S.R. weak.

Mr. BOLDYREFF. To reduce the financial power of the Soviet Union.

Mr. SHIFRIN. They gave to them, to all of these officers death sentence and then changed to 25 years. And I met with Gurevich in the concentration camp. He was a hero of the U.S.S.R. He was in Spain, in the civil war in Spain, in the days of this war. He was a Russian military attaché in England. He was a big general, but he was in the same condition like all of the prisoners. After three heart attacks, he was paralyzed in 1956 and he lay in the barrack, and all of the excrements were under his body, and after some days we put him with his mattress on the floor in the special room near the morgue. And he died on this rotten straw, this hero of the Soviet Union, in April 1956.

Senator GURNEY. Well, what you are saying, then, is that during the Stalin era, people were arrested and thrown into concentration camps on the slightest whim, without any real trial or anything?

Mr. SHIFRIN. Yes. I explained here that they have two sorts of trials. You have criminal court-martial. It was like a trial. It was not a trial in your sense; in my case it was without jury, only three people which have spoken with me half an hour. That is all. Without lawyer. Without nothing. But, in U.S.S.R. they have also another "court" which works in another way. The three people sit with a secretary, and the secretary has big, so big, a pile of files, and he says to these three "judges:" "This man have dreamed in the night that someone kills Stalin." "That's a potential terrorist—give him 10 years," answer the judge.

And they go through these files in 3 minutes each, in 2 minutes for each file. They don't see people which they send to prison. In this way they sent these millions to camps. It is big work to send millions to concentration camps, very big work. Because of this when came this commission of Khrushchev to the concentration camps and released these prisoners in millions they were not afraid to release so many "criminals."

Mr. BOLDYREFF. It was without any danger for themselves.

Mr. SHIFRIN. Yes, without any danger, because what's the danger? They know very well that these people are like angels with wings, absolutely innocent.

I want to tell you about these prisoners. One of them Sergei Krasilnikov explained to me that they beat him so much and pressed him to admit that he is a spy. He decided that it is better to confess because they would beat him to death. And he said: "Yes, I am a spy." Investigators answered: "Very well, now tell us for which country you are spy?" "Please write what you want," said Krasilnikov. "No, you must tell us," said these sadists. And he decided that to be American or English spy, that is too big, and he said: "Guatemala." As a spy of Guatemala he received a sentence of 25 years.

Senator GURNEY. I wonder if we can go to the Khrushchev era?

Mr. SHIFRIN. Now we come to this time of Khrushchev.

Senator GURNEY. Let's talk about the students now.

Mr. SHIFRIN. They released these prisoners in millions in 1956. Before Khrushchev, all of the nations was in the concentration camps, without any difference, without discrimination, as I told before. After this commission our concentration camps was half empty; and then came in 1958 a new wave of prisoners. We were astonished because it was young people. They were educated: professors, students and cadets from officers' schools. And we asked them: Why do you come—because we were anti-Soviet people, and you are Soviet people, with Soviet Communist mentality?" And they answered us: "Yes, we came here because we are Communists, but we are against this communism which kills people."

Senator GURNEY. But we are what?

Mr. SHIFRIN. We are Communists inside the heart, but we are Communists of Lenin's time.

Senator GURNEY. I don't understand.

Mr. SHIFRIN. Well, they——

Mr. BOLDYREFF. Well, they said they were Communists who didn't recognize or approve the regime that was in power, that they were Leninists, and, therefore, were better.

Mr. SHIFRIN. Some say Trotskyites, some say Leninists, and they do not want to be Stalinists, and that is why—they sent letters to Khrushchev, and they made little groups to learn, to study Trotsky, Bukharin, Lenin, Mao Tse-tung, and so on. And this government was so frightened with these little groups that they decided to give orders to the KGB to arrest all of the suspicious people among the students, professors, army officers, soldiers, and so on. And in these times they arrested I don't know how many thousands of people. But in each concentration camp it was hundreds and hundreds of new prisoners which came in under this charge, "anti-Soviet propaganda."

Senator GURNEY. What is that?

Mr. BOLDYREFF. Anti-Soviet propaganda.

Senator GURNEY. And what year was this?

Mr. SHIFRIN. It was 1958–59.

Senator GURNEY. In other words, because they were talking about some slightly different brand of communism than the present regime believed in, they were thrown into jail for that reason?

Mr. SHIFRIN. Yes.

Senator GURNEY. Now, tell me more. Were they just studying communism, or were they speaking out against it, or making speeches against the regime or what?

Mr. SHIFRIN. Real example: One group in Moscow, four boys and one girl which only finished school, 18-year-old boys and girls——

Senator GURNEY. Eighteen years old?

Mr. SHIFRIN. Eighteen years old. They tried to study Trotsky, and they tried to print leaflets against methods of rule against Khrushchev. They got 25 years. Mitreiko, the head of the group was in the prison 18 years. Now he is released after 18 years.

Now, another case: Bukovsky—all of the world now know this name. He was only among people, which tried to understand this situation in the U.S.S.R.; and, without any crime, they gave him his first sentence. In your opinion, in the opinion of all of the world, to think it is not a crime, to speak it is not a crime. But it is a crime in U.S.S.R. Bukovsky was arrested.

Another case: In Moscow, Ilya Bokshtein and Edward Kuznetsov, organized a little group and they began to read poems of Mayakovsky, Russian Communist poems, in the Mayakovsky Square, each Sunday. They read these poems, and the KGB had seen that they read official poems, and permitted them. But, little by little, people came to them, and each Sunday you can see in this square some hundreds of people, big meetings. And they read these poems of Mayakovsky. But when they seen that is maybe 1,000 people one day, Bokshtein climbed to this monument—the head of Mayakovsky and made a speech, made an open speech that we live in a slave country—we must think about this,

91

because it is not good to be slaves. And he came to us in the concentration camp. He was with me.

It is also not a crime in your opinion to say that we live in not a good country, but they gave this man, a little hunchback, heavy sentence.

And also there came to concentration camps many cadets from the officer schools. Why government send them? They made a group in their cadet officers' school, and they also tried to understand is our Government right, or is our Government not right in the way of ruling of this country. And they came to us.

Now, fate of ordinary worker, A. Marchenko. All the world now knows his name; he wrote a wonderful book "My Testimony." I ask very much that some pages of this book be put in the record, because he said the same thing which I now tell you, exactly, word for word in this book. He came to us in 1960 only, in 1960 after this big wave. He was a plain worker. He was man with little education. He was not an intellectual. He worked like plain worker in digging tunnels, and they arrested him because he said to other workers, "Why we live in such a situation? We have nothing, we work like slaves, 10 hours a day, and we have not bread. That is not good." Really that is not good. And this man was sentenced to prison, and after prison, he wrote this book, "My Testimony." This book, some of his friends printed in the U.S.S.R. It is also not a crime in your opinion, but they gave to Marchenko now another sentence because he wrote this book. Marchenko after the first sentence, was half deaf, he was very ill, and he came to the prison in very bad condition.

Senator GURNEY. Did he write the book while he was in prison?

Mr. SHIFRIN. No, after, when he finished prison, he wrote this book, wonderful book. You can see this book in English, and if you would read it, you would see that I tell truth and only truths, like you asked me.

Senator GURNEY. I am interested, how did the authorities find out in the first instance about his complaining about hard work and nothing to show for it? Did the person that he talked to tell the authorities?

Mr. SHIFRIN. You see—how did they know about his complaints? Because all of you must know that they have many informers in all of Soviet society, and in U.S.S.R. you can hear such sad joke: Man stay in front of a mirror and say: "One of us is informer . . ."

Senator GURNEY. A whole lot of people are spying on other people?

Mr. SHIFRIN. Yes. And also Marchenko when he understood that it is not a good country, he wanted to go to another country—and it is a big crime in the U.S.S.R. to say that you want to go to another country—that is his crime—they sent him to a concentration camp.

Some other cases: Two young boys and one girl, Ginzburg, Galanskov and Lashkova—these youths, they tried making a magazine with a typewriter, only it was not a big magazine. Only some poems which you cannot find in the official magazines of U.S.S.R., some articles about life in U.S.S.R., something about our real life. It was not anti-Soviet, it was only truths about life. This magazine was called "Phoenix." You know, like this bird that goes into flames and rises up again, Phoenix. And they made the first number of this magazine—and then they came to the prison.

Senator GURNEY. What was the article about?

Mr. SHIFRIN. What sort of articles? Only articles about real life in the prisons and real life in the country. Nothing against the regime, nothing, not one of them said, "We must destroy the regime." Nothing like this. Only a literary magazine.

Senator GURNEY. Just describing the prison life?

Mr. SHIFRIN. Prison life and life in the U.S.S.R.; yes. It was not a political magazine.

Senator GURNEY. When were they?

Mr. SHIFRIN. Only idiots or very brave men would make a political magazine in this country.

Senator GURNEY. When were they arrested and thrown in jail?

Mr. SHIFRIN. Yes; they were sentenced for 7 years.

Senator GURNEY. In what year?

Mr. SHIFRIN. Well, 1965.

Senator GURNEY. Go on.

Mr. SHIFRIN. You see, these cases, are real cases of prisoners which came to us in these years.

Also these came to us students from Leningrad, from Moscow, from Tomsk, from Tbilisi, when there was the uprising in Hungary. Students did not understand why the U.S.S.R. drown in the blood these innocent people, and they make speeches, and they ask our Government why they do this. There were meetings in universities, student meetings, Government sent students from the meetings to concentration camps. It was really new, a brandnew wave of prisoners. They changed the whole situation in the prisons.

Senator GURNEY. They sent a lot of these students because they were there at the meeting?

Mr. BOLDYREFF. Yes.

Senator GURNEY. They sent many of these students to camps?

Mr. SHIFRIN. Yes; thousands only because they were at the meetings. Without any crime, only that they came two or three times to the meetings to discuss these problems. Some of them came to concentration camps with charges that they were in the meetings, and they did not say anything in way of anti-Soviet propaganda, they did not make anything. You see, in U.S.S.R., you can see things which for lawyers here sound like idiocy. I made once here special lecture for lawyers. They were astonished because our law in U.S.S.R. is so different from yours. What can you say if someone would come to you in the night in your home, and would tell you, "I am hungry, and it is frost in the street, and I am traveling. Permit me to sleep in your home and give me something to eat." The law of hospitality tells you that you must permit this man to sleep and to eat. In U.S.S.R.—I have seen a thousand such prisoners which was sentenced to 25 years only because they permit such people to sleep and to eat in the night. And then the next day came to them KGB and said: "It was this man in your home?" "Yes, he was." "And why did you permit him to sleep and to eat?" "What is the question? He is a stranger on his way." "No, you helped two partisans"—because there was a big movement against communism. "You are a collaborator of theirs, 25 years in concentration camp."

I have seen thousands of such people, not hundreds—really, innocent people. How can I explain here to lawyers that these people can be sentenced to 25 years in the U.S.S.R.? And that is why it is hard to explain all of these real cases.

Senator GURNEY. You mentioned——

Mr. SHIFRIN. Excuse me, I did not finish. This political resistance will grow in the U.S.S.R. because the Soviet Government made, in my opinion, a very big mistake, not one mistake, maybe three mistakes. Our arrests, arrests of Zionists in the U.S.S.R. was maybe one of the first mistakes of the government in this field.

Senator GURNEY. Why was that?

Mr. SHIFRIN. What?

Senator GURNEY. Why is that?

Mr. SHIFRIN. Yes. Now I understand. Really, when they arrested us, we was innocent, because our fathers never told us that we are Jews. They never told us about our history and religious questions. In the U.S.S.R., communism destroyed absolutely, absolutely destroyed all of the Jewish community. You cannot find in the U.S.S.R. any Jewish newspaper, any Jewish magazine, you cannot find any Jewish club. They do not permit all of this. And also they have for 3 millions Jews, they have three synagogues in all of the country—four synagogues, Leningrad, Moscow, Kiev, and Odessa. They are little synagogues in which they implant many KGB informers, and that is why Jews know that it is very dangerous to go to the synagogue. In all of these ways they destroyed Jewish society. You cannot speak in your language. I can show you we have here witnesses letters; they were sent to the prisons only because the KGB found in their home a prayer book and also a book of Hebrew, study book of Hebrew—you know, they wanted to study to learn the Hebrew language. This is crime. They were sent for 3, 4, 5 years to the prison. Such people like Aleksandrovich and Voloshin and many others were sent to concentration camps with sentences.

In the days after Stalin and in the days before Stalin's death, they sent people to concentration camps with sentences to 25 years, like I was sent, only because we was Jews. Because we tried to understand what is it—Israel? It was like an atomic explosion when we have heard about Israel in 1948. We never have talked before 1948 about Israel and this problem, and what is it Israel, our state. But we were Jews, and for us it was sensational, and that is why we made little groups, not special groups, and we tried to tell each other what we know about this Israel, and we tried to find materials. You know, you find in all Bible texts, in private libraries, encyclopedias, dictionaries, the encyclopedia dictionary, about our Jewish history. And we found this and we tried to read it, and to explain to each other what is our ancient history. Believe me, we did not know in 1948 why they gave this name Israel to this state. We were absolutely without Jewish education. I was "very educated" because once I had read the Bible, and that is why I told my friends about our ancient history. And it was a crime in the eyes of government, and they sent us to prisons as Zionists but we were not Zionists in serious meaning of this word, believe me; and we became Zionists in the prisons. Prisons teach us; and in the prisons Zionism became very strong. In the prisons, Zionists decided to work again, when they would be free, and when we came from the prisons, we began to work—only then—and that is why it was a mistake of the government.

Senator GURNEY. When did these arrests of Jews begin? What year?

Mr. Shifrin. Oh, you should ask me when it was that they did not arrest Jews? It would be better. My friends and I were arrested from 1949 to 1953. First were released in 1956.

Senator Gurney. Well, I will ask that, then. Was there ever a time . . .

Mr. Shifrin. Always, always killing, arrests, pogroms. If you would read novels of 1918, about the days of the revolution and civil war, when they had these Red troops of Budenny and Voroshilov which killed Jews, and also the troops killed Jews. Now Communist propaganda tells that in 1918 only the Ukrainian people killed Jews. Try to understand that in the U.S.S.R. Jews in days of the past and today the Jews of the U.S.S.R. are always in danger, always. They obliterated all the Jewish culture in the U.S.S.R. You cannot find any sign of Jewish culture in this country.

Senator Gurney. Now, that was after the revolution?

Mr. Shifrin. Yes; in all of these 50 years they tried to obliterate Jewish culture.

Senator Gurney. From the very beginning of the Russian Revolution?

Mr. Shifrin. Yes; from 1918.

Senator Gurney. 1918.

Mr. Shifrin. Yes; 1918.

Senator Gurney. Let me ask another question, though. You said you didn't know you were Jews, and I expect you were saying there that——

Mr. Shifrin. No, we did not know about our Jewish history.

Senator Gurney. That is what I mean, because there were no synagogues, no religion, or schools.

Mr. Shifrin. No, no nothing about our cultures. I never have known our ancient history, and I have known nothing about the ancient people in my nation. It was a very big mistake of our fathers that they did this, but it was——

Senator Gurney. Is that because they probably were afraid to teach anything to you?

Mr. Shifrin. They were afraid to make from us people which would feel themselves not like part of the Soviet society, but like part of Jewish society.

I can tell you another thing. I must tell you. I have known that I am a Jew. I have known it very well, believe me, because in my childhood when I came at 6 years old to the school, first words I have heard was "dirty Jew" from children. These children, which do not understand anything, they have heard from their fathers and from their parents that Jews are "dirty people," and they have this special word, "*zjid*," that is 10 times worse than "dirty Jew," and that is why I understood very well and immediately that I am not part of these people. I was alone in this school. I understood that I am Jew, and that it is very bad to be Jew. And the mistake of our parents was because they did not give us some shield. I did not know anything about my religion, about my history, and I thought perhaps that all of the Jews were cowards, that all of the Jews were thieves, that all of the Jews were stinking people because I have heard this each day. Yes, I believed that I am stinking because I have heard it from day to day. You can believe in this if you are a child and they tell you this from day to day. And it came, believe me, from the top of the society, from Stalin—he was the biggest anti-Semite—and all in his government were anti-Semites; and the Jews which were in his government, they were so assimilated that they also were implanted with this anti-Semitism. And just like Stalin—a Georgian man—killed Georgians, like Brezhnev—Ukrainian man—killed Ukrainians, you see, so these Jewish Communists killed our Jews.

I told you about my childhood, and now I will tell you about childhood of my daughter—interval 25 years.

When I came to prison my daughter was a little girl, and when I returned from the prison, she was 19 years old. I did not see my daughter all of these 10 years. They did not permit me to see my relatives. I have seen, after 9 years, my mother. They permitted me to see my mother for 2 hours after 9 years in prison. And my mother was so astonished with all of this complex of concentration camps that she returned home and died. You must remember that my father was arrested and my mother waited for my father 10 years. My father died, and then she waited for me 9 years, and she met me, and she was so astonished because I was wearing the number, and with stripes, in starvation and she, after seeing all of this horror, she had gone mad and she died 2 months after this meeting. I did not see my mother when I came home.

And I met my daughter, 19 years old—and what did this girl tell me? "Father, you know what the worst day was in my life?" "What was the worst day?" I asked. "It was when I have heard in school that I am a Jewish girl." Mother never told her anything about my arrest, about all of these things. And this girl went unprotected in school, and she explained to me that she had heard from day to day, "dirty Jews," "stinking Jews," and so on. "And one day came to me one boy and told me—'You are also dirty Jew, I have seen in the papers of our teacher that you are a dirty Jew.'"

You see, they have nationality in all of the student questionnaires, and the teachers have lists with names and nationalities of each pupil. And this boy had seen, had come to my daughter and shouted "dirty Jew." She told me—"It was the worst day in my life."

It was an interval of 25 years, and nothing has changed. You can see now in the U.S.S.R. provocators which go in the street, provocators of the KGB, which go in the street like drunken people and shout, "We must kill Jews because they make all of this starvation in the U.S.S.R."

Senator GURNEY. This is even today?

Mr. SHIFRIN. It is today. I have here these letters, and I hear it by telephone. My friends shout to me by telephone, as one did some days ago. "You must remember and tell the people that we are like hostages in the hands of killers." They are in such desperation that they shout it by telephone, without fear. Try to understand what is the braveness of these people. They sent now Vladimir Markman to 3 years in the concentration camps only because of these conversations by telephone with Israel. They try to frighten people. But they cannot frighten them.

Now about Jews in prison. Jews were in concentration camps when I came in 1954, by thousands and thousands. In all of the concentration camps in which I was, I have seen was 30, 40, 50 Jews in each concentration camp. Try to understand if in all of the concentration camps you see 40, 50, 60, sometimes 100, Jews in each concentration camp, that is very big percent of Jewish population of country. It is not big among 3,000 or 5,000 prisoners, 50, 60 Jews, but you must remember there are 2½ million Jews, and among 256 million population, and that is why was high percent of the Jews. I am not able to count this, but it was a big percent of Jews in concentration camps.

Senator GURNEY. What was the Jewish population in the U.S.S.R. at the time of the revolution; do you know?

Mr. SHIFRIN. You see, all of these figures which they gave in their books are absolutely lie, and that is why I do not believe they have 2½ million Jews. I think there are more.

Senator GURNEY. This is what the Soviets say they have now?

Mr. SHIFRIN. Yes, they say 2½ million. I think that it is not right, but I do not know really.

Senator GURNEY. Those that you encountered in the prison camps that you were in, the Jews, were they there simply because they were Jews? What were they charged with?

Mr. SHIFRIN. Oh, yes; they were without any crime. There were many rabbis, I have seen hundreds of rabbis that they sent only because they believe in God, and they told the people that they believe in God, and they told us about our ancient history. They were wise, clever, good people. They sent them to concentration camps. Why they sent my father—he was a civil engineer. I am sure that he was not anti-Soviet because I was a grown boy, 14 years old when he was arrested. He never told in my presence anything about anti-Soviet propaganda. Never have I heard this. He was a good father of the family, he works without interruption all of his life, and they killed him. And I have seen many of such prisoners—Jews.

Why they killed these 28 Jewish poets and Jewish actors in 1952? Why did they kill this biggest Jewish actor in the world, Michoels? I remember that people came from the United States to see this actor, and one day they announced that Michoels was killed by a car in the street in Minsk. All of the people were very sad, not only Jews. And then I was very close in the camps with the first adviser of General Procurator of U.S.S.R. Lev Sheinin. He was a big general in the U.S.S.R. He was also a Jew. He was one of the biggest criminal investigators. He was at the head of all of the department of investigation of the U.S.S.R., criminal investigators. This Sheinin they sent to Minsk to investigate this case with Michoels.

Senator GURNEY. To investigate what?

Mr. SHIFRIN. To investigate, to see who killed Michoels because he was so important, this Michoels in the U.S.S.R., that they sent this General Sheinin on this investigation. And after 4 days Sheinin returned from Minsk, did not tell anything to us. He came to General Procurator and talked about this case, and then he was arrested. The KGB arrested him in 2 days. I met Sheinin in the concentration camp after some years, and he explained to me that in 4 days in Minsk he found that the KGB killed Michoels, and he came step by step with his investigation to the KGB building. And he explained this to General Procurator, head of all of the law enforcement in the U.S.S.R.; and this head of law enforcement told it to Stalin, and Stalin gave order to KGB to arrest General Sheinin.

After many years, in 1962 to our concentration camp came a Jewish boy which was an actor in 1962 in Minsk. And he came to us because they made a line of actors to put flowers in this place in Minsk in which was found the body of Michoels. From day to day Jews and also non-Jews, actors, in Minsk, put flowers in the sidewalk, in the place where killers put the body of Michoels in the night.

Sheinin told me that all of the body of Michoels was black from beating, and also it was stabbed many times with a pen. Yes; they tortured him with a pen and there was ink on the body from pens, and then they put this body on the sidewalk and announced that a car killed him. After many years they arrested this new generation of Jews because they organized these flowers on the place of the killing of this man.

Senator GURNEY. Let me ask you this, as you know much better than I, what I read in the press, as other people do, but Jews are trying to leave the Soviet Union.

Mr. SHIFRIN. Yes.

Senator GURNEY. Why is it that the authorities prevent these people from leaving when they do not want to stay?

Mr. SHIFRIN. You see, in the U.S.S.R., excuse me, please, for jokes, but, in the joke you can see the real situation in the U.S.S.R. In the U.S.S.R. you can hear such a joke. One man asked another: "How many Jews want to leave from U.S.S.R.?" Answer: "300 million." This example of free Jews is bad for the Government—very dangerous—because the Jews, they are people which cannot be slaves from ancient years. From our history you can see that we were in all of the rebellious causes, in all of these causes there were Jews, in all of the revolutions, Jews. And Jews now show to the people in U.S.S.R. this way of freedom. When Jews came from the prisons, these Zionists, decided that they cannot go in the open way, against Government, they must be very cautious and that is why they told to the Jews only about their right to go to Israel. It is not a crime, you see. It is a constitutional right in the U.S.S.R. But, no one in the U.S.S.R. in these 50 years, no one tried to enjoy this right. And Jews were the first national group which were told, "We have our own country, and we want to go to this country." And we explained to our Jews:

In these after-the-war years, the U.S.S.R. made the biggest propaganda in all of the world among Armenians to return to the "motherland." These Armenians came to France, United States, and to other countries some 100 years ago, some after World War II, and Communists made propaganda, told them, "You are Armenian, you must live in your motherland—in the U.S.S.R.—Armenia." And we Zionists in our propaganda, did the same thing. We told the Jews, "Armenians must live in Armenia, and Jews must live in Israel." You see, government cannot tell us nothing straight, and government was too weak to send us again to the prisons.

Second mistake of the U.S.S.R. Government was that they sent some of the Jews, and I was so happy that I was in this group in the autumn of 1970, they sent us to Israel. They decided that if they would cut off the "head of this movement," they would disturb this movement. But they was mistaken, because then our Jewish boys and girls understood that only if you would be active, you could come to Israel. After our departure, they became very active.

Senator GURNEY. How many in your group?

Mr. SHIFRIN. Well, maybe 60, 70 people only. And when we came to Israel we tried to explain to Jews here that they must be active, and we asked the American people to make demonstrations against the U.S.S.R.—demonstrations here; and your people helped us. The Russian Government was in 1970 too weak to send these activists to the prisons, and that is why in January and February of 1971 they sent to Israel in 2 months 6,000 Jews, because they know these Jews are activists.

Senator GURNEY. Why do you say they were too weak to imprison the activists at that time?

Mr. SHIFRIN. You see, in the U.S.S.R. they have had some periods of weakness. Khrushchev was weak when he came to government at first, and in the first 4 or 5 years, he was too weak because many pretenders wanted to be at the head of country. He became powerful. Then Brezhnev threw him from the post. Kosygin and Brezhnev was also weak because they have enemies inside the government. It was not enemy opposition; it was people which wanted to be at the head of government. And that is why they had not power to struggle with us.

My language is so bad. I only try to explain you the situation in the U.S.S.R. They were too weak against us, and we were very careful in our actions, and that is why they have not really reasons to arrest us. And when they send these 6,000 Jews to Israel, it was the biggest mistake in their policy because from this day on, all of the Jews in the U.S.S.R. decided to be active, because it is only way to come to Israel.

Senator GURNEY. We have an expression for it, that the squeaky wheel is the one that gets the grease.

Mr. SHIFRIN. Pardon?

Senator GURNEY. We have an expression, the squeaky wheel is the one that gets the attention.

Mr. SHIFRIN. Oh, yes. You are right. Also we know very well that only noise, only big noise in the world, only pressing on the killers, can help our friends in concentration camps, Jew and non-Jews and descendants of all people of the U.S.S.R. Only in this way—because the Communist government understand only power—you must tell them openly your opinion, tell them that Jews have right to go to Israel.

Now, I want to tell you about other dissidents because it is not good to talk only about Jewish questions. Impossible to understand all of the situation in the U.S.S.R. if I would tell only about Jews—I must tell you about danger of communism. And that is why, permit me, please, to tell you what happened from 1958 to now, 1972, with other dissidents in U.S.S.R. I told you that young dissidents came to concentration camps very "rosy," and sometimes very red inside, like some of your students which Communists try to cheat here in the United States, and in all of the world. My own opinion that your society is in a very dangerous situation because the Communists try to kill your society with all of these left movements, with all of these Trotskyists and New Left. They implant this movement here. They give money to these movements because they know that no one in the world believes in Soviet communism. I know very well that if you would tell to a good boy or a good girl "we must go to kill some people," this good boy or girl would answer you, "I don't want to kill people." But, if these

Communists came to your boys and girls and talked to them, "Do you want to save all of mankind?" and your boys and girls are so good-hearted, and they answer "Yes," because they want to help mankind. "Come with us. We will teach you how to help mankind," say these Communists. "Kill these men. In this way you can help mankind."

Communists now cannot go straight. They will always go in sideways, from the corner. These boys, these girls which they arrested in the U.S.S.R. in 1959, they were very young. They were really good boys and girls which believed in socialism.

Senator GURNEY. Believed in what?

Mr. SHIFRIN. In socialism. But when they came to concentration camps, they had seen this situation inside the camps, and they have seen these millions of prisoners, and they understand in which way this government has gone all of these 50 years. What they have seen? I must tell you what it was in 1958 in the concentration camps. Once in the year in concentration camps they make a medical commission. What is this medical commission in the concentration camp? In a room sit three, five, six KGB officers in white dress like physicians, and naked prisoners go in a line through this room, prisoners with only bones and skin, and these "physicians," they never try to examine your heart or your lungs. Now I would tell to my friend in Russian, and he will tell to you because it is too hard for me to explain in English.

Mr. BOLDYREFF. Well, what the doctor actually did instead of checking your lungs and so on, he would put a hand on the person's butt, so to speak, and if he felt there was some meat still there, then he would send the prisoner to work. If he would feel that there is just bones, and, you know, the coccyx or tail bone is sticking out, then he would send him——

Mr. SHIFRIN. This spine end, like the tail.

Mr. BOLDYREFF. He would send him to the hospital.

Mr. SHIFRIN. No, no. Not to the hospital. To the concentration camp without work.

But, you can see in a book "Country of Prisoners" by Margolin, a man which was in concentration camps in U.S.S.R., he said in his book: "You must not be envious to these prisoners which go to the concentration camp without work because they would give them half food, and these prisoners would die. They do not need them." These boys and girls which came in 1958, they have seen these concentration camps and they were astonished. They have also seen these prisons. I will tell you after about this prison in which I was. Inside the cell you can see the frost on the walls. They have seen this rotten cabbage, rotten potatoes, this bread like clay. They have seen this and they were astonished. And they lost this red and rosy color, and they became strong anti-Soviet fighters. They understood in some weeks that they were not right. You cannot help this government with advice. This government of Communists makes all of the crimes in full conscience, and that is the line of the government. They understood that they cannot help, that they must destroy this government. And these new prisoners, they have not like we have, sentences to 25 years—they were sentenced to 3, 5, 6 years in 1958, and that is why they came to their freedom in 1962, 1963, 1965.

It was in those years, you remember, when it was these new riots in U.S.S.R., for example, in Novocherkask, and there were many demonstrations in the U.S.S.R. What happened in Novocherkask? Simple people who live in a simple town, not big city, population some 100,000— worked in the plants and the mines. They were hungry. They have not had anything to eat, and it was in these days when government made prices again higher. And these people cannot find in shops bread and meat. But these people work, and they need food. I do not know who organized this, but they came to the committee of the party, to big building—men, women with children together and all the workers. They came with the slogan, "We must eat." "To work we need to eat." And these Communist killers in Novocherkask in 1962, what did they do? They sent troops, and the troops stayed around this meeting with tanks. An officer from the tank with a loudspeaker said, "Citizens, you must go home because I have orders to shoot." And they shout: "You are a Russian officer, you are a Russian man, and we are citizens of this country. You would shoot us simple workers?" And this officer has a "walkie-talkie" and on this "walkie-talkie" he heard orders from the Communist Party commissar: "Shoot, shoot, shoot." And he took out his pistol and shot himself in his head because he was not able to shoot the people.

And then immediately these soldiers left this place after this suicide. And these workers on the square shout "We need bread, we need meat." And these killers from Communist Party Committee sent other troops, not Russian troops, nor Ukrainian. They sent Asiatics from Todjikistain, Mongols—and these Mongols shoot these people. But these workers run against these troops and tore these troops to pieces. And it was 3 days battle in Novocherkask. And it was other battles, riots, in Krasnodar and Rvazan and Kaunas. Now it has been brand new riots in the U.S.S.R. Why? Because people understand these dissidents. They understand that the only one way that they have in the U.S.S.R. is way of real battles. Some of dissidents go in another way. Some weeks ago came to United States former member of an active committee of dissidents from Moscow, Mr. Chalidze, who said that they want to go in the way of law and to defend human rights, only without uprisings. You can see among these dissidents many streams, but all of these dissidents understand now in U.S.S.R. that these regimes, that it is the regime of killers, and especially understand this these youth. Now in concentration camps of the U.S.S.R. you can see members of two very big underground organizations which KGB arrested. One of them is the Christian Democratic Council of the U.S.S.R., the Social Christian Council of Democrats in the U.S.S.R. They arrested hundreds of these people and sent them to concentration camps.

Now, they arrested another big underground group, officers of Russian Army and Baltic Fleet. Officers made big organization in all of U.S.S.R.—in Leningrad, Vladivostok, Riga, Tallin.

Senator GURNEY. What is the name of the second group?

Mr. BOLDYREFF. The Baltic Fleet.

Mr. SHIFRIN. The Baltic Fleet group. They arrested these officers. I can tell you names in this Democratic Christian Society where they arrested the head of the group, Sado. And in this fleet, too, we have real names, and prisoners sit now in concentration camps in Potma and Ural.

I have here letters, articles from concentration camps from such people like Krasnov-Levitin and Petrov-Agatov who met with these people, and they bring their articles in underground—to these self-publishing groups in the U.S.S.R.—and we have now translation in English, and I gave to your committee these materials to see because you can find there all of the details about this fleet, dissidents, and about these other organizations.

Senator GURNEY. What kind of prison sentences are they giving these dissidents today, do you know? What kind of prison sentences?

Mr. SHIFRIN. Sentences? These people have 7, 10, 15 years. They gave to them full sentences. Now the biggest sentence is 15 years.

Oh, yes, I forgot to tell you a very interesting detail. In 1958 they made a brand new law in the U.S.S.R. that the biggest sentence in the U.S.S.R. would be not 25, but only 15 years. And all of the sentences of 25 years would be changed to 15-year sentences.

Senator GURNEY. Was this for political crimes or all crimes?

Mr. SHIFRIN. Political crimes and all other crimes. The biggest sentence, 15 years.

Senator GURNEY. Do they have death sentence any more?

Mr. SHIFRIN. Yes. They have sentences to the death. If you kill people, they would sentence you to death, and also for espionage, for diversion—for all of these crimes they give death. You remember that they give death sentence to Jews in 1970 in Leningrad trial. But they have 15 years as biggest sentence when they send to cencentration camp. But what is interesting is that they, with this new law, must change sentences for all of the prisoners who were sentenced to 25 years to 15 years. But, I can tell you real names—Pirus, Zarickata, Horbovoy, Soroka, Azbel, and many others—who were sentenced to 25 years, and were in concentration camps up to 1972 and finished their 25 years without changing of sentence.

Senator GURNEY. Why did they not change these?

Mr. SHIFRIN. Who knows? Many people sit with sentences of 25 years now. What to do? Communists do what they want. In U.S.S.R. law is not for people, but people for law. That is the danger in this country.

Senator GURNEY. In these present-day arrests of dissidents, are they mass arrests? Do they involve tens of thousands?

Mr. SHIFRIN. I cannot tell you that now in 1972 we have mass arrests, no. But, they have now in 1972 a new wave of arrests because they want in two ways to destroy these dissidents. First they want to frighten them. And people which they cannot frighten—to arrest.

Senator GURNEY. Are they accomplishing this mission?

Mr. SHIFRIN. What?

Senator GURNEY. Are they accomplishing this?

Mr. SHIFRIN. I am not now there, but in these telephone conversations I have heard that they are very brave, very brave.

Senator GURNEY. They are very brave?

Mr. SHIFRIN. Brave, yes.

Senator GURNEY. The dissidents?

Mr. SHIFRIN. They try to frighten them but they are brave. I will explain to you what is the new wave of arrests we have now. And then I would return to other movements; to the Baltics and the Ukrainians because I must tell also about them. It is very important to understand these movements.

In which way they try to frighten people now? First, in the past KGB made searches only in the night and without any witnesses. Now in 1972 they came openly to the same research institutes to the plants. They know that this man, this dissident, works in this place in Kiev in Leningrad or Moscow, and they came openly in the daytime, in full uniform of the KGB with witnesses and talked to this man: "We know that you are dissident and that you have publishing materials and reading materials which you publish underground—'Samizdat.' We know that you read these materials and we came to make a search of your desk at work and on your body." They search his desk and they know that they cannot find anything. They only want to frighten all of the institute or plant, because to make one search at the place it is enough. All of the people would talk about this for months. With these open searches they try to frighten people now in Kiev, and in Moscow, and in Leningrad, and in all the country. We have news from many towns.

What is very dangerous is that KGB now arrests—I know many names—dissidents as criminals. Boris Kochubievsky came in 1972 from the prison, where he was incarcerated as a criminal. What he did? He took part in open meetings in his plant and when it was a meeting against Israel—yes, they make many meetings in the U.S.S.R. against Israel, and the people in these meetings speak, and they say that they hate Israel and that Israel is aggressor, and all of these people talk this way because they give to them these prepared speeches. They do not think in this way. People in the U.S.S.R. know very well that Israel is not aggressive and that it is not U.S.A. blame in Vietnam. And this Kochubievsky stands openly among the people and says: "Friends it is not right that Israel is aggressor, with 2 million people in Israel and 100 million in Arab countries." And he explained his position and truth about Israel. And they sent him to a concentration camp not as political dissident but as a criminal. Yes, and they sentenced to 3 years imprisonment only 3 or 4 months ago a few from Sverdeovsk. He has spoken with us by telephone, and he explained to us the new wave of anti-Semitism now in the U.S.S.R., and they sent him to prison for 3 years as a criminal for "hooliganism." They send people to the camps from Lithuania—from little town, Ukmerge, one of my friends, Stasis Brokas, Lithuanian dissident was sent as "thief." They brought to his door in the night stolen lumber. You cannot buy openly lumber in the U.S.S.R. In the night they brought 3 or 4 cubic meters of this lumber. In the morning they came and said, "Good morning, thief." And they sent him for 7 years to the prison again. In this way they send now tens and tens of dissidents.

In the U.S.S.R. you must have a stamp in your passport from the police that they permit you to live in this town. You cannot live in a town without this stamp. If you came to your friends for some weeks or a month, and here they know that you are a dissident, they would come to you and ask for your passport. If you have not the stamp in passport, they would send you for 1, 2 years to concentration camp. We have now such cases.

Mr. BOLDYREFF. They would sentence you for the breach of the passport regulations.

Mr. Shifrin. So, they send in this way Zeev Wolf now to 2 years imprisonment from Odessa. He came to visit people only. In this way they also try to frighten people to stay away from dissidents.

They have sent now to prison Amalrik. He wrote his book——

Mr. Boldyreff. "Will the Soviet Union Survive Until 1984?"

Mr. Shifrin. They sent him to concentration camp. They sent to the concentration camp, General Grigorenko, well-known man in the world. This General Grigorenko tried to act in the defense of human rights in the U.S.S.R. He was the head of cibernetic department in Frunze Academy. That is the Army Academy in Moscow. He was a very big scientist and a very big general, and they have seen that he tried to defend the right of Jews, and Ukrainians, and Russians and Tartars, and they threw him from his position, and then they took away his rank of general, and he worked like a simple longshoreman. And then they arrested him when he came to Tashkent to testify in the trial against Tartars.

They try to frighten people in all of these ways in the U.S.S.R.— and they try to finish this dissident movement. And I told you that it is very dangerous for all of mankind because if the Kremlin would have free hands, they would be very powerful against you, against all free mankind.

Now, another movement. I want to tell some words about this Baltic movement, and Ukrainian movement. You see, they occupy these Baltic countries: Estonia, Latvia, and Lithuania; these countries, they occupy them because they have an agreement with Nazism, with Hitler, and they seize these countries and they arrest all people which they know where anti-Soviet and shoot them. And then it was an uprising there of a partisan movement, and they sent maybe 50 percent of adult population of these countries to concentration camps in Siberia. I have seen in concentration camps many thousands of Estonians, Latvians, and Lithuanians. With many of them I was in very friendly relations. Some of them KGB has now arrested again.

Senator Gurney. They were arrested about the World War II era?

Mr. Shifrin. Yes. They were arrested during war, in the last years of Stalin, and after Stalin's death also. There were many, many hundreds of thousands of these Baltic people.

Senator Gurney. Did you run into prisoners of war in the camp?

Mr. Shifrin. Oh, yes. I will tell you about prisoners of war. I would finish now with these prisoners from these countries, the Baltic countries and Ukraine. They are now in concentration camps. Now you can see in Baltic countries also these anti-Soviet movements there. There were some big demonstration only some months ago. You know this. There are now four cases where people burned themselves in Baltic countries in sign of protest against this Government. But, in Baltic countries they are like one man, all of these Baltic people, and they were from beginning anti-Soviet, and they are now anti-Soviet. It is not like with the dissidents from the U.S.S.R. who became anti-Soviet fighters after camp experience.

And in Ukraine, there is also another picture. They were caught by Communists in this agreement with Hitler: to U.S.S.R. came part of Poland, and this part of Poland in reality, was Ukraine—West Ukraine. And in U.S.S.R. already was East Ukraine. Ukraine, you see on the map, is a big part of the U.S.S.R., but they have there West Ukraine and East Ukraine.

And then came Hitler, in 1941, and there was an uprising against Hitler, and leaders of movement were sent to concentration camps of Hitler.

And then came our Communists, and they released them from concentration camps of Hitler and sent them to concentration camps of Stalin; leaders and thousands and thousands of these people from West Ukraine. After, in the west part of Ukraine, from 1945 to 1953, there were partisan movements with weapons, and they fought openly against the Communist government. But in East Ukraine it was quiet. They never engage in this national activity. They were assimilated in these 50 years of communism. They don't understand that they must help the Ukrainians in this struggle against communism. And Communists drown this uprising in West Ukraine in blood. This uprising was 8 years to 1953. Try to understand—8 years with weapons against all of the Red Army. But, KGB arrested from this West Ukraine, I do not know, maybe 50 percent of male population and sent them to concentration camps. They made a big mistake when they released them. KGB released them after 10, 15 years. These boys, which came in the concentration camps noneducated, without knowing history, and they became intellectuals after the concentration camps. Then KGB sent these Ukrainians to exile to the east part of Ukraine, to this assimilated Ukraine. They sent these dissidents there because they do not want them to go to the west part of Ukraine, and make again this uprising. And these former prisoners made in East Ukraine propaganda, these Nationalists, they make now nationalism in East Ukraine also. You know, this last uprising when KGB killed people, was now in the east part of Ukraine. It was in Dneprodzerzhinsk, where Brezhnev was born. Now in all of the Ukraine you can see anti-Soviet national movement.

You know, they arrested only in 1972, in Ukraine—we know the names—maybe some 300 Ukrainians. Among them such intellectuals like Moroz, Peusch, Dzuba, Karavansky and many others. They also arrested a great friend of mine—Yuri Shukhevich.

Now, I should tell you about POW's.

Senator GURNEY. I wonder if this is not a good time to recess and then we can start on that afterward. So, the subcommittee will recess until 2:30.

[Whereupon at 12:50 p.m., the hearing was recessed, to reconvene at 2:30 p.m. this same day.]

APPENDIX

I. PARTIAL LIST OF SOVIET CONCENTRATION CAMPS

[Source: *Posev*, Mar. 1969, p. 3–4]

Location:	Address
Abkhazskaya ASSR, Gal'skiy rayon, s. Sida	P/ya 123/35
Alma-Atinskaya oblast, st. Chemolgan	P/ya 154/9 "Zh"
Altayskiy, Barnaul 23	P/ya UB 14/1
Altayskiy, Barnaul 37	P/ya UB 14/2–2
Altayskiy kray, Barnaul, pos. Kusta	P/ya UB 14/3**
Altayskiy kray, Zimeinogorsk	P/ya UB 14/10**
Altayskiy kray, Novoaltaysk	P/ya UB 14/1
Altayskiy kray, Novoaltaysk	P/ya UB 14/4
Altayskiy kray, Novoaltaysk	P/ya UB 14/8
Altayskiy kray, Rubtsovsk 9	P/ya UB 14/9
Arkhangel'skaya oblast, st. Ertsevo	P/ya 233/3**
Bukharskaya oblast, Navoi	P/ya 64/29 "M"
Vibebskaya oblast, Novo-Polotsk	P/ya UZh 15/10 "I"
Vitebskaya oblast, Orsha	P/ya UZh 15/6 "B"**
Vitebskaya oblast, Orsha	P/ya UZh 15/2 "B"
Vitebskaya oblast, Orsha	P/ya UZh 15/12
Vitebskaya oblast, Orsha	P/ya UZh 15/12–1
Vitebskaya oblast, Orsha	P/ya UZh 15/12—"E"
Vitebskaya oblast, Orsha	P/ya UZh 15/12–"Zh"
Gorkovskaya oblast, Gorkiy 28	P/ya UZ 62/5 "E"
Gorkovskaya oblast, Dzerzhinsk	P/ya UZ 62/9 "B"
Gorkovskaya oblast, st. Sukhobezvodnoye	P/ya UZ 62/3**
Grodnenskaya oblast, Volkovysk	P/ya UZh 15/11
Dnepropetrovskaya oblast, Zheltye Vody	P/ya YaE 308/26
Dnepropetrovskaya oblast, Solonyanskiy rayon, St. Privol'noye	P/ya YaE 308/21
Donetskaya oblast, Shaktersk	P/ya Yu 312/57, d 5/13
Zaporozhskaya oblast, Berdyansk	P/ya YaYa 310/20a
Zaporozhskaya oblast, Berdyansk	P/ya YaYa 310/77 otr. 7
Ivano-Frankovskaya oblast, Kolomyyskiy rayon, s. Tovmachik	P/ya YaA 128/41–4
Kabardino-Balkarsk, ASSR, Nal'chik, Gazovay Str.	P/ya OL 49/1*
Karagandinskaya oblast, p/o Dolinskoe	P/ya 154/40**
Kemerovskaya oblast, Kemerovo	P/ya 16/12/5**
Kemerovskaya oblast, Kemerovo	P/ya 49–39/1**
Kievskaya oblst, st. Belichi, p/o Kotsyubinskoe	P/ya 128/75
Kievaskaya oblast, Borispol'skiy rayon, s. Martusovka	P/ya YaA (No. unknown)
Kirgizovskaya SSR, Frunze, pos. Kainda	P/ya 36/1 "B"
Kirgizovskaya SSR, Frunze, sovkhoz Prigorodnyy	P/ya 36/2 "P"
Kirgizovskaya SSR, Frunze, sovkhoz Prigorodnyy	P/ya 36/12–3*
Kirgizovskaya SSR, Frunze, sovkhoz Prigorodnyy	P/ya 36/12–9*
Kirgizovskaya SSR, Frunze, sovkhoz "Prigorodnyy"	P/ya 36/12–6
Kirgizovskaya SSR, Frunze 9	P/ya 36/12–8*
Kirgizovskaya SSR, Kirovskiy rayon, Kirovo	P/ya 36/6
Kirovskaya oblast, Verkhnekamskiy rayon	P/ya 231/23
Kirovskaya oblast, Verkhnekamskiy rayon	P/ya 231/25
Komi ASSR, Mikun', p/o Vezhayka	P/ya 400/4–II
Komi ASSR, Knyazhpogostskiy rayon, st. Veslyana, p/o Zaimka	P/ya 248/3–5*
Krasnodarskiy kray, Abinskiy rayon, pos. Novosadovyy	P/ya 68/1 "A" **
Krasnodarskiy kray, Krasnodar	P/ya 68/6 "I"**
Krasnodarskiy kray, Ust'-Labinsk	P/ya 68/3

I. PARTIAL LIST OF SOVIET CONCENTRATION CAMPS—Continued

Krasnodarskiy kray, Primorsko-Akhtarskiy rayon, st. Ol'shinskaya	P/ya 68/12
Krasnodarskiy kray, Primorsko-Akhtarskiy rayon, st. Ol'shinskaya	P/ya 68/12/9
Krasnodarskiy kray, Kurganinskiy rayon, pos. Pervomayskiy	P/ya UO–68/19
Kurskaya oblast, Kursk	P/ya OK 30/1 "I"
Kurskaya oblast, Kursk	P/ya OK 30/1 "D"
Kurskaya oblast, Kursk	P/ya OK 30/1"E"
Mariyskaya ASSR. p/o Mar'ino	P/ya OSh 25/1
Minskaya oblast, Minsk 47	P/ya UZh 15/7–1
Minskaya oblast, Minsk	P/ya 35/6*
Mogilevskaya oblast, Bobruysk	P/ya UZh 15/2
Mogilevskaya oblast, Bobruysk	P/ya UZh 15/2 "A"
Mogilevskaya oblast, Gorki	P/ya UZh 15/9–6*
Mogilevskaya oblast, Mogilev	P/ya UZh 15/15
Mordovskaya ASSR, p/o Yavas	P/ya ZhZh 385/17–7*
Mordovskaya ASSR, st. Pot'ma, p/o Yavas	P/ya 385/2
Mordovskaya ASSR, st. Pot'ma	P/ya 385/5
Mordovskaya ASSR, st. Pot'ma	P/ya 385/7**
Mordovskaya ASSR, st. Pot'ma	P/ya 385/17
Nikolayevskaya oblast, p/o N. Grigorovka	P/ya YaA 128/53
Odesskaya oblast, Odessa	P/ya YuG 311/74
Omskaya oblast, Omsk	P/ya UKh 16/3 "A"**
Omskaya oblast, Omsk 29	P/ya UKh 16/3 "N"**
Orlovskaya oblast, Kromskiy rayon, s. Shakhovo	P/ya 22/3
Pavlodarskaya oblast, Pavlodar–12	P/ya 154/25
Pavlodarskaya oblast, Ekibastuz	P/ya 154/53 "D"
Pavlodarskaya oblast, Kizel, p/o Talyy	P/ya 201–10 "A"
Permskaya oblast, Kungur	P/ya 389/18–4
Poltavskaya oblast, s. Kustolovo-Sukhodolka	P/ya YaA 128/9
Pskovskaya oblast, Sebezhskiy rayon, pos. Kuritsa	YaYa 61/3 "V"
Rovenskaya oblast, s. Rafelovka	YaYa 128/76 st. 5
Rostovskaya oblast, Sal'skiy rayon, p/o Yulovskoye	YaYa 398/3
Rostovskaya oblast, Matveevo-Kurbanskiy rayon, pos. Novykovka	YaYa 398/5
Rostovskaya oblast, Aksayskiy rayon, p/o Grushevskoye	YaYa 398/6 "B"
Rostovskaya oblast, Aksayskiy rayon, p/o Grushevskoye	YaYa 398/6 "V"
Rostovskaya oblast, Shakhty 19	YaYa 398–9–1**
Ryazanskaya oblast, st. Sten'kina	YaYa 25/6
Sverdlovkaya oblast oblast, Nizhniy Tagil	P/ya UShCh 349/6 E–12
Tashkentskaya oblast, Tashkent 5	P/ya UShCh 64/7
Kharkovskaya oblast, Kharkov 35	P/ya UShCh YuZh 313/54–5
Khersonskaya oblast. Kherson	P/ya UShCh YuZ 17/61–4*
Chelyabinskaya oblast, Chelyabinsk 51	P/ya UShCh YaV 48/5
Chelyabinskaya oblast, Satkinskiy rayon, Bakal	P/ya UShCh YaV 48–9–5
Chelyabinskaya oblast, Katav-Ivanovsk	P/ya UShCh YaV 48–12–7
Chitinskaya oblast, Karymskiy rayon, p/o Tyrgetuy	P/ya UShCh 14/2
Chuvashskaya ASSR, Alatyr	P/ya UShCh YuL 34/2 "A"
Chuvashskaya ASSR, pos. Kozlovka	P/ya UShCh YuL 34/5 "A"
Chuvashkaya ASSR, pos. Kozlovka	P/ya UShCh YuL 34/5 "V"
Chuvashkaya ASSR, pos. Kozlovka	P/ya UShCh YuL 34/5 "G"

NOTE. One asterisk denotes intensified regime camps, two asterisks denote strict regime camps. In addressing mail these asterisks should not be used.

II. STATEMENT OF FORMER SOVIET CITIZENS NOW IN ISRAEL

In July 1971, I Alexander Krimgold, now residing in Israel at No. 121/15 November Twenty-Ninth St., Bat Yam, had occasion to visit Pot'ma while escorting Nina Lotsovaya, the wife of Anatoliy Altman who had been sentenced to imprisonment during the first Leningrad trial. Going to Pot'ma with us were Mary and Aida Khnokh, the wife and sister of Leib Khnokh, who had been sentenced at the same trial.

Pot'ma is only 7 hours away from Moscow. A narrow gauge railroad, on both sides of which like so many boils lie scattered the terrible labor camps of Mordovia, runs deep into the forest from the main junction.

Our destination was camp No. 19, where besides Altman were also incarcerated Boris Penson and Mikhail Shepshelovich (at present in Beit Milnam, Ramat Aviv, Israel).

Upon arrival we stopped at the so-called "Guest House"—a dirty, ramshackle, two-room log cabin, where those visiting the prisoners stayed without differentiation as to sex.

After many hours of nerve-wracking harassment, tears, and insults, and threats on the part of camp authorities, Nina was at last allowed to see her husband in the evening . . . for 4 hours only, and from 6 to 10 p.m. The visit had to start precisely at 6 p.m., and only after the prisoners had shaved, thereby reducing their visiting time by 20 minutes. The meeting was attended by a guard, who from time to time "amused" himself with remarks such as "your Israel, we'll crush it", "you'll rot here in prison", etc. Half an hour before the end of the visit, the guard proposed a deal—end the visit now, and he would arrange for the prisoner to receive some of the things [brought by the visitor], or continue the visit until the end, and be deprived of permission to receive the things.

Nina and Tolia [diminutive for Anatol] chose the former. Nina and I had hastily packed a trunkful of things, and we gave it to the guard. He rummaged through the things, accompanying this dignified operation with select oaths and invectives . . .

A few months later we found out that Tolia was given two handkerchiefs and a pair of socks. The suitcase with all the other things apparently went to improve the standard of living of the guards.

Pot'ma is a fearful place which readily evokes Nazi concentration camps. Barbed wire fences. watchtowers, dogs set in pursuit of people. Escape from there is almost impossible. Besides, the destitute inhabitants of the surrounding Mordovian villages receive a sack of potatoes as their reward for intercepting a prisoner; this places their "ideological" standard on a higher level than that of any of the guards.

The humiliation of the prisoners and their visitors is conducted . . . with a sophisticated appreciation of human psychology. All visitors to Jewish prisoners are regarded as potential prisoners.

Natasha Yuriy Fedorov's wife, came to Pot'ma because she was upset and disturbed by Yura's letter in which he spoke of his very low morale because of continuing run-ins with the camp administration. She, however, was refused permission to see her husband, under the pretext that Yura was not and could not possibly be depressed as he was receiving the magazine "Inostrannaya Literatura ["Foreign Literature"] and attended movies one a week. Viktor Yakhota, who escorted Natasha, was searched without any previous warning and subjected to humiliating questioning and coarse threats.

The red flags of the "most democratic of states", the pompous slogans announcing "Peace to the World", "The People and the Party Are One", the various "catch-ups and overtakes" [referring to Soviet slogans on catching up and overtaking the U.S. in industrial production—Translator's Note] flutter and soar over Pot'ma.

The reality of life of the Jewish prisoners in Pot'ma is terrible in its everyday drabness, full of indifference to human beings as individuals, and humiliation on the part of the guards. All this is magnified by the unbridled and savage anti-Semitism of the camp's criminal elements, types who cooperated with the Facists. Nor does the camp administration lag far behind in its anti-Semitism.

The gloom of Pot'ma can hardly be exaggerated. The world should know that in the second half of the twentieth century, in a country which at every turn proclaims its humanitarian domestic and foreign policy, there exist terrible prison camps where political prisoners are incarcerated only because of their convictions.

These camps are the worthy heirs of Hitler's and Stalin's work.

ALEXANDER KRIMGOLD,
121/15 November Twenty-Nineth St.,
Bat Yam, Israel.

Jerusalem, December 26, 1972.

Reyza Palatnik, born 1936, librarian, arrived in Israel on 21 Dec 1972, after serving a two-year sentence both in a prison and a corrective labor camp.

Reyza Palatnik tells the following story: it all began on 14 October 1970 when my apartment was raided under the pretext that the authorities were looking for stolen goods. . . They found three folders of Samizdat materials. Before the arrest, which took place on 1 December 1970, I was called three times to the KGB. They tried to associate me with one of the Zionist groups in Leningrad, Riga or Kishinev, but since I categorically refused to support their lies, I was arrested and accused of distributing slanderous information on the Soviet state and particularly the Soviet legal system. Witnesses were called: these were my friends, who had been threatened that if they didn't testify against me, they would be arrested. Seven months after my arrest, on 24 June 1971, I was tried and sentenced to 2 years in a standard regime corrective labor colony.

The trial itself was a mockery. The verdict was decided upon in advance. Even the defending attorney refused to carry on the defense in view of the obviously prejudiced attitude of the court.

As of 11 October 1971 I was in the Dneprodzerzhinsk camp in the Dnepropetrovskaya oblast. This was a women's camp for criminals, and I was the only political prisoner.

The camp was located in a swamp (indicative of the special "care and concern" for women . . . .). The buildings were damp. . . A continuously semi-cold and hungry existence. No medical service. Grippe and quinsy were not considered illnesses. . . One had to lose consciousness to be allowed off for a day. . . Only the prison uniform was allowed: in summer, a cotton dress, in winter, the same dress and a padded jacket, which provided no warmth. . . The camp had approximately 1100 persons, despite the fact that it was designed for only 700. The result—terribly crowded conditions. I was intentionally placed in the venereal diseases ward. . . Hot water for laundry and bathing was available only once in 10 days. The food—garbage. . . Pigs are fed better by good masters!

Despite the fact that the camp was called a corrective-educational labor colony, only 4 of the entire staff had any higher education. When, and who could ever conduct this educational work remains a mystery. . . I was specially treated to endless instructive talks praising socialism and denigrating Zionism and Israel's aggressive policies. Attempts were made to induce me to participate in the "social life" of the camp's "society" . . .

Even before my arrival at the camp, people were warned that no one was to help me because I had connections with enemy Zionist organizations, that I was a dangerous criminal, and any assistance rendered me would be strictly punished. . .

At the camp, people worked twelve hours a day instead of eight, and often on holidays too. From the start I refused to work more than 8 hours a day and thereby provoked the anger of the camp administration.

But the main thing that struck me from the very start was the prisoner's complete lack of any rights in the camps and prisons. The duties of the procurator were purely ficticious: he completely supported the administration. For instance, upon arrest, I asked for the Criminal Code of the Ukrainian SSR and a book on criminal law—a request which was refused! I wonder how many people know that in the Soviet Union, an arrested person may not meet with his lawyer until the case is over with! This means that a person is entirely at the mercy of the authorities conducting the investigations; ignorant of the law and his rights, not equipped to defend himself, the prisoner is often himself instrumental in getting himself into prison.

Insults to human dignity are infinite. For example, since last year (1971) identification insignia on the chest became mandatory: family name, father's name, unit and brigade numbers. If the identification was not worn, the person was punished severely: permission was withdrawn to use the camp store, to receive visitors or parcels.

A widely used method for controlling prisoners is to instigate them against each other . . . There are also so-called activists who carry out the camp administration's orders and create the desired atmosphere. Jews, of course, are the principal and primary objects of persecution. An attempt was made to provoke me [against the administration] so that I could be given a beating, but it did not succeed. . . .

It must be emphasized that the morale of the prisoners, particularly the Jews, is severely undermined. Human rights are infringed upon at every step. For instance, I was deprived of more than half the letters sent me. Letters from my parents were more or less allowed through, but only a fourth of even my sister's letters were ever delivered. (I checked the number after my release).

To achieve anything, the prisoner needs contact with the outside world: this is his only opportunity of alleviating his condition, and the only one that the administration has any regard for, both the prison and camp authorities. . . .

It is not only a matter of the Jewish prisoners, fighting for their right to leave for their native land: these people are the defenders and representatives of the Jewish masses, deprived of their national social organizations. To a great extent the all important question of the prospects of the Jews in Russia for mass EXODUS, depends on world opinion, and particularly on Jewish world opinion and *on their active support.* The Soviet government not only does not observe its own laws, but doesn't even observe the basic principles of the Declaration of Human Rights, signed by its own representatives. Thus, this is more than just an internal Soviet problem, it is a violation of an international Declaration of Human Rights, which concerns all the peoples of the world. It is therefore a moral obligation of the free world to react to this situation.

REYZA PALATNIK,
Jerusalem, Katamon Tet,
Merkaz Klita.

Written down by T. Elina
[Seal with Hebrew letters]

DECEMBER 24, 1972.

Jewish prisoner Yuriy Vudka, sentenced at the Ryazan' trial to 7 years in a strict regime labor camp and at present in a camp in Perm, left the intensified regime ward on 30 Nov. 1972 where he spent 6 months in solitary confinement for having celebrated his birthday in the company of other Jews, refusing to disband (when ordered to do so).

His brother, Valeriy Veniaminovich Vudka, who had been sentenced at the same Ryazan' trial to three years, and who had already served all three years (including one and a half years in one of the most terrible prisons in Russia, the Vladimirskaya), had been released on 10 Aug. 1972 and was at the camp in Perm on November 30th. With Valeriy Vudka were his wife Mara Ulman-Vudka and Yuriy Vudka's fiancee, Khana Gurevich. All of them had applied for the regularly authorized visit, which is granted twice a year. However, they were refused permission under the pretext that on one of his days of confinement in Bura, Yuriy Vudka got up too early from his bed: for this he was deprived of his prescribed visit, whereas the next visit was due only in four months time.

Valeriy Vudka, Khana Gurevich and Mara Vudka spent two days travelling from Chernovitsy to Perm, but were not granted the visit. On the same day, November 30th, they requested a visit with another Jewish prisoner, Shimon Grilyus, sentenced at the Ryazan' trial to 5 years of confinement to a strict regime labor camp (February 1970). But permission for this visit was refused, despite the fact that Sh. Grilyus' parents were in Israel and he had no relatives in the U.S.S.R. to visit him.

Lately, the Jewish prisoners have had it very hard. At the labor camp in Perm they work in three shifts: day, evening, and night. Since the camp is new, many work on construction under the open sky. Some work in machine shops. A number are engaged in making flat irons and in the extremely harmful work of stamping asbestos linings for the flat irons, when great amounts of injurious dust are generated; the Jewish prisoners, however, are not given the special rations which normally go with such work. Many of the Jewish prisoners are ill. Sil'va Zalmanson is getting *deafer* every day! Almost all the prisoners are ill, but receive no medical treatment. For example, Dymshits, who suffers from rheumatism of the arms (fifteen years of strict regime labor camps) works on construction under the open sky. The health of the other prisoners is also very bad.

The situation regarding visits and letters from relatives is continuously getting worse—what should be normal contact with the Motherland and relatives! At present, a request for a visit must be submitted to the camp authorities several months in advance. This provides [the authorities] with the opportunity of cancelling the visit just several days before it is due. "Give us a man—we'll always find a law to take care of him", was the saying in Stalin's time. Now it is: If you have permission for a visit, there will always be a reason for rescinding it. . .

All this information was obtained in a telephone conversation with Valeriy Vudka. The call was made to Chernovitsy on December 19.

KHAIM GEILYUS,
Holon, Kiriat Sharet,
Block 74/21,
Israel.

True copy: [Stamp with Hebrew lettering]

TEL AVIV, *December 18, 1972.*

As told by former prisoner Aleksandr Guzman: Was sentenced by the Military Tribunal (was an officer in the Soviet Army) for his attempt to escape to Israel from Poland (while serving on the territory of the Polish People's Republic). Article 19–58–1b. Term—10 years. After the (Penal) Code was amended, the Article specified a maximum of 7 years. Wrote several petitions to the Supreme Court and his case came under review. A decision from the Supreme Court arrived at the camp stating that his sentence was reduced to 6 years and 10 months. Served his term in the Temnikovskiy labor camps—camp 385/7. Commandant of the camp—Medvedev; deputy for political affairs—Tolbuzov.

LABOR CAMP CONDITIONS OF PRISONERS

In 1954, conditions in the labor camps became unbearably harsh and riots took place in several camps. Prisoners were machine-gunned from watchtowers. In some places tanks were used to flatten the camps. However, later conditions were relaxed and became better; prisoners were allowed to let their hair grow, to write and receive an unlimited number of letters, receive monthly package, etc. But soon things again changed for the worse.

The first blow came with the abolition of the system of so-called "credits" for hard labor, which allowed prisoners to count one day of hard labor as three days towards reducing their term. Actually, however, many prisoners ruined their health with hard work, never attaining their freedom in advance of their term . . . The number of packages was reduced to one in three months; all civilian apparel was forbidden (whereas prison clothes provided very poor protection from the cold); hair no longer was allowed to be grown. Food was low in nutritional value, bread resembled plasticine.

In 1960 a new wave of restrictions was instituted, including a strict classification of camps by the severity of their regulations.

I was in an intensified regime camp, where the following rules prevailed:

One package, not exceeding 5 kg. allowed once every 6 months, but only after half of the term had been served.

Two letters a month, only.

A 10-hour working day and the mandatory fulfilment of the daily norm, otherwise strict punishment.

Only five rubles worth of goods per month allowed to be purchased from the camp store: jam or margarine, low-grade tobacco, cigarettes or tooth-paste—but neither bread nor salami! The unit commandant often deprived the prisoners of the permission of making even these small purchases.

Visits from relatives were allowed only after half the term had been served, and then only once a year for three days. But the unit commandant could always deny permission for even this visit . . .

At camp 385/7 out of a total of 1500 prisoners only 10–12 were Jewish. The majority of the prisoners were former Ukrainian policemen who had engaged in mass genocide of the Jews upon instructions from the Nazis.

I remember an interesting episode from my camp life : Following a change in the Criminal Code, the maximum term was reduced from 25 to 15 years. A visiting representative from the Court, in conjunction with the Court, could, at the request of the camp administration, free a prisoner who had already served two-thirds of his term. The trial took place within the camp compound, and the prisoners could attend it. On one occasion a Ukrainian policeman who had killed 200 people was recommended for release. During the trial he behaved cynically and to the judge's query: "Will you ever again kill Jews?", he answered : "Of course I will! Just give me a gun! . . ." The Court was lenient with the murderer, his term of punishment was reduced to 15 years, and he was set free.

The same Court investigated the case of the Jewish prisoner, Teplitskiy, sentenced for embezzlement. But the Court's decision in this case was—not to be released ! . . .

LIFE OF THE CAMP'S JEWISH PRISONERS

Camp 385/7 (a camp in the Temnikovskiy region) had a group of Jewish prisoners. Several were only beginning their terms, others had already gone through the concentration camps of Karaganda and the North. Unlike the other prisoners, they not only wanted to be set free and get out into the outside world, the "Large Zone", but also to emigrate to the land of their forefathers and forever escape Soviet tyranny. Not a single day passed in the camp without the Jewish prisoners talking about Israel.

Prisoner Rafalovich had learned Hebrew to a point where he could converse with old man Teplitskiy, accused of "sabotaging the economy of the U.S.S.R."— he had been sentenced to 25 years in a corrective labor camp. I met him after he had already served 15 years; he had a prayer book and a Torah. Rafalovich used these books to compile not only an alphabet, but a large dictionary as well. (It was strictly forbidden to have prayer-books or Torahs, and insubordination to this rule was punished severely !)

My teacher of Hebrew was the prisoner Semen Moiseyevich Podol'skiy, a great aesthète, a graduate of the history and art history departments of the Moscow State University, who had served as school inspector for the city of Moscow. His entire family—wife and son, were incarcerated in a labor camp for many years because he had had contact with members of the Israeli diplomatic corps.

The Jews secretly celebrated all the Jewish holidays, and even secretly baked matsoh.

The group also secretly studied the ancient and modern history of the Jewish people. The group's instructor was Avraham Shifrin. I was one of his students— Shifrin had the uncanny ability to present his material in such a way as to arouse the national pride of his listeners in their people and country.

I am proud of having helped Shifrin translate in great secrecy from all, except the Jewish prisoners and several Ukrainian nationalists, the book "Exodus", from English into Russian; it later crossed the camp's borders and was published extensively in Russia by Samizdat. The Jewish prisoners in the camp were on very good terms with each other, sharing their bread and spending their free time together.

My friends were Boris Podol'skiy, Boris Khatskevich, Edik Kuznetsov, Adolf Rafalovich, Zolya Kats, and Iosif Shnayder, but my best and closest friend was Avraham Shifrin.

A true copy : [Seal with Hebrew lettering]

140/48 Jaffet St.,
Tel Aviv—Jaffo,
Israel.

[Top address] To: Rosa Kogan, Rech. Sireni 28, Givat-Rambam, Israel.
From: Dr. Wolodymyr Horbowyj, Village of Obolonja, County of Dolyna, Iwano-Frankiwska Oblast [Region], USSR.
[Bottom, Address] To: Rosa Kogan, Rech. Sireni 28, Givat-Rabam, Israel.
From: Igel N. Kogan, Uchr. No. 5110/1 Zh. V. Moskow.[1]
[Translator's note: This letter was apparently written by Wolodymyr Horbowyj, the sender's name on the envelope on top of page one.]

---

[1] Translator's note: The sender's address expressed in abbreviations and figures may be that of a prisoner.

DEAR MRS. ROSA: I received your valuable letter dated October 7, of the current year [1972]. Thank you very much. Already in my postal card I indicated that your letter is in my possession. Your handwriting alone allowed me to establish who was its author.

I like very much your courageous attitude in view of the difficult situation of your life. The fact that you are alone, continue to work and keep everything the way it was in spite of Jehuda's absence, speaks for itself. This allows Jehuda to keep his spirit high and cheers him up. He sees and realizes that there is somebody for whom to like and bear the life's misfortunes.

I am hopeful that Jehuda will be able to return to his longed for home country and enjoy the fascination of a happy married life. He knows well what he wants and he is able to pursue his goal. Already in December he is going to file an appropriate petition with the authorities, stating his citizenship, the place of residence of his wife, the source of his former and future livelihood and the fact that he wishes to return there. The reply should come in about three months or a little more. I am certain that his Government or its substitute will undertake appropriate steps in regard to his timely return. However it is necessary to see to it that these endeavors be started in proper time.

My life is running its course as usual. I stick to a rigid daily routine. Everything is normal with me, too, although that "everything" is now very modest. My main endeavor is to keep my heart under strict control. Although its [my heart's] machinery is rather worn out, I am trying to maintain its functioning without letting it wear out for good. It is my impression that my endeavors have a temporary success.

I was pleasantly touched by your noble offer to help me. Although I have always been in my life generous not only in my profession but also in society, i.e. I kept my heart and my purse open for any deserving neighbor, I will gladly take advantage of Mrs. Rose's kind offer. Two persons were vitally instrumental in improving my fate. They are my two girl cousins. The first one saved me from the plague of Asian rodents and insects, the other one keeps kindly filling my "horn of plenty". I would like to reward them with a nice gift. They are both middle aged (30–40 years of age), slim, one of average height and the other slightly taller. They need handbags dark in color and of various styles, as well as blouses. I know that they have been looking in vain for embroidery yarn "DMC". I regret that I do not entertain close friendly relations with your sister, since it is there that the yarn factory is located. What I need is a billfold for documents and bank notes. My beautiful billfold decorates the pocket of a dignitary. My request, however, is qualified. It means that it can be carried out only if it does not strain considerably Mrs. Rose's finances. Also, I cannot promise to settle my accounts now, because I still do not know how my personal situation will develop in the future. I can only say that this request will be the only one and will not be repeated.

Should you happen to meet Mr. Abraham, please tell him that the reason of my delay in answering his letter is the photograph which he wants of me. The problem is that I sat twice in front of a camera and both pictures turned out poorly. If the third picture is good, I will not fail to forward it to my good colleague. I wish to add that I'll take the liberty of sending one copy of my good photograph to the Kogan family. Mr. Jehuda's photograph is in my album.

Please convey my best regards to Jehuda along with sincere wishes for a happy return to his dear wife.

At the same time, please accept best wishes from your devoted friend.

WOLODYMYR.

Voloshin, Arkadiy. Born in 1946 in Kishinev. Arrested 17 Aug. 1970. Trial on 21 June 1971. Sentenced to 2 years. Accused of distributing literature:

1. Exodus (by Uris), an article by Amos Kenan, satire by Kishon, information on Jewish holidays, a prayer book, a 1903 Jewish encyclopedia, a textbook on Jewish history by Graetz and Dubnov, information on the political economy of Israel.

2. Accused of establishing plans for the study of Hebrew and the history of the Jewish people up to the time of the establishment of the State of Israel.

3. Accused of printing such literature and distributing testbooks on the Hebrew language, which were described as Zionist and anti-Soviet.

My Hebrew prayer book was taken away from me and burned by the KGB in accordance with a statute which stated that prayer books are reactionary and may not be distributed in the USSR.

I stayed imprisoned in the Mordovskaya ASSR from 18 Aug. 1971 to 17 Aug. 1972.

The aim of the camp administration was to destroy everything Jewish that the prisoner may have had. We were prevented from studying Hebrew, despite the fact that according to Soviet law we had the right to study our own language, and therefore had the right to books and textbooks in Hebrew.

Prisoners of all other nationalities were allowed their own national songs and allowed to celebrate their holidays. The Jews however were not allowed to celebrate the Sabbath or their national holidays. We were forced to do so illegally and in a different place each time.

A large number of letters which were written to us never reached us. If a letter which was written contained any information on the conditions of daily life at the camp, these letters were confiscated.

Whenever possible, the authorities insulted the human dignity of the prisoners and particularly that of the Jews.

For example: A food parcel arrived from Switzerland addressed to one of our friends. He was required to pay postage, but was not allowed to have the package; six months later he was called in and given the package, but in as much as after half a year's time everything in the package had spoiled, an official statement was prepared in his presence, ordering that the package be destroyed.

ARKADY VOLOSHIN,
Rehov Hameginim 131,
Merkaz Klita.

———

December 21, 1972.

I, Ruth Aleksandrovich-Averbukh, was born in Riga in 1947. On 7 Oct 1970 I was arrested by the KGB. The trial took place in May 1971. I was sentenced in accordance with Article 70 of the Criminal Code which specified deprivation of freedom for one year. I was accused of passing out books: Hebrew language textbooks, books on Jewish history, handwritten collections of information on Israel and Jewish culture, etc. All this was described by the prosecution as "anti-Soviet literature".

After the sentence was passed, I was sent to a women's camp in Pot'ma, Mordovskaya ASSR (Address: ZhKh 375/3. Camp commandant—Vorontsov; security officer—Pichugin.)

This women's camp was adjacent to a hospital for prisoners from camps in Mordovia and was under a single security system.

The daily schedule was as follows: arise at 6 a.m., breakfast at 6:30 a.m., begin work at 7 a.m., lunch at 12:30 p.m., then continue working until dinner at 6 p.m., lights out at 10 p.m.

The work consisted in sewing mittens. The norm—60 pairs a day. This could only be done in 10 or more hours. If the norm were not fulfilled, punishment followed: loss of right to receive visitors, to write and receive letters, to purchase items from the camp store (five rubles' worth of goods per month: for example, half a kilogram of jam, half a kilogram of cheap candy, a bottle of low-grade vegetable oil, and tobacco). Systematic failure to comply with the required norm was punishable by confinement to a cell for up to 6 months. Punishment could be meted out quite arbitrarily.

The food was of low nutritional value. In the morning—gruel (a thin watery soup made from a handful of grain and a few rotten, dry potatoes). Bread was handed out in the morning, 600 grams for the entire day. For lunch—once again gruel (from rotten vegetables and, sometimes, bones), and a portion of boiled buckwheat porridge. In the evening—boiled buckwheat porridge and a small, 30 gm, piece of fish.

Correspondence—two letters a month were permitted to relatives. There was no restriction on the number of letters one could receive, but actually the number depended on the censor's mood.

There was practically no medical aid. For instance, while suffering from a toothache, pulpitis [?], I received no medical aid for three and a half months.

The prisoners included those persecuted for their religious beliefs, Ukrainian nationalists, persons who had attempted to cross the border, and those who had cooperated with the Nazis.

———

TEL AVIV, *December 12, 1972.*

Gilel Shur—Jewish prisoner, who had served two years in Soviet concentration camps and who arrived in Israel about three weeks ago, repeated and reaffirmed a declaration he addressed to the Presidium of the Supreme Soviet of the USSR.

DECLARATION

I don't want to be silent. A feeling of indignation fills me, indignation at the tyranny of the investigatory agencies which conducted the preliminary study of my case. Indignation at the unfair and unfounded sentence of the judge. On 5 Aug 1970, in violation of legal procedure, I was brought into court by the KGB of the city of Leningrad (who appeared early one morning in my apartment and literally lifted me off the bed) to attend a cross-examination in the capacity of a witness. Since I refused to testify as a witness at the cross-examination, I was placed under arrest, first as a suspect and then as a defendant, and charged under Article 70 (part 2) and Article 72 of the RSFSR Criminal Code. Thus, by refusal to serve as witness was the immediate cause of my arrest; I was duly informed of this by the KGB officers who accompanied me to the cross-examination. I was accused of membership in a Leningrad Zionist organization, whose aim presumably was the "undermining and weakening of the Soviet government".

The questions which I refused to answer concerned Mogilever, Dreyzner and others, whose arrest on 15 June 1970 I and Grigoriy Vertlib, currently residing in Israel, protested in our letters of 2 July 1970 to the Procurator General and to the Presidium of the Supreme Soviet.

Thoroughly convinced that these people had no other object in mind than their own departure to Israel and the assistance to other Soviet Jews who desired to do likewise, in addition to the popularization of Jewish culture, i.e. language, literature, history, and music, I became thoroughly aroused by the numerous arrests and raids conducted on the homes of persons (including myself) aspiring to emigrate to Israel and therefore naturally refused to testify about anything.

The purpose of my present deposition is to draw attention to the flagrant violation of Soviet law in the course of the preliminary investigation and the court examination of case 6628 in the Supreme Court of the Moldavian SSR.

On 1 Oct 1970, in violation of due process of law, my case was withdrawn from case No. 15, which was then being reviewed in Leningrad, and sent for review to Moldavia. This was done despite the fact that none of those accused in case No. 15, and none of the witnesses testifying, indicated that I was at all involved in the crime committed in Moldavia or knew anything of it.

In Moldavia my case was artificially incorporated into criminal case No. 6628, despite the fact that I knew none of the residents of Kishinev involved in the case, and that none of the witnesses testifying in my case resided in Moldavia.

The KGB officers concerned themselves exclusively with problems concerning my activities in Leningrad, since they knew all too well that I knew nothing of any one's activities in Moldavia, despite the fact that the indictment contained a profound philosophical deduction, unfortunately completely unsubstantiated.

Thus the law, specifically articles 28 and 182 of the Criminal Political Code of the RSFSR, in my case was blatantly subverted.

My appeals to the Procurator General asking him that my case be placed under the jurisdiction of, and be reviewed by, Leningrad did not reach him and did not produce any results. Preliminary investigation of criminal case No. 6628, conducted in Kishinev by a group of investigators headed by major Kulikov, Head of the Investigation Division of the KGB of the Council of Ministers of the Moldavian SSR, was conducted in crude violation of the law and most unprofessionally.

I feel it is my duty to cite a few actual facts in support of my statement, so that the officials who took advantage of their official positions be punished and justice triumph. The investigators went so far as to use physical measures against me. Thus, upon arrival in Kishinev, when my ulcers flared up painfully, I could not obtain any medication for 10 days. My pains increased; I could neither eat nor sleep, but despite my remonstrations, I was called for questioning, and major Kulikov, in reply to my appeals for medication, advised me: "Provide the evidence and you will feel better immediately."

Neither did an appeal to Poluektov, Senior Legal Counsel and Head of the Division for the Supervision of the Investigative Organs of the KGB of the Procuratura of the Moldavian SSR, help. Poluektov appeared in court as the State's prosecuting attorney. The question arises : whose interests was he defending when he helped Kulikov humiliate me in such a subtle way?

Kulikov even went so far as to disobey the orders of Chaban, the Deputy Chairman of the KGB of the Council of Ministers of the Moldavian SSR, regarding medical assistance to me, orders which he gave Kulikov in my presence. Only after submitting a complaint to the Procurator of the Republic, did I get my medication, and then only 10 days later.

During the trial I was consistently intimidated. Kulikov set the tone. He threatened me with a maximum sentence and subsequent exile for 5 years, spent his time figuring out how old I would be when finally released, threatened that I would be serving my sentence at Spitzbergen or some other such place, where, as he expressed it, "the devil never set foot". He threatened me with permanent confinement to a mental hospital. I was continuously blackmailed with the arrest of my youngest sister.

The day after the news of the hijacking of a Soviet passenger plane and the killing of a stewardess appeared in the papers (October 1970), my interrogator informed me that this was the work of Lithuanian Jews, and that severe punishment awaited all the defendants in case 6628, who were all Jews.

A few days later, after a detailed description of the incident had appeared in the papers, when I asked why he brought up the subject of the Lithuanian Jews, he referred to the "Voice of America" broadcasts.

As to how "qualified" Major Kulikov's brigade was to conduct a preliminary investigation of so serious a matter as the commission of particularly dangerous state crimes, the documents in criminal case No. 6628 bear witness.

The following items demonstrate the kind of material evidence proving the "criminal activity" of the defendants—of which the case was full.

On 5 Aug 1970, when my mother's apartment was searched for the second time (the first time being on 19 June 1970). a Russian language literary review called "Ariel", published in Israel in 1965 and sent to the USSR through the mails, plus a travel brochure entitled "This is Israel", published in England by a travel agency and printed in Holland, were confiscated.

During the first search of the same apartment, the above mentioned publications were not confiscated by the KGB officers. However, after my arrest and during the second search they were confiscated and appended to the criminal case. This "consistency" can only be explained in the following way : nothing of a criminal nature was found during the search, but it was somehow necessary to justify the arrest.

The magazine "Ariel's" content is well illustrated by the titles of the articles in it: "Shakespeare on the Israeli Stage", "The Institute of Bibliography of Publications in Hebrew", "Israeli Cancer Research Methods". "Mstislav Rostropovich's Concert Tour of Israel", etc.

It should be pointed out that "Ariel" first came out and was sent to the USSR in 1965, i.e. when normal diplomatic relations existed between Israel and the USSR, and when both sides expressed a desire to develop cultural relations. The article in "Ariel" on the Israeli concert tour of the Soviet musician Mstislav Rostropovich is witness thereof.

As to the brochure "This is Israel", it an ordinary advertising travel brochure containing essentially illustrations and views of historic monuments and natural sites in Israel.

Furthermore, as I already mentioned, this brochure was published not in Israel but in England. Nevertheless, in the statement of 26 Oct 1970 which attached the brochure to the case as material evidence, Chief Investigator Savel'yev asserted : "The book 'Ariel' is nationalistic and pro-Zionist, and the book 'This is Israel' is a nationalistic Zionist publication. These books may not be brought into or distributed in the USSR. Since these works, kept in the home of defendant Shur. portray him as a member of an anti-Soviet underground organization. the books 'Ariel' and 'This is Israel'. confiscated during the search of G. Z. Shur's home. are decreed under Article 67–68 of the Code of Criminal Procedure of the Moldavian SSR as material evidence to be appended to and retained with the case".

After reviewing my case. I petitioned for the appointment of additional expertise to determine the true nature of the above named publications. But my petition was refused.

I cite another document of the same kind (Vol. 19, page 46 of the case). "Decree of 11 Jan 1971 Regarding the Attachment of Material Evidence to a Case. city of Kishinev". Captain Nagovitsyn, Senior Investigator of the Investigation Division of the Ukrainian KGB of the Council of Ministers of the Ukrainian SSR for the Donetsk oblast, stated: "A search of the home of Volf Moiseyevich Gruman on 29 Sept 1970 showed up a book entitled 'Brothers of Mine—Illustrious Heroes' ('The Maccabees') by H. Fast. The book presents the revolt of the Jews against domination by Greece and Antioch (150 B.C.) from a nationalistic point of view. A photostatic copy of 'A Textbook of Jewish History for Self Study' by

S. M. Dubnov, part III, published in Russian in 1918 by Kadima Ltd. in Petrograd. An examination of this book showed it to be replete with nationalist and Zionist ideas. Therefore Fast's and Dubnov's books are to be considered as material evidence and appended to case No. 6628 and retained with the case".

It is of course difficult to comment on the insistence that a description of the exploits of the national heroes of the Jewish people, the Maccabee brothers, who led the struggle of the Jews against foreign oppressors during the second century B.C., as correctly noted by the investigator, is material evidence of anti-Soviet activity on the part of persons typing this book on a typewriter and distributing it.

Such an assertion could hardly be taken seriously by any normal person, and would even appear funny, were it not part of such an important document as a criminal case.

As to Professor Dubnov's "Textbook of Jewish History", published in Soviet Russia, it was for many years used in Soviet Jewish schools. Dubnov's multivolume "History of the Jews" is known the world over. It is also generally known that Dubnov was not a Zionist. Had the persons preparing case No. 6628 examined the documents which they included in the case more carefully, they would have noticed that the case contained material showing that Dubnov's "History of the Jews" was available to the general public in state libraries. Perhaps this would have kept them from passing the resolution they did.

Basic ignorance characterizes a similar document (Vol. 7, page 265) "Resolution Regarding the Attachment of Material Evidence to a Case, 22 Jan 1971, City of Kishinev". Captain Ivanov, Senior Investigator of the Investigation Division of the Ukrainian KGB of the Council of Ministers for the Chelyabinskaya oblast, after examining the materials in the case 6628 on the accusation of Voloshin and others, stated:

During a search conducted on 15 June 1970, the following were found and removed from the possession of defendant Voloshin:

1. Three volumes of the "Jewish Encyclopedia" (vols. 6, 15, 16), a prerevolutionary edition published in Russian, edited by Dr. Katsenelson and Baron Gintsburg;

2. The book "History of the Jews in Europe", vol. 1, pp. 382, by the former Bundist Dubnov, published in 1936 in Riga.

3. The book "A Thousand Words" (textbook "Elef Milim") part 1, 140 pages, in Hebrew, published in 1954 in Israel.

4. The book, "A Thousand Words" (textbook "Elef Milim") part 2, 136 pages, published in Israel in Hebrew in 1964.

5. A. Rozen's book "A Thousand Words and Two Thousand More" 155 pages, published in Israel in Hebrew in 1960.

The above material is described in detail in the protocol review of 18 Sept 1970. The examination showed the above books to be nationalistic and Zionist. The books "A Thousand Words" (part 1 and 2) and "A Thousand Words and Two Thousand More", published in Israel, furthermore did not have the imprint of "Soyuzknigtorg" [Soviet Book Trade Association], indicating that they had entered the Soviet Union illegally. In view of the fact that the above indicated materials reveal the crime and the circumstances of the case, and guided by articles 55, 67, and 68 of the Ukrainian Criminal Code, it is resolved: to consider the literature enumerated in the present statement as material evidence and attach it to criminal case 6628 and retain with the case".

It is true that the "Soyuzknigtorg" stamp appears on none of the above mentioned Hebrew language textbooks because unfortunately textbooks on Hebrew are never for sale in the Soviet Union. But the absence of the stamp by no means indicates that they entered the Soviet Union illegally, and the proper officials know full well that such textbooks frequently arrive in the USSR from Israel by mail, passing through customs inspection.

As to Ivanov's contention that the "Jewish Encyclopedia", a thoroughly scholarly work containing basic information on the life of the Jewish people for the last several thousand years, one can only express surprise at any one with no knowledge of the subject so cavalierly attacking this problem and giving an opinion on so basic a learned work about which probably only a specialist has the right to judge.

I would like to point out that the materials contained in the case make it evident that the encyclopedia was purchased from "Staraya Kniga" ["Old Books"] in Leningrad, and that when searches were conducted in Leningrad, this encyclopedia was not usually confiscated.

Investigator Ivanov's statement also mentioned Dubnov's "History of the Jews". I would not have returned to this point, had not the investigator shown once again his ignorance, his complete lack of familiarity with the subject involved. He called Dubnov a Bundist; if so, the book could not have contained any Zionist ideas.

An investigator working on such important resolutions should know these basic facts. But Captain Ivanov is not just ignorant. His ignorance is militant and takes on the aspects of hooliganism. On that very day, 22 Nov 1971, he prepared one more document, which he appended to the case in addition to the first.

In this "Decree on the Determination of Materials for a Search" he states: "Destroy, as having no relevance to the case, as being in its content reactionary, the 'Compendium of Prayers, Rites, and Religious Laws of the Jewish People', 538 pages published in Hebrew and Russian before the Revolution".

The book was destroyed, as shown by the following document, appended to the case: "27 Jan 1971. Statement. City of Kishinev. We the undersigned, Captain Nagovitsyn, Senior Investigator of the Investigation Division of the Ukrainian KGB of the Council of Ministers of the Ukrainian SSR for the Donets oblast, Captain Kozlov, Senior Investigator of the Investigation Division of the KGB of the Council of Ministers of the Moldavian SSR, and Captain Ivanov, Senior Investigator of the Ukrainian KGB of the Council of Ministers for the Chelyabinskaya oblast, did this day, in accordance with the decree of 22 Jan 1971, destroyed by burning the 'Compendium of Prayers, Rites, and Religious Laws of the Jewish People'."

A savage, barbarian act! I wonder whether Jewish prayer books have been burned since the Spanish inquisition. As the documents show, investigator Ivanov and Major Kulikov, who was in charge of the investigation, in their fervor to destroy any book on any Jewish topic, did not even stop at violating a basic article of the USSR Constitution, guaranteeing the freedom of conscience of citizens. In accordance with legal procedure, the above Compendium shouldn't have been removed from the home of defendant Voloshin, since in conducting a search, the investigator must limit himself to confiscating items and proofs which have a direct bearing on the case. How this requirement of the law was complied with in Kishinev is evident from inspector Fedotov's "Decree on the Determination of Materials for a Search" of 11 Jan 1971 (Vol. 19, page 72 of the case). Having examined the items confiscated while conducting a search of witness A. B. Zhenin, he ordered that "literature and writings of nationalist and Zionist content—a book in Hebrew entitled 'Grammar for Reading and Study in a Cheder, at School and at Home', part 2, by Dr. Shtaynberg, published in Warsaw in 1915—be forwarded to the KGB of the Council of Ministers of the Moldavian SSR for its work".

The same Fedorov in the "Decree on the Determination of Materials for Search and Confiscation", dated 14 Jan 1971 (vol. 20, p. 49 of the case), ordered: forward to the State Republican Library imeni Krupskaya the "Jewish Encyclopedia", as one forbidden to be distributed in the USSR (published by a society for the publication of learned Jewish works and the publishing house of Brokhaus & Efron of St. Petersburg).

In searching my mother's home after my arrest, a Hebrew language textbook and a Jewish-Russian Dictionary by Pevsner (not confiscated during the first search) were confiscated. Thus investigator Savel'ev decrees that the books be forwarded to the state republican library, without even deeming it necessary to justify his action. The order simply stated "forward", but why "forward"— well, for this he apparently had no explanation.

Kulikov, who was in charge of the investigators, apparently recognized the illegality of his actions, because when upon reviewing the case I protested and demanded that the textbooks and dictionary be returned, he ordered the books to be sent back by the republican library.

Thus, the law does not exist for Kulikov. Those working under him systematically confiscate all books on Jewish topics, be they a textbook on the Hebrew language or the "Jewish Encyclopedia", and no matter whether the books had been seized at the home of an arrested person or that of a witness. There are many such examples in criminal case 6628.

No matter that the "Jewish Encyclopedia" and "History of the Jews" by Graetz, the material evidence in the case, were obtained from the "Staraya Kniga" ("Old Books") ; no matter that books which couldn't possibly have had any connection to any criminal case, such as case no. 15 in Leningrad, were not confiscated.

Kulikov does everything to root out "Jewish sedition" and sent an official letter to the director of "Lenknigtorg" [Leningrad Book Trade Assoc.] with the request that such books be neither accepted by nor sold in the shops of "Staraya Kniga". His actions reek from afar with anti-semitism. He is ready to forbid Soviet Jews to study their language, history, and literature, and to celebrate their religious holidays. He appended the poems of Byalik, the great Jewish poet and a classic of Jewish literature as material evidence, i.e. instruments in the commission of crimes.

What purpose will such an investigation serve? What good will it do the Soviet State or for that matter anyone?

Having exercised the power bestowed on him, Major Kulikov did everything to denigrate and humiliate the human and national dignity of dozens of Soviet Jews.

At the beginning of this deposition I already pointed out that my case, in violation of law, was sent for trial to Moldavia. This fact and the methods used by Kulikov and his associates during the preliminary investigation, suggested to me that I was sent to Moldavia on purpose, as the KGB could more conveniently deal with me in Moldavia than in Leningrad for refusing to serve as a witness.

A review of the documents in criminal case 6628 convinced me of this. In such an atmosphere of arbitrary lawlessness on the part of the investigative authorities of the Moldavian KGB I could not count on an objective study of my case by the Moldavia court—under whose jurisdiction it did not come anyway.

As I already mentioned, my appeals to the Procurator General regarding this matter did not reach him. On 28 Apr 1971 I appealed to the Supreme Court of the USSR with a petition in which I again asked that my case be tried in Leningrad. However, the administrative personnel in charge of the cell in which I was confined during the inquest refused to forward my petition and returned it without any explanation.

After familiarizing himself with criminal case 6628, Bordyuzha, a member of the Supreme Court of the Moldavian SSR, began reviewing my case, which obviously did not come under the jurisdiction of the Moldavian court. My challenge to the Court at the beginning of the trial, and my appeal to transfer my case to Leningrad, were refused by the Court.

Under these circumstances I was obliged to decline from participating in the work of the Court, and the court examination proceeded without my participation.

As I anticipated, the trial was a direct continuation of what was begun at the preliminary hearings, i.e. an undisguised attack on me.

In violation of the law, all incriminating elements ascribed to me were accepted by the court as having been previously established. Everything, which during the course of the trial contradicted the accusations of the presecution, was simply ignored by the court, as though this evidence just didn't exist.

At the trial, witness Galilov very definitely showed that the young woman who gave him the home-made Compendium (Iton-1) didn't say anything about the fact that she transmitted the Compendium at some one else's request. Exactly the same evidence was given at the questioning and at the confrontation during the preliminary hearings. However, in the indictment I was accused of passing anti-Soviet literature to Galilov. The investigation needed no proofs. Neither did the court.

However this is not the only thing that arouses indignation. Even more so is the statement in the sentence indicating that evidence supplied by witness Galilov supports the prosecution's contention that I engaged in disseminating "anti-Soviet literature". During the course of the trial the defense demonstrated conclusively that the identification of the sports bag containing the literature was conducted contrary to established legal procedure. In violation of this procedure bags of different color were submitted for identification (dissimilar objects). Of the three witnesses who were shown the bag for identification, one, Erastov, did not recognize it at all, another one, Mikhaylov, recognized only the color. Despite this fact, the sentence affirmed that this bag belonged to me, and referred to the evidence given by Erastov and Mikhaylov.

The Court in its sentence following the indictment repeated, without any proof, that I had manufactured, reproduced, and disseminated a large amount of anti-Soviet literature—though not a single piece of evidence was submitted during the trial, or the preliminary investigation, to support this contention.

Certain incidents were included in the indictment only on the strength of the evidence given by witness Mogilever, who was sentenced earlier in another case,

120

and then [these incidents were] automatically included in the sentence, though
evidence given by one witness, and completely unsubstantiated, is definitely insufficient to establish anyone's culpability.

Such action is all the more improper in view of the fact that some of the evidence given by Mogilever at the trial did not agree with evidence given at the
preliminary hearings.

Unfortunately, I cannot in this deposition argue at greater length in favor of
my complaint regarding the unfairness of the sentence. And for the following
reason (and another blatant violation of the law) which states: "A copy of the
sentence should be handed the accused or the acquitted not later than three days
after its announcement". I was given a copy of the sentence for thirty minutes
only, and only on the ninth day following the completion of the trial. I was not
given a copy of the sentence while in solitary confinement in Kishinev during
the investigation, nor at the corrective-labor colony where I am now.

Immediately following the end of the trial, right there in the court-room, a representative of the KGB took away from me (as from the others who had been
sentenced) my copy of the indictment. Apparently the authors of the sentence
and the indictment aren't too comfortable about their work, and are "shy" about
handing copies of these documents to the accused, as required by the law. But
not too "shy" to break the law once again, the law which they are called upon
to defend.

GILEL SHUR,
Jerusalem, Beit-Giora, 33 Rabinovich St.

THE CASE OF YURI GALANSKOV

TO THE INTERNATIONAL RED CROSS AND UN HUMAN RIGHTS COMMITTEE

AN APPEAL

[By Yuri Galanskov]

On January 19, 1967 I was arrested. The sixth year of my imprisonment has
now begun.

I am ill and am suffering from duodenal ulceration.

I am able to eat only a fraction of the food that is being given to me in the
camp and I am, therefore, daily exposed to malnutrition. At the same time, due
to the rules of strict regime imprisonment, I am virtually deprived of any possibility to receive the food I need from my parents and relatives.

Suffering from nightly excruciating pains. I am never able to get enough sleep.
I have been denied sufficient food and sleep for more than five years now. At
the same time I was obliged to work 8 hours a day.

Every day for me was a torture, a continuous struggle with my illness and
pains. For five full years I maintained this struggle for my health and life.

For five years I remained silent. Not for a moment during these five years have
I lost faith that the competent judicial and state authorities will finally take
a realistic view of the conditions as they have come to be. Now the sixth year
of tortures has begun.

My health is continuously deteriorating. As a result of many years of malnutrition, lack of sleep, and excessive nervous strain the progress of my ulcerous afflic-
tion has become aggravated by hepatic lesion, intestinal and heart diseases, and
so on.

Five years I was tormented in prisons. I endured this in silence.

During the remaining two years I am to be gradually exterminated and I can no longer keep quiet, for not only my health but my very life is now endangered.

In addressing this statement to the International Red Cross and the Human Rights Committee I would like through these international organisations to address my request to the international community to draw the attention of the pertinent state and legal authorities in the USSR to the insufferableness of my position.

> YURI GALANSKOV, *Mordovian ASSR,*
> *Zubovo-Polyanskiy rayon,*
> *Poselok Ozerniy,*
> *Uchrezhdeniye ZhH 385/17–a.*

February, 1972.

AN UNHEEDED APPEAL

Only now—three months after the tragic death of Yuri Galanskov—a hardly legible photocopy of his hand-written appeal to the International Red Cross and the UN Human Rights Committee has reached us and is being printed [above]. The letter requires no comment. The reader himself will assess the importance of this terrifying human document, this outcry for help, in which Yuri Galanskov, who always stood up in the defense of others, for the first time asked for assistance to himself.

We draw the attention of the readers to the fact that this letter was written in February 1972, that is nine months before Galanskov's death. And we ask ourselves, why is it that this document had not appeared in the press until now? Why is it that the world has not learned about its existence before, when there was still time to save the dying man?

The Soviet authorities, of course, do not permit such letters to go through. We know that they are directly responsible for Galanskov's demise, and there is nothing new in the fact that they've done their best to prevent this letter from being published. But Galanskov's friends, of course, did all they could to make it available to the free press. And now, after his death, they have sent a copy of it to the West.

We are under the impression, that the original has in its time reached a journalist abroad, but failed to "arouse his interest". In the best case, he had sent it to the addressee, but chances are that he may have simply kept it in his files. It is also possible that he had tried to use it, but the matter was not found sufficiently newsworthy by the editors. However the case may be, those who knew of the existence of this appeal and concealed it from the public will have to face the judgement of their conscience, for they have become willing accomplices of a most hideous crime.

The deceased can no longer be helped. He cannot be brought back to life. But should this document—belatedly as it is—be made universally known and cause the world community to raise its voice in the defense of those whose lives are still threatened in Soviet prisons, concentration camps, and psychiatric institutions, then a worthy tribute would be paid to the man who never tired to fight for the rights of others, and was always ready to help his neighbors.

Possev, No. 3, March 1973.

GRIGORIY BERMAN

Grigoriy Berman of the city of Odessa was sentenced to three years for refusing to serve in the ranks of the Soviet Army.

Grigoriy Rafailovich Berman, born in 1946, graduated from the Beltskyi Pedagogical Institute, Ukrainian SSR, having majored in Russian language and literature. After graduation he worked as instructor in the Okirosh village, Anayevskoy region, Moldavian SSR. A year later, Berman became director of the school where he began teaching. In April of 1972 Berman filed an application to emigrate to Israel. Before applying for permission to emigrate, Berman left his job and requested a transfer of his draft registration from the Novo-Anayevskoy Region. Moldavia SSR to Kiev. When he returned to Kiev to appear before his draft board, he was told that since he had applied for emigration, he had no need to report to the military registration board.

In submitting his documents for emigration, Grigoriy Berman joined the struggle for free emigration of all Jews from the USSR to Israel. In company with other activists of the city of Odessa. Berman signed telegrams and petitions originated by international organizations, pleading for the rights of Jews to emigrate to the land of Israel. One month after applying for emigration, an agent of the Odessa KGB (Krasnov) summoned Berman. He was accused of anti-soviet activity and the dissemination of Zionist propaganda. He flatly refused to give any written or oral testimony and rejected the accusations against him as unfounded.

At the end of the interrogation, after many threats, Krasnov informed Berman that he could not go to Israel since he was going to be drafted.

Two days later a lieutenant Moshinskyi visited Berman, presenting a draft notice from the Novo-Anayevskoy Region. Berman refused to accept the notice and explained that he had already transferred his military registration from the Novo- Anayevskoy Region. Then Lt. Moshinskiy ordered Berman to accompany him to the military commissariat of the Kiev Region in Odessa, under the pretense of clarifying the matter.

At the military commisariat the commissar, Dybrovetskii, (who a month earlier had refused to register Berman), at this time ordered Berman to be drafted into the army. Berman refused to sign for the induction notice. The next day, Lt. Moshinskiy again visited Berman and forced him to accompany him to the military medical commission.

The military medical commission drafted Berman for a year's service with the infantry. Berman protested against being suddenly drafted without consultation of his prior records, which had shown him disqualified for reasons of health. The doctors who had earlier examined Berman and exempted him for reasons of health now consider his previous medical record, and informed him that he must immediately begin his tour of military service.

Berman informed the authorities in writing that he refused to serve the Soviet army, since he considered himself an Israeli citizen, and he felt that the USSR was an adversary of Israel.

On Nov. 11, 1972 Berman was arrested, tried and sentenced to 3 years imprisonment. At present Berman is confined to a labor camp at Berdyansk, Zaporozsky Region, Ukrainian SSR.

HADERA, *December 21, 1972.*

ADDITIONAL STATEMENTS BY FORMER SOVIET CITIZENS NOW IN ISRAEL

I, a former Colonel-Engineer in the Soviet Army, who had given twenty-five years of my life to the army, who had fought German fascism, who had been wounded six times in battle and received two contusions, losing my right arm as far as the shoulder and the fingers of my left hand, whose both legs had been broken, etc., was under treatment in a hospital until 1948.

On 5 Feb. 1948 I was arrested and accused of being a member of a counter-revolutionary military organization, whose aim was to overthrow the Soviet government through an armed uprising, and of other crimes punishable by death. At several so-called cross-examinations, I was beaten and subjected to tortures, which Tolstoy, Dostoyevsky, Mirabeau and Hugo all together could hardly describe. On 15 May 1948, by a decree of a special session of the Ministry of State Security of the U.S.S.R.. I was sentenced to 25 years in a special regime labor camp with the disenfranchisement of rights for 5 years and banishment for 5 years after the completion of my sentence.

On 29 June 1959 I was rehabilitated and freed.

At present I am residing in the State of Israel, in the town of Hadera, Shikun PER 5%4 [sic., 554]. I receive no pension from the Soviet government and live on a pension accorded me by the State of Israel for which I had never fought.

The above was set forth by me, in witness whereof is my signature below.

S. YA. KRAPIVSKIY.

TEL AVIV.

Kokhnover, Iosif, born 1896, at present residing in Tel-Aviv, Derech Ashalom, No. 98/35, Israel, states:

THE LIFE OF THE PRISONERS IS IN DANGER!

In the West, people have become accustomed to infringements on human rights and the humiliation of people in the Soviet Union. This has prompted me to share my recollections of life in labor camps, where I had spent so many, many years.

I began my life in a labor camp on the Kolyma, in 1936, and ended it in famous Tayshetlag in Eastern Siberia. "Ozerlag" was also there, and its name is deciphered as follows: Special Closed Regime Camp [*Osobyy zakrytyy rrzhimnyy lager*']. This camp had a variety of "socially-related" prisoners: dangerous thieves, and other criminals.

There were also those listed under the term, "enemies of the people", who had not committed any crimes. The authorities simply thought that these people were potentially dangerous to the totalitarian regime.

As "enemies of the people" there were also some very, very old men, former priests and rabbis, and adherents of other faiths (evangelists and others); scientists, men of letters, and members of the Soviet intelligentsia. There were also a few Soviet government and communist party men, who had become suspect. The latter tried to show their complete, 100% loyalty to the regime and emphasized this with the following statements: "I was sentenced by mistake, and soon will be released, but 'you' ('you' meaning you all) have been justly sentenced, and 'you' are an opposer". Nevertheless they—like the "enemies of the people"—also died of hunger and backbreaking labor.

Correspondence with relatives at best was allowed twice a year. The few parcels received fell into the hands of the criminals, but frequently the owner of a parcel would himself give away most of it, just to get out of work for a day or so.

At the camp the work day was 12 hours or longer, and the 5–6 kilometers to the place of work was made on foot under the heaviest of escorts. Prisoners were entitled to 3 days off a month, but did not always get them. It was worst of all in autumn, when prisoners had to work all day long under a driving rain. The more privileged were the "socially-related". They were better fed and had many privileges. The authorities at the camp were more or less afraid of them.

Much has been written about Soviet labor camps, so I will limit myself to a brief outline of the pertinent factors of life in a labor camp.

The small amount of food consists of 700 grams of badly baked black bread, 13–18 grams of sugar, 17 grams of vegetable oil, 40–45 grams of cereal (mostly oats or barley), a very small amount of potatoes, several grams of onions, the same amount of mix flour, and 100–125 grams of fish or meat—these are the rations of the prisoner. Fish and meat is of the poorest quality, but often there is neither fish nor meat, and nothing in their place. It should be added that 700 grams of bread is the portion of a prisoner fulfilling his daily norm. Those who work extra well receive an additional amount, called the "premium dish". The "premium dish" is based on a complicated arithmetic formula: one-one. one-two, two-two, and the rarely received three-three. The rations are given out for each day on the basis of the work performed the previous day.

The labor camp is a place where gangsters walk around with large knives (made from broken saws, pieces of steel or iron). Situations often arise when camp authorities are afraid to enter a zone inhabited by prisoners.

The place—this is where the heads of brigade leaders roll at the hands of those who carry out the camp's administrative functions (those who hand out the work, superintendents, brigade leaders, and so-called cultural-educational officers). These fights result in a large number of killed—often more than ten. Individual killings occur constantly.

The place—this is where the heads of brigade leaders roll at the hands of camp workers, and where the new brigade leader from among the criminals has the right to humiliate the men in his brigade in every way possible: beat them with a stick, repeating meanwhile: "I am like Stalin to you, and it is useless to complain against me."

At the camp they play cards not only for your jacket, but for your very head. No matter who loses, he'll pay at your expense. To "over-play", i.e. to lose and not pay—is worse than death for a prisoner. He lives in constant fear of death.

The camp is a place where in some enclosures a thief or gangster with a full belly can come up to a woman who has struck his fancy and demand that she have relations with him right there on the spot, and if she does not satisfy his demands immediately, he begins beating her up, repeating all the while: "What did you come here for, to drink my blood!"

Camp authorities can organize transfers (transfers to neighboring camps) and pack off newly arrived political prisoners together with criminals just to relieve the "greenhorn" of his expensive fur coat or new suit. These recidivists who deprive the prisoners of their belongings pass them on to the camp superiors for several loaves of bread, some sugar, low-grade tobacco, or fish.

The medical service has the right to free a sick prisoner with a very high fever from work, but at the same time must not exceed the number of persons that may be relieved of work for the day as established by the camp administration. As a result, those suffering from high blood pressure, heart disease or other diseases, are frequently brought into the dispensary already dead, having dropped dead on the job.

A camp superintendent may not set free a prisoner who has completed his court appointed term despite the fact that the prisoner's prison form indicates the exact date of the end of the sentence. Release from camp must come from above. Until such a release statement comes, the prisoner who has completed his term is sent out to work together with the other prisoners. This can continue for many long months and even years.

At the camp a young kid of an overseer may order a prisoner to undress and leave him in his undershirt and underpants for a whole night in winter in a cold cell, and always find an excuse for this. This is often done to make fun of a prisoner and to demonstrate the overseer's power over the miserable creature, who is totally deprived of any rights. Early in the morning the "culprit" is let out of his cell and sent out to work. The prisoner, who has shivered the whole night long in his cell, grabs his ration of bread, eats his morning soup (a thin gruel), in which "one grain chases another with a stick", and runs to join his brigade. The barracks must be left on the double, as the last one out gets the overseer's curses and oaths. Only those relieved of work by the medical service may stay in the barracks.

Alimentary dystrophy, scurvy and even pellagra are prevalent at the camp. The prisoner suffering from dystrophy reaches a state of complete physical and psychic exhaustion. A sort of dotage comes upon him. And it is the rare person who manages to stay alive. A person in such a state of emaciation can devour at one sitting two or more kilograms of bread and an enormous amount of buckwheat porridge. Such a person then walks around with an enormous belly, but in his other, rear part there is nothing.

The pain killers used at the camp are opium, morphine, pantopon [?] and others—but the doctors, afraid for their lives, are forced to give these to the drug addicts among the criminals.

This outline should be sufficient to increase our concern for the lives of the Jewish prisoners, who are in camps on trumped up charges.

IOSIF KOKHNOVER.

FORM "A"—THIS MAY NOT SERVE AS A RESIDENCE PERMIT; NOT RENEWABLE UPON LOSS

USSR
Ministry of Justice
- -
p/ya 120
13 May 1955
5–I–AA

REPORT NO. 0043364

Given to citizen Kokhnover, Iosif Abramovich.
Date of birth—1896, place of birth—Gomel.
Citizenship: USSR   Nationality: Jewish.
Sentenced by: Special ? Court [Illegible].
            Ministry of Internal Affairs of the Khabarovskiy Kray.
            28 Nov 1946, Article 58—[illegible] Ukrainian SSR.

To the deprivation of freedom for 8 years, and disfranchisement of rights for 5 yrs.

Having in the past been sentenced for [illegible] in 1932, in 1935, in 1936, in 1937.

For having served his sentence in places of confinement until 13 May 1955 and having completed his term is released [?].

Freed on 13 May 1955 and going to his selected place of residence: UMVD, Smolenskaya oblast.

- - - - - - - - - - - - - - - - - - - -
[Signature]
Head of Camp (ITK).

- - - - - - - - - - - - - - - - - - - -
[Signature]
Head of Division.

TEL AVIV., *January 1, 1973.*

Shepshelovich, Mikhail, born 1943, student. Sentenced 27 May 1971 in Riga to 2 years, in accordance with Article 70 of the Criminal Code. Served his sentence in Pot'ma.

On 4 Aug 1970 my place was raided: they were looking for literature—Samizdat materials and material on Israel. They found some film containing excerpts from the book "Exodus", and this was added to the case against me and used in the accusation. After that I was called for questioning at which I was to give an account of the publication of "Samizdat". But I said that I knew nothing. On 15 Oct 1970 I was arrested and placed in solitary confinement at the KGB.

It should be noted that there was absolutely no defense present at the preliminary hearings: the accused is even refused access to the code of laws used in the preliminary investigation. Thus, a person who had not been acquainted with the law prior to his arrest is unable to defend himself.

The trial took place on 24–27 May 1971. By this time the Jewish trials gained widespread notoriety in the free world and the authorities, afraid of adverse publicity and further leaks on what was taking place, conducted the trials with great haste: the trial took *two and a half days instead of ten days*. Departure from established procedure consisted above all in continuously interrupting the accused and preventing them from expressing themselves. The accused were: A. Shpil'berg (sentenced to 3 years), R. Aleksandrovich (1 year), B. Maftser (1 year), and myself (2 years). I believe that we received such short terms only because of the widespread publicity and support given our trial in the free world. Without this support all of us would have been sentenced to 4 to 7 years. Initially, Article 65, which carries sentences ranging from 10 years to the death penalty, was to be applied in sentencing us. The government, noting the publicity that the trials were accorded in the free world and desirous of maintaining an appearance of judicial propriety, substituted Article 65 of the Criminal Code by Article 70, which provides sentences ranging from 6 months to 7 years. Even in terms of this article the sentences imposed were *mild*. The effect of public opinion in the free world on the course of our trials and on the sentences imposed must be stressed once again, and compared with the sentence meted out at the first Leningrad trial of December 1970, whose severity, in my opinion, was due to the insufficient attention and support the trial received in the West before the sentence were passed. The protest by the West after the sentences were passed helped prevent the imposition of death sentences, but did not essentially reduce the severity of the sentencing since the article under which the sentences were passed and the terms imposed remained practically the same.

I served my sentence in Pot'ma (formerly Dubrovlag). The network of establishments in Pot'ma is known as "Institution ZhKh 385". The ZhKh Institution includes camps for both political prisoners and criminals, and men as well as women. The political prisoner camps included zones 19, 17, and 3, and were strict regime zones. Zone 3 also included a camp for women political prisoners. The above mentioned zones had approximately 2000 prisoners. The complex of institutions for political prisoners also included the Vladimirskaya prison, where prisoners particularly distasteful to the authorities are held.

Conditions of confinement

The factor which determines the nature of confinement in political labor camps at present is that their aims and objectives are still the same: as before, confinement in political labor camps is designed not only to remove a person from society, but to force people to renounce their views and convictions, give up all participation in public affairs. Thus the objective of a labor camp remains unchanged; what has changed are the means for achieving the objective; for at present the quick physical annihilation of political prisoners is no longer possible in the Soviet Union, so that annihilation is achieved through a slow process of destruction over a period of many years.

Continuous malnutrition, and the constant nervous tension to which the prisoner is subjected in his environment, is the essence of this method. As the years go by, this inevitably leads to physical and psychic disabilities. The physical illness of a prisoner means that the first state of his subjugation has been attained. The prisoner's medical treatment depends very much on his attitude toward his political views. A person who does not renounce his political convictions receives practically no medical aid. In a labor camp such people are condemned to slow deterioration and death. The best example of how this method works is the death of Yuri Galanskov. He held out for 6 of the 7 years of his sentence (he was forced to work when his physical conditions was extremely bad—until the very end!)

Jewish prisoners who do not renounce their convictions, who do not repudiate their desire to leave for Israel, are in a similar position. Some of these prisoners are seriously ill. *Actually they will suffer the same fate as Galanskov, if no special interference is made on their behalf!* The attention of the authorities is directed particularly toward the Jewish prisoners, for they not only don't renounce their political convictions, but, on the contrary, protest actively.

The best of the political prisoners of other nationalities understand and respect the struggle of the Jewish prisoners for their national liberation.

MIKHAIL SHEPSHELOVICH.

Taken down by G. Elina.

___

To: The Senate of the United States of America.
From: Roza Kogan, 28 Sereni Street, Givataim, Israel.

REQUEST

My husband, Idel' (Yehuda) Kogan, a citizen of Israel, born in Poland in 1922. Was arrested on 7 June 1963 in Kiev during a tourist trip to the U.S.S.R., for which he received a visa-permit from the Soviet Embassy in Israel.

He was arrested and sentenced to 10 years of prison, accused of deserting from the Soviet army. During the war (World War II) my husband was in the Kovel ghetto, then with the partisans, then served 6 months in the Soviet army until July 1945, and after that left for Israel.

Now my husband has now served 9 years and six months! We are both ill; ten of the best years of our lives have been snatched away from us! I beg your intercession in obtaining his release in advance of the six remaining months of his sentence, and thereby help reduce the additional and undeserved suffering of a family!

(My husband's address is: Moscow, UChR No. 5110/1, Zh. U. Idel' Kogan)

Respectfully and gratefully,

· ROZA KOGAN.

DECEMBER 22, 1972.

Mrs. Golda Meir, [Israeli] Consul, arrived in Moscow on the day of Zhdanov's death; I was then working as a translator in one of the offices of the MVD (Ministry of Internal Affairs) in Odessa. On the day of her arrival I was sent to the Metropol Hotel in Moscow to participate in a reception for the guests in the guise of a waiter; I was instructed to eavesdrop on everything Mrs. Meir was to say in Yiddish. Since the guests were amiably received, I took the liberty of asking her in Yiddish what the country which she represented was like. She replied in Yiddish that it was the first Jewish state in history for Jews throughout the world. After the reception was over, I was sent directly to a prison in Odessa, for someone had eavesdropped on me during the conversation and denounced me to the KGB, saying I was a Zionist. I was arrested, served a great deal of time in prison, then released but thrown out of my job, victimized for more than ten years, finally arrested again in 1958, thrown into prison, and without any trial sent to the Amurskaya ASSR, and from there to Wrangel Island, where I remained until 1962.

At the camp I made the acquaintance of Rudolf Trushnovich, a former physician, Vasiliy Ivanovich Polyakov, a former member (colonel) of the Vlasov army, a large number of SS and Gestapo Germans, and many Italians, who had long been declared dead, but who are actually still living on Wrangel in the Belopolyar'ye. Among them:[1]

1. Kremer Ernest
2. Mgoler Paul
3. Kristover Otto

___

[1] The list of names of POWs on Wrangel Island requires further clarification, which the subcommittee is trying to obtain. Spellings are in question, first, because the names were written in by hand and some were not legible; and, second, because inaccuracies in spelling inevitably arise when German and Italian names are transliterated from Latin script to Cyrillic script for the camp record, and then transliterated back into Latin script. According to Shifrin, who has discussed the Wrangel Island matter several times with "kozlov," "kozlov" was in a position where he had access to camp records, but only in rare cases was he able to get to know the POWs personally. The listing of Italian names suggests that in the camp records the name was given, together with the rank, the city of residence, and the date of birth. In the case of name number 6, "Milaneso Tradati. 1903." the adjective "Milaneso," meaning "from Milan," was probably used instead of "Milan." Shifrin reported to the subcommittee staff that a representative of an Italian committee which is still seeking information about missing POWs had come to Israel to interview "kozlov," and they had been able to match some of the names of Italian POWs whom "kozlov" had met, or whose names he had seen listed in the camp records, against the list of missing Italian POWs believed to be in the Soviet Union.

4. Ambrozio Verito—55 years old—Gestapo
5. Zulvazino Cordion—65 years old—died there
6. Milaneso Tradati—1903—
7. Gracianeca Verona—1899—chief of police
8. Toretto Firenze—1901—captain
9. Giovanni [?] Lassa—1905—SS Lieutenant
10. Rasteliano Vivzina—1900—colonel
11. Lecio Vivaus—1910—colonel
12. Pyairetta Piacenza—1900—died
13. Joradello Padova—1903—SS
14. Giovani Bianchi—
15. Luigi Campanella—1901—SS
16. Lucca Brantyi [?]—1905
17. Messina Donato—1914—SS

The camp on Wrangel Island was an experimental camp, where experiments were conducted on living people. The experiments were in the form of injections, diets, oxygen tests on people who were long declared dead but were alive at that time (1962) and were working very hard in the camp. The guards and the administrative staff were former convicts, such as V. N. Rudnikov, A. I. Vasil'kov, a former convict and big-time bandit; Iv. Nik. Ivanov, Nikolay Artemevich Pitanov. The camp also had a military guard for a special camp in which people were trained for spying abroad. That camp was headed by Ivan Ivanovich Shevilov, a veteran MVD trooper. There were also many others, including Italian war prisoners. There was also Raoul Wallenberg, who had been Swedish consul in Budapest during the war and who under the German occupation, aided by money, helped Jews escape from Hungary, through Switzerland, into other countries. When the Russians entered Budapest, Raoul Wallenberg was immediately arrested at the request of the military commandant of the city of Budapest and sent by special train to Moscow. He was then 27 years old, and was a handsome, educated young man.

These are a few of the many facts which I know, having witnessed them personally. Unfortunately I cannot sign my real name [to the statement], as I still have some close relatives in Russia.

"KOZLOV"

A true copy: [A stamp with Hebrew letters]

U.S.S.R. LABOR CAMPS

U.S. SENATE,
SUBCOMMITTEE TO INVESTIGATE THE
ADMINISTRATION OF THE INTERNAL SECURITY ACT
AND OTHER INTERNAL SECURITY LAWS
OF THE COMMITTEE ON THE JUDICIARY,
Washington, D.C.

The subcommittee met, pursuant to notice, at 2:30 p.m., in room 2228, Dirksen Senate Office Building, Senator Edward J. Gurney presiding.

Also present: J. G. Sourwine, chief counsel; Samuel J. Scott, associate counsel; A. L. Tarabochia, chief investigator; David Martin, senior analyst.

AFTERNOON SESSION

Senator GURNEY. The subcommittee will come to order.

This subcommittee is charged with assessing all possible threats to our Nation's internal security . . . and this is a most important duty . . . one which will be fulfilled with propriety . . . with an honest attempt to get at all the facts . . . and with a sense of responsibility to the American people.

The testimony we have heard yesterday and today shows the tenacity of the human spirt . . . the ability of men of faith to survive almost unimaginable ordeals when they believe in freedom, and have a burning desire to tell the world of what they have undergone, so that the world may someday be rid of this cancer of communism.

More important yet, the testimony reveals how one group of human beings is subjected to almost complete degradation by a totalitarian form of government. It shows how Soviet Jewry . . . those articulate people who believe in the freedom and dignity of mankind . . . have been subjected to gross abuse in an effort to stifle their voices.

This tactic of suppression of a vocal segment of a population is not distant in time and geography . . . it is happening today . . . and it is drawing closer to our Nation.

The same Communist tactics used to repress great groups of people are now being used in Cuba . . . at the doorstep of our Nation.

This story of Communist repression of dissent and brutal imprisonment of dissidents from minority groups must alert the world to the failings of that form of government.

Mr. Shifrin has spent the last 2 days telling that story, and I now ask him to continue to work with this subcommittee, and at an appropriate time to assist in making appropriate recommendations as to what might help to free these prisoners of a political regime so hostile to individual rights, that it is repugnant to the entire free world.

Slavery ended in this Nation and most other civilized countries over a hundred years ago.

Yet, the testimony here in these last 2 days indicates that millions, probably tens of millions, of people in the Soviet Union are slaves to their brutal government. Why? Because they have dared to speak out against the brutal policies of a totalitarian government and proudly proclaim their belief in their God and their faith.

Counsel has some housekeeping details he would like to present for the record at this time.

Mr. SOURWINE. Mr. Chairman, first we have a chronology of Mr. Shifrin's imprisonment in the U.S.S.R. prepared by the staff but checked with Mr. Shifrin as to accuracy. I would like to have the order be that it will go in the record at this point, and Mr. Shifrin will have the right when he corrects the record to make any corrections that he finds that he thinks he wants to make.

Senator GURNEY. It will be so ordered.

[The chronology referred to appears on p. 35 of pt. 1.]

Mr. SOURWINE. We have several lists categorized by prisons of other prisoners met by Mr. Shifrin in some of the various prisons he has been in and this is by no means in any case a comprehensive list, but these are names of people that have been identified and may be of some interest, and I would like to ask that these lists by prison go in at this time with these small paragraphs of identifying materials respective to people's names.

Senator GURNEY. They will be received in evidence and be placed in the record.

[The biographies referred to can be found in chronological order, in the staff summary printed in pt. 1 of the hearing.]

Mr. SOURWINE. Thank you.

Then I have a few questions which I think will fill in possible blanks in the record.

Mr. Shifrin, I do not believe it has been brought out yet in the record, certainly not clearly, that you were by no means an ordinary prisoner; that you were an officer of grade in the Army of the Soviet Union and that you are by way of being a war hero. And I would like to cover this briefly with a few leading questions if the Chair will permit.

You were conscripted in 1941 and immediately assigned to a penal battalion because your father was a class enemy?

Mr. SHIFRIN. No, he was not class enemy. He was arrested without any crime.

Mr. SOURWINE. I understand that.

Mr. SHIFRIN. And they told him that he is enemy of the people. That is big difference.

Mr. SOURWINE. This was their words and not mine.

Mr. SHIFRIN. Yes; I understand you.

Mr. SOURWINE. All right, now, a penal battalion was a battalion that was sent to the front lines?

Mr. SHIFRIN. Yes.

Mr. SOURWINE. The penal battalions were short on weapons?

Mr. SHIFRIN. Yes. It was maybe 1 out of 10 who have rifles.

Mr. SOURWINE. As you told it when the staff interviewed you, you were told: "Your weapons are in the hands of the Nazis; go get them."

Mr. SHIFRIN. Yes, this officer—not officer, some sergeant told to us: "Your rifles in the hands of the Nazis; you must catch them."

Mr. SOURWINE. Thank you. All you had to do was say "Yes." Please forgive me. I am trying to cover time fast.

Mr. SHIFRIN. Yes; you are right.

Mr. SOURWINE. It sounds better when you say it, but it reads just the same either way in the record.

Now, you were wounded?

Mr. SHIFRIN. Twice.

Mr. SOURWINE. Several times?

Mr. SHIFRIN. Twice.

Mr. SOURWINE. Twice?

Mr. SHIFRIN. In 1941 and 1942.

Mr. SOURWINE. Now the first time you were wounded, were you sent back to the penal battalion?

Mr. SHIFRIN. Yes.

Mr. SOURWINE. The second time also you were sent back to the penal battalion?

Mr. SHIFRIN. No, sir.

Mr. SOURWINE. How did you become an officer?

Mr. SHIFRIN. I have seen after the second wound that they want only to kill me, and that is why on the way to central hospital, I changed my identification. I gave another date of birth, I gave another place of birth, and I changed my name from Avraham to Ivrahim. And that is why I came after hospital to regular regiment, and in this regiment, in first battle, when our officer was killed, I became officer; battlefield promotion.

Mr. SOURWINE. You got a battlefield promotion and you eventually became a major, did you not?

Mr. SHIFRIN. Yes: a major in 1943.

Mr. SOURWINE. How serious was your wound?

Mr. SHIFRIN. Both times they said it was serious. In the first, it was my hand——

Mr. BOLDYREFF. In the joint.

Mr. SHIFRIN. And in the second, my legs were full with the iron. In many places I was wounded in the legs.

Mr. SOURWINE. Yes, sir. You were decorated, were you not?

Mr. SHIFRIN. Yes.

Mr. SOURWINE. And you fought through the whole war?

Mr. SHIFRIN. Yes; to the end. I was demobilized after the end.

Mr. SOURWINE. After the war you went to Krasnodar region as an investigator of banditry?

Mr. SHIFRIN. Yes, banditry.

Mr. SOURWINE. You were promoted to chief of the investigative unit?

Mr. SHIFRIN. Yes.

Mr. SOURWINE. You were transported to headquarters of the department to combat banditry in Moscow?

Mr. SHIFRIN. Yes, sir.

Mr. SOURWINE. You took a correspondence course in law?

Mr. SHIFRIN. Yes, sir.

Mr. SOURWINE. You were made chief investigator at Tula?

Mr. SHIFRIN. Yes.

Mr. SOURWINE. You there became chief legal adviser in secret war plant number 535?

Mr. SHIFRIN. Yes; you are right.

Mr. Sourwine. That plant was making automatic guns for fighter aircraft?

Mr. Shifrin. Yes.

Mr. Sourwine. It also made antiaircraft guns for the navy and mine launchers?

Mr. Shifrin. Yes.

Mr. Sourwine. You served there from 1948 to 1952?

Mr. Shifrin. Yes.

Mr. Sourwine. You were then transferred to Moscow to the Ministry of Defense?

Mr. Shifrin. Yes.

Mr. Sourwine. As chief legal adviser in the Contract Division of the Juridical Department?

Mr. Shifrin. Yes.

Mr. Sourwine. You received your law diploma in 1953. You got your law diploma in 1953?

Mr. Shifrin. Yes.

Mr. Sourwine. You are a lawyer?

Mr. Shifrin. Yes.

Mr. Sourwine. I thought that material should be in the record. You were not an ordinary prisoner.

Now, you served in defense plants in the Soviet Union. What can you tell us about Soviet defense plants? Are there many instances where the plants produced both war material and civilian goods?

Mr. Shifrin. You see, it is very interesting that in U.S.S.R. I have seen it myself, that many war plants, they officially listed as plants in another ministry but not in Ministry of Defense. Such cases; in Tula, they have big plant, maybe 40 shops in the plant, and they make weapons and ammunition. But 39 shops make weapons and ammunition, and one shop make samovars. You know, for tea.

Mr. Sourwine. Civilian items?

Mr. Shifrin. Yes. That is why this plant has name "Samovarniy"—Samovar factory—not army plant, and they have money from Ministry of Light Industry.

Mr. Sourwine. Similarly, at Chelyabinsk they had a pipe plant which really made ammunition?

Mr. Shifrin. Right, in Chelyabinsk—barrels for guns.

Mr. Sourwine. In Izhevsk they had a motorcycle plant that made tractor vehicles armed with guns and rifles and motorcycles equipped with machineguns?

Mr. Shifrin. Yes.

Mr. Sourwine. You have personal knowledge of these things because in some of the cases you drew the contracts; didn't you?

Mr. Shifrin. Yes, I drew contracts and also I have seen plants.

Mr. Sourwine. Is similar camouflage used with respect to atomic plants in the Soviet Union?

Mr. Shifrin. Yes, they have special committee of atomic energy, and under command of this committee they have Ministry of—how do you say it? Medium Machinery.

And this Medium Machinery Ministry, gave money to them. And that is why in U.S.S.R. you can see millions which go in budget to machinery but in reality it goes to weapons plants.

Mr. SOURWINE. Now, your first-hand knowledge of those matters was before you went to Siberia. Now, do you know whether the situation has changed since then?

Mr. SHIFRIN. No; this situation didn't change. Many of my friends, which work with me in the days before my arrest, they work now in the same ministry, and I have seen them in 1965, 1969, 1970, and they told me that the situation didn't change.

Mr. SOURWINE. Thank you.

Now I want to go to another matter. You have discussed the anti-Jewish terror, the Doctors' Plot. Now, is it correct that your boss was arrested before you were at the time you were arrested in 1953?

Mr. SHIFRIN. No; he was not arrested. KGB secret service, came to arrest him in Ministry of Defense and said to him—his secretary explained to me later—that he lost secret paper and when he have seen that he would be arrested by these killers, he sprung from the window from this big building, six stories high to the courtyard, and committed suicide.

Mr. SOURWINE. That was 2 days before you were arrested?

Mr. SHIFRIN. Yes; 2, 3 days before my arrest.

Mr. SOURWINE. Now, another matter. While you were in Lubyanka you met the screen writer Makliarsky?

Mr. SHIFRIN. Yes; he was twice winner of Stalin prize.

Mr. SOURWINE. He had specialized in scripts glorifying the KGB?

Mr. SHIFRIN. Yes; he wrote big scenarios and they made big films of the work of KGB—and then they arrested him.

Mr. SOURWINE. But even though he was almost a hero of the Soviet Union and the favorite of Stalin, he was put in jail because he wrote one pro-Zionist poem?

Mr. SHIFRIN. Yes; this was in 1922, or 1921, when he was ordinary journalist in Odessa he wrote in some newspaper Zionist poetry, little poetry.

Mr. SOURWINE. And years later they found it?

Mr. SHIFRIN. And they found it in 1949 or 1950.

Mr. SOURWINE. More than 20 years later?

Mr. SHIFRIN. Yes. In 1950, and they arrested him only for this crime. Then they released him in 1954. He was in freedom after. I got from him a letter.

Mr. SOURWINE. Now, at the time of your move from Butyrskaya, do you remember telling us they moved you in an ice cream van?

Mr. SHIFRIN. Oh, yes.

Mr. SOURWINE. Tell us about that.

Mr. SHIFRIN. They don't want to show to foreigners these special cars for prisoners. They have special built cars—vans for prisoners. And that is why on the wall of these vans you can see "Bread," "Butter," "Meat." And we always make jokes that we are good meat—fresh meat. And also I was once in the car with words "Ice Cream" and with the picture of a big bear eating ice cream.

Senator GURNEY. This is so the people wouldn't know that prisoners are being transported?

Mr. SHIFRIN. Yes; these cars go in the street, and people think that it is ice cream.

this forest and built highway, and then near this highway they built railway. And they told me that now in my time—in 1954—it is here like resort. But I here heard this from living corpses. In 1945, 1946, 1947, 1948 it—they told me—was days when people died in hundreds each day from starvation. They showed me kilometers of cemeteries on the side, and then, I told you, I have seen these cemeteries which go near the railway. They explained to me that along this railway was the Kwantung Army and hundreds of thousands of other POW's. And it was truth. I don't know how many died there—maybe million and maybe more because it is a 600 kilometers railway and highway, and on both sides cemeteries without intervals.

When I came I met not millions of POW's; I met only thousands. But we know that in Kwantung Army was million soldiers.

In 1956 when they released these prisoners, I have seen how they put them in the trains near our concentration camp. They brought them from all along the railway; from all the concentration camps, and I have seen that it was only some 10,000 people: Germans, French, Spanish, Japanese,

Now, try to understand how many died here.

I have seen only maybe hundreds of these German officers, and they told me that most of these prisoners of war died there. After 1956 KGB released other foreigners from Tayshet, it was citizens from Czechoslovakia, Poland, Iran, and other countries.

It was also Belgian officers. Was maybe 12 to 15 of these officers. I don't know why they didn't release them in 1956. I don't know. They were there to 1962. At the end of 1962 they released them.

When Queen of Belgians came to U.S.S.R.. she asked to see these officers and in big hurry came, KGB, to our concentration camp. The Belgians was in concentration camp No. 7 in Potma because in these days we was not in Tayshet; we was in Potma.

I told you yesterday they brought us from Tayshet to Potma in 1960, and these Belgians came together with us. Only in 1962 KGB sent them home.

Also in 1963 once I have met with group of criminals which came to our concentration camp, No. 7, and when I asked them in which place they were, they told me we were in Island of Wrangel. I asked, "Island of Wrangel? KGB has concentration camps there?" They answered me, "Yes; there is three concentration camps for prisoners of war and there sits only big officers from Germany, Italy, France, and Spain."

I didn't believe them, but now in Israel I met with one man in 1971—we have his letter; I would show his letter—and he explained to me, this man, that he was also in Island of Wrangel in 1962 and he have seen there three concentration camps with thousands of prisoners of war, and he explained to me that they have in one concentration camp atomic reactor, and they make experiments on the live people with radiation. In another concentration camp, they have experiments with physicians on the people and in third they have submarines and they have experiments with live people under water. And it is big secret, and he was there in the group of prisoners which gave to the prisoners food; he was not inside secret camps. He have heard from other prisoners about this work, and he sent to you letter and I gave to you this letter in which he wrote real names of these prisoners in Wrangel.

Also he told about two big people which he met on Wrangel. One of them, Alexander Trushnovich, head of anti-Communist Russian organization, NTS; he was kidnaped in 1953 from West Berlin. And another man which he have seen there and all the world don't know nothing about his fate; this man is Raoul Wallenberg, diplomat of Sweden, consul in Budapest, who save many thousands of Hungarian Jews from Nazis. They kidnap him in 1945, this man, and they always answer to free world that they don't know nothing about this man.

Senator GURNEY. Do we have the letter?

Mr. SHIFRIN. Yes; you have letter.

Senator GURNEY. Proceed.

Mr. SHIFRIN. No; I think that is all I can tell about prisoners of war.

Senator GURNEY. In summary, then, what you have said was that the Russians kept their prisoners—and they probably captured hundreds of thousands during the course of the war—for a period of 10 to 15 years after the war and used them for slave labor all during that time?

Mr. SHIFRIN. Yes; they also was in slave labor.

Senator GURNEY. And probably a majority of them died in prison camps?

Mr. SHIFRIN. Yes; I am sure a majority.

Senator GURNEY. And then the other significant point was that in this prison camp in Island of Wrangel there was——

Mr. SHIFRIN. Italian, French, Spanish, and German.

Senator GURNEY. And they used prisoners for medical experiments, which were atomic medical experiments, I suppose, to see what the effect of radiation would be upon the human body?

Mr. SHIFRIN. Yes.

Senator GURNEY. Do you have any other points that you want to cover, Mr. Shifrin, not on prisoners of war, but any other points?

Mr. SHIFRIN. Yes; I wanted very much to tell you something about this Jewish process in Leningrad, this Jewish trial in Leningrad. When they arrest these 12 people and 1 girl in 1970, crime of these people was only one; they want to go to Israel. And all of these 12 have two and three times refusal from Soviet Government when they gave documents and ask permission to go to Israel. Then these people decided to steal Russian plane, not hijack, but steal plane and to go to Sweden from Leningrad. It was their goal, and they arrest them before they committed this crime. They arrest them on land, not in the plane. They arrest them before they came to this plane, and they gave to these people death sentence, to two of them, and two others 15 and 10 years in prison.

Among those people was Silva Zalmanson, a brave Jewish girl, which is now in such situation that we wait maybe her death from day to day because she cannot swallow food. Something is wrong with her throat, and they don't permit the physician to see this girl. And permit me to tell that only some weeks ago we got letter from the prison from another prisoner, Galanskov, we also told to all the world that Galanskov maybe would die; that he is ill. And no one hear our voice. Now Galanskov died some weeks ago. Maybe it will be same with Silva; maybe it will be with her husband, Eduard

Kuznetsov, he is very ill. He cannot eat this food because he has ulcer and he is now in starvation. He cannot eat this rotten food.

And we have letters from their relatives about all this. I must tell you that these people showed the way to others—these people were so brave but they now are in desperation. And I ask you very much to make something—I tell you because your opinion very great in the world and I tell you about this terror.

I must tell you about them. These people in such situation—permit me to explain to you. I also was in this concentration camp No. 10 and I know that in reality it is prison. That is strict concentration camp in which now sit Eduard Kuznetsov. I was there 1 year (pointing to the map). Now here in the cell are 20 people. In this concrete barracks thin walls. Inside concrete they put railways——

Mr. BOLDYREFF. No, rails.

Mr. SHIFRIN. Rails, excuse me. Rails. And that is why in summer you cannot breath there. It is like in the oven in the cell. In the winter inside this cell on the wall where window it's front, 5 or 7 centimeters and sometimes 10 centimeters of frost inside the cell on the wall. On the ceiling always drops of water—because we were alive.

In each cell they have one, sometimes two, people with tuberculosis. In our cell was prisoner Baranov; he spit with the blood always.

Here you see on the map is women prison. Here I have seen once in winter of 1960 when chief of the prison, Buryak—his second name, Buryak—nickname "Hitler"—made something impossible. Once I was here preparing wood for the stoves in the courtyard of prison, and I have seen when Buryak and soldiers—overseers came to this women's prison in the Sunday and they shout to these women, go to wash——

Mr. BOLDYREFF. The shower.

Mr. SHIFRIN. To showers, to wash. And it was on Sunday, It was there nuns from convent, and they ask permit to pray on Sunday. But Buryak and soldiers tore from them clothes and pulled them on their backs through snow to shower.

In this prison I have seen each month that one, two prisoners go mad. My friends in desperation, in starvation now—and I must tell you about all this—there is the other map.

Mr. BOLDYREFF. Yes, here.

Mr. SHIFRIN. That is cell in which I was in another, strict concentration camp No. 10 in Potma and in this camp—which is in reality prison—now my friends, they sit here in these cells; that is also concrete barrack. Here it was very little cells. Here you have cell 3 meter by 3 meter. It were here in the cell, three Ukrainians, three from Baltic, and I—Jew—international. Seven people here in cell 3 on 3 meters. You can here lie only on your side. You cannot lie on the back.

Here you see a little table and only 30 inches from a common bunk in which we lie together to the door. And in this place near door two prisoners make work because they permit in this way to other prisoners to lie on the back on the bunk. [See diagram, part 1, page 61.]

In starvation, with hard labor on the brick plant, they are now here 1973. And here in camp No. 10 I have seen not one time but many times, when prisoners open their veins in desperation. They tried to commit suicide. And if you think that guards bring in these cases physicians, you mistaken. They tell: "You opened your own veins yourself. It is not our task." And so only friends try to help these people in such cases.

139

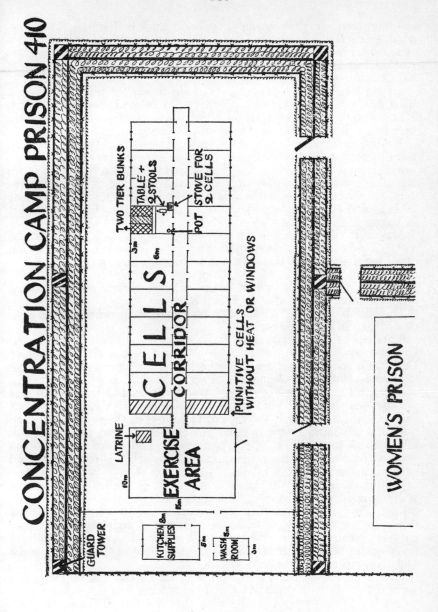

CONCENTRATION CAMP PRISON 410

GUARD TOWER

KITCHEN SUPPLIES — 8m — 5m

WASH ROOM — 5m — 3m

LATRINE

EXERCISE AREA — 60m — 15m

CELLS — 3m — 6m

TWO TIER BUNKS

TABLE + 2 STOOLS

STOVE FOR 2 CELLS

POT

CORRIDOR

PUNITIVE CELLS WITHOUT HEAT OR WINDOWS

WOMEN'S PRISON

I have seen many times when people cut their bellies here. They beat glass from the window and with this glass they cut their body. I remember one prisoner, he was in such desperation he want to commit suicide, but he cannot. He have not power. And he asked me: "Avraham, cut my belly; cut me."

I have seen when people cut part of the meat, yes, part of the meat, flesh, and try to boil it on flame with paper from the books and eat it. I have seen people open veins and put in the pot blood and put their bread—our black bread—and then eat this bread.

Really, they were not in full conscience these prisoners because they were in such desperation: from year to year, from year to year, from year to year, without hope . . . I have seen in this concentration camp No. 10 one simple boy, Nikolai Shcherbakov. He was in such desperation, that it is hard to find words. He lost his parents in the days of War II and he was without parents—how do you say? I would tell it in Russian.

Mr. BOLDYREFF. He was without parents. All his life was on the streets, and then he became thief. And when he was in concentration camp for thieves, 3,000 thieves make a tattoo on their forehead, "Slave of Communism."

I have seen people which make tattoo—rocket on the breast, atomic rocket, with words, "To U.S.S.R."

They explained me, "We want to be killed with rockets but to stop this killing in this country."

This Shcherbakov with this forehead, with this tattoo "Slave of Communism," came to our camp No. 10 and before 22d Congress of Party ask another prisoner to make tattoo on his ears: "Present to 22d Party Congress; Communist Party." And then when we was in courtyard for exercise—courtyard was with barbed wire with dogs outside, with machine guns on towers—he cut with right hand left ear and throw this ear in the face of this chief of the prison, and then with the left hand he try to cut right ear and he was not successful. Blood came to all sides, he cut big vessels, and all of the prisoners was in the blood in this courtyard. But he cut this second ear and throw it in the face of this killer.

In this camp-prison in the same situation prisoners now. Eduard Kuznetsov, Yuriy Fedorov, Murzhenko, Dymshits and hundreds others. They sit now in this concentration camp-prison for second time—in first time I were with them. I cannot understand how they survive, because I do not know how I survived. And that is why I don't understand how it is possible to come second time to this place and live without any hope.

Excuse me for my nerves. But you see that I speak not only with the words; I speak with my heart and I want with this testimony all the world try to understand me because this Nikolai Shcherbakov, this noneducated person, this man which never finished school, man without parents, this boy, when I asked him: "Why, why you make it?" He answered me: "Avraham, when I would come to the freedom and when I would tell to the people that we were in this desperation, they would not believe me. And then I would show them my head without ears. Maybe then they would believe me."

You see what the thought was in this man? He want to prove to the world all of this awful situation. Excuse me—I have my ears.

Senator GURNEY. I understand a man must be totally desperate to undertake that.

Mr. SHIFRIN. Pardon?

Senator GURNEY. I said I can understand how a man can be totally desperate to want to do that.

Mr. SHIFRIN. Thank you very much that you understand. I know that you was in the army. I know that you was in the war. I know that you man which can understand me. That is why I talk so openly.

Senator GURNEY. There is one point on these prisoners of war that we didn't discuss that I think is worthwhile discussing to complete that picture.

When you were in these prisons, these camps, did you ever run across Russian prisoners of war who had been captured by the Allied Armies?

Mr. SHIFRIN. I have seen many thousands of them.

Senator GURNEY. Why were they in Russian prisons?

Mr. SHIFRIN. You see these people became prisoners of war in the hands of Nazi in the days of the war.

Senator GURNEY. Yes.

Mr. SHIFRIN. Because these Russian Communist commanders in this Communist army, they lose army in first days of the war. You remember this. And millions of these soldiers came in the hands of the Nazis. After the war many of these people don't want to return to U.S.S.R. They didn't want to return to U.S.S.R. because they know what await them.

Senator GURNEY. You mean they would rather stay in Germany than go back to Russia?

Mr. SHIFRIN. No; when after the war you released these people from the hands of Nazis, they told you that they don't want to go to U.S.S.R. because they know——

Senator GURNEY. You mean they would rather have stayed in Germany? They would rather stay in Germany than return to Russia?

Mr. SHIFRIN. Yes; excuse me. I cannot speak so well. Ask please, Mr. Boldyreff to translate when you cannot understand me. I want very much that you understand me to the point.

Senator GURNEY. I understand you. Go ahead.

Mr. SHIFRIN. They didn't want to return because they know what is the brutal government they have in U.S.S.R. They know that concentration camps await them. But the U.S.S.R., the Communists, and all the world want to return prisoners of war. It was very big mistake because you returned—and England and France returned—they returned these people. You brought them under machineguns to the border of U.S.S.R., and when Communists catch them, they immediately brought them to concentration camps. They explained to me, these people, that when KGB brought them to concentration camp, it was big announcement on the gates, "Motherland Awaits You." Such hypocrisy words. And when they came inside gates in another side of these gates was words, "Stay, I Would Shoot Without Warning." It was concentration camp. From these concentration camps, after investigation—they tried to show that KGB make investigation why these soldiers were caught. What was the investigation? I have heard it from many people. They asked: "Why you became prisoner of Nazi?" "I was wounded; I was in the battlefield with bullets in my legs." "We don't believe you. Why you didn't shoot this Nazi when they catch you?" "I have not gun."

"But you must catch them with your teeth."

That was answer of KGB. And once my friend told me such story that he was in so desperation in these investigations that he make a little pistol from the bread. He was officer. He made it wonderful. And when he made pistol he brought pistol to investigation room. And when investigator came to him with the fists again, he took out this pistol and told him, "Stand on the knees!" This investigator immediately stand on his knees, this KGB officer immediately stand on knees. And prisoner told him: "Kiss my feet!" And he kissed. And then this prisoner told him, "Why you don't catch me with your teeth?" [Laughter.]

They sent all of these people for 25 years to the prisons. It was— I don't know how many hundreds and hundreds and thousands of such people.

Senator GURNEY. Well, you saw them 10 years or more after the end of the war, after they had been returned, isn't that correct?

Mr. SHIFRIN. Oh, yes. They were in there 1956, 1958, and 1960. They were there in concentration camps many years, some of them 25 years.

Senator GURNEY. So these Russian soldiers——

Mr. SHIFRIN. Russian soldiers, decorated soldiers.

Senator GURNEY. These soldiers were slaves for 10, 15, 20, and 25 years after they were returned?

Mr. SHIFRIN. Yes; in this way they gave to them "salary" for this war.

Senator GURNEY. Do you have anything else you want to add?

Mr. SHIFRIN. Yes. I did not tell you about this new slavery tax for Jews when they want to go from this country to Israel. In my days, when I came from U.S.S.R. to Israel, I paid to government tax 40 rubles—half of month salary. When I came to Israel they made tax after some months in 1970 from 40 rubles in 1 day to 1,000 rubles. Now what is a thousand rubles? In the U.S.A. you have here salary of $1,000 in the month, sometimes $2,000 in the month. Your people can have such a salary. In U.S.S.R., salary of the worker is 100 rubles in the month. Big engineer or good physician sometimes have 120 or 150 rubles in the month. That is why 1,000 rubles, that is your year's salary without eating, without dress, without nothing. In 1971 tax was 1,000 rubles. And then from 1972 this robber have seen that all free world keep silence and made another slavery tax for Jews which want to go home, to Israel from 5,000 to 25,000 rubles, for engineers, physicians, and doctor professors. And that is why they put people in such position that they cannot pay and cannot go to Israel. With all your life you cannot have 5,000 rubles. It is impossible.

Senator GURNEY. This is in order to prevent any of them from leaving?

Mr. SHIFRIN. Yes. And now only people without education can go to Israel. They stopped educated people. And now we have cases when Jews committed suicide; they have permission to go to Israel but had no money to pay this slavery tax. And I know that my Jewish friends in U.S.S.R. try to fight now against this slavery tax and defy them and we have now victims. They put in the prisons and in the concentration camps some of Jews which try to fight against this slavery tax. I know them. They now in the prison because they told that they don't agree with this slavery tax; that there is slavery in 20th age——

Mr. BOLDYREFF. Twentieth Century.

Mr. SHIFRIN. Twentieth Century. And really that is slavery. And I think that all people with education in free world must tell to these robbers that they don't permit them to make slavery in 20th Century, and send people for this crime to the prisons. I would give you documents about these fighters.

And also, I want to tell you that when I came to your world, to the free world, I have heard about this intention to make trade with U.S.S.R. When my friends I told you shout to me by the telephone: "We are hostages in the hands of killers." They also told me by telephone conversations and in letters that free mankind should boycott trade with U.S.S.R. Only boycott of U.S.S.R. can help them.

That is only one way to help these people which live in desperation.

It would be good to tell you one sentence of Lenin: "Capitalism would sell to us—to Communists—the rope on which we would hang them." And now your Wall Street tries to sell to them rope on which they would hang you.

You, free world, built for them all these big plants for U.S.S.R. You, free world, build for U.S.S.R. all these tank plants, iron craft plants. All this is work of free mankind and then these killers from U.S.S.R. would go against you with the war.

Now you try to make trade with U.S.S.R. Wall Street discussed problem of how many billions they would loan to U.S.S.R.: $100 billion, or $150 billion.

I can tell you that I have heard in concentration camps sometimes from prisoners in desperation that when these Communists would catch these Americans, which helped U.S.S.R. and would send them to concentration camps, they, political prisoners, would go to the towers of concentration camps to be overseers because free world now try to help the Communists against these people which live in desperation. Simple people cannot understand your politic because you work against your interests.

Mr. SOURWINE. Who is it who says if the Communists catch the Americans and put them in concentration camps, they, the speakers, would be willing to go and be with the guards? Who said that?

Mr. SHIFRIN. I have heard these words many times from simple uneducated prisoners which were in desperation. They see that Americans try to be friendly with the Communists and Communists oppress them and they in desperation in these cells. You must understand these people which told in desperation such bitter words.

Senator GURNEY. In what way do they think that we are helping the Communists oppress them?

Mr. SHIFRIN. First, I must tell you, I am sure you must go against these killers. You must be open and brave in the struggle against communism. If you don't struggle with Communists—you help them oppress these people in U.S.S.R. I know that communism is not so powerful like you think. I have seen them all my life and you know that in my work I have known much. And I am sure that if you would understand only one simple thing: Communists understand only language of power. If you would go against them with power, they would stay on their knees.

Please remember about Cuba case when they brought to Cuba rockets. Please try to remember this case with Taiwan when they try to catch Taiwan. Only in these two cases your United States talked openly and straight, with full power: "Stop; or it would be war." And they stopped in one day. You remember? They threw out those rockets from Cuba on the ships, these killers, and they stopped attacks in China-Taiwan immediately.

But in all the cases when you try to speak with these murderers, they understand and they could understand only one thing—their mentality is very simple—"If I would have power to kill these hateful United States—think man like Brezhnev—I would kill them without any hesitation. I speak with this America only because I not have power to kill them today. When America speak with me, I must understand that they have not power to kill me." Communists cannot understand that you are people with another mentality; that you want peace; that your war in Vietnam was a war of peace.

Believe me, that in U.S.S.R. people understand your war in Vietnam more better than your students, which make these demonstrations. In U.S.S.R. simple people understand you. But Communists understand only one thing: you, free world, didn't do nothing to help the Czechoslovakians—free world not just only the United States—free world didn't help Hungary; free world don't want to help these dissidents in U.S.S.R. which died now in the prisons, concentration camps, and mental asylums. And that is why they understood that they now have power to throw to the prisons these dissidents. They now understood that you don't want to do nothing to help these dissidents. Only because of this they now throw to the prisons so many dissidents and life of Solzhenitsyn and Sakharov in danger. Believe me. They build now new, big concentration camps. They can finish with this Jewish movement and with another dissidents now because they see that free world don't want to help to these brave people.

Mr. SOURWINE. So it is all the fault of the United States, is that what you are saying?

Mr. SHIFRIN. Not fault of the United States, excuse me. It is fault of free mankind. People in the free world don't remember about responsibility in mankind. This I must tell to free mankind because your liberals don't know socialism and communism and think that they can build socialism with human face. They make mistake. Communists would kill them first.

In Czechoslovakia intellectuals also thought that they can make communism with human face. You see their end. So it would be here when these Communists would destroy your society with all these New Lefts and new Trotskyists. Then they would have power to kill this free mankind. That is their goal.

Senator GURNEY. Well, I think I recognize their goal as closely as you do, Mr. Shifrin. Many of us in this country do.

Let me summarize by saying this, that your testimony has been most startling. It has been revealing, illuminating, shocking. It will be made a part of the public record of this committee and of the U.S. Senate. I hope many will read it. That is one of the reasons why I was so anxious to chair these hearings and be sure that you did have a chance to make your voice heard.

I share your same fear about the ultimate goal of communism. I think many of our people, not only in this country but also in the free world, are not aware of the fact that concentration camps, political prisoners, slave camps, are pretty much the same in the Soviet Union today as they were during the reign of Stalin. That is why I think this testimony is so important.

It is hard to believe that over a century or more after most civilized countries have done away with slavery, that we have slavery in one of the most powerful nations in the world and on a scale such as never existed before at any time in the history of the world.

This I think is the important part of your testimony, your very important testimony, and I want to thank you very much for coming here. I think you have done a real service. As I said, I hope people will read this and become aware of the things that are happening in Soviet Russia and perhaps that will contribute to some change some time down the road. I certainly hope so.

Thank you very much.

Mr. SHIFRIN. Thank you very much also for work of your Internal Security Commission, I have read in the U.S.S.R. many times in Russian newspapers, articles against your Internal Security Commission, and I am sure that you make big work and you try to defense your society.

I told you all this because I am sure that only with all the power of all the free mankind, we can make something, do something with these murderers who try to kill free people on all the Earth.

Thank you very much.

Senator GURNEY. Your comment about their awareness of what goes on in this country by the way of news dissemination in the U.S.S.R. is certainly correct. I recall when I first came to Congress as a young Congressman about 10 years ago—as you know, I come from Florida—this I think was back in 1963—and I made some comment about the Soviet threat to Cuba. The next day or 2 days after that, it was picked up in Prague, I believe, and they commented on it. They commented on this crazy man from Florida and what he had to say about what was going on in Cuba. So I am aware of the fact that shedding light and publicity on what the Soviets are doing is important in this country and that the Soviets are aware of it and they do react to it.

Thank you very much.

The hearing of the subcommittee is adjourned.

[Whereupon, at 3:30 p.m., the subcommittee recessed, subject to the call of the Chair.]

APPENDIX

SOME BIOGRAPHIES OF SOVIET POLITICAL PRISONERS

[From Grani, Nos. 79, 80, 82 and 84]

1. IVANOV, Nikolay Viktorovich, b. 1937, art historian, instructor at the Lenningrad State University. Sentenced 5 Apr 68 in Leningrad to 6 years in a strict regime labor camp for his membership in the All-Russian Social Christian Union for the Liberation of the People. Is serving his sentence in Dubrovlag. (Grani No. 82, p. 120)

2. KONOSOV, Mikhail Borisovich, born 1937, metal worker at Lengaz, poet, student by correspondence at the M. Gorkiy Literary Institute in Leningrad. Sentenced 5 Apr 68 in Leningrad to 4 years in a strict regime labor camp for his membership in the All-Russian Social Christian Union for the Liberation of the People. Served his sentence in Dubrovlag. Released upon completion of sentence. In February 1971 registered for residence at the city of Luga in the Leningradskaya oblast. (Grani No. 82, p. 120)

3. BOCHEVAROV, Georgiy Nikolaevich, b. 1935, engineer-economist. Sentenced at the 5 Apr 68 Leningrad trial to two and a half years in a strict labor camp for his membership in the All-Russian Social Christian Union for the Liberation of the People. Served his sentence at Dubrovlag. Released after serving his time. (Grani No. 82, p. 121)

4. SLUTSKIY, Boris Abramovich, b. 7 May 1919 in Slavyansk (Donbass), studied in Moscow at the Law Institute and the M. Gorkiy Literary Institute. Member of the Communist Party since 1943. First poems published in 1941. Other works published in 1953, 1955, 1961, 1964. Much work censored and remains unpublished. (Grani No. 82, p. 121)

5. BOGORAZ-BRUKHMAN, Larisa Iosifovna, b. May 8, 1929 in Kharkov. Married Yu. Daniel in 1950. Participated actively in the defense of her arrested husband, and appeared in the defense of Yu. Galanskov, A. Ginzburg, A. Dobrovol'skiy and V. Lashkova. Also appeared in the defense of Anatoliy Marchenko and her sister Irina Belogorodskaya. Arrested and beaten for her participation in a demonstration protesting the entry of Soviet troops into Czechoslovakia and sentenced to 4 years of exile which she served in the Yakutskaya oblast. According to foreign sources, was released conditionally in December 1971 before completing her term and sent to Kaluga where her husband settled upon his release from camp. (Grani, No. 82, p. 125)

6. NAGORNIY, Valeriy, b. 1938, engineer with the Leningrad Institute of Precision Mechanics and Optics. Sentenced at the Leningrad trial of 5 Apr 68 to 3 years in a strict regime camp for his membership in the All-Russian Social Christian Union for the Liberation of the People. Served his sentence at Dubrovlag. Released March 1970 upon completion of term.

7. BARANOV, Yurity Petrovich, b. 1938, electronic engineer at the Clinic of Hospital Surgery of the First Leningrad Medical Institute. Sentenced at the Leningrad 5 Apr 68 trial to 3 years in a strict regime camp for his participation in the All-Russian Social Christian Union for the Liberation of the People. Served his sentence at Dubrovlag. Released 10 Feb 1970. Died shortly afterwards. (Grani, No. 82)

8. SUDAREV, Anatoliy, b. 1939, translator, graduated from the Leningrad State University. Sentenced at the Leningrad 5 Apr 68 trial to 2 years in a strict regime labor camp. Served his time in Dubrovlag, whereupon released in March 1970 . (Grani, number and page not given)

9. DOL'NIK, Solomon Borisovich, b. circa 1900. Arrested early in 1966 in Moscow and accused of distributing Zionist and anti-Soviet literature. Served time in labor camps in Mordovia. Upon release immigrated to Israel with his wife. (Grani, number and page not given)

10. GENDLER, Yuriy L., born 1936. Arrested 1 Aug 1968 for planning to express his sympathy to Czechoslovakia. Sentenced in Dec. 1968 to 3 years in

(147)

a strict regime labor camp. Was to be released in August 1971 upon completion of term. (Grani, number and page not given)

11. VERETENOV, Vladimir, born 1936, chemist from Tomsk. Graduated Leningrad State University. Arrested for his participation in the All-Russian Social Christian Union for the Liberation of the People. Sentenced 5 April 1968 to 2 years in a strict regime labor camp. Served his sentence in Dubrovlag. Released March 1969 upon completion of term. (Grani, number and page not given)

12. GABAY, Il'ya Yankelovich, born 1925, philologist, poet, scriptwriter, teacher, editor. Author of "At the Closed Doors of an Open Court" and many other works challenging the arrest and imprisonment of Soviet dissidents. Arrested 19 May 1970 for possession of documents regarding the struggle of the Crimean Tatars for their rights. Sentenced to 3 years in a standard regime labor camp. His address: Kemerovo 28, p/ya 1612/40, br. 44. (Grani, number and page not given)

13. KRASIN, Viktor, born 1929, economist, worked at the Central Economics and Mathematics Institute. A graduate of Stalinist labor camps. Member of the Action Group for the Defense of Civil Rights in the USSR. Active protester of Stalinism. Author of numerous documents on civil rights in USSR and countries of the Soviet bloc. Arrested 20 Dec 1969, tried on 23 Dec 1969 and sentenced to 5 years of exile in the Krasnoyarskiy kray. Address: Eniseyskiy rayon Makovskoye village, general delivery. (Grani, p. 92)

14. TALANTOV, Boris Vladimirovich, born 1903, son of a priest. Father and brother perished in labor camps. Graduated Pedagogical Institute in Kirov. Taught mathematics. Long record of dissent and struggle for civil rights and freedom of religion. After many years of persecution, finally arrested in Kirov on 12 June 1969, tried on 1 Sept 1969 and sentenced to 2 years in a concentration camp. As of 6 Nov 1970 in a prison hospital in Kirov. Died on 4 Jan 1971 of heart attack. (Grani, No. 79)

15. SHAVROV, Vadim, born 1924, Moscovite, from the family of an old bolshevik. Member of VLKSM and graduate of military-naval school. Arrested in 1948 with his father and sentenced to 10 years. While in camp in 1954 became religious. After rehabilitation completed a religious seminary. A friend and co-author of A. Levitin. (Grani, No. 79)

16. BURMISTROVICH, Il'ya Evseevich, born 1938, candidate of physical-mathematics sciences, author of 9 scientific works; had been a senior member of the staff of the Academy of Pedagogical Sciences. Arrested 16 May 1968. Tried in Moscow 21 May 1969. Sentenced to 3 years in standard regime corrective labor camps. Sentenced for duplicating and distributing the works of Sinyavskiy and Daniel, information on the trial of Yu. Galanskov and A. Ginzburg, and Samizdat materials. At present in a concentration camp. Address: Krasnoyarskiy kray, st. N. Ingash, p/ya 283/1-5-3. (Grani, p. 95)

17. KUSHEV, Evgeniy Igorevich, born 1947, a Moscovite, from the family of artists. Author of the poem "Decembrists", one of the founders of "The Ryleyv Club", an editor of the literary magazine "Russkoye Slovo" (Russian Word) and the magazine "Sotsialism i Demokratiya" (Socialism and Democracy). Arrested and spent some time in a mental hospital for his participation in a demonstration protesting the arrest of Sinyavskiy and Daniel. Met A. Krasnov-Levitin in 1965 (his godfather when Kushev became baptized). Arrested and sentenced to 7 months for his participation on 22 Jan 1967 in a demonstration protesting the arrest of Yu. Galanskov, A. Dobrovol'skiy etc. Tried together with V. Bukovsky and V. Delone on 30 Aug-1 Sept, 1967 and sentenced conditionally to 1 year of deprivation of freedom. Testified on the behalf of Yu. Galanskov, A. Ginzburg, A. Dobrovol'skiy and V. Lashkova on 8 Jan 1968 at their trial. One of the authors of the magazine "Phoenix-66". (Grani, p. 95)

18. GINZBURG, Aleksandr Ie'ich, born in 1936, Moscovite, poet, publicist. Edited 3 issues of an underground literary youth magazine "Sintaksis"; arrested and sentenced to 2 years in a concentration camp for this work. Arrested again in 1964 for allegedly harboring anti-Soviet material. Following the arrest of Sinyavskiy and Daniel in 1965, compiled a "White Book on the Trial of Sinyavskiy and Daniel" during 1966 and sent copies to the KGB, to members of the Supreme Soviet, N. Podgornyy and other government officials. Arrested, tried, and sentenced on 8 Jan 1968 to 5 years in a strict regime camp for demonstrating on behalf of V. Lashkova, Yu. Galanskov, and A. Dobrovol'skiy. While in camp participated in a variety of protest acts. Tried on 18 Aug 1970 in Yavas for these protests, and

moved from Dubrovlag to the Vladimirskaya prison [reputedly one of the most terrible], operating under strict regime conditions. (Grani, no. 79, p. 100)

19. BOGACH, Nikolay Pavlovich, b. 1944 in the Kuban. While a student of the Nikolayev Agricultural Technicum tried to establish the "Organization for Social Justice", for which in the spring of 1969 he was sentenced by the Nikolayev City Court to 4 years at a correctional strict regime labor camp; the term was subsequently reduced to 3 years. (Grani, no. 84 p. 91)

20. VASILYAN, Ovik M., b. 1936, an Armenian, non-party. Engineer of the Erevan Electric Lamp Plant. Sentenced by the Supreme Court of the Armenian SSR in February 1969 to 6 years in a corrective labor camp; accused of criticizing life under the Soviets, of spreading slanderous information on the domestic and foreign policy of the USSR, of agitating for an independent Armenia, etc. In camp participated in strikes against brutalities inflicted by camp guards and administration. (Grani, no. 84, p. 91)

21. GYUNASHYAN, Shirak, b. 1939, an Armenian, non-party. Engineer and designer. Sentenced in Feb 1969 by the Supreme Court of the Armenian SSR together with O. M. Vasilyan for the same reasons to 4 years. (Grani no. 84, p. 92)

22. KHACHATRYAN, Ayk Karaevich, b. 1920, Armenian, non-party. Artist-painter. Sentenced by the Supreme Court of the Armenian SSR to 5 years according to article 70. (Grani, no. 84, p. 92)

23. FEDOROV, Yuriy Ivanovich, b. 1936, from Leningrad. Worked with the Komsomol, then the MVD, then a captain in the police force. Sentenced in July 1969 by the Leningrad City Court to 6 years for illegally organizing the "Union of Communists". After a two-week stay in solitary confinement in Dubrovlag, transferred to a camp in Mordovia (17–a, Ozernoe). In 1971 participated in a hunger strike on Human Rights day, demanding amnesty for all political prisoners. (Grani, no. 84, p. 92)

24. GREBENSHCHIKOV, Vasiliy Fedorovich, "Chronicle", No. 21, 1971 calls him Grebenshchikov, Viktor Orestovich and states that he is from Alma-Ata. Arrested on 27 June 1967 for his attempt to throw onto the grounds of the American Embassy a typed text of his work, "History of the collectivization of agriculture in the USSR". Released 26 June 1971 from a camp in Mordovia. (Grani, no. 84, p. 92)

25. IVANOV, Yuriy Evgenevich, b. 1927, of Leningrad, son of the artist-painter E. Sivers, shot in 1938 and rehabilitated after his death. While attending the Academy of Arts, arrested in 1947, with two others, for not attending lectures on Marxism-Leninism. Sentenced without trial to 10 years in a concentration camp. After 1 year, acquitted and released. Arrested again in 1955, accused of spreading anti-Soviet literature, etc. Sent to work on the construction of the Kuybyshev Hydroelectric Power Station where at that time approximately 8,000 prisoners, charged according to Article 58 (same as Ivanov), were working. Was not released as many others after Stalin's death; caught during an attempt to escape and sentenced to another 10 years. Spent 1 year at the Vladimirskaya prison, in solitary confinement. In 1963 again sentenced for another 10 years for spreading "anti-Soviet propaganda" in the camp. Of these spent 3 years at the Vladimirskaya prison, then 2½ years in a special regime camp (camp 10 in Dubrovlag). In the summer of 1968 transferred to strict regime camp no. 11, then 4 months in solitary confinement at the Saransk KGB, then camp 17 at Dubrovlag, etc. etc. In 1969 an exhibition of his painting was held in London. According to rumors he was released from the Mordovian camps in advance of his term. Present address unknown. (Grani, no. 84, p. 94)

26. KALNYN'SH, Viktor Yanovich, b., 1936, Latvian. Graduated Moscow Pedagogical Institute. Journalist. Arrested 18 Apr 1962. Accused of membership in an "underground anti-Soviet, nationalistic organization", the "Baltic Federation". Sentenced to 10 years in labor camps. The sentence was protested by the Procurator of the Latvian SSR, the Procurator General of the USSR, and numerous Latvian intellectuals, but to no avail. Sent to camp 17–a in Mordovia. Participated in various camp protests and punished accordingly. In 1969 transferred to BUR for protesting the transfer of Yu. Daniel and V. Ronkin to the Vladimirskaya prison. (Grani, No. 84, p. 95)

27. CHERDYNTSEV, Ivan Alekseevich, b. 1938. Teacher. In 1964 was tried by the Supreme Court of the Moldavian SSR for participating in the organization of the "Democratic Union of Socialists" and sentenced to 6 years in a labor camp; received another 4 years while in camp. In Sept 1971 participated in a hunger strike at camp 19 in Dubrovlag. His mother, Efrosiniya Nesterovna [Cherdyntseva] lives at No. 84 Krasin St., Petropavlovsk, Kazakh SSR.

150

28. IVANOV, Anatoliy M. (Real name—Novogodniyy), Moscovite, poet. Arrested 6 Oct 1961 together with V. Osipov and E. Kuznetsov for their participation in the magazine "Phoenix–61". Sentenced by the Moscow City Court on 9 Feb 62 to 7 years in a intensified regime labor camp. Served his sentence in labor camps in Mordovia. Released in October 1968. According to Osipov, spent part of his sentence in a mental hospital.

29. KHAUSTOV, Viktor Aleksandrovich, b. 1938, Moscovite, poet, member of SMOG, an upholsterer by trade. Participated in the 22 Jan 67 demonstration protesting the arrest of V. Lashkova, Yu. Galanskov, and A. Dobrovol'skiy for their work on the magazine "Phoenix–66". Arrested and sentenced by the Moscow City Court to 3 years in an intensified regime camp. Served his term in labor camps in the Orenburg oblast. Released in Jan 1970. (Grani, no. 80, p. 141)

30. KUZNETSOV, Eduard Samuilovich, b. 1941, Moscovite, student of philosophy at the Moscow State University. Arrested along with V. Osipov and A. Ivanov for their work on the magazine "Feniks–61". Sentenced by the Moscow City Court to 7 years in an intensified regime labor camp. Served his term first in camps in Mordovia, then in the Vladimirskaya prison. Released in October 1968. Settled in Riga and married S. Zalmanson. On 15 June 70 together with his wife and 9 other friends apprehended by the KGB and accused of an attempt to hijack an airplane from the "Smolone" airport in Leningrad. Kuznetsov and Dymshits were sentenced to be shot, the others got 4 to 15 years in concentration camps. As a result of protests the world over, Kuznetsov's and Dymshits' sentences were changed to 10 years in concentration camps. Kuznetsov arrived in June 1971 at camp 10 (Station Udarnaya Lepley), a special regime camp, i.e. living in a prison and going out to work. (Grani, no. 80, p. 141)

31. BOKSHTEIN, Il'ya Veniaminovich, Moscovite, spinal tuberculosis since childhood, student at the Library Institute, poet. Arrested 6 Aug 61. Sentenced by the Moscow City Court to 5 years in concentration camps for his participation in "Phoenix–61". Released after serving his sentence. (Grani, 80, p. 142)

32. GEDONIY, Aleksandr Gidoni. A menber of the All-Russian Social Christian Union for the Liberation of Peoples, denounced this organization to the KGB. Remained in the organization at the instruction of the KGB until the first arrests of its members in Feb–Mar 1967 and their trial in Nov 67–Apr 68 at which he appeared as witness for the prosecution. (Grani, No. 80, p. 142)

33. BORODIN, Leonid Ivanovich. B. in Irkuts. Student at the Irkutsk University. First arrested in 1956 for membership in an illegal student group, "Free Speech" and for listening to the radio station "Baikal". Expelled from the University and the Komsomol. Later finished the University. Specialty—historian of education. The last few years was director of a secondary school in the Luzhskiy rayon in Leningrad oblast. In 1964 established the "Democratic Party". In 1965 became a member of the All-Russian Social Christian Union for the Liberation of Peoples. Arrested in Feb–Mar 1967. Sentenced by the Leningrad City Court in 1968 to 6 years in strict regime camps. Served his sentence in the camps of Mordovia. While in camp participated in a variety of protests. Address: Vladimir-Oblastnoy, p/ya OD/1–st. 2. (Grani, no. 80, p. 143)

34. IVOVLOV, Vladimir, b. 1937, economist. Member of the All-Russian Social Christian Union for the Liberation of Peoples. Sentenced by the Leningrad City Court in 1968 to 6 years in a strict regime labor camp. Served his sentence in Mordovian camps. Address: Mordovskaya ASSR, Potma, p/o Yavas, p/ya ZhKh 385/11. (Grani, no. 80, p. 143)

35. OGURTSOV, Igor Vyacheslavovich, b. 1938/9, philologist, translator (Japanese). Main leader of the All-Russian Social Christian Union for the Liberation of the People. Arrested Feb–Mar 1967. Sentenced in Nov 1967 to 15 years: 5 years in prison, 10 years in a strict regime camp. Place of incarceration—the Vladimirskaya prison. Address: Vladimirskaya oblast, p/ya OD/1–st. 2. (Grani, No. 80, p. 144)

36. SADO, Mikhail Yukhanovich, b. 1934 in Leningrad into a family of bootblacks. Of Assyrian origin. Grandfather, father, two uncles persecuted during the 1930s, with only father, who spent 16 years in prisons and labor camps, surviving. Sado himself, one of the founders and one of the four principal leaders of the All-Russian Social Christian Union for the Liberation of Peoples. Arrested in Leningrad in 1967 for his political activities. Sentenced to 13 years: 5 years in prison and 7 years in strict regime concentration camps. First—the Vladimirskaya prison, then labor camps in Mordovia. According to latest information he is serving his sentence at camp 17–a. Address: Mordovskaya ASSR, p/o Ozernyy, p/ya ZhKh 385/17–a. (Grani, No. 80, p. 144)

37. VAGIN, Evgeniy Aleksandrovich, b. 1938/39, literary historian and editor of note. One of the four leaders of the All-Russian Christian Social Union for the Liberation of the People. Arrested in 1967. Sentenced in Nov 67 to 10 years: 2 years in the Vladimirskaya prison and 8 years in strict regime labor camps in Mordovia. Address: Mordovskaya ASSR, st. Potma, p/o Yavas, p/ya ZhZh 385/11. (Grani, no. 80, p. 145)

38. AVEROCHKIN, Boris, b. 1940, lawyer. One of the four principal leaders of the All-Russian Christian Social Union for the Liberation of People. Arrested in 1967. Sentenced by the Leningrad City Court in Nov 67 to 8 years in strict regime camps. Serving his sentence in camps in Mordovia. Address: Mordovskaya ASSR, st. Potma, p/o Yavas, p/ya ZhZh 385/11. (Grani no. 80, p. 145)

39. PLATONOV, Vyacheslav, b. 1941 in Leningrad in a workers family. Studied at the Leningrad State University. Assistant in the African Dept. Upon return from a tour of duty in Ethiopia, arrested by the KGB for active membership in the All-Russian Christian Social Union for the Liberation of the People. Sentenced by the Leningrad City Court to 7 years in a strict regime camp. Serving his sentence in Mordovia. Participated in a series of protests while in camp. According to latest information, is at camp 17-a. Address: Mordovskaya ASSR, p/o Ozernyy, p/ya ZhZh 385 17-a. (Grani, No. 80, p. 146)

40. KRASNOPEVTSEV, Lev. Moscovite, studied at Moscow State University, member of "Union of Patriots of Russia" (illegal Marxsist group). Arrested in connection with the trial of the Moscow University Group on 30 Aug 1957. Sentenced by the Moscow City Court to 10 years of strict regime camp. Served his sentence in Mordovian camps. Released 30 Aug 1967. (Grani no. 80, p. 146)

41. RENDEL', Leonid A., Moscovite, historian, studied at the Moscow State Univ. Member of the "Union of Patriots of Russia". Arrested in connection with the trial of the Moscow University Group on 30 Aug 1957. In Feb 58, together with Krasnopevtsev sentenced to 10 years in a strict regime camp. Served in Mordovian camps. Released 30 Aug 67, but remained until the end of 1968 under administrative supervision for "repeated disobedience of camp regulations and for harboring anti-Soviet convictions". (Grani, no. 80, p. 146)

42. OBUSHENKOV, N. G., CHESHKOV, M. AND SEMINENKO, M., Moscovites, former students at the Moscow State University and members of the "Union of Patriots of Russia". Arrested in Moscow 30 Aug 1957, sentenced by the Moscow City Court in Feb 1958 to 10 years in strict regime labor camps. Served their sentences in Mordovian camps, together with Krasnopevtsev and Rendel. Released 30 Aug 67. (Grani, no. 80, p. 146)

43. SINYAVSKIY, Andrey Donatovich, b. 1925 in Moscow. Writer and literary critic. Graduate of Moscow State University. Father arrested in 1951, at which time son's diary confiscated. In 1952 appointed senior associate in Soviet Literature Section at the Institute of World Literature. In 1956 wrote his now famous "The Trial Goes On", "What is Social Realism", in 1961–62 a novel "Lyubimov". Towards the end of 1956 began sending his works abroad, where they were published under the pseudonym of Abram Terts. In 1961 became a member of the Union of (Soviet) Writers. On 8 Sept 1965 arrested by KGB in Moscow. Tried together with Yu. Daniel (Sept–Dec 1966). Sentenced by the Supreme Court of the RSFSR to 7 years in strict regime labor camps for publishing "anti-Soviet" works abroad. Serving his sentence at camp no. 11 in Mordovia. (Grani, No. 80, p. 147)

44. DANIEL', Yuliy Markovich, b. in Moscow in 1925, into the family of a well known Jewish writer, Mark Daniel (literary pseudonym). Severely wounded in 1944 during the war. Studied at Kharkov University, then at the Philology Department of the Moscow Regional Pedagogical Institute. Taught for 6 years. In 1951 married Larisa Bogoraz. Began writing in 1952. First novel, "Escape", published by "Detgiz" (Soviet publishers of children's literature), but not allowed to be sold. Other works followed. Most works eventually published in the USA by "Inter-Language Literary Associates". Beginning with 1957 earned his living by translating poetry: approximately 40 volumes of his translated works appeared before his arrest. On 12 Sept 1965 arrested in Moscow by KGB. Accused of anti-Soviet propaganda. Tried together with Sinyavskiy Sept–Dec 1966. Sentenced by the Supreme Court of RSFSR to 5 years in a strict regime camp. Served his time in Mordovian camps. In 1968, his wife Larisa Bogoraz, arrested and sentenced to 4 years of exile for demonstrating against the entry of Soviet troops into Czechoslovakia. Served her time in the Irkutskaya oblast [see her biography, No. 5 of this report]. While in camp Yu. Daniel continued to write and to protest the cruelties and unfairness of the camp administration toward other prisoners.

Participated in hunger strikes, appeals, and complaints. In July 1969, together with Ronkin tried for his activities and sentenced to serve the remainder of his term at the Vladimirskaya prison, to which duly transferred. Released on 12 Sept 1970. Denied right to live in Moscow. Settled in Kaluga. Addressed an appeal to the Presidium of the Supreme Soviet for the release of A. Sinyavskiy. (Grani, no. 80, p. 348–150)

45. MARCHENKO, Anatoliy Tikhonovich, b. 1938 in Siberia. A driller by profession. While working on the construction of the Karagands Hydroelectric Power Station, arrested in a local brawl and sentenced to a labor camp in the Karaganda oblast. On the way to the camp escaped, but was caught 40 km from the Iranian border. Accused by the KGB of treachery to the Motherland. After 5 months of solitary confinement, the Supreme Court of the Turkmen SSR sentenced him to 6 years in a concentration camp for political prisoners. Served his sentence in Mordovia. For attempted escape, transferred to the Vladimirskaya prison, then returned to a camp in Mordovia. In camp suffered terrible physical hardship. Physically was reduced to an invalid, spiritually transformed into a politically conscious fighter. While in camp started writing about the life of political prisoners there and of conditions at the Vladimirskaya prison. In 1967 finished "My Testimony", which was immediately published and distributed by Samizdat. The book was written while he was for 5 months at a hospital undergoing two very serious operations and the next 5 months while he was looking for work and moving from one town to another: Kursk, Kaluga, Maloyaroslavets, Vladimir, Kalinin, Barabinsk (Siberia) and finally the town of Aleksandrov in the Vladimirskaya oblast, where he has lived since May 1968, working in Moscow as a stevedore, despite his extremely poor health—no other work was available to him. Despite various acts of persecution by the KGB, continued his stand against political injustice and repression. One month before the entry of Soviet troops into Czechoslovakia, addressed a letter to the leading Czech newspapers, praising Czechoslovakia for its political policies, and warning of possible intervention by the USSR. Two days later, on 29 July 1968, he was grabbed on his way to work, arrested on false charges, and sent to the Butyrskaya prison. His arrest and imprisonment initiated a series of protests on the part of many, including Larisa Daniel-Bogoraz, N. Gorbanevskaya, P. Litvinov, V. Krasin, Academician Sakharov. More than 60 letters of protest were sent. Samizdat published a statement summarizing his case. Larisa Daniel's sister, engineer I. Belogorodskaya, arrested in connection with Marchenko's case, was sentenced to 1 year in a concentration camp, which she spent in Mordovia—released 8 Aug. 1969. Marchenko himself was sentenced to 1 year in a strict regime camp. In Dec. 1968 after a long march, he arrived at a concentration camp in the Permskaya oblast. Despite all medical evidence as to his extremely bad health he was sent to work on construction jobs of great hardship. When his term was almost completed the Perm procurature instigated a new case against him and he was transferred to the prison in Solikamsk. On 20 May 69, the USSR Human Rights Committee sent a letter, signed by 54 petitioners, to the United Nations, in defense of political prisoners in the USSR, including Marchenko and Belogorodskaya. But the U.N. staff in Moscow refused to accept the letter on the pretext that it was from private persons. On 30 June 1969, a second letter was sent regarding Marchenko and the use of mental hospitals for dissenters. A new trial was held on Marchenko on 22 Aug. 1969 in the village of Nyrob on the camp grounds. False witnesses were called; Marchenko was sentenced to another 2 years in a strict regime camp. Though the sentence was passed in Sept. 1969, Marchenko remained at the Solikamsk prison until Feb. 1970, at which time he was transferred to a camp at the following address: Perm oblast, Solikamsk region, XXX p/o Krasnyy bereg, uch. AM 244/7–8.

According to the latest information, he was transferred by the camp administration in Feb–Mar 1970, with temperatures ranging 45–50°C below zero, [54–60° F] into a tent, and assigned, despite his state of health—bleeding ulcers, anemia, terrible headaches due to unattended meningitis while at camp, two serious operations (one of them brain surgery)—to unloading firewood for train engines and digging foundation pits. He was refused a visit from his mother and lawyer, deprived of letters and books, paper, pen and even a text-book in physics, as having no "politically educational value". His health has greatly deteriorated, and in addition to everything else he has developed hypertension. His friends fear that he may not survive.

But his dream—for which he is paying with his life—has come true: his book "My Testimony", through Samizdat, appeared abroad, where it was published both in Russian and in all the major languages of the world.

Marchenko was released upon the expiration of his term. (Grani, No. 80, pp. 154–157)

46. RONKIN, Valeriy Efinmovich, b. 1936 in Murmansk, in the family of a workman. Engineer. Studied at the Leningrad Technological Institute. Worked on the construction of petroleum plants throughout the USSR, thereafter at the Institute for Synthetic Rubber in Leningrad. In 1963, together with S. Khakhaev wrote the book "From the Dictatorship of Bureaucracy to the Dictatorship of the Proletariat". Both Ronkin and Khakhaev are Marxists and came out for "true Marxism against its perversion". Criticized the party and its leadership as responsible for the tragedy of the Stalinist dictatorship. Khakhaev and Ronkin formed a group with several others, called "Union of Communards", which issued two issues of a typewritten magazine, the "Bell" ("Kolokol"). Arrested on 12 June 1965 and sentenced by the Leningrad City Court to 7 years in a strict regime labor camp. Served his sentence in Mordovia. In camp participated in various acts of protest, including hunger strikes, and appeals to the higher authorities. Like Yu. Daniel continuously and systematically fought for the rights of prisoners, thus gaining the animosity of both the camp administrators and the higher authorities. Due to these activities both Ronkin and Daniel were tried on 7 July 1969 and sentenced to serve out the remainder of their terms in the Vladimirskaya prison. According to latest reports, Ronkin, together with 27 other prisoners, took part in a hunger strike to mark the approaching Constitution Day and Human Rights Day, and to protest the unbearable conditions of life in labor camps. His address is: Vladimirskaya oblast p/ya OD/1—st. 2. (Grani, no. 80, pp. 157–159)

47. KHAKHAEV, Sergey. Formerly student at the Leningrad Technological Institute and member of the All-Union Lenin Young Communist League. In 1963, together with Ronkin wrote the book "From the Dictatorship of Bureaucracy to the Dictatorship of the Proletariat"; also articles criticizing Stalinism, the party, and the leadership. Together with Ronkin and others formed the circle "Union of Communards" and the magazine "Bell" ("Kolokol"). Arrested 12 June 1965 together with Ronkin, and sentenced by the Leningrad City Court to 7 years in a strict regime camp, followed by 3 years of exile. (See Ronkin's biography for additional details.) Is serving his sentence in a camp in Mordovia. (Grani, no. 80, p. 159)

48. DRAGOSH, Nikolay Fedorovich, b. 1922, from Odessa, non-party. Graduated the Odessa University. Was director of a school for working youth in the Tarutinskiy region of the Odessa oblast, and taught mathematics. Accused by the Supreme Court of the Moldavian SSR in 1964 for establishing the "Democratic Union of Socialists" and for printing a brochure "Truth to the People". Sentenced to 7 years in a strict regime camp. Served his sentence in Mordovian camps. Transferred to the Vladimirskaya prison for his participation in a hunger strike at the camp in the summer of 1970. While at the Vladimirskaya prison again participated in a hunger strike to mark Constitution Day and Human Rights Day, celebrated Oct 5–10, 1970. Released 15 May 1971. (Grani, no. 80, p. 160)

49. ZAITSEV, Valeriy. Ship's mechanic (naval engineer?) on a repair-and-rescue ship. Arrested in 1962 with 7 other crew members of whom nothing is known, for trying to escape to America while near the coast of Alaska. Sentenced to 10 years. Serving his sentence in Mordovia. (Grani, no. 80, p. 160)

50. BERG-KHAYMOVICH, Yakov, metal worker, Moscovite, non-party. Accused by the Moscow City Court of an attempt to establish an illegal printing shop (together with V. Aydov). Sentenced in 1968 to 7 years of deprivation of freedom. Served his sentence in Mordovian camps. In 1969 transferred to the Vladimirskaya prison for participating in protests and hunger strikes, where he again, together with 27 others, participated in a hunger strike to mark Constitution Day and Human Rights Day. His address: Vladimirskaya oblast, p/ya OD/1 st. 2. (Grani, no. 80, p. 160)

51. AYDOV, Vyacheslav. Accused of an attempt (together with Berg) to establish an illegal printing shop. Served his sentence in Mordovian camps. Participated in hunger strikes in Nov. 1969. Took part in another three-day strike in 4 May 1970 to protest the killing of a mentally ill prisoner by the guards. Together with other prisoners demanded that the procurator general investigate the killing. For this was transferred to the Vladimirskaya prison where he together with 27 others participated in a hunger strike to mark Constitution Day and Human Rights Day. His address: Vladimirskaya oblast, p/ya OD/1–st. 2. (Grani, no. 80, p. 160–161)

52. MOSHKOV, Yuriy. Probably MOSHKOV, Sergey. B. 1939 into a family of physicians in the village of Nadbel'ye in the Leningrad oblast. Graduated from the School of Biology of the Leningrad State University. Became a member of the

illegal circle "Union of Communards". Arrested 12 June 65 in connection with the case of "Union of Communars" and the magazine "Bell" ("Kolokol") (together with V. Ronkin, S. Khakhaev, and others. See Ronkin's biography for details.). In the summer of 1965 sentenced by the Leningrad City Court to 4 years in a strict regime camp. Served his sentence in Mordovia together with Ronkin, Yu. Daniel, and others. Together with Daniel and Ronkin went on a 10-day hunger strike in Feb. 1968, and then came out in the defense of A. Ginzburg who was on a hunger strike in May-June 1969, Released 12 June 1969. (Grani, no. 80, p. 161)

53. KHANZHENKOV, Sergey. Born 1942 in Belorussia. Completed 4 years at the Belorussian Polytechnical Institute. Arrested in 1963. Accused of being a traitor to his country: cf attempting to establish anti-Soviet organizations and of the preparation of diversionary tactics. Sentenced to 10 years in a strict regime camp. Serving his sentence in a camp in Mordovia. (Grani, no. 80, p. 161)

54. TARNAVSKIY, Nikolay Andreyevich. Born 1940. Ukrainian by origin, a native of the Kirovogradskaya oblast. Secondary school teacher in a school where Dragosh [see biographical note] was the director. Arrested in Odessa and accused by the Supreme Court of the Moldavian SSR in the same case as Dragosh. Sentenced to 7 years in a strict regime camp. Served his sentence in camps in Mordovia. Participated in hunger strikes in Nov 1969 and in the summer of 1970. On 13 July 70 transferred to the Vladimirskaya prison, where together with 27 others conducted a hunger strike to mark Constitution Day and Human Rights Day. Released 19 May 1971. (Grani, no. 80, p. 162)

YURI ANDREYEVICH TREGUBOV—writer, born in 1913 in St. Petersburg, Russia. Emigrated with his parents to Berlin, Germany, in 1926, where he completed his education. In 1934 he joined the NTS. In October 1944 he became aide-de-camp to General Trukhin, Chief of Staff of the Vlasov Army. Gen. Trukhin, as well as Gen. Meandrov, Commander of the Second Vlasov Division— formerly both senior Red Army officers—were also NTS members. They were forcibly delivered by the Americans to the Soviet Union, where they were executed together with General Vlasov.

After the capitulation of Nazi Germany, Tregubov returned to West Berlin where he worked actively for the NTS. On September 19, 1947, he was kidnapped by the KGB. After three years of captivity in the Lubyanka, Lefortovo and Butyrskaya prisons, he was tried and condemned to death. Later the death sentence was commuted and he was sent to serve 25 years in concentration camps. He worked two years in the Vorkuta mines, then in Dubrovlag and Potma. After the establishment of diplomatic relations between West Germany and the USSR, Tregubov, as a German citizen, was repatriated with German POWs.

Mr. Tregubov has written several books, describing his experiences in the concentration camps and the conditions of life in the Soviet Union.

VALERY PETROVIC TREMMEL was a teacher by profession. He joined the NTS in Russia. To avoid reprisals by the Gestapo for having provided shelter and saved a number of Jewish children, whose parents were exterminated by the Nazis in the occupied territories of Russia, V. Tremmel, through underground channels, escaped to Poland. In 1954 he worked for NTS in Lintz (Austria). On October 20, 1954 three Soviet agents broke into his apartment, drugged him, and abducted him to Urfar (Soviet zone of Austria). The circumstances of his abduction were investigated by the American authorities and reported to the State Department by the First Secretary of the American Embassy in Vienna, Mr. M. Gordon Knocks.

According to some unconfirmed information V. Tremmel has died in Soviet concentration camps.

NIKOLAY SERGEYEVICH KOZOREZ, born in 1898 in Kremenchug. As an officer he fought in World War I and in the White Russian Army against the Bolsheviks. In 1920 he emigrated to Yugoslavia, where he received his engineering degree at the Belgrade University. A member of NTS since the early 1930's, he was forcibly repatriated by the British in 1945 from Lintz, Austria, with a large group of Cossaks. Kozorez has spent 11 years in Soviet concentration camps of Vorkuta, Yaya, Inta, Mordovia, Potma, and Bykov

DR. ALEXANDER RUDOLFOVICH TRUSHNOVICH was born in 1893 in Postoyna, Slovenia, then part of the Austro-Hungarian Empire. In 1914 as a graduate medical student he was mobilized and sent to the front, where in 1915 he succeeded to defect to the Russians and joined the First Serbian Volunteer Division to fight for the liberation of his native land. After the Bolshevik Revolution in Russia, Dr. Trushnovich fought in the Civil War in the White Russian Army. Twice wounded, he was awarded several medals for bravery. In 1920 his unit was encircled and captured by the Reds, and as an officer he was condemned to be shot. Luckily some Serbian soldiers who served under his command in World War I protested and he was released. To avoid further persecution by the Cheka (Secret Police) Dr. Trushnovich assumed the maiden name of his mother, and in 1927 completed his medical training at the Kubansky Medical Institute. In 1934 he finally succeeded in obtaining an exit visa to return to his native Yugoslavia. In Yugoslavia he worked as a physician and joined the NTS. After the Nazi invasion of Yugoslavia, the NTS went underground, and Dr. Trushnovich directed its operations in that country until September 1944 when he joined the Vlasov Army to become Chief of its Medical Service. In 1946 Dr. Trushnovich was elected to the NTS Council. Actively working against forcible repatriation of former Soviet citizens, he moved to West Berlin to head the NTS-sponsored Committee for the Protection of Refugees. The Committee, among other services, provided shelter and support to many defectors from the Red Army. In West Berlin Dr. Trushnovich organized the Free Russian-German Friendship Union, whose honorary President was the late Prof. E. Reuter, mayor of West Berlin. Dr. Trushnovich became a prominent leader among anti-communists in West Berlin. He published a number of books, wrote in newspapers and lectured extensively in West Germany, England, Switzerland, the Scandinavian countries, France and Italy. On April 13, 1954 he was brutally kidnapped by the KGB from West Berlin.

THE CAMP REGIME

LIFE IN DUBROVLAG

(An interview with Iosif Shneider, correspondent of "AMI" [1])

Q. Please tell us about the camp itself. I heard that you served your sentence somewhere in Mordovia.

A. Yes, I was sentenced to four years in a corrective-labor camp. I was in Dubrovlag. There is a small station on the Kuybyshev railroad line called Pot'ma. A branch line, not shown on any map, leads from there to Dubrovlag. Dubrovlag consists of 36 camps, with two to three thousand people in each camp. I was in camp No. 7. There was no escape, because all around there were camps. The entire Mordovskaya ASSR is one network of corrective labor regime camps.

Q. Were there many Jewish political prisoners? How in general did the Jewish prisoners behave? Did they feel that they belonged together, did they understnad the significance of what was happening, did they know about Israel?

A. Altogether there were about 100 Jews in our particular camp [No. 7]. But besides Zionists there were "economic counter-revolutionaries" and "revisionists". We carried on Zionist work among them, told them what we ourselves knew of Israel and the Jewish people, explained what remained obscure in "official Soviet sources". We carved out and distributed Stars of David, using twenty kopek coins (it was strictly forbidden to keep money or fret-saws). Generally speaking, the Jewish prisoners lived in harmony, and I would say, with a sense of personal dignity. When in 1959 Khrushchev declared in New York that there were no political prisoners in the Soviet Union, the authorities began liquidating the enormous concentration camps in Siberia and Kazakhstan, and concentrating political prisoners in one place—specifically, in Mordovia. It was then that Jews, many Jews, oppressed and miserable, who had already served many long years and who had experienced all the horrors of "camp anti-Semitism"—for the guards in the camps of Vorkuta and Tayshet were former cops—arrived in our camp.

Q. How did the non-Jewish prisoners feel about you? Was there any anti-Semitism among the prisoners?

A. You know that among the prisoners, I practically never felt any anti-Semitism. On the contrary. For instance on Israel's Independence Day we did not come out to work, and of course got 10–15 days of solitary confinement. But all day long that day we were continuously congratulated by the political prisoners: Ukrainians and Lithuanians, Estonians and Georgians, Armenians and Tatars. We in turn supported their national liberation movements.

Q. Was there any anti-Semitism in Dubrovlag from above? How did they behave with you personally? For weren't you sentenced for "Zionist propaganda"?

A. In this respect we had it easier, though the authorities—they were the same everywhere. I remember my first day at the camp. Lieutenant-colonel Fatkin (head of camp No. 7) and Colonel Tolbuzov, nicknamed Göbbels, head of the Cultural Educational Division (KVCh) sat around on their chairs like old-time merchants receiving live goods—slaves—that is us. When he found out about my profession, the chief of the cultural-educational section declared condescendingly: "A photographer—that's good. We need a photographer in the cultural-educational section." "But I am here not to photograph you, but to serve my sentence", said I. Citizen chief Fatkin lazily half opened one eye and inquired condescendingly: "And what is your nationality?" "An Israeli" I answered, upon which citizen chief Fatkin and citizen chief Tolbuzov became agitated and shouted: "What? What?" So I had to repeat my answer but accompany it with an explanation. This is how I ended up in the crash brigade.

---

[1] "AMI"—Association of Israeli Youth. The first issue of this journal appeared in December 1970; it is the organ of an Israeli association of students and youth who had emigrated from the USSR. The journal is of interest not only to Jews, because it has a great deal of recent information on Russia, good articles, prose and poetry. We are reproducing here part of an interview, published by AMI, with Iosif Shneider, a photographer now living in Israel, who was formerly an active member in the Zionist movement in the USSR.

Now I recall this with amusement, but then it wasn't funny. Cement, night and day. Hellish work. Luckily the brigade chief was Jewish (25 years for "economic counter-revolution"). After a while he figured out that I was "not suited" for this strenuous work.

Q. How long was the working day in an ordinary brigade?

A. Eight hours. But after the work was finished, there was always more to do. For example, very frequently we had to "fry the trolley" (i.e. destroy the bed-bugs in the plank beds), etc., etc.

Q. Did the resolutions of the Twentieth Meeting of the Party have any effect on camp food?

A. If you didn't fulfill your norm you received 400 grams of bread and hot food only every other day. If you did, the daily rations consisted of 600 grams of bread and a thin watery gruel which only faintly resembled soup.

Q. In other words, the principle of material incentive about which they now shout so much in the USSR was already being applied in concentration camps? Tell us please, what were your last impressions in camp and your first impressions when released?

A. During the last few months I was sent out to work on the so-called "no-guard" shift. They knew that a political prisoner would not try to escape when there were only a few hours left to be served. The first thing I did when I was "free" was to break my camp spoon and throw the pieces as far away as possible. This was the custom. What was priceless inside the camp lost all its value on the outside. Once freed, I re-examined all my hitherto held values. I said, "when freed", but upon release I didn't feel very much freer. There were many reasons for this. For instance, I was given a "wolf's passport", with which nobody gave you a job.

Nevertheless, despite this passport I managed to apply for an exit permit for Israel as soon as I returned. But my application was refused. I felt that I was just as far from my objective as in the camp.

MY RETURN

by A. Krasnov-Levitin

[Translated from Grani, No. 79, 1971]

After 1969 it became certain that I would be arrested. It is difficult to say on what this conviction was based. But the conviction was unmistakable and definite. Was it intuition?

Not entirely. It was also the ability to grasp quickly the political situation, an ability acquired through years of obsession with politics (I could only thus describe my intense, lifelong interest in politics).

At the end of 1969, there occurred a regular periodic swing of the political pendulum, a swing to the right—to the Stalinist era. There were several such swings after 1956, and they were all short-lived, (a self-evident truth—the wheel of history does not turn back), but each such swing had cost a certain number of people their freedom. However, now is not the time to analyze the situation—this should be left to the historians. At present I am just reaffirming the fact.

My political intuition did not betray me. In March 1969 Ivan Yakhimovich (chairman of a kolkhoz in Latvia), a wonderful person and a convinced democrat, was arrested.

In May, the trial of the Crimean Tartars in Tashkent was to take place. In May the epic of General Grigorenko and Gabay began with their arrest.

Meanwhile the clouds thickened: in June, B. Talantov, a talented and original, sixty-five year old religious writer was arrested in Vyatka (Kirov), then my friends began coming under attack, rumors began circulating about my arrest, and people began warning me that I may be arrested in autumn . . .

And then on the twelfth of September [1969] at five o'clock in the afternoon, the bell rang, sharply and persistently—I immediately understood what was the matter, for nobody ever rang my bell that way. I opened the door. An officer in police uniform, and behind him—a tangle of people. The police officer quickly disappears. Several civilians enter. A little middle aged woman jokes prettily:

So many guests at one time!—and shoves a little book under my nose. The book has her photograph, family name, and profession: "Akimova. Senior investigator of the Moscow procurature". I say:—I've heard about you.

Somewhat surprised: Really?

Actually I did hear that she sometimes handled political cases, that she liked to play the liberal, but nevertheless promptly executed the orders of those standing behind her.

So it happened! I'm again in jail.
This is already the third time.
On April 24, 1934—at eighteen—the GPU, Leningrad—the Shalernaya [prison].
June 8, 1949—at thirty three—the MGB, Moscow—the Lubyanka [prison].
September 12, 1969—at fifty-four—the police—Moscow.
At one a.m. I was led out of the police station and squeezed into a paddy wagon.
Heavens! What a sight: gloomy, distorted, unshaven faces, hats with bashed in
crowns, thieves, gangsters, debauchers of the young. I was to live in their midst for
eleven months. There was time to consider one important problem—the problem
of political prisoners. But first of all, to avoid all misunderstanding, I wish to
point out that I wasn't at all bothered by the fact that I was among criminals. I
got along very well with them. When I was asked whether they bothered me—I
answered: "No, it was more so I who bothered them." And really, I was often
ashamed that I could not return the respect, attention, and concern which they
showed me, not to mention my irritability and fits of temper (the more difficult
and unpleasant aspects of my character) which I visited upon them.
Nevertheless, the question arises: should political prisoners be kept together
with common criminals?
Jurists the world over would unanimously say: "No." No—because living among
criminals—the dregs of society, rough, cruel, and completely undeveloped intellectually and morally, is for an honest man a form of disguised torture. Nowhere
are people brought so close to each other as in prison or a labor camp—here they
share not only their food, their work, but even their bed, sleeping side by side.
And so all along you are in the midst of dreadful people, capable of everything,
people whom you would avoid on the street at night. In addition to mental torture,
the political prisoner feels humiliated: he has been placed on the same level with
the thieves, the gangsters, the murderers.
At present political prisoners are kept separately; however, the following
fantastic trick is being carried out to keep them with the criminals: those charged
under Article 70* are considered as political prisoners; however, those charged
under article 190** are regarded as criminals. There is nothing more stupid than
this "classification". Actually, who is to be considered a political or state criminal?
A person whose actions are directed directly against the state. A person who
ideologically opposed the state. But aren't persons charged under article 190, not
ideological opponents of the state? No less so than persons charged under Article
70. So how can one explain why they are housed with the criminals?
There is no and cannot be any other reasons but to inflict pain. Not everyone
gets along with people as easily as the writer of these lines. For example, how should
someone like Boris Vladimirovich Talantov, a sixty-five year old teacher of
mathematics, now in a camp for his writings, or thousands of others like him,
feel, thrust among criminals?
Finally we were brought to the prison in Matrosskaya Tishina (instead of the
Butyrki, as promised by Akimova). We approach. Our first night in prison. How
difficult it is to describe a prison to someone who has never been in it. Imagine a
large building something like a railroad station, in which the lights burn all night
long, in which like in a giant ant heap people scurry night and day—then you will
have some idea what a prison is like in a large city.
And so—night has come. Electric lights. Crowds of people. A great deal of
activity. It is at this hour that people are taken there and back, from cell to cell,
in expectation of some new formality to go through. The cells are relatively small,
about twenty meters each, with bare iron two-tier bunks and a flush toilet: the
air is stuffy and close, men swearing, filth . . . You are taken to the medic,
brought back from the medic, led to hand in your belongings, given receipts;
continuously taken in and out of cells; and all around—yelling, commands, oaths—
and everywhere people, people and people . . . "How many are there of you?",
burst out one of the officers who met us at Matrosskaya Tishina. *And truly, how
many?*
Here I had my first encounter with a representative of the administration. This
was Major Ivanov, head of solitary confinement block No. 1. It is extremely
painful to recall the interrogation of dozens of undressed men standing before
women interrogators, swearing no less foully than any man. These women interrogators relieve us of our keys, money, and all personal possessions, entering them
on the spot into a register. I was wearing a cross. A cross is usually taken off the
prisoner, entered in the register, and returned when the prisoner is transferred to
another prison or released. This time the cocky young girl who took away my
cross announced:

—We won't enter it in the register—we'll throw it away. And she repeated once again:—We'll throw it away.

In response I kicked up a row. The girls became embarrassed. One of them began arguing with me:

—Do you think the cross will help you get out of here any sooner?

Another one said:

—Well I just don't know. How can we enter a cross into the register? I just don't think that's possible. Speak to the head of the prison. As a matter of fact he is here right now.

A giant of a major came up to me. The following conversation took place between us:

—What do you want? What do you need the cross for? [Using the familiar Russian "thou", as with an inferior—Translator's note].

—First of all, don't "thou" me. You are talking to someone who is older than you.

—How do you know? [Still using the familiar "thou"]. Maybe I am older. (He wasn't even forty.)

—Not judging by your intellect. You've got the mind of a five-year old child. The cross belongs to me, and like all personal belongings should be entered in the register.

—Not for you, but for the priest (?!—A.K.) Don't register the cross—throw it away.

So that's how I lost my cross.

[Several lines on pages apparently missing from the xerox copy—Translator's note]

There I again settled into one of those famous "Stolypin" railroad cars (I certainly spent enough time in these cars in my day). But perhaps not everyone knows what a "Stolypin" car is. On one occasion P. A. Stolypin became incensed when F. I. Rodichev, a well-known orator in the Duma and a member of the State Duma representing the Kadet Party, ended his speech with the exclamation: "A Stolypin necktie!", outlining a gallows in the air with his hand. Stolypin challenged F. I. Rodichev to a duel; did the famous statesman ever think that his name would be remembered only in connection with prisoner railroad cars? The famous Stolypin "otrubs" (peasant land allotments), his founding of the Land Bank, the "June 3rd" Duma—all is forgotten. Only prisoners continue to remember his name in association with those dreadful railroad cars.

What a sad fate, but what a lesson! A lesson for many statesmen. But as Bernard Shaw said: "History teaches lessons which nobody ever applies". I said that the Stolypin cars were dreadful; but the term is not mine—it appears in the poems of my godson, Yevgeniy Kushev "the dreadful Stolypin cars." They are really dreadful: a shiver overtakes you as you enter the car. The car is divided into two compartments, separated by a grate from the floor to the ceiling. The first impression—a cage for wild animals. The part intended for the prisoners has no windows, and is divided into small cages (cell-compartments) containing three tiers. These compartments are sometimes occupied by fifteen to twenty people. Their most unpleasant feature is their lack of sanitation. If you are thirsty—the guard won't give you any water. Only after many reminders will he hand you an aluminum mug of water—one for every five to six prisoners. The mug passes from mouth to mouth (and by the way, syphilis is a very common disease among the criminals, nevertheless medical examination is very superficial in all prisons). [Xerox smudged and illegible, and apparently several lines missing—Translators note].

Meanwhile life went on.

The conditions, as I already said, were very harsh: the cell (a twenty meter room) was filled with people—between eighteen to twenty-five or twenty-six. Continuous smoking, and the toilet located in the cell, poisoned the air; the unending clatter of dominoes and the roar of the loud-speaker were deafening, and never stopped for a moment from six in the morning to ten at night.

The food—very meager, but at my age, generally speaking, sufficient; six hundred grams of black bread and, in the morning, two teaspoons of sugar and a thin gruel: a soup with noodles; at mid-day—lunch: a frightful cabbage soup (I almost never ate it), porridge, usually millet; in the evening—hot water without sugar and some soup.

The most difficult thing to bear were the awful sanitary conditions: the prisoners slept on two-tier plank-beds (welded metal bunks) which almost touched each other, on mattresses which were never changed (on the day of the public bath they were simply taken out into the yard and sprinkled with dust): there are no bed clothes—the prisoners are only given a mattress cover, a blanket, and a pillow. The only ones changed during the day of the public bath are the towel and the pillow case. The underclothes were taken for wash only until January, and then for some reason that stopped, so that the underclothes had to be washed in the cell under the cold water tap.

The public bath in the Armavir prison is a nightmare: the prisoners carry their mattresses and bed clothes which are then left outdoors. The prisoners are then led into the fore-bath entrance where they are invariably met by a yelling elderly woman who is said to have grown up in the prison at that job. (The story goes that her mother also had the same job). One had to see that woman with one's own eyes, yelling thunderously among those dozens of naked men—it is difficult to convey the picture. A sliver of black soap, sliced as thin as cheese, was given each prisoner for his bath; but the shower under which the prisoners washed operated for not more than ten minutes. It was almost impossible to get washed in this time.

However, above described conditions are a real paradise compared to the trips from Armavir to Sochi for the hearings. After an exhausting trip in a "Stolypin" car, which I already described, one is brought to Sochi to the local police station (on the main street of the town) because there is no prison in Sochi. Here a "room for those awaiting trail" (KPZ) greets you—a tiny room about ten meters, in which seven to eight fully clothed people lie side-by-side on the bare floor. At times the place is so crowded, it is impossible to stretch your legs. I spent eighteen days in such a place: between October 15 and November 4, 1969, and a second time, from January 10 to January 29, 1970. When after my first stay in Sochi I wrote to the local procurator, I received a reply from the assistant procurator of Sochi, Goncharov, that the conditions in which I found myself complied with the law.

Any comments are probably extraneous. I won't even go into it. I only want to bring attention to the following. Sochi is a beautiful resort town, to which people from all over the world flock for cures, rest, and amusement. There are dozens of sumptuous hotels, restaurants and cafes. And right there in their midst people are subjected to such dreadful conditions. People! What can those who permit the above say in their justification?

Nothing.

Two months had gone by. And now before me lies the opinion of the experts. This is truly a classic document. I will discuss it in greater detail.

The first question which the experts were asked was the following:

"What is the religious affiliation of the author?" The answer: "The author belongs to an extremist group within the Russian Orthodox Church. The aim of this group is unlimited religious propaganda, the abolition of all laws regulating the conduct of religious worship, religious education (including the establishment of Sunday schools), and the prohibition of antireligious education."

After reading this, I was, for a moment, dumbfounded. I must say, that I am not easily taken aback. I remember both the Stalin, the Yezhov, and the Beria periods; I am familiar with the utter unscrupulousness and deceit of the antireligious propaganda of the Khrushchev period, but I never expected such blatant lies.

The experts were so carried away with their illegally self-appointed judicial functions, and so taken with their role, that at the end of their report they took it upon themselves to sentence me:

"Levitin, along with other dangerous sectarians, should be imprisoned."

TRANSFER BETWEEN TWO POINTS

(POTMA PRISON CAMP TO PERM)

1972

[The following account was smuggled out of a prison camp a short time ago]

(1) There were fifteen people in a compartment; sweat pouring down in streams; foodstuff has gone bad; for two days we have not been let out to relieve ourselves. People have been forced to relieve themselves in the corridor. They have ordered us to take soap and toothbrushes for the journey, even though they knew in ad-

vance that prisoners would not be allowed to use these things. They poured water from above (but) wouldn't open the air vents; only toward the end of the trip they opened them a little bit which was of little help. Naked people were lying on the floor; filth, stench, a lack of air. One man died en route. Terrible torment.

(2) In Perm the prisoners submitted a complaint about the conditions of the transfer. The reply (A general's reply was passed on to us that "everything was in accordance with the law". Conclusion: either he is covering up a crime or everything was in accordance with his instructions. Everything was planned.)

(3) To Rodionov: "Hey, beard, come here!" Ten days in solitary. Twenty people went on a hunger strike (Jews also). Izza was deprived of his visiting privileges. Wolff was deprived of his canteen privileges, visitors were cut off earlier.

(4) On the 4th of September all prisoners addressed a petition to the Red Cross requesting that the 4th of September be considered a day commemorating the 40 million who had perished during the 1930's, so that families could display photographs of their dead relatives and light two candles: one for their relatives and the other for the 40 million. Jews participated the first day. (However), they did not take part in the memorial ceremony.

(5) For refusal to attend political indoctrination sessions people have been deprived of visiting rights. There is an intention of declaring a one day hunger strike and write a petition about compulsory communist indoctrination.

Requests for prisoner

(6) Organize adoption of prisoner by Kibbutzim—Dymshitz, Osher, Frolov, Zeidilfed, Yakov Suslinsky.

(7) Aid Lila Dreisner and Bronya Chernoglaz to emigrate to Israel.

(8) On the 12th of September for refusal to attend political indoctrination session Chernoglaz was deprived of visiting rights. Earlier Yefrem Mendelvitch was deprived of visiting rights fot the same reason.

(9) As a sign of protest against further imprisonment of Sylva Zalmonson on her birthday the 25th of October, the following people have declared a hunger strike: Wolff, Izza and Eduard Kuznetsov for three days; Dymshitz and Chernoglaz for three days beginning 27 October; Mendelvich and Grengauz for three days from 29 October; Frolov and Suslinsky for three days from 1 November.

The text of the declaration when hunger strike announced:

Sylva is not guilty, since she was forced to what she did by the unlawful actions of the authorities; she is a woman; the condition of her health is constantly deteriorating and she has been imprisoned long enough.

(10) They confiscated for investigation the Chernoglaz Hebrew notebook and won't give it back.

(11) When they shaved off the beards, they handcuffed the prisoners, and even though there was not resistance, they were deprived of visiting rights and put in solitary.

(12) Chernoglaz, Dymshitz and several others have not worked now for two months.

SELF-MUTILATION AND ATTEMPTED ESCAPES

[Excerpts from "My Testimony" by Anatoly Marchenko, E. P. Dutton Co., New York, 1969]

Here is one out of a number of similar stories, from which it differs only in its originality. It took place before my very own eyes in the spring of 1963. One of my cellmates, Sergei K., who had been reduced to utter despair by the hopelessness of various protests and hunger strikes and by the sheer tyranny and injustice of it all, resolved, come what may, to maim himself. Somewhere or other he got hold of a piece of wire, fashioned a hook out of it and tied it to some home-made twine (to make which he had unravelled his socks and plaited the threads). Earlier still he had obtained two nails and hidden them in his pocket during the searches. Now he took one of the nails, the smaller of the two, and with his soup bowl started to hammer it into the food flap—very, very gently, trying not to clink and let the warders hear—after which he tied the twine with the hook to the nail. We, the rest of the cons in the cell, watched him in silence. I don't know who was feeling what while this was going on, but to interfere, as I have already pointed out, is out of the question: every man has the right to dispose of himself and his life in any way he thinks fit.

Sergei went to the table in the middle of the room, undressed stark naked, sat down on one of the benches at the table and swallowed his hook. Now, if the warders started to open the door or the food flap, they would drag Sergei like a pike out of a pond. But this still wasn't enough for him: if they pulled he would willy-nilly be dragged towards the door and it would be possible to cut the twine through the aperture for the food flap. To be absolutely sure, therefore, Sergei took the second nail and began to nail his testicles to the bench on which he was sitting. Now he hammered the nail loudly, making no attempt to keep quite. It was clear that he had thought out the whole plan in advance and calculated and reckoned that he would have time to drive in his nail before the warder arrived. And he actually did succeed in driving it right in to the very head. At the sound of the hammering and banging the warder came, slid the shutter aside from the peep-hole and peered into the cell. All he realized at first, probably, was that one of the prisoners had a nail, one of the prisoners was hammering a nail. And his first impulse, evidently, was to take it away. He began to open the cell door; and then Sergei explained the situation to him. The warder was nonplussed.

Soon a whole group of warders had gathered in the corridor by our door. They took turns at peering through the peephole and shouting at Sergei to snap the twine. Then, realizing that he had no intention of doing so, the warders demanded that one of us break the twine. We remained sitting on our bunks without moving; somebody only poured out a stream of curses from time to time in answer to their threats and demands. But now it came up to dinner time, we could hear the servers bustling up and down the corridor, from neighboring cells came the sound of food flaps opening and the clink of bowls. One fellow in the cell could endure it no longer—before you know it we'd be going without dinner—he snapped the cord by the food flap. The warders burst into the cell. They clustered around Sergei, but there was nothing they could do; the nail was driven deep into the bench and Sergei just went on sitting there in his birthday suit, nailed down by the balls. One of the warders ran to admin to find out what they should do with him. When he came back he ordered us all to gather up our things and move to another cell.

I don't know what happened to Sergei after that. Probably he went to the prison hospital—there were plenty of mutilated prisoners there: some with ripped open stomachs, some who had sprinkled powdered glass in their eyes and some who had swallowed assorted objects—spoons, toothbrushes, wire. Some people used to grind sugar down to dust and inhale it—until they got an abscess of the lung. . . . Wounds sewn up with thread, two lines of buttons stitched to the bare skin, these were such trifles that hardly anybody ever paid attention to them.

The surgeon in the prison hospital was a man of rich experience. His most frequent job was opening up stomachs, and if there had been a museum of objects taken out of stomachs, it would surely have been the most astonishing collection in the world.

Operations for removing tattoos were also very common. I don't know how it is now, but from 1963 to 1965 these operations were fairly primitive: all they did was cut out the offending patch of skin, then draw the edges together and stitch them up. I remember one con who had been operated on three times in that way. The first time they had cut out a strip of skin from his forehead with the usual sort of inscription in such cases: 'Khrushchev's Slave'. The skin was then cobbled together with rough stitches. He was released and again tattooed his forehead: 'Slave of the USSR.' Again he was taken to hospital and operated on. And again, for a third time, he covered his whole forehead with 'Slave of the CPSU'. This tattoo was also cut out at the hospital and now, after three operations, the skin was so tightly stretched across his forehead that he could no longer close his eyes. We called him 'The Stare'.

In the same place, in Vladimir, I once happened to spend several days in a cell with Subbotin. This was a fellow the same age as myself and a homosexual. There were few homosexuals in Vladimir and everyone knew who they were. There was nothing they could earn there. He had been classed as a 'political' after being in an ordinary criminal camp and making an official complaint—thus 'letting the tone down'. One day, after having sent about forty or fifty complaints to Brezhnev and the Presidium of the Supreme Council and to Khrushchev and the Central Committee of the Communist Party of the Soviet Union, he swallowed a whole set of dominoes—twenty-eight pieces. When the whole of our cell was being led down the corridor to the exercise yard—he had swallowed the dominoes just before our exercise period—he clapped himself on the stomach and said to one con from camp maintenance who was coming the other way: 'Listen, Valery!' I don't know whether Valery really heard the sound of dominoes knocking together in Subbotin's stomach, but he asked him: 'What have you got there?' and Subbotin drawled 'Dominoes'.

The doctors wouldn't operate on Subbotin. They simply ordered him to count the pieces during defecation, saying that they would have to come out on their own. Subbotin conscientiously counted them each time and on his return to the cell ticked off in pencil on a special chart the number that had come out. No matter how diligently he counted, however, four pieces still remained unaccounted for. After several days of agonizing suspense he washed his hands of them: if they stayed in his stomach it was all right as long as they didn't interfere, and if they were out already, then to the devil with them.

I should point out that Tkach believed in Keshka's story not only because he was cracked; everyone who had done time in Vladimir knew of cases even more horrifying than cannibalism. In one cell, for instance, the cons had done as follows: they had got hold of a razor blade somewhere and for several days collected up paper. When everything was ready they each cut a piece of flesh from their bodies—some from the stomach, others from the leg. Everybody's blood was collected into one bowl, the flesh was thrown in, a small fire was made from the paper and some books and then they started to half-fry, half-stew their feast. When the warders noticed that something was wrong and burst into the cell the stew was still not cooked and the cons, falling over themselves and burning their fingers, grabbed the pieces from the bowl and stuffed them into their mouths. Even the wardens said afterwards that it was a horrible sight.

I can well imagine that this story is hard to believe. But later I personally met some of the participants in that terrible feast and talked with them. The most remarkable thing of all was that they were fully normal people.

I have already mentioned self-mutilation in the cooler and such cases are even more frequent on special regime. Men gouge their eyes out, throw ground glass in them, or hang themselves. At night sometimes they slit their veins under the blankets; and if their neighbor doesn't wake up soaked in blood, yet one more martyr is freed of his burden.

One day three cons agreed to put an end to themselves in the usual way, that is with the help of the sentries. At about three in the afternoon they took three planks from the brick factory and placed them against the wall. The sentry in the watch tower shouted:

"Stand back or I'll fire!"

"By all means, and deliver us from this happy life," replied one of the cons and started climbing. Having reached the top, he got entangled in the barbed wire there. At this moment there was a burst of tommy gun fire from the tower and he slumped across the wire and hung there. Then the second man climbed up and calmly awaited his turn. A short burst of fire and he fell to the ground at the foot of the fence. The third man followed and he too fell beside the first.

I was told later that one of them had remained alive, he had been seen in the hospital at camp three. So at least he had escaped from special regime for a time. The other two, of course, had escaped for ever, shot dead on the spot. In general this suicide was just like many others, differing only in that it was a group affair. Individual instances are common, and not only in special regime camps.

A sentry who picks off such an 'escaper' in this way gets rewarded with extra leave to show admin's gratitude. But the attitude of the other soldiers to the marksman doesn't always coincide with admin's. Once, in camp seven in the autumn of 1963, a sentry shot a routine suicide case, a fellow who was ill, when he was on the wall. He got his leave all right, but he was black and blue when he set off for home: that night the other soldiers had organized a little farewell party for him, though under a different pretext, of course.

Once I saw two former criminal cons, then politicals, who were nicknamed Mussa and Mazai. On their foreheads and cheeks they had tattoos: 'Communists=butchers' and 'Communists drink the blood of the people'. Later I met many more cons with such sayings tattooed on their faces. The most common of all, tattooed in big letters across the forehead, was: 'Khrushchev's slave' or 'Slave of the CPSU' (Communist Party of the Soviet Union).

Here in the special regime camp, in our hut, there was a fellow called Nikolai Shcherbakov. When I caught sight of him in the exercise yard through the window I almost collapsed; there wasn't a single clear spot on his whole face. On one cheek he had 'Lenin was a butcher' and on the other it continued: 'Millions are suffering because of him'. Under his eyes was: 'Khrushchev, Brezhnev, Voroshilov are butchers'. On his pale, skinny neck a hand had been tattooed in black ink. It was gripping his throat and on the back of the hand were the letters CPSU, while the middle finger, ending on his adam's apple, was labelled KGB.

Shcherbakov was in another corner cell similar to ours, only at the other end of the hut. At first I only saw him through the window when their cell was taken out for exercise. Later, though, we three were transferred to another cell and we often exercised simultaneously in adjoining yards. In secret conversion, unnoticed by the warders, we got to know one another. I became convinced that he was normal and not cracked, as I had thought at first. He was far from stupid, he used to read quite a lot and he knew all the news in the newspapers. Together with him in one cell were Mazai and the homosexual, Misha, both with tattooed faces!

In late September 1961, when our cell was taken out for exercise, Nikolai asked us in sign language whether anyone had a razor blade. In such cases it is not done to ask what for—if somebody asks, it means they need it, and if you've got one you hand it over, with no questions asked. I had three blades at that time which I still had from camp ten, before landing in the cooler, and I had hidden them in the peak of my cap as a necessary precaution; in spite of all the searches they had never been found. I went into the latrines, ripped open the seam under the peak with my teeth and took out one blade. Back in the yard, when the warder's attention was distracted, I stuck it into a crack on one of the wooden fence posts to which the barbed wire was secured. Nikolai watched me from his window. The blade stayed there in the crack all day long. Many other cons saw it—the boys used to scour every corner of the exercise yard while outside, every pebble, every crack, in the hope of finding something useful. But once a blade has been placed somewhere, that means it already has an owner waiting to pick it up; in such a case nobody will touch it. Furthermore Nikolai spent the whole day at the window, keeping watch on the blade just in case. While exercising the following day he picked out the blade and took it back to his cell.

Later that evening a rumor passed from cell to cell: 'Shcherbakov has cut off his ear'. And later we learned the details. He had already tattooed the ear: 'A gift to the 22nd Congress of the CPSU'. Evidently he had done it beforehand, otherwise all the blood would have run out while it was being tattooed. Then, having amputated it, he started knocking on the door and when the warder had unlocked the outer door, Shcherbakov threw his ear through the bars to him and said: 'Here's a present for the 22nd Congress.'

This incident is well known to all cons in Mordovia.

The next day we saw Shcherbakov at the window of his cell. His head was bandaged and in the place where his right ear should have been the bandage was soaked with blood, and blood was on his face, neck and hands. A couple of days later he was taken off to hospital, but what happened to him after that I do not know.

And that is the reason why cons always have to be without their caps during inspection and to uncover their foreheads, so that they can be checked for tattoos. Men with tattoos are first sent to the cooler and then put in separate cells, so as not to corrupt the others. Wherever they go after that they are. . .

One of the prisoners here in camp number ten was a Lithuanian, Richardas K. He had once taken part in an escape bid and he told me how they had been caught. Three of them, all Lithuanians, had somehow managed to elude their escorts while at work in the fields and had only been noticed when near a wood. They came under fire, but it was already too late. Then the tommy gunners were called up from division headquarters; they put a cordon round the wood and soldiers with dogs began to hunt the fugitives. It was not long before the dogs found the scent and soon Richardas and his comrades heard the chase almost at their backs. They realized that come what may they could not avoid it, but still they tried to hide in the hope that the guards with the dogs would plunge straight past them. The other two shinned up an oak tree and hid in the foliage, while Richardas buried himself in fallen leaves (the time was autumn) beneath a bush. The scene that followed happened literally before his very eyes.

He had not even had time to camoflage himself properly with the leaves when two soldiers appeared with dogs. The dogs circled the oak trees and clawed at the bark with their front paws. A further six tommy gunners ran up together with an officer holding a pistol. The young men in the tree were discovered at once. The officer shouted: 'So you wanted freedom, you mother——? Come on, get down!'

The lowest branch was about six feet off the ground. Richardas saw one of his companions put his feet on the branch, then crouch down and ease his stomach on to the branch so that he was hanging across it, with his hands on the branch and his legs in the air, ready to jump down. At that moment he heard the sound of several bursts from a tommy gun and the young man fell to the ground like a sack. But he was still alive, he writhed and squirmed with pain. The officer fired another shot into him and ordered the dogs to be unleashed. The man on the ground, meanwhile, was unable even to defend himself. When the dogs had been dragged off, he remained lying motionless on the ground. The officer ordered him to be picked up and carried away. They dug the toes of their boots into him, but he did not rise. Then the officer said: 'Why spoil your boots on him? What do you think your weapons are for?' The soldiers started stabbing the wounded man with their bayonets and jeering: 'Come on, come on, stand upon, don't try to pretend!' The wounded man labored to get to his feet. His bullet-riddled arms flapped like empty sleeves. His tattered clothes had slipped off down to his waist. He was completely smothered in blood. Prodding him along with their bayonets, they led him to the next tree. The officer called out: 'Guard halt!' The fugitive collapsed at the foot of the tree. Two soldiers and a dog remained to keep watch on him while the rest turned their attention to the second youth. He too was ordered to climb down from the tree. Having decided, evidently, to be more clever, he did not go as far as the lower branches, but plummetted on to the ground at the very feet of the soldiers. No one had time to fire. As he lay there on the ground the officer bounded over to him and fired several shots into his legs. Then he received the same treatment as the first; he was kicked unconscious, savaged by the dogs and then stabbed by bayonets, Finally the officer ordered the beating to stop, went over to the youth and said: 'All right, free and independent Lithuania, tell me, where's the third?' The youth was silent. The officer swung his boot into him and repeated the question. Richardas heard his comrade croak: 'I'd call you a fascist, but you're worse than that.' The officer was outraged: 'I fought against the fascists myself! In the front line. And with fascists like you as well. How many of us did you shoot back home in Lithuania?' Again they threw themselves on the wounded youth and started to beat him. Then the officer ordered him to crawl on his hands and knees to the tree where the first man lay: "If you don't want to walk you can crawl!"

And the wounded youth, with his legs broken, started to crawl, egged on by bayonets like the first. The officer walked along beside him and jeered: "Free Lithuania! Go on, crawl, you'll get your independence!" Richardas told me that this youth was a student from Vilnius and had got seven years for distributing pamphlets.

When the two fugitives were together they were beaten and bayonetted again, this time to death. Finally there were no more groans or cries. The officer assured himself that they were dead and sent to the settlement for a cart. He evidently counted on dealing with the third one by the time the cart arrived. Richardas, however, took quite some time to find. Whether it was the dogs who were tired, or perhaps the smell of decomposing leaves that threw them off the scent, they were quite unable to find him. Soldiers ran about the wood, almost stepping on him and the officer stood no more than two yards away from his bush. Richardas said that on several occasions he was ready to leap up and run for it. And it was only when Richardas could already hear the sound of cart wheels grinding along the road that the officer came up to the pile of leaves, prodded them with his toe and instantly yelled: "Here he is, the bastard! Get up!" At that moment the cart came along. "Where are the escaped prisoners, comrade major?" Richardas stood up. The major was aiming his pistol straight at him. Instinctively Richardas jerked round at the very instant the shot rang out, then felt a searing pain in his chest and shoulder and fell to the ground. He did not lose consciousness, but lay there motionless, trying not to stir or groan. Other men gathered around and somebody asked "Maybe he's still alive, comrade major?" And the major replied: "Alive my foot! I shot him point blank in the chest." He could not have noticed how Richardas had turned away.

Richardas was thrown into the bottom of the cart—even then he managed not to groan—and the two corpses were piled on top of him. The cart moved off towards the camp. Richardas heard someone approach the cart and heard the major say: "Killed while trying to escape."

But a trial's only a trial and escaping prisoners are intentionally killed while being caught so as to put off the rest from trying. And the injured and beaten are purposely not healed. Seeing someone like Richardas without an arm, many men think twice about whether it's worth the risk. But a trial, a prison sentence—that would stop nobody under the conditions that exist in our prison camps.

But even without Richardas's story I well remembered the incident at the Bukhtarma power station. There the officer had fired practically point blank at an unarmed fugitive. I had seen that myself. And I and all the others knew that if we were caught the odds were against us remaining alive. But nonetheless we decided to take the risk.

This old man of ours was not only cracked but also very weak physically. He was always complaining about pains in his head, pains in his spine, pains in his heart. One day the two of us applied to see the doctor. During her rounds the nurse always asks through the food trap: "Is anybody sick?" Almost all the cons complain about some ailment or other, especially in winter and then the nurse, not bothering to examine the patient, gives him some sort of powder. But if the complaint exceeds her competence she registers the con hospital block. The doctor came, looked at Tkach, felt his pulse and quietly laid the limp arm across his breast. Then, after questioning us as to what had happened, she called the senior warder outside. She never appeared again, but the senior warder came back and ordered Kekshtas and me to carry the old man out. I took him under the arms. Kekshtas took the legs, and we dragged the body into an empty cell that was indicated to us. There the warder ordered us to lay the dead man on a bare cot and then hurried us out again. The cell was locked. I said to the warder:

"I suppose Tkach can lie on his cot till lights out now, can he?"

"Do you want to go in the cooler?" roared the warder as usual.

Tkach was dead. He had been completely alone, nobody had ever helped him and he never ever received any letters from anyone. But maybe he has relatives somewhere who lost touch with him and don't know what became of him. And so: old man Tkach starved for many years, suffered, fell ill, froze and died in Vladimir Prison in the winter of 1962.

LETTER FROM CAMP No. 17 DUBROVNYY DIRECTORATE OF CORRECTIVE LABOUR CAMPS (MORDOVSKA ASSR)

[Translated from Samizdat]

Camp No. 17 under the Dubrovnyy Directorate of Corrective Labour Camps is located in the village of Ozerne in the Zubovo-Polans'kiy rayon of Mordovia. The camp has two zones: the main one holds approximately 700 women convicted for ordinary crimes, and a second holds 276 male political prisoners. The chief of Camp 17 is Captain Novikov; chief of section 17–A (the men's zone) is Captain Annenkov; chief of the medical section is first lieutenant Zabaykin; the representative of the KGB to Camp 17 is Captain Ivan Romanovych Krut'.

The majority of the male prisoners are invalids. There are 208 invalids of the second category and 51 of the third. In this zone there are only two crowded, cold and badly ventilated barracks. Food is brought in from the women's zone and in spite of the fact that the prisoner's food ration is very small to begin with, he never receives a full portion anyway. Even a healthy person cannot eat the sour, half-raw bread—not to mention sick people who make up the majority of the camps inmates.

Medical aid is virtually non-existant. For example, on January 7, 1967, the prisoner Mykhailo Soroka, who has spent 31 years in Polish and Soviet prisons (24 years in Soviet prisons), fell seriously ill with myocardium infarct. In such cases immediate qualified medical aid is essential. But a medical assistant arrived only four days later, on January 11th. On the seventh day after his attack, Soroka was taken to the medical station. Up to this time he had remained in the barracks and was looked after by Mykola Yevdokimov, one of the prisoners who is also an experienced medical assistant but who was helpless without drugs and instruments.

The so-called hospital contains only 7 beds—to accomodate 22 invalids the majority of whom are seriously ill and quite old. There are no drugs and the prisoners are not allowed to receive any from their families (not even vitamins, although the diet is so poor). No one even thinks of dentists and such. Theoretically, the seriously ill should be transferred to the central hospital (in camp No. 3 in the village of Barashevo). But this is not always possible, as in Soroka's case, if the sick man cannot be moved (especially over these terrible roads).

Often directing a man to the central hospital brings no results. On several occasions when the camp doctors sent prisoners to the central hospital with diagnoses of cancer, the doctors at the central hospital, instead of releasing the prisoners on the basis of their illness (they have full right to do this), sent them back to the camp with a diagnosis of severe gastritis. Only the prisoners' death and autopsy confirmed the initial diagnosis. Prisoners are released only in cases where death is expected to come a few days after the release. What else can one expect from people who will not take one step without orders from the KGB and the operational department?

In Camp No. 3 (the central hospital), the deciding voice is that of the chief of the regime, Captain Kitsayev, who released and sent back to camp Dr. Horboviy although his treatment was far from being finished. Similar cases occur quite often. During Karavansky's hunger strike, the chief of the medical section in Camp No. 11, Yeremeyeva, stated that she knows about the hunger strike but she cannot do anything because she has no orders from the operational department. The prisoner Ivan Maksym applied several times for medical aid to the surgeon in Camp No. 11, but the latter refused to talk to him, calling him a simulator. As a result, the prisoner died.

The medical personnel chosen from among the prisoners is not much better: only people who cooperate with the KGB and the operational department are selected. Medical training plays absolutely no part in the selection. For example, such medics-prisoners as Yaroslav Hevrych and Dmytro Verkholyak, were transferred from their jobs in the medical section and put to work in the workshops, although there is a shortage of medical workers. But men who have no connection with medicine, as for example Malykhin, and those who are in the good graces of the KGB and the operational department, have worked and still work in the medical center. If there is an experienced and conscientious medical worker in Camp No. 17, this is only because he did not please someone with no medical training at the central hospital and was sent to Camp No. 17.

On the whole, Camp No. 17 is organized as a penal camp. The administration does not hide this in their conversations, although officially it is not considered as such. In addition to invalids, they have brought to this camp people who had no inclination to submit to the so-called educational work among prisoners and thus could by their actions or examples negatively influence other prisoners to the same end. Therefore a policy of repressions towards the prisoners is severely applied here directed at undermining health and suppressing the least display of rebellion or protest. With this aim in mind, the organized manufacture (sewing of gloves and construction) is based on a system of compulsion, arbitrariness and repressions. Prisoners who work on construction do not have the required warm clothing (felt boots, quilted jackets); the temperature in the shop stays between $+5°$ C and $+9°$ C and the floor temperature is usually under $0°$ C. Thus any talk of normal work, when one has to hold metal machine parts in one's hands at such temperatures, is absurd. Nevertheless, the prisoner is expected to fill a quota which would be impossible to fill even under normal circumstances, whereas here the equipment is broken down and the premises where the prisoners are forced to spend 9 hours are unheated (the prisoners are supposed to work an 8-hour day).

One hour is reserved for a so-called lunch break and rest period. But not only is this not a rest, it is an additional punishment, because people are forced to spend an extra hour in the cold building. Lunch and supper are served in unsanitary conditions, in generally dirty premises, without tables—so that the prisoner has to eat at his machine. There is nowhere to wash one's hands because the tiny wash-basin cannot hold enough water for everyone, and in the work area there is neither water nor towels. Smoking is prohibited in both the workshop and in the corridor. As there is no place where smoking is allowed, the prisoners are forced to smoke in the hallway leading to the street where doors are continually being opened and there is a constant draft (here temperatures are at $-30°$ C).

The administration constantly threatens those who do not fill their quotas with repressions (at this time there is no one who fills his quota) and they will put these repressions into force as soon as the training period is over (at the beginning of February, 1967). Because invalids of the second category do not have to work and there are not enough people to do the work, the administration has announced that it will form a local medical commission to re-categorize the invalids and put them to work. Captain Annenkov, chief of section 17-a has spoken openly about this.

The reason for this is that prior to our arrival there was a camp for female political prisoners here. The majority of the prisoners was comprised of women convicted for religious beliefs—in other words, a group which was least capable of opposing the arbitrariness of camp administration or even of protesting various pressures. In addition, these were mostly old women. The guards say that they were exhausted, ragged creatures, who were forced to work in cold premises where the temperature seldom rose 2 or 3 degrees above zero and more often remained below zero. In so far as the system of compulsion had become a tradition here, they intend to maintain it for the future. No wonder that the guards state quite openly that the more we complain about their violations of our legal rights, the more the authorities praise them—and vice versa.

Have the prisoners tried to complain about these numerous violations, pressures, and injustices? They have done so more than once with no results. The chief of the camp, Capt. Annenkov, shouted that things would remain as they are. The head engineer, when he was told that we are forced to eat in the cold, in unsanitary premises, replied that this is not his concern and suggested that we direct our appeals "Vanka Vyetrov" (an expression meaning "talk to the wind"). After numerous complaints, a medical inspector arrived from the medical sector of Dubravlag Directorate. In the first place he did not believe that the temperature in the work shop was much too low (he refused to measure on the spot), and stated that "quotas were always filled and exceeded here". After we had told him that we had recently sent out a number of complaints signed by the foreman (a free man) in which we mentioned the temperature in the workshop, he only asked to whom we had addressed them and showed dissatisfaction that we had sent these complaints to the Prosecutor General rather than to the Directorate.

With regard to the complaint written by the writer Daniel about the shocking attitude to Mykhailo Soroka's illness, the same medical inspector stated that all these matters were irrelevant (the sick man had not died during the time when he had received no medical aid) and tried to force Daniel to acknowledge that everything was in order in the camp (he needed this for his report). Daniel refused. Small wonder then that when prisoners demand what is theirs legally, the representatives of the administration do nothing and assure them "You may complain", because they know that no one will pay the slightest attention to the complaints. To whom can we address our complaints when our educators of the past sit in all the departments? Their caliber is obvious from such facts as that in Camp No. 7, the man who was doctor there for two or three years, had before been the representative from the operational department to Camp No. 19, from where he had been transferred for attempting to rape a nurse. At present he is working as an orderly officer in the prison in Ruzayevka in Mordovia. In Camp No. 1, the chief of section is first lieutenant Nekrasov who had previously been a medical worker in the same camp. Our attorneys supervision is similar to the medical care we receive. (Our attorneys often switch from positions as lawyers to positions as chiefs of camps, Directorate officials and vice versa. This is what happened to our present assistant chief of Dubrovnyy Camp Directorate, Nekachan.)

We have already mentioned our letters and packages. I want to add that our reception of packages of books which is legally permitted to us, depends (as do our letters) on the will of the KGB operative (in this case, Capt. Krut') who makes our right an illusion.

The camp holds representatives of various nations of the Soviet Union. There are Latvians, Lithuanians, Estonians, and Russians. As might be expected, there are also quite a few Ukrainians.

Who are they?

(Here follows a list of Ukrainian prisoners. The author (or authors) of this letter groups them into the following categories: "participants of national liberation movements 1942–1954 and of various illegal groups of similar nature"; "those convicted for religious beliefs (Catholics, Baptists, Jehovah's Witnesses, etc.); "those convicted for so-called anti-Soviet agitation, for attempts to cross the border, and similar crimes"; "those convicted of crimes committed during the war". The list gives the name of the prisoner, the oblast he comes from, his date of birth, date of arrest, date of sentence. There is a total of 114 names on the list. However, this is obviously not a complete list of Ukrainian prisoners in Camp No. 19 becasue at the end of some categories, there appears "and others".)

. . . . Although all the Ukrainians listed here were sentenced by UkrSSR courts, they are held (and always have been held) in Russian camps. This is only one more unnecessary proof of UkrSSR's rejection of her sovereignty—carrying out the sentences of her courts.

. . . . There are only 17 categorical prisoners—that is, prisoners capable of work—in the camp.

The chief of the Dubrovnyy Directorate of Camps is Colonel Gromov, known for his arbitrariness in the 40's and 50's in Kamyshlah (Kemerovo Oblast). The chief of the KGB section attached to the Dubrovnyy Directorate is lieutenant-colonel Blinov.

THE KINGIR UPRISING—KINGIR PRISONERS FIGHT AGAINST TANKS

[From "The Profits of Slavery" by Adolphs Silde, Latvian National Foundation in Scandinavia, Stockholm, 1958]

The most dramatic of all uprisings occurred in the Kingir copper mine region in Central Asia. Nine thousand male and four thousand female camp inmates participated in it. Only a few, possibly a hundred, avoided the fight; most of them were MVD informers who had to stand aside in the interests of their personal safety. A year earlier, the Ukrainian resistance organization—the largest in this camp—had killed about 100 stool pigeons. In cooperation with the Balts and other national groups there evolved, in time, a special "counter-intelligence service" which managed to unmask every informer and traitor. This enabled the Kingir rebels to open their fight in a spirit of greater unity than in Vorkuta.

The Kingir strike developed from the very outset into a well-organized uprising. Leadership of the strike was assumed by Colonel Kuznetsov, one of the most popular Soviet officers, who had acquired undeniable merit in storming Berlin at the end of World War II. In 1952, he was arrested on charges of having attempted to escape to West Berlin with an entire tank regiment. After having been kept in various prisons, he was sent in 1954 to Kingir—a place which, according to the MVD, housed only "fascists." The Soviet security authorities had a hard time with these "fascists." As stated above, the political prisoners in Kingir had gotten the better of the MVD agents, and the MVD therefore tried to regain its influence.

It formed a plan. In April 1954, about 600 criminal prisoners were sent to Kingir which since 1949 had only had political internees.

"You see," an MVD officer told one of the newcomers a few days after their arrival, "the fascists plan to attack and do away with you. Unless you forestall them, your days are numbered. Try to teach them a lesson; we shall back you up in every possible way."

However, men who have spent long years in interment develop a special instinct. This particular man and other criminal convicts understood that the MVD was using them. One of them went to see a representative of the political prisoners and told him frankly what he had been told.

It turned out that the new arrivals had been imprisoned with political prisoners a few years previously, and, under their guidance, had seen through the Soviet methods of terrorism.

The spokesman of the criminal interned said they favored solidarity with the political prisoners, especially where the common interests of all interned were at stake.

Who were these criminal prisoners?

Many were youths whom grim Soviet life had left without parents, school or home. Not so many years ago they were called *bezprizorniye*, meaning "those without home and shelter." There was no one to help and take care of them. Some of them had been sent—at the age of 16—to the Kingir camp branded as habitual criminals. Their chests and hands were tattooed. These children of Stalin's dictatorship, interned behind barbed wire or thick walls, listened, perplexed, to stories about the "sunken world" which the October Revolution had replaced by the dictatorship of the proletariat. One thing, however, seemed quite clear to them—the Chekists could not possibly be their friends and therefore they did not even covet the benefits promised by the MVD.

It was soon found that the MVD planned to incite the criminal internees against the political prisoners; the subsequent clash would disclose the leaders of the latter, something the MVD had so far failed to achieve with stool pigeons or otherwise in Kingir.

One of those who enjoyed authority from the very outset was the aforesaid Colonel Kuznetsov.

He not only spoke but wrote frankly, showing no respect for or fear of the Soviet power. And so, for having described the prison cell of the camp in a letter to his wife, he was confined there himself, joining 400 other prisoners.

The true reasons behind the activity of the newcomers were not clear, but one Sunday they dismantled the heating tube of the camp bath and used it to break through the separating wall of the neighboring camp. It was one of the internal walls designed to separate the different camps. An outer wall, eight meters thick, encircled the whole camp area.

The wall was two brick-lengths thick. It would have been impossible to break through it with a pipe, unless a place had been chosen which was formerly a passage way. This was done and the passage was reopened.

Eye-witnesses have reported that the guards were amazed. They had orders to shoot, but did not do so. As they hesitated, it was possible to free 400 internees and 200 held in the penal barrack. Kuznetsov, too, was released. He may even have imagined that the prison was forcibly opened because of him. Having thus regained partial freedom, Kuznetsov assumed the leadership of the political prisoners. He ordered the capture of the camp guards.

The criminal prisoners meanwhile continued their task. The wall which separated the two men's camps from the women's camp was pierced within an hour. Four thousand women were no longer separated from the rest of the camp inmates.

By next morning the situation could be seen more clearly. The guards had been captured, but their officers had escaped. Food warehouses and other strategic places in the camp were guarded by lookouts selected by the prisoners themselves.

Another day passed, and the Soviet administration and the MVD prepared countermeasures. At three o'clock the next morning, MVD units entered the camp from three sides. The MVD guards had been drinking. With shouts, they attacked everyone who crossed their path, using bayonets or rifle butts. Shots were heard from the women's camp. As the internees of neighboring camps were driven out from the women's camp, they were fired on. Some 60 or 70 dead were counted. The number of wounded was higher. The MGB hurriedly transported the dead to nearby Dzhezkazgan.

Kuznetsov, who now grouped around him representatives of all nationalities, protested against this action. He was supported by Balts and by Ukranian partisans known as *banderists*.

The regulations forbade armed guards to enter the camp, but this night whole military units had broken into it.

"We demand the punishment of the guilty! Armed units had no right to penetrate into the camp area." This was the slogan under which the Kingir camp inmates began their strike. They knew that the military action had been taken without Moscow's knowledge and that the law, even if it was Soviet law, was on their side. In the case of any setback, the Soviets always look for scapegoats; if the strike looked like ending in favor of the interned, Moscow would blame the Soviet officials in Kingir and this event would not pass unnoticed. The strikers knew this, and therefore stressed the illegal character of the camp administration's action.

The strikers also demanded that the bodies of their fallen comrades be brought back to the site of the clash. Only in this way could they prove that their fellows had been killed by MVD bullets and had not—as the administration might allege—been killed by the strikers themselves. Another demand was that no internees be transferred to another camp during the coming weeks.

The local Soviet officials promised to fulfill the strikers' demands and in addition undertook to summon a public prosecutor. The acceptance of their demands made the strikers call off the strike which had lasted three days.

However, as soon as the work brigades began work, the guards rounded up the criminal convicts and drove them out of the camp. Since the original scheme of the MVD had failed, it had been decided to send them elsewhere. The MVD men behaved so brutally that this alone caused new trouble.

One of the criminal convicts succeeded in reaching the camp siren and sounded a warning which was heard by political prisoners working on a building. Their prompt decision was to return to the camp. The guards stopped them, but work ended.

On their return to the camp in the evening, the political prisoners learned about the administration's failure to honor its pledge and indignantly resumed the strike.

A new, enlarged "strike committee" was formed. Of its 15 members, 14 were designated by the men's camps and one by the women. The women's representative was a "counterrevolutionary" who had spent 17 years in forced labor camps. Kuznetsov again played a leading role.

From that moment on, the Kingir camp cluster was turned in a truly autonomous republic of a type not known in the Soviet Union since the October Revolution. The strike committee supplemented the old demands with new ones. These were:

1. Review of indictments and sentences.

2. Amnesty for juveniles and the aged.
3. Release of foreigners to their home countries.
4. Conversion of the camps from regime camps into ordinary labor camps.
5. Removal of bars from barrack windows.
6. Removal of numbers from clothing.
7. An eight-hour work day.
8. A wage raise.
9. Reduction of sentences by up to seven days for each work day performed.
10. Right to choose residence after release.
11. Right to correspond more often with family.
12. Promise not to punish the strike committee, and
13. Review of sentences imposed in 1953 and punishment of officials responsible for imposition of these high sentences.

With respect to demand No. 13, it should be noted that in 1953 a strike broke out in protest against the brutal treatment of political prisoners by the guards. One day, as they returned from work, a guard opened fire without reason, killing four and wounding 16 internees, including three Latvians. To "justify" himself, the guard later alleged that an internee had grinned in the work column. The prisoners' indignation was so strong that it took the form of a protest strike which went on for three days. For participation in that strike a number of prisoners received heavy sentences. In 1954, as a token of solidarity with their comrades, the strikers demanded a review of their sentences and restitution for wrongs suffered in 1953.

The main demand was that a representative of the Soviet Communist Party Central Committee come from Moscow.

To preclude the possibility of accusing the strikers of being "counterrevolutionaries," Kuznetsov advised them to abstain from anti-Soviet slogans. He suggested instead that the suppression of the strike be made more difficult through slogans, such as "Long live the Soviet Constitution," and "Down with Beria's terror methods."

Invocation of the Soviet Constitution was merely a parody. Article of the constitution starts with the words: "Considering as its main task to end any exploitation of people and the elimination of classes, without pitying the exploiters . . ."

If the Kingir mutineers demanded the same, they spoke a deep truth and their slogan was actually not so strange. Only, those who live in the Soviet Union need no explanation what the Constitution and the law means—they know it too well. The Kingir rebels who rose against the Soviet exploiters belonged to the lowest class in the Soviet police state and they seriously wished that their exploitation cease. However, their slogan was not the result of naivete.

They chose the sign of the Red Cross as their flag. The Red Cross and Red Crescent are the traditional signs of a humanitarian spirit. Why couldn't these principles be applied in Kingir, the strikers thought?

Then one day the loudspeakers in the watchtowers sounded: "Attention, attention! Representatives from Moscow have just arrived. They want to talk to you. At three o'clock they will come to the camp."

The strike committee placed tables in the yards of the two camps, and the inmates of three individual camps, both men and women, gathered there.

An eye-witness describes the ensuing events: "Punctually at three p.m., four of us went to meet the Moscow representatives. Clad in bright uniforms, they came to the gates. Their gold braid and medals shone in the sun. One of the generals was called Dolghish, and a few moments later we were told that he was Assistant Public Prosecutor General of the MVD. The second man, called Bychkov, was Deputy Chief of GULAG, the main administration of the forced labor camps. One of them, accompanied by numerous Soviet officers, went to one courtyard, and the other to the yard of the neighboring camp. Kuznetsov sat down at the side of Dolghish. There was a moment of silence. "It looks as solemn as Red Square (in Moscow) during a troop review," said one of the men. Then Bychkov rose to his feet. "Comrades, you have made several demands," he began. "Some of the demands are justified and deserve acceptance. However, the Government implemented them even before you wrote them down. Look, here I have the texts of decrees issued by the Government in April. That was only a few weeks ago, and evidently news of them has not reached Kingir yet, but you may rest assured that these instructions will be carried out even here. I am choosing one at random—a decree of April 24, 1954 on the amnesty for juvenile delinquents. Another decree, issued on the same day, provides for the release of invalids and old or sick people before the expiration of their term, provided they submit their petition for pardon to the camp administration. The same applies to reduction of sentences for good work. The decree does not foresee, it is true, sentence reduction by seven days for each work day, as you demand, but those fulfilling or exceeding the work norm will have their sentences shortened by two or three days for every workday. There is no need to speak of the eight-hour day—it has already been approved. You see, on its own initiative, the Government has worked out plans to alleviate your work and reduce your sentences. Unless I am mistaken, what with the envisaged reductions in sentences, most of you have only a small portion of the term left and have just to prepare for leaving the camp. But you should keep in mind one thing—don't gamble away all these advantages offered to you by some rash action. Be sensible, comrades! Comrade Kuznetsov, who is no doubt a clever man, would give you the same advice. Wouldn't you?" Bychkov turned with a forced smile to Kuznetsov, watching at the same time the other members of the strike committee. One of them asked: "What about a review of the indictments and sentences?"

"Well, comrades, you see, we have also come here to receive your applications for review of sentences. I and General Dolghish will accept them beginning tomorrow."

"When will the bars disappear from the windows?" a woman shouted.

"Will those who shot at us last year be punished?" another voice was heard.

"Will we be permitted to return to our homeland after our release?" asked a man with a Baltic accent.

"There were many questions.

"We shall discuss quite a lot of things during the next few days. We are staying here two more days,' said both Soviet generals, as soon as they heard questions concerning the 17 killed and several hundreds crippled in the Kingir camp.

"Bychkov and Dolghish tried to close the meeting, but the prisoners insisted on prompt arrival of members of the Soviet Communist Party Central Committee.

"What is the use of your asking for the appearance of central committee members,' said one the generals indignantly. "Both we and your camp commandant act on behalf of the central committee. This is why we have come here to listen to you. Don't imagine that the central committee has so little to do that it can send one of its members here. Before we discuss other matters, we want an answer concerning the discontinuance of the strike. We shall come back tonight to hear your answer and to decide further steps.'

"This was the end of the meeting. However, the final word had not been spoken. In the evening the camp inmates gave it:

"Comrade General! Our imprisoned comrades have authorized us, the strike committee, to declare that we insist on the fulfilment of our demand for the arrival of members of the Party Central Committee. Until their arrival, we refuse to resume work.'

"The Moscow representatives evidently had not expected such an answer. They considered new steps. One of them was dividing juvenile camp inmates into different groups. The next morning, 180 of them were summoned out of the camp. All of them believed they would be released, but only 30 were freed, while the rest were sent to a work colony near Kingir and promptly assigned to work brigades, Youths who had not yet left the camp refused to appear before the Moscow committee.

"Thereupon the Moscow men tried their hand at categorizing invalids and tuberculosis patients. After five percent had been declared to come under the category of those to be freed, all activities in this respect were halted.

"The next day, a host of Soviet public prosecutors arrived from Alma Ata, the capital of Kazakhstan, from Karaganda and other distant places. They interrogated the political prisoners on the bloody clashes of last year, prepared minutes, took pictures of whatever material evidence was left on the scene of events and told the prisoners that the culprits had already been imprisoned.

"Several days passed. The camp inmates did not spend them idly.

"In order to inform others about the uprising, they started building a radio transmitter. In their opinion, this would enable them to inform not only other areas of the Soviet Union, but also the free world about the events in Kingir, 'We shall contact the International Red Cross,' said some. 'We shall refute Moscow's lies that no forced labor camps are left in the Soviet Union,' suggested others.

"The claim that all slave camps had been liquidated in the Soviet Union was published in 1954 in some Western newspapers. Only Moscow's campaign of lies could bring about the publication of such a statement in the press of the free

173

world. We should not let Moscow get away with such a brazen lie, we must have a radio transmitter which can be heard in all of Europe and non-Communist Asia. The voice of the Kingir rebels should pierce the Iron Curtain.' And so it was decided

"There were outstanding specialists in the Kingir camp. As soon as the need for a transmitter arose, a radio engineer was found. Of course, he was a political prisoner, as was also his young assistant, a Lithuanian.

"X-ray equipment and medical supplies provided the technical basis for the construction of the transmitter. The Lithuanian hastened to perfect himself in the use of the Morse code for English-language broadcasts. An excellent hiding place for the transmitter was found in a remote corner of the women's camp.

"Early in June the first SOS signals of the Kingir mutineers were broadcast, telling of the fate of 13,000 internees.·

"The engineers understood that the audibility of their broadcasts would not go far beyond the Kazakhstan steppes. The lack of suitable equipment precluded the building of a more powerful transmitter. |Moreover, it was realized, that as soon as a more powerful transmitter started operation, there would be bolshevik interference with its broadcasts.

"Even as things were, the rebel transmitter had to compete with the camp loudspeaker used by the administration. Several times a day, it addressed the rebels and it was clear that the administration knew fairly well what was going on in the camp although it held only a defensive position. Kuznetsov ordered the erection of barricades. In addition, weapons were forged. Bars removed from the windows were forged into spears, and carbide lamps and explosives were adapted for repelling invaders.

"All this activity was observed from airplanes which flew over the camp every day.

"You will see, we shall stamp out all of you,' barked the administration's loudspeaker in the watchtower.

"Freedom or death' replied the prisoners' loudspeaker. 'If we have to die, we shall die. We would rather blow ourselves up than surrender to you.'

"Moscow watched the developments in Kingir closely, and very seriously appraised every action and statement by the prisoners. For the reports on the disastrous events in Karaganda, Salekhanda, Norilsk, Kolyma and Vorkuta had been piling up in Moscow during the past few years.

"The local administration knew that there were excellent chemists among the prisoners, and that the internees had been able to smuggle explosives into the camp from mines and stone quarries.

"Food reserves were available for 40 days. The strike committee rationed them strictly.

"Members of the Party Central Committee did not come, but on the other hand nobody paid any attention to the two generals sent from Moscow.

"Midsummer came. Life in the camp followed the newly established routine; the internal walls were no longer any obstruction. Both men and women did guard duty. The women's post stood at some distance from the armed men whose weapons were however so miserable that Kuznetsov, the one-time Soviet tank commander in Berlin, feared that panic would break out during the first moments of the expected attack. Women mounted guard for the sole reason of encouraging the men during the fight, as it was believed that the latter would not retreat under the eyes of the women. The barricades, built of bricks, clay, scrap iron and wood, could only resist infantry attack. The headquarters of the strike committee were surrounded by a specially built barbed-wire fence.

"In the early hours of June 26th, Bychkov's voice was heard over the loud-speaker:

"Attention! Attention! Troops are entering the camp. I order everybody to leave the barracks!'

"At the same time, hundreds of rockets flared up, casting a ghostly light over the camp area. Tanks emerged from several directions. Some rolled in through the camp gates, crushing the barricades like matchwood, while others broke through the walls. It is not known for sure whether there were seven or more tanks, but within a few moments they controlled the camp. Hiding behind them, infantry men fired at whoever happened to be in the courtyard. One of the first bullets struck Villis Rozenbergs, a former Lativian legionary, while another killed an Estonian woman who stood on a sentry post.

"The tanks set fire to the barracks, smashed their walls and rolled over whatever was in their way. Infantry followed in their wake, dashing into the barracks and firing at the prisoners whether these were still in their beds or had risen, awakened by the noise.

"Although taken by surprise and half-awake, the most courageous among them fought back. The sound of firing and shouts of fear mingled with the cries of the wounded. The MVD men bayonetted even those who lay on the ground, pierced by bullets. Tank crews fired at prisoners who were at some distance from them.

"Camp No. 2 put up the fiercest resistance. Twice it repelled the attack. Carbide bottles were hurled and home-made grenades exploded against the walls and turrets of the tanks. When the supply of these weapons was exhausted, the men and women in prisoners' garb threw stones against the invaders.

"The desperate fight had been going on for almost four hours. Lithuanian women tried to save the transmitter which a few moments ago had broadcast the the last SOS signal, surprising the enemy.

"A few Latvian girls continued the fight in another corner of the camp. One after another they sank down to the ground. The bullet of an MVD man struck Biruta Blums, the daughter of a Latvian war hero, who stood side by side with another Latvian of whom it is only known that she was the mother of two children. The surviving women joined hands and advanced against the tanks. They had neither carbide bottles, nor stones. They marched towards the enemy singing. It was difficult to tell what they sang. Maybè a hymn, maybe a song about their country. The rattle of the tanks drowned their voices.

"The huge tank, grim and ominous, lifted its steel belly in front of the girls. And a moment later it rolled over them. The drunken tank crew laughed.

"General Bychkov, Deputy Chief of the central administration of the forced labor camps, watched the scene from a fourth-floor window in the administration building and directed the 3000 men and the tanks. Only a few hours ago these were opposed by 9000 men and 4000 women, but a four-hour fight had thinned their ranks.

"Bychkov did not act on his own initiative. When Moscow had been asked a few days previously how to proceed against the rebels, it had answered: 'Liquidate them!'"

K., a returnee, who told the story of this terrible night at Friedland in the fall of 1955, added: "All the Balts took part in this fight. The number of their fallen and wounded was therefore relatively high."

Five hundred were killed. Another returnee said that if the attack had not come at night, the number of victims would have been much higher. In the darkness and confusion some were eliminated from the ranks in the first moments of the clash, being taken by surprise and disabled for the fight.

The Kingir uprising lasted 42 days.

On June 26th it was ruthlessly quelled. Casualties equalled those of a major battle.

Many of the seriously wounded died of their injuries. On the other hand, many a man whom his comrades had seen fall to the ground during the fight proved to be only wounded and God's grace helped him to recover. This was evidently also the case of Biruta Blums who was considered dead. In the spring of 1956 the news was received in Latvia that she had survived. Little information is available on the fate of the other fighters.

It is only known that the surviving were arrested, tried, and brought in special trains to Kolyma. A special trial was staged for the members of the strike committee who became the leaders of the rebels.

A solidarity strike with the Kingir mutineers commenced in Dzhezkazgan on June 10th. After the Kingir massacre of June 26th, General Bychkov arrived with his tanks in Dzhezkazgan. "Do you want to suffer the same fate as the Kingir rebels?" asked Moscow's executioner.

The twenty thousand Dzhezkazgan camp inmates were not prepared for a fight and called off the strike.

Nevertheless, great changes followed.

A few mutineers who, as foreigners, were due for an early release, returned to the Kingir camp some time after the terrible night; they were greatly surprised at what they saw in their former camp.

Work no longer began at six o'clock in the morning but at eight and ceased at five p.m. Window bars which had disappeared during the mutiny had not been replaced. Numbers had been removed from the clothing of the prisoners. Invalids, disabled persons and juveniles were being released from the camp at a fairly rapid rate. Those who were not released, had their sentences reduced. However, because of the extremely severe sentences most of them had to spend in the camp an additional five or more years.

The administration began to invite theatrical troupes and orchestras to the camp. Men and women were allowed to meet a few times a month at concerts, theatrical performances or dances.

The general mood, however, was still so low that nobody could really enjoy all the new things. It felt strange to dance at a place where not long ago blood had flowed in streams.

The heroism of the persecuted people in Kingir was a hymn to modern man's yearning for freedom and this place became a new link in the chain of freedom uprisings which broke out spontaneously in Soviet camps where terrorism and exploitation resembled that practised in the cemetery of living people in Kazakhstan.

STRIKES AND UPRISINGS IN SOVIET FORCED LABOR CAMPS

[This list is not exhaustive]

Region and Punitive area	Year	Month or season	Duration
KOMI S.S.R.:			
Ust-Ukhta	1940		
Ust-Vym	1947		
Vozhael	1952	Summer	
Vorkuta	1953	do	
	1955	do	
URAL REGION:			
Salekharda	1950		
Molotov (Perm) area	1952	June	
Fabrichnoye			
Revda/Sverdlovsk	1954		
Karabash	1954	Summer	
Solikamsk	1955		
SIBERIA:			
Krasnoyarsk region	1952	Fall	
	1956	April	
Norilsk	1953	March–August	100 days.
Tayshet	1950	Winter	
	1954		
Reshoty	1954	October	
CENTRAL ASIA:			
Dzhezkazgan	1947, 1951		
	1953, 1954		
Kingir	1954		
Karaganda	1947, 1951		
	1953, 1954		
Sherubay Nura	1954		
Balkhash	1954	Spring and summer	
FAR EAST:			
Kolyma	1946, 1953		
Sakhalin	1954		
EUROPEAN RUSSIA:			
Potma	1955	Summer	

THE SUPPRESSION OF THE DISSIDENTS

[Excerpted from "Uncensored Russia"]

by Peter Reddaway

American Heritage Press (New York 1972)

THE ALL-RUSSIAN SOCIAL-CHRISTIAN UNION FOR THE LIBERATION OF THE PEOPLE

Between March 14th and April 5th [1968] seventeen Leningrad intellectuals were tried in the Leningrad City Court. Procurator Guseva and Judge Isakova (deputy chairman of Leningrad City Court) took part in the trial.

All the accused were charged under articles 70 and 72 of the Russian Criminal Code. The essence of the charge was participation in the All-Russian Social-Christian Union for the Liberation of the People. [Photographs on p. 279.]

BRIEF EXPOSITION OF THE UNION'S PROGRAMME

The establishment of a democratic system. The head of state is elected by the whole population and is accountable to Parliament. The upper chamber—a *Sobor* (representatives of the clergy)—has a right of veto vis-a-vis the head of state and Parliament. The land belongs to the State and is allocated to private people or collectives (exploitation forbidden); hired labour only permitted on a basis of equality. Enterprises are mostly owned by worker collectives, but the main industries—transport, electronics, etc.—to be state-owned. Basic principle of the economic system—personalism.

STATUTES OF THE UNION

Strict conspiracy, members operating in "groups of three"; each person knows the senior member of his "three" and its second member. In addition, each person recruits new members, creating a new "three" in which he becomes the senior. The head of the organization is not known to the members—in case of need they communicate with him in writing through the senior member of their "three".

In practice the organization engaged only in recruiting new members and distributing literature (the books and copies of books confiscated in searches included those of Djilas, Berdyayev, Vl. Solovyov, [G. von] Rauch's *History of Soviet Russia*, Tibor Meray's *Thirteen Days that shook the Kremlin*—on Hungary in 1956, Gorky's *Untimely Thoughts*, etc., and even [Evgenia] Ginzburg's *Into the Whirlwind*).

The organization was formed in about 1964. By mid-1965 it had some ten members. By this time the Leningrad K.G.B. already knew it existed but did not stop its activities and allowed it to develop and expand (in court Alexander Gidoni appeared as a witness: he had denounced the organization to the K.G.B. in 1965 but was advised to continue to keep in touch with its members).

In February/March 1967 some sixty persons were arrested or detained (not only in Leningrad but also in Tomsk, Irkutsk, Petrozavodsk, etc.).

In November 1967 the Leningrad City Court tried four leaders of the organization (under articles 64, 70 and 72) and sentenced:

Igor Ogurtsov (translator from Japanese, 30 years old) to 15 years of imprisonment; Mikhail Sado (orientalist, 30) to 13 years; Evgeny Vagin (literary critic from Pushkin House [a literary research institute], 30) to 10 years; and [Boris] Averochkin (jurist, 28) to 8 years—all to be served in strict-regime corrective-labour colonies.

The second trial lasted from March 14th to April 5th, 1968. The difference between the people brought into court as accused and those brought in as witnesses consisted basically in the fact that those on trial had engaged in recruiting people— even if only a single person—for the organization. All the accused admitted their guilt (evidently in the sense of admitting the facts of the charge) but not all of them recanted (particularly Ivoilov, Ivanov, Platonov and Borodin).

The following were sentenced (term of imprisonment shown after each entry in years with term demanded by the Procurator in parentheses):

1. Vyacheslav Platonov, born 1941, orientalist—7(7).
2. Nikolai Ivanov, born 1937, art critic, teacher in Leningrad University—6(7).
3. Leonid Borodin, born 1938, school headmaster from the Luga District in Leningrad Region—6(6).
4. Vladimir Ivoilov, economist (Tomsk), graduate of Leningrad University—2(2) [in fact six years—see *Chronicle* 19].
5. Mikhail Kolosov, born 1937, fitter employed in the Leningrad Gas organization, correspondence course student of the Gorky Literary Institute—4(5).
6. Sergei Ustinovich, born 1938, Leningrad University graduate—3½(4).
7. Yury Buzin, born 1936, engineer, agricultural institute graduate—3(4).
8. Valery Nagorniy, born 1943, engineer in L.I.T.M.O. (Leningrad Institute of Precision Mechanics and Optics)—3(4).
9. Alexander Miklashevich, born 1935, engineer (agricultural institute graduate)—3(3).
10. Yury Baranov, born 1938, engineer (graduate of institute of cine-technicians)—3(4).
11. Georgy Bochevarov, born 1935, Leningrad University graduate—2½(3).
12. Anatoly Sudaryov, born 1939, translator, Leningrad University graduate—2(2).
13. Anatoly Iylev, born 1937, chemist, Leningrad University graduate—2(3).
14. Vladimir Veretenov, born 1936, chemist, Leningrad University graduate—2(3).
15. Olgerd Zobak, born 1941, L.I.T.M.O. mechanic—14 months, the time already served while under pretrial investigation (1 year).
16. Oleg Shuvalov, born 1938, L.I.T.M.O.—14 months, the time already served (1 year).
17. Stanislav Konstantinov, librarian—14 months, the time already served (1 year).

The trial was characterized by violations of legality similar to those in the Moscow trial [of Galanskov and Ginzburg]:

1. The terms of pre-trial detention exceeded the legal maximum in the case of some of the accused.
2. Admission was by permit to an 'open' trial (although the court was half empty).
3. Most witnesses were ejected from the courtroom immediately after testifying.

It is also not clear why the leaders of the organization were tried separately and why they were tried under article 64 (treason), as well as articles 70 and 72. Was the programme they had drawn up defined as 'a conspiracy aimed at seizing power'? If |so, this was clearly illegal. In the circumstances of the trial of the first group of four every kind of illegality could have been committed, since nothing was known of the trial until it was over and it was, apparently, completely closed.

It is reliably known that no one was charged with having connections with N.T.S., nor with engaging in currency transactions, nor with possessing arms.

This account of the two trials fits well with the only other substantial source yet available, an anonymous article of 1969 apparently written by a member of the Union. This confirms that twenty-one people were sentenced, adding that twenty-nine in all stood trial and that the case materials filled over a hundred volumes. It also states that Union members were indeed charged with participation in 'a conspiracy aimed at seizing power', and that the Union's programme stood for armed revolution, although its activity had not reached the stage of acquiring any arms. The article provides a fascinating analysis of the Union's social composition, ideological development, programme and activities, and of the reasons for its betrayal. There is sufficient similarity between its programme and that of the 'Democrats of Russia, the Ukraine and the Baltic Lands' (see p. 173) to make it possible that the latter group includes people previously associated with the Union.

In any case, the next development was predictable enough:

In May and June 1968 the Russian Supreme Court considered the appeals of the Leningrad members of the All-Russian Social-Christian Union. The sentences on all those convicted were confirmed. Ogurtsov, sentenced to fifteen years' imprisonment, and Sado, sentenced to thirteen years' imprisonment, will, according to the sentence, spend the first five years of their terms under a prison régime. They are in the prison at Vladimir.

178

The other accused are now in camp 11 of the Mordovian camps: their address is: Mordovskaya A.S.S.R., st. Potma, p/o Yavas, p/ya ZhKh 385/11.

We have already met Ogurtsov, Sado, Platonov and Borodin in Vladimir prison and the camps (see pp. 207, 220). In addition, No. 9 recorded in 1969: 'Sado has been transferred from Vladimir prison to camp 3 of the Mordovian complex', but it did not explain why the transfer took place early. No. 10 then reported his further transfer to camp 17-a. This was where he became friends with a man of whom the Chronicle *wrote:*

Alexander Petrov (pseudonym Agatov), the Leningrad poet and author of the words of the song 'Dark Night' (from the film *The Two Warriors*), was convicted in Moscow in February 1969 under article 70 of the Russian Criminal Code for a book he had written (the title is unknown).

In a document written in Mordovia in late 1969 Petrov gives the date of his closed trial as January 7th–8th and the basis for his seven-year sentence as his 'poems about the tyranny of the Beria times, written in that period'. Here he also describes Sado as 'a man with a wonderful heart, a fine mind and an unbreakable will', and in a later document he writes in detail of Sado's remarkable life-story. In autumn 1970 Petrov was transferred to Vladimir for his pains, along with Borodin. Earlier he had served over twenty years in camps, getting out in 1967, having a year of freedom and publishing a few works, before returning.

PRISONER ENCOUNTERS

(A true story by Aleksandr Petrov-Agatov)

[Excerpts translated from Grani, Nos. 82–84, 1972]

In the year of our Lord, The summer of 1969.

Trouble comes unexpectedly. Arrests are no exception. Nobody warns of them either. Particularly in a Soviet country, where there are very many beautiful words about freedom and brotherhood, and very little conscience and honor.

Having already spent more than twenty years in prison and having just come out a year ago, I never imagined that I would be arrested again. But no. I was grabbed and arrested.

"Do you know what you were arrested for?", asked Major Khabibulin, after introducing himself, and looked meaningfully at the manuscripts. I understood that he decided to make things clear from the start.

"Is it possible that it's on account of my poems?" I said with surprise.

"These poems are worse than an atom bomb", he cut me short. "Right now we won't discuss anything. I would like you to gather your thoughts and simply rest. Here is the order for your arrest signed by the procurator. Times have changed, we don't just grab people, don't be afraid. You won't be imprisoned in the Lubyanka. Generally speaking, we don't have any people in prisons. You will be taken to Lefortovo. It is now an isolation ward for political prisoners."

"You mean to say . . . a prison . . .", I corrected him.

"An isolation ward. We don't have prisons any more."

I was taken to Lefortovo not in a "Zim" [brand name of a car made in the USSR] but in a "paddy wagon". I hope the reader will not miss the opportunity of learning of this "marvel of the twentieth century". Those friendly first-aid cars, equipped with sirens, which go everywhere. In Stalin's time they were disguised with the words "BREAD", "MEAT" or simply "FOODSTUFFS" written on them, and not without reason, I believe: these cars, loaded to the gills, transported from prison to prison the "products of the epoch" [a play on words, the Russian word for foodstuffs being "produkty", meaning also products—Translator's Note].

This was my first time in Lefortovo. I already knew that this was a political prison. Rumors had it that here as in Lubyanka and at the Butyrki people were shot without trial or investigation. However, people were also sent to the next world after being tried.

. . . Sado was also soon taken away from me, but I had time to find out from him that a large group of Social-Christians was arrested in Leningrad in February 1967. This group was headed by Igor Vyacheslavovich Ogurtsov, who according to Sado was a very pure, courageous, well educated and—above all—religious man.

"All the people in this group are believers and are highly intellectual", Yuriy Yukhanovich assured me. "My brother Mikhail, who is Ogurtsov's first assistant, is an orientalist. Platonov is one too. Nikolay Viktorovich Ivanov is an art historian who taught at the Leningrad University and who not long before his arrest had returned from Ethiopia. A clever fellow! What a clever fellow! Vladimir Fedorovich Ivoylov taught political economy at the Tomsk University. Mikhail Borisovich Knosov, a poet, was a student by correspondence at a literary institute of writers. Georgiy Nikolayevich Bochevarov is an historian. And Vanin? Evgeniy Aleksandrovich [Vanin]—well he is a very special person! I was shaken. In Russia, in the sixties, and a military-political organization! [Following sentence smudged and illegible—Translator's Note] "Don't be obstinate, Aleksandr Aleksandrovich," repeated Major Sedov for the nth time. "Why should you protect Boris Slutskiy? He is a Jew and a Zionist. And you are a Russian. After all we know that he is anti-Soviet. Just confirm this to us. And tell me what you know about Tvardovskiy."

"But I saw Tvardovskiy only once, and then only in his official capacity as chief editor of 'Novyy Mir' [a literary journal—Translator's Note]. As to Slutskiy, I know him only very superficially.

"My goodness, Aleksandr Aleksandrovich," interrupted the procurator, "aren't you tired of being in prison? What good is all this to you? Help us—and you'll be a free man."

It all ended with Lieutenant-General Lyalin, Head of the Moscow Committee on Security, appearing one day in person at the interrogation. This obese swine was infinitely frank.

"Here is my party card," and he pulled a blood-red little booklet from his pocket. "See? If you will tell us all about the writers and how the manuscripts get abroad, I guarantee you your freedom tomorrow. This card is my assurance to you."

. . . I was tried at Christmas in the old manner. Naturally, in camera. Besides Zagryaznina who transmitted my manuscripts to the KGB, my daughter, who in her innocence admitted that she had heard my poems, and a large number of guards, there was nobody else. Also, there were two security committee characters. Of course, in civilian clothes, silent, but their spirit hovered above the procurator's and judge's armchairs. I say "armchairs" because the impression was that the ones who conducted the trial were not the people but the armchairs. I refused the services of the attorney. The day before the trial, a middle-aged woman with large yellow teeth, brightly painted lips, and a thick cigarette in her mouth, came to the prison (she was the defending attorney) and said to me: "I advise you to admit your guilt. . . . You will then get less time."

The procurator made a long speech. Time and again he pronounced the cast iron words: ideology, ideologic diversion, class struggle. . . ."

Then came the verdict: "I ask for 7 years."

Naturally, I would not admit that I was guilty. And I told the court everything that I thought of it and the investigation, and that long ago I came to the conclusion that the worst enemy of the Soviet state was the Soviet state itself. The greatest reward for my critical outpourings were my daughter's words. Aleshka's voice rang out in the hall:

"Marvellous, Daddy!"

There were the three of us: in Ryazan' the two Armenians were put into a stolypin (a passenger railroad car divided into cages). They were still very young men, and had been brought from Armenia. I only found out that they were both engineers, graduates of the Erevan Technological Institute, the first one, Ashot Khachaturyan, sentenced to ten years for betraying his country, the second, Stepan Zatvokhyan, to four years for anti-Soviet agitation. Both were from good families, used to the good things in life, and throughout the trip continuously expressed their indignation at the inhuman, as they said, ways of the KGB.

As soon as we had changed into prison garb and entered the zone, they were whisked away by some Armenians (for here there was a great variety of nationalities), and I began to be besieged by the Slavs. Naturally, I was anxious above all to meet Andrey Donatovich Sinyavskiy, who as I found out while still at the transit prison, was here and about whom I had heard so many different reports. Therefore, when one of the messengers, who said that his name was Mikhail Konukhov, said: "We invite you to join our group of three: Sinyavskiy, engineer-designer Derunov, and myself," I had no reason to refuse. But Konukhov's appearance somewhat disturbed me. He looked like a criminal: shifty eyes, an earthen complexion, the expressionless face of a drug addict, tatooed arms. "He probably shouted off some anti-Soviet slogans or wrote a leaflet in blood, just to get out of the criminal prisoner's camp," I thought to myself.

"Andrey Donatovich will soon be here. Please sit down," greeted me a young man with a small reddish beard like a child's spade, soft features, and blue eyes which, it appeared, nothing could astound, since they had seen everything. "I'm very grateful to you for having come. I myself am from Moscow. My family name is Derunov, my name and patronimic, Mikhail Evgen'evich. My father is a professor. I am a design engineer. A leader of a small group. Of course, democratic. I've been given seven years, charged under article 70. And here now is Andrey Donatovich. . . ."

The conversation was hard in getting started, and during the first few minutes I almost openly scrutinized Sinyavskiy. He was a bit cross in one eye, his teeth were yellow and, I thought, disintegrating; his face exhausted and deeply lined, long before its time (he was forty-five)—an intelligent, spiritual face. He spoke little and was modest in his behavior. Nevertheless he remarked:

"When I arrived, I had no respite from the curious. . . . I was being scrutinized like a bride brought before the bridegroom and his relatives."

"A well-known name," I remarked not knowing exactly what to say.

"Well-known, yes. But undeservedly so. I myself appreciate that this isn't honest fame which comes to a real writer. I was brought in on a wave, and as everyone knows, a wave brings in anything."

I did not sense any posing in Sinyavskiy's words and I liked his sober evaluation of himself.

On that occasion, I believe, we parted without any definite ideas about each other, but a grain of sympathy for Andrey Donatovich was planted in my heart.

. . . The next day, when I returned from work (I was sent to do some of the most difficult work there) I was called to the headquarters, to the office of the chief of operations. A major in horn-rimmed glasses was at the table, and nearby, next to the wall, a lieutenant-colonel. Both were in the uniform of the cavalry, but without spurs: Soviet gendarmes shouldn't make too much noise, they move silently.

"You've been invited, Aleksandr Aleksandrovich, so that we may get acquainted. Please sit down. I am the chief of the KGB Administrative Office. My name is Postnikov. And this," he nodded in the direction of the lieutenant-colonel with his balding head, "is my deputy."

I didn't hear the name. Anyhow it had no meaning. I already mentioned that the secret police have no face. Neither do they have names. Like dogs, they have only nicknames and go from one master to another.

"How was the trip? Did you settle down?"

Each one of them had a piece of paper before him.

"I would prefer it if you didn't trouble youself with polite questions. Can anyone have any doubts about the cultural level of our gendermerie? Please come to the point."

"Are you upset about something?" screeched Postnikov.

So I had to answer the questions. The questions were mostly those of the curious: how many copies of my books had been printed abroad, how much money did I have in my bank account, which journals in the Soviet Union had published my works? I was also asked to state my political and philosophical positions.

I took advantage of the situation and painted a picture of near catastrophe for the Soviet regime.

"Alright, but don't express your ideas to any of the other prisoners. Bear in mind that anyway we will find out what you said and to whom and this will only add to your problems."

And again as in Lefortovo:

"What good are they to you? And by the way, I can tell you with whom you had met yesterday and today and what you had talked about . . ."

And he repeated almost the entire conversations I had with both groups.

"So you see," concluded Postnikov didactically, looking me fixedly in the eye, "we know everything and we will continue to know everything."

During the next few days I became convinced that the camp was swarming with informers. It was especially this that created an atmosphere of nervous tension, distrust, and was responsible for the formation of small, tight, closed groups. Everyone feared each other. Suspicion reached schizophrenic proportions, and people often warned one another:

"Be more careful with that one."

"Don't say too much."

"He's not a bad fellow, but he works for the management, and one does not work for the management for nothing."

181

"That one there is always getting cigarettes and coffee in his parcels."

At the conclusion of the conversation I asked Postnikov to return to me all the manuscripts which were taken away from me at the entrance to the zone. These manuscripts were already checked by the Security Committee in Moscow, and there was a special statute in the prison regulations which covered this.

"Moscow manages its own affairs, and we manage ours. . . . We'll take a look and will then return them. Don't worry. If you have any problems, let us know; we are not putting you in the same category with the military criminals."

"By the way," said I, "why don't you let them go. They've been sitting here for twenty years and more. They are living corpses. . . ."

"Dear me, Aleksandr Aleksandrovich. You don't know what dangerous people they are. They can't be let out. They are in blood up to their necks . . ."

But several months later one of these "dangerous" fellows admitted to me his spying and told me frankly:

"Do you know what Postnikov told me when he recruited me into his service? You, he said, are not dangerous to us. The ones who are dangerous to us are those. . . the educated ones . . . with the lily-white hands. Those who are in for four or seven years, not for twenty-five. The thinkers and talkers. But you— you are our fellows."

And these were not empty words.

All services in the camps for political prisoners are rendered by former policemen and Beria men. They are in the councils of the collectives and are the trustees for the communist party.

Next day I was visited by Nagorniy and Ivoylov. They were the first swallows of that military-political arm of the Social-Christian Party of which Yuriy Yukhanovich Sado spoke to me in Lefortovo. I spent the entire first three days inquiring about them, did obtain some information, but was too shy to approach them myself. Both were young and somehow glowing; radiating warmth, they brought a breath of something fresh and pure into my corner (my cot was in a corner at the end of the barracks).

"Valeriy Ivanovich . . ."

"Vladimir Fedorovich . . ."

The first one, with blue eyes and very fine, almost transparent features, was Nagornyy. The second one, reserved and more subdued and gloomier, was Ivoylov.

All of them who were in that zone had gathered together. I say "that zone" because there was yet a seventeenth camp. Several from the group were there. Three of them were: the orientalist Vyacheslav Mikhaylovich Platonov, the literary historian Evgeniy Aleksandrovich Vagin, and a former director of schools, Leonid Ivanovich Borodin, who according to hearsay was a very interesting person who had been in Saransk for so-called "prophylactic treatment": every year three to four persons were brought there for a period of two months for re-education in order to change their convictions.

The leaders [of the group] Igor Vyacheslavovich Ogurtsov and Mikhail Yukhanovich Sado were serving their sentences in a prison in Vladimir.

. . . Seven persons seated behind a large table, brought in from somewhere especially for the occasion. Besides Nagornyy and Ivoylov there were Boris Anatol'evich Averechkin, a grandson of one of the first Soviet admirals, with a reserved expression and a face framed in a thick dark beard; Mikhail Borisovich Konosov, still just a boy, with soft cheeks and beautiful brown eyes, very charming, a poet, who admitted that he would prefer being addressed not only by his first name but his patronimic also; Georgiy Nikolayevich Bochevarov, an historian, very kind and frank but trying to appear withdrawn and very much a man of principle; and Yuriy Petrovich Baranov, an engineer, about thirty-three to thirty-five years old, phlegmatic, with a tattoo on his right arm, with an elongated, well-groomed face, grey before its time. There was also a man who looked very much like czar Nicolas the Second, with purblind, runny eyes, whose name we did not know. And finally, there was Sudarev, a man of medium height, who was continuously steeped in thought, and as I found out later, dreaming of becoming a writer.

Later I found that the questionnaire played an important role in the organization. They had some very substantial archives and personal files, which affected the organization adversely when it was uncovered and crushed. My compatriots at first meeting obviously did not want to reveal all about themselves. After some "questioning" they asked me to tell them what I thought of their organization, to share with them my prognosis of the future, to read some of the poetry for which I had been arrested.

The next day I made the acquaintance of Vagin. Unfortunately Platonov and Borodin were driven right past our camp straight to camp no. 17.

Evgeniy Aleksandrovich [Vagin] made a very pleasant impression on me. Tall, graceful, neat even in prison garb, he radiated nobility of character, intelligence, and grace of manner. Is it possible to radiate a grace of manner? Judging by Vagin, yes.

Together with Sinyavskiy, Derunov, and the ever-present Konukhov, I spent no less than two hours with Evgeniy Aleksandrovich. We discussed literature, art, politics. Despite all his modesty it was impossible not to notice his erudition and high intellect. One felt that this man did not select a world outlook which was popular at the moment, but had worked it out for himself. It was the first time I heard a literary historian (and Evgeniy Aleksandrovich was a highly qualified literary historian, specializing in Dostoyevskiy) evaluate Gorkiy correctly:

"Awful language," said Vagin. "Is it possible that a Russian writer can use such language? Furthermore, he's so nasty, that Gorkiy."

I asked Evgeniy Aleksandrovich to describe, in the few minutes that remained, the "prophylactic treatment" in Saransk. What was it?

"A joke," smiled Vagin. "Local writers and other Mordovian luminaries come by at the request of the KGB, naturally, and try to convert us. Sometimes they even take us in private cars to restaurants and shops in town. Look how well and in what a civilized manner the Soviet people live. There is bread, the movies are spinning away, no charge for entering a restaurant. Jazz. And sometimes there's even cognac. . . . What more could one want?"

Platonov asked to be taken to church. He wanted to confess and to receive the eucharist.

Colonel Arbuzov (deputy chief of the Mordovian KGB) was momentarily non-plussed by Vyacheslav Mikhaylovich's [Platonov's] request. Then he smiled jauntily and said firmly: "We will take you! Certainly we will take you!"

But of course he [Platonov] never did go.

"A Chekist [a member of the Cheka, i.e. the secret police—Translator's note] lies the way a thief steals, the way a friar. . . ." said Konhukhov.

This time Mishel was in his element. He obviously knew what he was talking about.

. . . Without exception, all the Petersburgers * in zone eleven had gathered around the Easter table. Andrey Donatovich and I were also invited. Besides coffee and candy there was nothing else on the table.

Evgeniy Aleksandrovich, who headed the table said thrice: "Christ has risen!"

Everyone rose, and crossing themselves responded in unison: "In truth He has risen!"

It was spring outside. The earth was warming up. Hearts too could not but warm up. I looked at the faces around me. They were all solemn; a ray of sunlight shimmered upon them.

Vagin made a short speech. Its gist was that those who had gathered around the table were Russia's salt of the earth, and that he believed in the country's rebirth. In the nation's rebirth. And of the people sitting at this table.

I don't know why, but I felt like crying. As before, I had a great affection for Vagin and all those who were here, and didn't for a single moment doubt that Evgeniy Aleksandrovich, Nikolay Viktorovich, Georgiy Nikolaevich, and Vladimir Fedorovich—all those sitting around the table—were destined to build a new Russia; but I still felt like crying.

King Solomon, when he learned that Kitovras [?] began crying on seeing a happy young pair of newlyweds emerge from a church, asked: "Why did you cry?" "I foresaw that one of them would perish the next day," answered the wise prophet.

I am not a prophet, and I cannot foresee people's futures. But even then, at that table, I knew that these were today's Russia's best people. Not yet the salt of the earth. Those around the Easter table were brothers.

They *could become* the salt of the earth, I thought, if they suffer much, become masters of themselves, and learn how to love.

Were there any other interesting people in the camp? In zone eleven alone, one thousand four hundred prisoners lived in misery. There were very few intellectually

---

* i.e. natives or residents of St. Petersburg, the pre-revolutionary name for Leningrad. The author uses this term instead of "Leningraders" to indicate their identification with pre-revolutionary Russia and their non-acceptance and opposition to the present Soviet regime—Translator's note.

interesting people, and none equal to the Petersburgers or to Sinyavskiy. Nevertheless, there were many people with interesting, and in some cases legendary lives. Vasiliy Illarionovich Stotsenko, a former communist and chief of the planning department of the Krasnodonugol' Trust, an engineer by training, mayor of Krasnodon under the German occupation, but at present a quasi-corps, has been languishing now in prison camps for twenty-three years. He was under interrogation for several years in the Lubyanka, questioned by a gendarme in a Chekist [secret police] uniform who looked like and resembled in spirit the writer Aleksandr Fadeyev, author of the notorious novel "The Young Guards".

Vasiliy Illarionovich, a rather intelligent man, swears that he had never heard of any "Young Guards", that he did not consider himself guilty nor ever would, because when the Soviet troops retreated, the party organization in Krasnodon ordered him to remain behind with the occupation forces for undercover work. But since nobody from the underground ever came to join him, he decided that he would rather become mayor than die in a concentration camp.

Ivan Nikolayevich Cherenkov, who served much of his time with Stotsenko, had been rotting in USSR MVD corrective-labor camps for just as many years. Until the occupation, he was chief accountant at the same Trust. Under the Germans he became senior investigator for the police, investigating political affairs only. "Communists and commissars," honestly admitted Ivan Nikolayevich [sic]. "I never had anything to do with "The Young Guards". And anyway there weren't any of them around. There were some young fellows, hooligans. They stole packages from cars and sold stolen cigarettes at the market. The police warned them several times. But they would not listen. Finally, shortly before Christmas, the hooligans stole some Christmas parcels sent to the soldiers and officers. Naturally they were arrested, and since this coincided with the retreat of the German armies, they were shot. Without my participation. I managed to evacuate. I was already in the American zone in Italy, and quite safe, when I was asked to the headquarters and told that in accordance with an agreement made between Stalin, Roosevelt and Churchill, I was to be handed over to the Soviet authorities as having committed especially grave crimes against humanity. I spent five years in the Lubyanka. They all wanted to know about the Krasnodon organization known as "The Young Guards". At the inquest I answered each time: There was no such organization. And each time I was told: You will stay here until you show us that there was such an organization. So I showed them. After all, in that famous joke about the 10th grade student who was grabbed by the Chekists (secret police) for unreliability, the student finally admitted that it was he who wrote "Eugene Onegin" [Pushkin's masterpiece—Translator's Note]. So I too admitted that there was such a thing as the "Young Guards", and that I had conducted an investigation of it. By the way, Koshevoy's mother became Fadeyev's mistress when the latter came there to write his story. She had a child by him" Thus ended his story—the quiet introvert with the horsy teeth.

Cherenkov is now in zone seventeen. He works in a clothes factory, checking for defects. The Chekists (secret police) asked him to keep his eyes open for anti-Soviet leaflets stuffed into dress and coat sleeves by malefactors.

The cool, calm, and collected Kalmyk, Erdni Batiyevich Dorozhiyev, a man of his word and scrupulous in his accounts with others, who had worked for "Smersh" (the military counter-intelligence) and the fascist Abwehr, had become a dental technician in camp. He always had money and even "no-loss promissory notes", as the three percent gold loans were called. He was not greedy, always willing to help, and hated cheating. His sentence—twenty-five years.

In general, there is a tremendous number of investigators, policemen, and secret service men. Soviet, German, those without any nationality, stateless, Beria men and Abakum men.

Anakhashiyev, the former chief of the Azerbaydzhan KGB, always very, very clean, and with a wedge-shaped beard, was here too; they say he had shot more than one person in his office. He walked around very little, preferring to sit in the corner like a safe. You couldn't get a word out of him, but his chest was decorated with an SVP pin, the internal security section's acronym. Some people without their insignia are like billygoats without horns—and what is a billygoat without its horns?

For my poems "In the Land of Mordovia" I was obliged to spend five days in solitary confinement. Following one all-camp search, which used to be performed regularly, I was invited in for a talk by Major Krut' and a young lieutenant by the name of Ershov, who had exchanged his teaching profession for a policeman's uniform, both of them with the KGB.

"We warned you, Aleksandr Aleksandrovich, that we would punish you for anti-Soviet poems or any form of anti-Soviet propaganda", began Krut' without any preliminaries, rolling his lackluster eyes. "You can't hide anything from us, Soviet Chekists [secret police men]. Are these your poems?" "Mine," I replied firmly, "How is it that you," interrupted Ershov, "a cultured person, a talented poet, can write something like this?" "Exactly," added Krut', approaching me. "I see no point in discussing this with you," I said. For a few minutes there was silence. "Then," said the major turning sharply and directing himself toward the table, "you will have to spend five days in solitary confinement." "I'm ready." "Just for a few poems, *these* poems!" he exclaimed.

The order that they showed me before placing me in the stone box stated: "For systematic anti-Soviet propaganda, which negatively affects the contingent."

This made me remember captain Kolodochka, chief of another forced-labor camp. Once when he walked into a Russian language class at the camp school, he saw this word, unfamiliar to the unlettered on the blackboard. "Contingent? Hmm?" And puffing up like a frog, he began squawking at the teacher: "I won't allow it! Revealing state secrets?! I won't allow it! Erase the word 'contingent' immediately."

In solitary confinement I went on a hunger strike, unable to reconcile myself with the thought that normal people could punish a person with solitary confinement for his poems. Lermontov was banished by the czar to Pyatigorsk [a famous spa in the Caucasus—Translator's note] for open incitement to rebellion, for urging the overthrow of the autocracy. Again I remembered Catherine, and her conversation with a prominent painter: it was not under the monarchy that the soul's high and noble aspirations were oppressed, that the creations of the intellect, poetry and the arts were victimized. The Shakespeares, the Molières flowered under their magnanimous protection; but Dante could not find any place in his republican motherland. True geniuses arose under the brilliance and power of monarchs and royal states, not under the hideous political systems and terror which never gave the world a single poet. Poets and painters are a special breed, they bring only peace and wonderful quiet into the soul, not agitation and grumbling discontent. The learned, the poets and the artists—are the pearls and diamonds in the imperial crown, they decorate and add to the brilliance of the age. . . . [words obliterated—Translator's note]

The next day after I declared my hunger strike, the head of the unit, a young puppet-like lieutenant came to see us: he turned whichever way he was pulled. He was later followed by Major Spirin, the deputy political administrator, a man with a face yellow and wrinkled like a dry pear.

I did not end my hunger strike, but neither was I released from solitary confinement before the specified five days had expired. This was for the best, as everything always is, wherein lies the ideal wisdom of the Creator.

On the day of the public baths I made the acquaintance of Yakov Berg, who at the time was confined to his cell for six months for his uncompromising anti-Soviet views.

This was a very honest and courageous Jew. He, too, had a beard, but a large one, like Marx's though of a more uncertain color—neither red, nor white, nor black, nor sandy. All these colors, apparently, had to be mixed to produce the color of Berg's beard. He treasured his beard as he did his convictions. On one occasion, when his eighty-year old mother arrived for a visit (which was before he was transferred to solitary confinement, when no visits are allowed) the Chekists propositioned Yakov, in the form of an ultimatum, to shave off his beard.

"If you don't shave it, you won't get the visit."

But he didn't shave it. And they gave him the visit. They had to give it to him, otherwise a certain group of political prisoners would have created a disturbance. Though not many, there were several prisoners, who, in defiance of Soviet obscurantism, were capable of honorable behavior. The Petersburger Leonid Borodin, a talented poet and an intelligent historian, was placed in solitary confinement for refusing to attend lectures in political indoctrination. The next day none of the Petersburgers appeared for work. They were supported by the communards headed by Khakhayev, a liberal group under Gragosh.

Arriving at a fast trot from Saransk came the KGB "cavalrymen", the procurator and the others.

Leonid Ivanovich who, even when roped in, refused to listen to the balderdash, was released from the cell, and for a while those who did not want to absorb Marxist-Leninist ideas were left alone.

I now return to Berg. He was the only person among the political prisoners, who ostentatiously refused to accept food on holidays celebrating the Revolution, and who refused to do any kind of work for the Soviet regime. He went on hunger strikes on any pretext, giving the Chekists to understand that his entire being was against the Soviet regime. Hunger was the only weapon left to him in his chains. And he used it continuously.

While in the eleventh zone I tried to make the acquaintance of the Tikhonovites. The reader no doubt knows of this Russian Orthodox group. My attempt was unsuccessful.

Orlovich, whom I approached, had a beard like all the other Tikhonovites. Their beards were all of the same color, dark red and long, some almost to the waist. He asked me: "Are you from the Cheka [secret police]?"

The always quiet and grave Orlovich worked as a male nurse in the infirmary barracks. Only a very few were willing to look after dying old men who could not control their bodily functions. There was a constant stench in the infirmary barracks, but Orlovich worked diligently and was kind to these unfortunates.

"What do you mean from the Cheka?" I asked without first quite understanding his question, because I was so flabbergasted by it. "Don't you know me?"

"Only God knows everything. You, of course are a prisoner. I can see that. But what's in your soul?" And answering himself, he said: "Well, that's another matter."

Resentment and pain overcame me. "You are no believer," I shouted. Then I left.

I was wrong. We are never right when angry and full of resentment. For then our senses are clouded. Orlovich was a very religious man, but I understood that only later when he and I were together in zone seventeen.

It was easier to get to know the Jehovah's Witnesses. There were quite a few of them in camp and they pursued their teaching with great zeal. They always had an enormous amount of religious material, mainly sermons, lectures and various issues of their publication, "The Watchtower" [published in Russian—Translator's note]. Of course there were also the Old and New Testaments which they knew how to hide. And when the Chekists found these books, the Jehovah's Witnesses never gave them up without a fight.

Karl Yasovetskiy told me that when they came to arrest him and began searching his place, his ten-year old daughter Galia grabbed the Bible from the table, clutched it to her breast, and shouted excitedly: "Kill me, but I won't let you have it! I won't let you take away God's Word!" And when the father was led away, she said: "Dad, remain faithful, otherwise death is better."

Dmitriy Zarubin and Vasiliy Patrushev were highly critical of the teachings of the Jehovah's Witnesses. "One of those very ancient old men," Dmitriy told us, "after he dared ask God: 'What are the Johovah's Witnesses? Explain, O Lord!' had the following dream: a man is carrying a vessel with milk. He then takes some manure and mixes it in with the pure milk—God's Word—and passes it out to the people. The old man then says: this is who the Jehovah's Witnesses are."

Despite all this they were mercilessly thrown into prison. All of them were in camp for the second or third time.

For several years now, but apparently without success, Igor Vasil'yevich Belik who was here for his participation in the Novocherkassk uprising, has been learning the facts of camp life. The other participants in the uprising, who numbered more than five hundred, were sent to Komi [Komi ASSR—Translator's note].

Zinoviy Anatol'yevich Troitskiy, a candidate of jurisprudence who before his arrest apparently worked at the Perm University, was one of my new acquaintances. He and his wife were arrested for their membership in the NTS [National Labor Union]. The wife recently completed her term.

I was extremely fond of Volodya Krivtsov. He grew up in the camp, having already served twenty years. He was about to be released, and charmed everyone with his ingenuity and optimism.

"It's the end for the communists! Don't you see my friends that these bastards are on the edge of a precipice? . . ."

He was very Russian, with no education, but quite intelligent. Watching and listening to him, one became once again convinced that understanding, enlightenment, and learning are God-given. Given only by Him. That is why simple people with God's light upon them are the bearers of true culture.

. . . Thus, I know not for what reasons, political or economic, it was decided in Moscow that the political camp in the eleventh zone should be closed down and that criminal prisoners should be moved into it. We found that out in the last days of June. We lived as though we were on wheels. On the twentieth we didn't even finish our day at the plant (which normally ended at five o'clock), and after lunch started shoving our stuff out into the living area, which became a veritable railroad station. Here and there were bags, suitcases, sacks, knapsacks. Everyone was trying to find out where we would be going. There were three destinations: the third zone, the seventeenth zone, and the nineteenth zone; criminal elements were being moved to our zone from the latter. All these zones were in Mordovia. This entire land is one continuous stretch of watchtowers, barbed wire, and wooden fences.

Ivanov and I were sent to the seventeenth zone, Andrey Donatovich [Sinyavskiy] to the third, and Vagin and Ivoylov to the nineteenth. On the evening of the last day and the entire next morning Sinyavskiy and I spent the entire time together, discussing just about everything. Both of us prayed, both of us cried. Before he reached the check point Andrey Donatovich looked back no less than ten times: he couldn't but feel my eyes on him as he moved away. I believe he won't forget my hands which blessed him either.

On the afternoon of June twenty-ninth, the prisoners were already loaded into twenty specially equipped trucks, and those who were heading for zone seventeen had started on their way.

I was in one of those trucks, sitting with my legs crossed under me. Next to me was Orlovich. Before us stretched the forest and the bumpy road ahead. To this day there are still very few roads in Russia. Right in front of us in the truck stood two men armed with machine guns. They were somehow ashamed to look us straight in the face and they kept glancing aside. The machine guns, like those in the court house, were directed at us at an angle. The machine guns were staring straight at us.

I was going to the seventeenth zone willingly, hoping to meet there both Galanskov and Ginzburg about whom I had heard so much. I also wanted to meet Daniel. I had met Yuliy Markovich [Daniel] only once; that was when I was escaping and managed to work illegally as a researcher for the minister of culture of the Chechen-Ingush republic. It was then that I was introduced to Daniel by the Chechen poetess Raisa Salgimuradovna Akhmatova, now chairman of the writers' organization of the republic, who was then very favorable to the poet. Working for the Chechen-Ingush Republic publishing house, I had, at Akhmatova's request, helped Daniel conclude an agreement for the translation of the poems of several Chechen and Ingush poets.

All the prisoners in the eleventh zone who knew Daniel spoke very warmly of him. Yuliy, they said, was uncompromising with the authorities, did not hide his convictions, and was honest and simple in his behavior with his friends. He was disliked by the Chekists, and he was continuously either in solitary confinement or restricted to his cell.

After hearing this I was naturally impatient to know Daniel better; furthermore, I also wanted to hear some of his poems.

I had heard much good of Platonov and Borodin too.

But this time the Chekists again played a cruel joke on us. They weren't such fools as to bring together political prisoners from the eleventh and seventeenth zones. It is the communists above all who know the formula for "divide and rule."

This was not very apparent in the eleventh zone, where there were 1400 prisoners but in a small zone such as ours, where there was only one two-story building for prisoners, several administration buildings, and only 350 prisoners, there were no secrets.

In the morning there was no water either in the wash-basins or drinking water in the barrels. The herring was rotten. Among the "seventees" (as those sentenced under paragraph 70 were called) there was grumbling. And when we came to work, a real shouting broke out.

Leaflets calling the prisoners to refuse work, to sabotage, etc., appeared in the living quarters. They were signed RPP—which immediately was deciphered as the Russian Progressive Party.

At work no one did anything. People gathered in groups, warming themselves in the sun. The administration was taken aback. After lunch members of the Cheka administration arrived, and towards the evening—investigators from Saransk. The officer of the day had no time to call out the prisoners. The informers who knew nothing, because everyone knew them, were the first to be called. Then, all those who in the eyes of the Cheka were suspect, that is the "Peterburgers," myself, and rebels of the type of Vyacheslav Kuzin were called. All had but one answer: we know nothing, we saw nothing.

In general I refused to answer questions, and demanded the procurator's sanction for our investigations. Ivanov and Bochevarov did the same. But the Chekists would not give up and called everyone systematically for questioning, using samples of handwriting as evidence. This produced another wave of protests: numerous appeals were sent to the procurator about the legality of the above action, as though legality ever existed in the USSR.

Finally the Chekists were obliged to give up. The investigation of the leaflets was dropped. But the camp administration didn't get anywhere about making the prisoners work; as before we sat in the sun and read books.

. . . On one occasion the enraged Garkushev tried to overturn a mug of coffee with his foot. He hardly made it out of the zone. And again a crowd of authorities arrived. This time the entire leadership of the Administration, except for Gromov, the chief. Great in the past, he was going down hill lately, and he tried to keep apart.

Whereas the influence of the "Peterburgers" was hardly felt in the overall mass of the prisoners, in the eleventh zone, here, Ivanov and Bochevarov immediately became the center of attention of the youth. People went to them, listened to them, imitated them. This could not but become known to the authorities, and the chief of the operations division with his retinue approached Nikolay Viktorovich. "What are your complaints toward the administration?" he asked.

Very objectively, supported by evidence, Ivanov outlined the situation: poor food, rotten herring, lack of food-stuffs in the camp store, irregular newspaper delivery, bad public baths, and the impossibility of fulfilling the work norm because none of the prisoners had ever sewn any mittens before. It was impossible for anyone of them to produce the required sixty pairs of mittens.

The lieutenant-colonel sniffed at the herring, which was shoved right under his nose and almost into his mouth.

"Yes, the herring is not too good," and turning to Garkushev he said: "Forbid its distribution." "Yes Sir."

"As to the work . . . We will provide you with two months of training. During this time the usual norms will not be required of you. Newspapers, the public bath, and bread—all these will be provided."

"Give us a guarantee!" demanded Ivanov.

"A man must be trusted" smiled the lieutenant-colonel.

"A man, of course . . . But you, forgive me, are a jailer," said Nikolay without losing his cool.

"Aren't you ashamed Ivanov?"

"But it isn't me who's the chief of the secret service department", the prisoner cut him short. And immediately, without letting the lieutenant-colonel get over the shock, he said:

"What about the food-stuffs in the camp store?"

"We ourselves eat almost the same stuff that you have in your store", the chief of the secret service blurted out the truth without thinking.

"It's indeed too bad that after fifty-two years of Soviet rule you still eat so badly . . ."

General laughter.

Losing control of himself, the lieutenant-colonel blurted: "Come on now . . . let's see if it will be any better when you'll be in charge!"

"To do that, we would have to change places right now," clinched off Nikolay Viktorovich.

Victory was complete.

The lieutenant-colonel and his retinue fled in the real sense of the word.

This was not only a prisoner's victory over a highly placed MVD functionary. This was the victory of one system of thinking over another. This was the victory of freedom over eternal bondage. The personification of freedom was Nikolay Viktorovich Ivanov, and the personification of bondage was the chief of the secret police, by the chains of Soviet bureaucracy.

Shaking Ivanov's hand, I asked permission to see the documents in the investigation and trial of the Social-Christians. Nikolay Viktorovich very kindly made it possible for me to do so. I read without stopping, rereading certain pages several times over.

No wonder that the lawyers who defended Ogurtsov, Sado and Vagin were suspected by the Cheka [secret police] of being favorable to the prisoners. Igor Vyacheslavovich Ogurtsov, about whom I had already heard many a flattering statement in the eleventh zone, had risen in my eyes to a gigantic figure after I had gone through the papers. Intelligent, well educated, pure in thought and heart and body (he was still chaste, at thirty-five), Ogurtsov rose like an eagle, even from the pages of the trial's transcript and I already saw his wings spread over Russia. Even Terekhov, the deputy procurator-general, and a representative of the Central Committee came to pay homage to this prisoner. They wanted to persuade him to renounce his convictions. When they encountered refusal, they tried to frighten him with death by shooting. To Russia's great honor, he did not tremble, but filled the cells of the Vladimirskaya prison with the white nights of St. Petersburg.

I embrace you my dear compatriots. I kiss the earth upon which you walk, Evgeniya Mikhaylovna and Vyacheslav Vasil'yevich—mother and father of Ogurtsov!

Our Igor, your "Gorik", will soon return to the city on the Neva. He will return to you, his parents. To have a son like that is happiness which can't be compared to any other.

I had the same good impression of Mikhail Yukhanovich Sado, Orgurtsov's first assistant within the organization. Like Igor' Vyacheslavovich, he behaved honorably both at the investigation and the trial. I had seen this man for only one hour. He came to zone eleven from Vladimir towards the end of April but was immediately transferred to zone three, and then to zone seventeen, then again back to zone three, either to "work" or for hospitalization.

The Chekists were obviously afraid to keep him too long in one place—so great was the attractive force of this Assyrian. Yes, indeed, an Assyrian who had accepted Russia with his entire being, who had gone forth to fight for her in the very front ranks and under the most dangerous conditions.

In his last year at the university Mikhail Yykhanovich was asked to the Leningrad office of the KGB.

"Your knowledge of Arabic is excellent," began the captain, "would you be so kind as to translate a short text into Russian . . ."

Sado translated the text. He was then asked to work for the KGB.

"Since you also know Hebrew very well, we will send you to Israel. You will have a brilliant career, Mikhail Yukhanovich. The only thing you'll be missing is bird's milk."

"I prefer the milk of truth. The milk of Christian teaching."

Blok [a Russian poet—Translator's note] once said: A poet has no career. He has only a fate. Learned men, truly learned men like Sado also have no careers. Such people are profoundly knowledgeable and have a clear conscience. Where are you Mikhail Yukhanovich? I would so love to see you!

"Everyone to work!" commanded Garkushev, lining up the armless and legless. "Those who don't go will be deprived of their store privileges, visiting rights, packages—everything!"

"Corpse-eaters! Savages!" came from all sides.

Nevertheless a few still went or rather crawled, because these aged men—between sixty and ninety—already could not walk.

Solomon Borisovich Dol'nik did not go.

"Why aren't you at work? " asked Garkushev the next morning.

"I'm an invalid. I won't go."

"I'll deprive you of your store privileges."

The next day the same question.

"I won't go," repeated Dol'nik.

On the third day again.

"I won't go."

"I deprive you of the right of a visit from your wife."

"I simply won't go."

"And I will deprive you . . ."

Once again the prisoner won. Garkushev did not deprive Dol'nik of anything—he was afraid. But the camp boiled and churned more and more.

New prisoners were arriving. Two engineers from Rovno, and a seventy-year-old Ukrainian priest—a uniat. And finally, Yuriy Ivanovich Fedorov, the former MVD captain who had worked as senior investigator in Leningrad.

All of us had already heard about this interesting affair, but of course we all wanted to know the details. All the more, because Yuriy Ivanovich—tall, with a kind, open face—charmed us. That same evening we invited him to coffee, the next day too, and on the third day again. We no longer drank coffee without him.

We found out the following: opposition had arisen in Leningrad to the Soviet regime among the hierarchy of the Ministry of Internal Affairs and Security [MVD]. All of them practicing communists, who nevertheless saw in the party's present policy a distortion of Lenin's teachings, and who therefore felt that Brezhnev and Kosygin should be removed and a two-party system, for which Lenin presumably fought, should be established, and freedom be given to the people.

Neither I, nor Ivanov, could of course in the least share Fedorov's point of view, but we had the utmost respect for Yuriy Ivanovich's courage to engage in the struggle.

On one occasion, during a recess in work, Yuriy Ivanovich gathered several of us in a group and said:

"Today the zone is going on a hunger strike. I know with certainty of three of the participants: Galanskov, Ginzburg, and Borodin. We must lend them our support."

"What's the reason for the hunger strike?" asked Ivanov.

"We should of course know the reason," seconded Bochevarov. "We should know the exact reason."

"I'm afraid there's not much of a chance for this. But each day counts in a hunger strike. I propose that we write a petition stating our demands. For the time being we won't declare a hunger strike. But we will give them to understand that if our demands are not met, we will go on a hunger strike."

On the first of December we dropped our petition into the mail-box, and on the second, the man in charge of distributing the work came to the factory immediately after lunch.

"Petrov, Bochevarov, Konosov, Fedorov, Dragosh, Dol'nik, Sokol'skiy, Ivanov, Khachatryan, Merkushev—get ready for departure.

In the residential zone we noticed Major Postnikov, the head of the KGB, with an unknown captain, also a "cavalryman".

"Some trick! Where are they taking us to?" we asked each other.

"Take all your things. Even those you have outside the zone . . ." came the order.

"Well, what do you know!"

We of course understood that the Chekists had decided to forestall the hunger strike, particularly because of the approaching anniversary of the Soviet constitution. Furthermore, the continuous unrest in our zone frightened them, at least worried them considerably. They selected nine prisoners who from their point of view were the most fervently convinced and important.

"We'll be scattered throughout the various camps," said Ivanov.

"Most likely we'll be sent to Saransk for brain-washing," suggested Fedorov.

"And I think that we'll be all sent to zone three. I believe there's a new factory there," declared Konosov.

Others too made a stab at it. I myself was inclined to think that more than likely it would be Saransk, or the Central Investigation Confinement Center.

. . . They took us to Ivas, to the investigation confinement center where each of us was placed in a cell. I was sent to zone three with Ivanov, Sokol'skiy and Dol'nik; Fedorov, Konosov and Bochevarov were sent to zone nine; Dragosh, Khachatryan, Merkushev to zone five. By the way, I had forgotten to introduce the reader to Merkushev. His first name was Slava. He was young—twenty-five. He was the son of an important MVD official. He rose not so much against his father as against the Soviet regime. He too, of course, wore a beard; he had a delicate face and a strong personality; in camp he was always rebelling and talking to his father's colleagues in a barking manner.

Restricted to our cells, we too, without exception, started barking.

"Who's in charge!" (Boom! Boom!—on the doors).

"Where's the chief of this institution!" (Boom! Boom! Boom!)

"Guard! Come here!" (Boom! Boom!)

The guard comes up. The officer of the day and the chief too. Each of us is handed a decree, which we proceed to read:

DECREE

On the basis and so forth, return so-and-so to solitary confinement for indoctrination. *For educational training.*

Signature: chief of the KGB, Chief of departmental operations. Approved by the procurator.

At first our eyes become large like saucers or like the eyes of Hollywood stars. Then there is general laughter; and finally again: boom! boom! boom!!!

The lieutenant-colonel who came the next day and who said he was Deputy Chief of the Administration was asked to leave, since he obviously wasn't able to explain anything at all.

Ershov appeared in the evening: he was congratulated for the star on his epaulettes, called a fascist, and promised that he would get it in the face from everyone in the ward if we were not immediately relieved of the indoctrination (the ward was dirty, there were plank beds instead of cots, and we had been deprived of everything, even pencils and paper).

"You'll have everything. Everything will be explained. Calm down." However they withdrew immediately and did not appear again.

The next day I did not accept any food, declared a hunger strike, and wrote a sharp letter to the secretary of the Mordovskiy regional committee party. Incidentally, I told them that my legs were in poor shape and that I needed medical treatment, not indoctrination in a solitary confinement cell.

Captain Afanas'ev appeared; he too was a "cavalryman". He called each one of us out in turn and explained that this measure was a temporary one and was due to our conflict with the administration.

"Not with the administration, but with the Soviet system," corrected Dragosh.

Two surgeons were asked to see me.

"Yes, you really should be hospitalized. Why don't you stop the hunger strike", suggested doctor Petrishevskiy, a major by rank.

"I won't stop it until you get me out of solitary confinement."

"This is up to the KGB," said the doctor, shrugging his shoulders.

"If the doctors prescribe it, we'll send you! "said Afanas'ev.

The coming Friday (in Mordovia the train for political prisoners runs between camps only on Fridays) we were taken to our various destinations. Dol'nik and I were taken to the hospital. He had some sort of heart trouble. Nikolay Fedorovich Dragosh and Slava were sent to zone nineteen, Sokol'skiy to zone seventeen, the lesser zone where Galanskov and Ginzburg were also kept. The Petersburgers were returned to their old place. Only Yuriy Ivanovich disappeared God knows where. We came to the conclusion that he was taken to Saransk. We decided that the Mordovian Chekists wanted to have a look at their former colleague from Leningrad and a chance to hear him speak.

More than a pleasant surprise awaited me at the hospital. While my belongings were being carefully scrutinized, Solomon Borisovich told me when we were in the waiting room which resembled a police precinct:

"Galanskov and Sado are here!"

"Really?" I was surprised.

"I already spoke to Sado. He works as a stoker in the kitchen. Galanskov is in the recovery ward. He has ulcers."

"And you, Solomon Borisovich, have an excellent sense of smell", I said jokingly.

No sooner had I entered the building (I was sent to the first, the surgical), when Mikhail Yukhanovich bounced in. We embraced and kissed. They say that everything in a person begins with the eyes. If the eyes are luminous, the person is luminous. If the eyes are clouded, the person is clouded. Mikhail Yukhanovich's eyes shone. Deep and dark, wisdom and sorrow was in their depth, and light from the soul and love shone on the surface. His face mat in color, his lips—full (a sign of a generous nature) and he wore a thick, black beard in a halfmoon.

"You don't know Yuriy Evgen'evich Ivanov! Ah! He is a painter of genius! I will tell you about him later. They took him to Saransk. Yura (that is Galanskov, who incidentally sends you his best regards) was sent here. They brought me too here. . . . It was very good that you supported us. It's only a pity that they sent back all our Petersburgers. Tell me please, in brief for the time being, how are Kolya, Mikhail Borisovich, Bochevarov?"

You could tell by the way in which Mikhail Yukhanovich pronounced the names of his colleagues that he felt closest to Nikolay Viktorovich Ivanov, but also he wanted to know everything about all the others.

"Yuriy Timofeyevich Galanskov and Vania Cherdyntsev will drop by. Cherdyntsev is a friend of Dragosh and a nice fellow. Like yourself, he is recently from Vladimir. As to Daniel, he was recently sent to Vladimir. Did you know that?"

Yes, I already knew this.

I liked Yuriy Timofeyevich immediately. He at the same time resembled both Dostoyevskiy and Belinskiy. He wore the democratic beard of the narodniks of the sixties of the last century; he was thin, walked slowly, did everything unhurriedly, and wasn't too ready with words for he spoke little. It was difficult to see his eyes: the glasses on his straight nose were in the way. Eyeglasses always hide the eyes, or somehow disguise them.

From a three-hour conversation at coffee, I understood that Galanskov and Sado were entirely different people, but were both honest, courageous, and could not dissociate their own personal happiness from that of their country's. But each understood happiness in his own way. I will say it again: there are as many roads [in life] as eyes.

Sado's erudition and high intellect were immediately apparent. Despite all his Russianness (Mikhail Yukhanovich grew up and was educated in Russia) he was a southerner. Looking at him, listening to him, I was involuntarily transposed in my imagination into the Assyria of the first centuries of Christianity, that Christianity of powerful unbending meekness which in pagan Rome [made its adherents?] walk into the lion's jaws, blessing the insanely aroused amphitheater.

Yes, Sado was a personality, a personality but not an organization.

Yes, Ogurtsov was apparently an even greater personality. But also a personality and not an organization.

On several occasions I saw tears in Mikhail Yukhanovich's eyes when I told him that many in their group were still not really ready for anything . . .

Sado wept with his entire being, and tried to counter me with argument, but I saw that his arguments held no water. And deep down in his own soul Mikhail Yukhanovich must have known this. He could not but know.

Galanskov was less emotional. Despite all his tenderness and kindness one sensed his rationalism. He did everything like he walked, slowly and surely. And he undermined Soviet power systematically and with persistence: articles and letters flowed from his pen. And he certainly knew how to write. I became convinced of this after reading his letter to the Procurator General about the position of political prisoners in Mordovia.

"In your account don't forget to write that Igor Vyacheslavovich is seriously ill. Attention should be drawn to him, the public should be taught that people like Ogurtsov must be treasured. This is the possession of the entire nation, not of an individual system."

"Just look—what an artist Ivanov is!" said Sado to me, when he brought me, shortly after we met, two of Yuriy Evgeniyevich's works.

The paintings were really magnificent: one, a portrait of Sado, another, entitled "Rus" [the ancient and poetic name for Russia—Translator's note], painted by a prisoner sentenced five times and now into his second decade behind a barbed wire fence.

"He has dozens of works! He is a giant! A titan! Do you understand?" Mikhail Yukhanovich continued convincing me.

To me his words meant:

"Here she is—Russia. This is our holy Russia, the Russia of Dostoyevskiy and Bunin. Of the archpriest Avvakum, and of Kutuzov. The Russia of Ogurtsov and Yuriy Evgen'yevich Ivanov."

In this respect Sado and Galanskov were of a like mind; they agreed because both of them were zealously devoted to Russia, as was Vagin, and the two Ivanovs, Platonov, and Borodin whom I never did get to meet; and Dragosh and his associate Ivan Cherdyntsev, a really wonderful man, who never pushed ahead of you but who was always ready to help a friend or any person in need.

I bow to you, Aleksandr Ginzburg. Until now, fate had not brought us together. But I always hear the beat of your heart. And I cannot think of Russia's tomorrow without you either, Andrey Donatovich Sinyavskiy. I believe that Konosov will write some beautiful verse. And Yuriy Ivanov Fedorov, having cleansed himself of materialism as of barnacles, will contribute towards the rebirth of a new Russia.

I believe in the Russian people.

———

THE TRIAL OF IRINA BELOGORODSKAYA

[Translated from Posev, March 1969, p. 2]

Moscow.

On 19 February, the case of engineer Irina Belogorodskaya was being heard in the people's court in the Bauman section of Moscow (28 Chernyshevskiy St.). Preliminary information on this case was given in the last issue of "Posev" (article entitled "New Trials are Expected").

Belogorodskaya was accused of "manufacturing and spreading fabrications and slander against the Soviet state and social order." The accusation was based on copies of an open letter found in Belogorodskays'a home, addressed to Soviet citizens, appealing to them to rise to the defense of Anatoliy Marchenko, who was arrested July 29 of last year; Marchenko is the author of the book "My Evidence," which describes conditions in Soviet concentration camps. This appeal was signed by Larisa Daniel, Pavel Litvinov, General Grigorenko, Pyotr Yakir, Anatoliy Yakobson, and Lyudmila Alekseyeva.

Irina Belogorodskaya was sentenced to one year in a concentration camp under article 190/1 and 15 of the Ukrainian RSFSR. Article 15 covers "responsibility for preparing a crime and for attempting a crime." Belogorodskaya did not admit her guilt, and defended her right both during the preliminary investigation and at the trial to come to the aid of an arrested person who was in trouble.

The judge at the trial was Monakhov, and the procurator, Biriukov. The defending attorney was Boris Romm; this attorney was approved by the investigating judge, and appointed against Belogorodskaya's wish.

The trial was not open to the public and was conducted for all practical purposes in camera. Friends of the accused and community representatives were not allowed at the trial. They congregated in front of the court building. There were about 150 people; among them were A. Yesenin-Volpin, P. Grigorenko, P. Yakir and others. When the accused was brought to the court a bouquet of flowers was thrown from the crowd.

Irina Belogorodskaya's case produced a new wave of indignation in the community. The outrageous highhandedness with which the case conducted was pointed out. The accusation was described as a blatant disregard of the law and the rights of citizens. The letter in Marchenko's defense contained no slander against the Soviet state. It stated the truth. During the entire investigation this letter was never described as anti-Soviet. None of the authors of the letter were called in to testify as witnesses, either during the investigation or the trial. Thus, Irina Belogorodskaya was tried for a letter, which was declared as "slandering the Soviet order" without any proof, and only at the trial.

Following Irina Belogorodskaya's arrest, the authors of the letter appealed many times to various offices, pointing to the fact that it was they and not Irina Belogorodskaya who was responsible for the letter. Recently they again presented a statement to the procurator and intend to continue their protests against the arbitrary sentence and the description of the letter as an anti-Soviet document addressed to Soviet citizens. In Moscow it is feared that the authors of the letter—General P. Grigorenko, P. Yakir, L. Alekseyeva, A. Yakobson—will now be subjected to repressions and arrest.

Foreign newspapermen in Moscow state that Irina Belogorodskaya is 29 years old. She is the fiancée of Anatoliy Marchenko and a step-sister of Larisa Daniel. She was denounced by a taxi-driver in whose car she left her purse, containing 60 copies of a petition in defense of Marchenko who was arrested on July 29 for addressing a letter to the Czechoslovak newspapers, criticizing the Soviet position on the democratisation of Czechoslovakia. On August 21, the day that Soviet troops began their intervention, Marchenko was sentenced to one year of hard labor.

Irina Belogorodskaya was again arrested on 5 Jan 1973 [Sentence penciled in—Translator's Note]

The trial of Il'ya Burmistrovich, also scheduled for February 19 (see the above indicated communication in the last issue of "Posev"), did not take place. It was presumably postponed on account of the judge's illness.

Il'ya Burmistrovich has been under guard since 16 May 1968. He was arrested for distributing the works of Sinyavskiy and Daniel (according to some sources, and in general for working for "samizdat"). He is about 30 years old; he is a candidate of physical-mathematical sciences.

Burmistrovich behaves very courageously and steadfastly at the investigation. He denies distributing literature not approved by the government, but categorically refuses to regard what he did as criminal, in as much every citizen has the right to express and proclaim his views, as stated by the Human Rights Declaration.

Burmistrovich refuses to name the people from whom he received Sinyavskiy's and Daniel's works, or the names of those to whom he had passed them on. It is expected that because of his courageous stand, Burmistrovich will receive a more severe sentence: that is, three years.

Information has been received from certain circles of the Moscow intelligencia on Larisa Daniel, Pavel Litvinov, and Konstantin Babitskiy.

Larisa Daniel is working at a wood-processing factory in the region of Bratsk, 808 kilometers from Irkutsk. Her address is: Irkutskaya oblast, Chuna Station, General Delivery.

Pavel Litvinov works as a machinist. His address is: Chitinskaya [Chita] oblast, poselok [village] Verkhne-Usuglin, General Delivery (the village is not mentioned in the list of populated places within the USSR: apparently it's a small village or settlement, perhaps newly established). P. Litvinov lives in a barrack; his wife has left to join him.

Konstantin Babitskiy works as a joiner, not far from the town of Syktyvkar, Komi ASSR. His oldest daughter has gone to join him.

FROM THE DIARY OF EDUARD KUZNETSOV SENTENCED TO DEATH AT THE FIRST LENINGRAD TRIALS

[From Tribuna (Israeli Russian language daily), 29 Dec. 1972]

This terrible human testament was written by one sentenced to death at the Leningrad trial of December 1970 for an attempt to highjack a plane to escape from the Soviet Union. The death sentence was commuted to 15 years of imprisonment. Prior to this, from 1961 to 1968, Kuznetsov served in a forced labor camp for having edited and distributed an underground political magazine. Excerpts from Kuznetsov's diary were miraculously brought to the West and published in the French weekly "L'Expresse", at risk to himself but with his full consent.

BEGINNING OF THE DIARY

The investigation ended on 27 Oct 1970. All the documents had been signed and I was left with only a pencil and some paper. Usually the prison guards look for every scrap of paper and every written word. I can't say that I had thought or wondered much; I derived my satisfaction from concentrating, smoking to my heart's content, and writing down all sorts of irrelevant things.

28 Oct: I refused the services of a lawyer. I know, and not only from my own personal experience, that in political trials the defense has no significance. I know that I won't be allowed to say everything I want, so it is best to say nothing at all. Each time I was sure I had led the procurator and the prosecuting attorney into a corner, I noticed that they were very pleased. They knew that they had my fate in their hands. Any attempt to force them to think logically was bound to fail in advance.

CONTACT WITH THE OUTSIDE WORLD

I assume that this trial too will be a parody of "socialist law" in its pseudo-legal proceedings. I did not commit any crimes against the USSR. Therefore I do not want to play their game before the judges. I am no longer twenty, and I cannot change the existing ways. (Despite this Kuznetsov's friends insisted on obtaining a lawyer for him.) The lawyer hired by my friends is no fool. We both came to the conclusion that my case was all but decided. In any case I will be sentenced to no less than 15 years in prison. Therefore it makes no difference whether I do or don't admit my guilt under no matter what paragraph of the indictment. Still, I am pleased that my lawyer provides me with some contact with the outside world. He is the only normal being in this world of bureaucratic despotism.

30 Oct: We were transferred from cell 347 to cell 242. Just above us is cell no. 193 where Lenin once sat. Now it is empty. It is something like a historic shrine which must not be profaned. At the beginning of the Revolution everyone used to shout in unison: let's destroy the churches and prisons. The churches have been destroyed with considerable success, but the number of prisons has increased.

11 Nov: Almost my entire life had been spent in communal quarters, barracks, and forced labor camps. How long can people live like rotten herring and dream of a private room as of a utopia? I would exchange 15 years in prison for 20 years in solitary confinement without any regret. According to Sinyavskiy, a forced labor camp is a cross between communal housing, a mental hospital, and a kindergarten. This is the prisoner's point of view. Of course there is also the administration's point of view. A labor camp is the closed shore of the Soviet empire. People may waltz around there completely naked without experiencing any shame.

FREE EDUCATION

Captain Kruglov once told me that if it were up to him, he would chase all the Jews out of the Soviet Union. In his opinion, Jews don't want to serve the Soviet government loyally. This point of view is very prevalent among party members, government officials and bureaucrats. This does not mean that those imprisoned are more anti-Semitic than those on the outside.

14 Nov: We were told that the standard of living in the United States had dropped, and that the situation there with respect to education is critical. Thank goodness education in the USSR is free. This is one of the reasons for forbidding emigration from the USSR. True enough, just think: the state had spent money educating you, and you want to give your knowledge to the enemies of the Soviet Union! Why should a master refuse to provide free education to his slave who can't leave him?

The sweat of an educated slave is sweeter. Economically, it is more advantageous. In the Soviet Union free education opens the doors of the universities to untalented though respectable people. They know that five years spent among students will assure them a living until the end of their days, without much effort on their part. Generally speaking the Soviet Union is a paradise for parasites. Where else in the world can a person continue to receive a salary without doing anything?

NO EXPLANATIONS OR ALIBIS

20 Nov: Since early morning I had been preparing for the trial. I had not eaten or drunk, and was on needles and pins. One, then two, then three hours had gone by. Finally, towards evening, I was informed that the trial was postponed until December 15. No explanations or alibis.

29 Nov: I believe that I found out why the trial was postponed. On November 25th the U.N. General Assembly adopted a special resolution against the hijacking of planes. Now they can sentence me to death.

4 Dec: Lenin spoke of bourgeois democracy the way St. Augustine spoke of idolators, whose good qualities are but potentially negative characteristics.

5 Dec: The heroes in Soviet novels have no bad qualities. Sometimes they do suffer from weaknesses, but these are only there to allow the author to show how they may be overcome.

10 Dec: At last I was able to speak to my lawyer. He demands that I restrict my participation in the trial to a minimum. He wants me to speak and behave like a repenting criminal resigned to his fate. I don't like his proposal. It is good to love people and Russia, but from afar. In the West they have no idea of what's happening in the Soviet Union. They don't know that here we seek bread, not butter. After lunch I was visited by Major Vasil'yev of the KGB. He told me (either intentionally or unintentionally) that a noise and din were raised in our favor in the West. I don't believe this will help us, but it will help raise our morale. There is nothing worse than an anonymous death. Vasil'yev asked me whether I intended to wear a skull-cap the way Mendelevich did, passing himself for a religious man. "I have never met a Jew who was religious," said Vasil'yev. "The only thing that they believe in is money!" I answered him with all possible courtesy: "Dear Sir, the ancient Jew lay on a sheep skin looking up into the sky, and thought of God, while people like you hung on branches swinging on their tails."

13 Dec: And so, the trial begins the day after tomorrow. Yesterday, to my own surprise, I suddenly decided to participate in it actively. For two days I wrote without stopping and only now have finished. I haven't yet decided how I will behave in court, but the pages I have written arouse in me a desire to read them out aloud in court. (Following are several passages from the statement which Kuznetsov intended to read at the trial.)

"I have long given up the thought of fighting the existing regime. The political traditions of the Russian people are tied to despotism. Think of Ivan the Terrible and Peter the Great. The Soviet regime is an ideal heir to these two rulers. I have no hope that the regime will become democratic in the near future. To me personally, it is clear why a person with my convictions would want to leave Holy Russia. However, I wonder whether the judges will understand me! I am a Jew, and want to live in Israel, the land of my forefathers. This does not mean that Russia is not my motherland. It is just as much my motherland as Israel. But I must emphasize that the concept of 'motherland' does not take first place in my scale of values. The main thing is—freedom! Israel attracts me, because it is both my motherland and a free country."

15 Dec: The first day of the trial has come to an end. The comedy lasted from 9 a.m. to 7 p.m. I am very tired and can hardly stand on my feet. Today was Dymshits', Iosif Mendelevich's, and Silva's turn. Tomorrow will be mine. Officially this is an open trial, but actually only the defendant's closest relatives are allowed in the courtroom. Iosif and Silva were O.K. They firmly denied all the accusations. The procurator behaved like an ass. On occasion his female assistant would get

him out of difficulties. I was revolted by the procurator's behavior, which prompted my lawyer to say: "He is duty-bound to act the way he does. As to the indictment, he is not under any obligation to delve into it. He is only asked to represent the will of the authorities in court."

16 Dec: I now remember that before going to the Riga airport to fly to Leningrad, Silva asked me: "What will happen to us?" And I answered: "If we are caught and the matter will not be made public, we will be sentenced to death," but when I saw the expression in her eyes I became ashamed of myself and added: "They will not put us to death. If they sentence us to death, it will be only to frighten others. You would be sentenced to about three years of imprisonment."

Silva's answer to this was: "I don't want this. I want to be treated like the rest."

Silva believes that she would help us if she took the whole blame for what we did on herself.

19 Dec: How did all this begin? Towards the end of February Silva introduced me to Butman. (Butman was sentenced to 10 years of hard labor in May 1971 at the second Leningrad trial.) On one occasion we approached a modest memorial marking the place where tens of thousands of Jews had been killed by the Nazis. Butman asked me: "What are the prospects of leaving this place?" I answered: "At present there aren't any, and probably there won't be any within the near future, unless." "Unless what?" asked Butman. "Unless everything they want to hide will blow up. As long as each one of us thinks only of himself, nothing will happen. Try to understand that this is not a problem of the emigration of individual persons, but a problem which concerns us all, the problem of free emigration from the Soviet Union for all those who want to leave. Only thus will we achieve anything; not by writing tearful letters to the Kremlin or the United Nations."

"So what do you suggest?" asked Butman. "A lot of people have lost all their patience after so many years of waiting and so many arbitrary decisions by the authorities in refusing exit permits. I suppose that one fine day a group of people, who have lost all hope, will do something unheard of. No doubt that they will suffer greatly for it. But this will be the first break in the Chinese wall".

"But, still, can this be done at the present time?"

"Thirty to forty people could get together in a group and go on a hunger strike to protest the fact that paragraphs 13 and 15 of the Declaration of Human Rights have become a 'dead letter'."

"I have a friend who is a good pilot. We have no other way out but to organize a group."

"The prospects for success are very small," I answered, "but if this turns out successfully, it will be the first time that personal considerations will contribute to the general welfare of all Soviet Jews."

So here we are now in prison. We made a serious mistake because our evaluation of the police system of our "beloved motherland" was amateurish and childish. In the Soviet Union pressure is applied on a disobedient prisoner in a forced labor camp in two ways: by decreasing the daily rations, and by sentencing the prisoner to solitary confinement. When a prisoner leaves the camp, he is obliged to co-operate with the KGB, otherwise he is threatened with a new term of imprisonment. For example, it is enough for a prisoner to see a young girl twice, but for her to be called in by the KGB, questioned, and given appropriate instructions.

Behind a barbed wire fence a person can say whatever he wants. It is true that he may then be given a maximum of 15 days of solitary confinement, or an additional three years in prison. This is socialist democracy. You are free to say anything you want, but they too are free to do what they want, and can throw you into prison. If you are listed as an opponent of the regime, they won't try to improve your behavior, but will want to destroy your personality. They have no need to transform you into a Marxist-Leninist. You don't have to have any principles. After three months of particularly harsh conditions in a corrective labor camp there are no two opinions on the usual question of whether you prefer a piece of sausage or a woman. Everyone wants the sausage.

22 Dec: Yesterday I found it difficult to write anything in my diary, as the procurator demanded that Dymshits and I be sentenced to death. He also demanded that both Yurity Fedorov and Aleksey Murzhenko, both of them non-Jews, be sentenced, the first to 15 years, and the second to 14 years of imprisonment. He demanded 15 years of imprisonment for Iosif Mendelovich and 10 years for Sil'va Zalmanson. When I returned to my cell, I asked my cellmate to leave me alone. Finally, I knocked my head against the wall three times. The prisoners in the next cell thought I was signalling them and answered me by knocking against the wall.

3 Dec: The comedy is over. The sentence will be carried out tomorrow at 6 o'clock in the evening. Until then I have a whole evening, an entire night, and the whole next day.

24 Dec: Sil'va's words were the best. She said in Hebrew, immediately translating it into Russian: "If I forget thee, O Jerusalem, let my right hand wither." Dymshits said: "I thank all my companions in misfortune. I had first met most of you at the time of our arrest at the airport. But we did not become spiders in a glass jar, we did not attack each other. This will come about in the middle of February 1971, and of course will not be a happy time."

5 May 1971: I begin at zero point.

We were searched on April 30th, on the eve of a holiday. As a result, I lost all my papers. One of the guards discovered the place where I had hid my notes. I jumped on him as though stung by a scorpion and grabbed the notes. I began tearing up the papers and threw them into either the Neva, the Fontanka, the Moyka, or some such other canal. Two guards manhandled me energetically. And now, one week after the incident, my face, hands, and neck are covered with bruises. Thus I destroyed my notes of four months. Only the fate of my very first notebooks, those for November and December, remains unknown to me. When I was transferred to death row, all my notes were wrapped in paper and I was told that they would be kept with my personal belongings.

(On May 10 Kuznetsov returns to his diary, going back to 31 Dec 1971.)

The door suddenly opened. Several prison guards walked in. One of them ordered: "Kuznetsov, put your hands behind your back and follow me." Then he said to the second guard: "Take his things." I put a pack of cigarettes in my pocket and went to the entrance. For a moment the whole thing seemed like a nightmare. New Year's eve—and here I am up against the wall with the guard's hands at my throat. The look in his eye is savage. I don't remember my heart beating, or what I was thinking of then. The third floor. The second floor. If we are going to continue descending like this. . . . But we stopped at the first floor and headed for Captain Kruglov's office. He got up and solemnly announced: "A humanitarian decision was made in your favor. The death sentence was commuted to 15 years of imprisonment in a special regime camp. My congratulations. I wish you a happy new year. What's so funny?"

He thought I was laughing. With great effort I refrained from humiliating tears; I was filled with scorn for the comedy played by the KGB.

"You're displeased?" asked the captain with an ironic smile. "If anyone asks me 20 years from now whether Kuznetsov had changed for the better, I wouldn't believe it." "You are quite right", I answered. [In Russian, a play on words having the following two meanings: 1) that Kuznetsov himself had changed for the better; 2) that Kuznetsov's life had changed for the better—Translator's Note]

18 June 1971: In 1963, on the day of my arrival at the special regime camp, I was called in to Major Garushkin to learn from him that here the enemies of the Soviet state, whose annihilation is demanded by the masses, are detested.

He also told me that those who in other camps were sentenced for disobedience to 15 days of solitary confinement, in this camp were physically destroyed. It should be noted that death sentences under paragraph 77(1) were quite common. In 1963 alone, nine prisoners were committed to death because they had tatooed parts of their bodies. They had tatooed the words "Soviet Communist Party slave", "Bread and Freedom", "Down with Brezhnev and Kosygin", "Down with Soviet Buchenwald" on their foreheads and cheeks.

One prisoner received 10 additional years for helping to make these tatoos.

21 June: I frequently witnessed the most terrible self-inflicted mutilations. Prisoners swollowed nails, metal wire, thermometers and other objects. They chopped off scrotums, swallowed hooks attached to doorknobs by wire so that when the door was pulled the entrails were dragged out; they sewed up their mouths and eyes, cut out pieces of flesh from their bellies and ate it; opened up their arteries, collected the blood into a plate, threw in pieces of bread and ate it up. They cut off fingers, noses, ears and even sex organs. It is simply difficult to describe all this.

31 July: It is getting more and more difficult for me to write anything. I am very tired.

24 Sept: For three days now I have had terrible pains in the stomach. Terrible pains and vomiting. Could it be that these are symptoms of stomach ulcers?

Major Tabakov, a paramedic, examined me and said: "You don't have any pains." "But what about the vomiting?" "You haven't been vomiting either," he answered.

27 Sept: The situation here is very bad. There are no laboratories, x-ray equipment, or doctors. People suffer excruciating pains for months before being sent to the hospital.

A CITIZEN OF ISRAEL

Today Yuriy, Aleksey and I sent out letters repudiating our Soviet citizenship. Following is the text of my letter:
"To the President of the Supreme Soviet of the Union of Soviet Socialist Republics—from prisoner Kuznetsov. For several years now I am no longer a citizen of the Soviet Union. Neither in accordance with my conscience nor my political convictions.
In 1968, I completed seven years of imprisonment, after being indicted for anti-Soviet activity. I had tried to realize through legitimate means the elementary right of a person to emigrate. When unsurmountable difficulties were placed in my way, I was obliged to use illegal means to get out of the country, specifically by hijacking an airplane.
At the trial in Leningrad this was unfairly described as treason. I was sentenced to death three times. But the Court of Appeals commuted this to 15 years of imprisonment in a strict regime camp. I consider myself a citizen of Israel. Not only because of my philosophy of life and my [national] origin, but de facto. Therefore I formally request that you annul my Soviet citizenship, as in fact I no longer am a citizen of the USSR. As of today and from now on I am not a Soviet citizen and request that I no longer be considered a citizen of this country."
In three days all of us will go on a hunger strike, begun by Aleksey. We must win, otherwise we are lost.
At present Kuznetsov is in comp No. 10, a strict regime camp. For two years now he has not been allowed any visits from his wife, Sil'va Zalmanson. However, even behind barbed wire, he and his companions had triumphed over their tormentors. The thousands of Soviet Jews who came out to Israel in 1972 are witness thereof.
Tribuna, 29 Dec 1972, p. 2, cols. 1–8 (Israeli Russian language daily).

PERSECUTION OF THE CHRISTIANS

[From "Uncensored Russia," Peter Reddaway, American Heritage Press, New York, 1972]

THE CHURCHES

In my fifty years, firm and clear convictions have formed in me; these are what I express in my articles. I write there the truth. You yourselves do not say that there is any untruth in them. I protest against the barbaric persecution of religion, which expresses itself in the destruction of churches and the humiliation of believers. I protest against a situation in which the Church has been reduced to scum, and comrade Trushin, who is present, is the dictator of the Moscow Church. He, an unbeliever and a communist, appoints and removes priests at whim. (The cause of this naturally lies not in him but in the existing system.) All this infringes every norm and even our Stalinist Constitution. Against all this I protest in my articles, which I have circulated, am circulating and will circulate, exercising my right to freedom of expression.
Anatoly Levitin, at a meeting with prominent atheists, May 1965
All three Soviet constitutions to date proclaim as a cardinal principle the strict separation of Church and State. On the other hand, the Bolshevik ideology, the fanatical intolerance of Lenin personally towards religion, and the close association of the Orthodox Church with the ancien régime all combined to make a live-and-let-live relationship impossible in practice. Almost immediately laws began to be passed undermining the separation principle, until, with the legislation of 1929, close state control of religious bodies was fully legalized in respect to everything except the supreme law, the Constitution.
Apart from the developments on paper, religious groups often suffered much worse depredations 'in the field'. The fact that these started under Lenin, and were not just another aspect of the Stalinist terror, has interested the Chronicle. *Here is how it commented on the appearance in* samizdat *of 'A Letter to the Members of the Politbureau':*
This letter, dated March 19th, 1922, is signed by Lenin and demands that *the most merciless measures* be taken to *crush* all opposition to the proposed confiscation of church treasures. The instructions contained in the letter do not

conform to the principles of socialist legality. They are the product only of the political and tactical requirements of the moment: 'We must appropriate at all costs this source of several millions—or perhaps even milliards—of gold roubles'; 'suppress their (the clergy's) resistance so brutally that they will remember it for decades to come'; send a member of the All-Union Central Executive Committee of the Soviets (V.Ts.I.K.) to the town of Shuya [NE. of Moscow, where clashes had occurred], with 'verbal instructions' to arrest no less than several dozen representatives of the clergy, the middle classes and the bourgeoisie 'on suspicion of direct or indirect participation in violent resistance to the V.Ts.I.K. decree concerning the confiscation of church treasures'; 'on the basis of his report, the Politbureau will issue a detailed directive, also verbal to the judicial authorities, so that a trial of the rebels of Shuya for resisting the campaign to help the starving can be held as quickly as possible and can end, unfailingly, with the execution of a very large number of the most influential and dangerous Black Hundreders of Shuya, and if possible not only of Shuya, but of Moscow also, and several other ecclesiastical centres'; 'the more representatives of the reactionary bourgeoisie and the reactionary clergy we manage to execute on this suspicion, the better'. The famine appears consistently throughout the letter as providing a convenient set of circumstances in which the confiscation of church treasures can be carried out without fear of resistance from the peasantry. The millions or milliards of roubles are required not for famine relief, which admittedly might have justified repressions; they are necessary so that the Soviet team may feel itself a power at the Genoa conference [on European economic reconstruction of April-May 1922].

The letter is a top-secret document, and the channel through which it passed into *samizdat* is unlikely to be discovered. Therefore one should not regard the document as indisputably genuine: it would be wise to carry out a detailed textual analysis of the letter. Obviously official propaganda will not miss its opportunity to declare such a document a forgery. But in *samizdat*, where there is complete freedom of research, one should not rush to the opposite extreme: if the authenticity of the document is confirmed, then the profile of the first Chairman of the Council of People's Commissars will become more clear-cut in the mind of the public.

No. 15 duly reported that the letter's authenticity was confirmed by the appearance of a brief summary of it in Volume 45 of Lenin's Complete Works. Further confirmation lies in the fact that recorded events fit closely with the letter; a crowd at Shuya had been machine-gunned in clashes on March 15th, Izvestia recording four people killed, and forty-five priests and laymen later stood trial, twelve of whom were executed.

In the 1930s Stalin turned to the forcible closure of places of worship on a massive scale, with the aim of eradicating public religion completely. The war, however, prevented him completing his task; in order to gain believers' support he had to reopen the churches. After this, the next big onslaught did not follow until 1958–64, under Khrushchev, when at least half the religious buildings in the U.S.S.R. were closed by deception or force. The number of open Orthodox churches, for example, fell in this period from about 20,000 to some 10,000. Since 1964 the situation has remained fairly static, but occasionally the Chronicle has carried reports like this;

In the town of Kolyvan near Novosibirsk [in south-central Siberia] the Orthodox church has been closed on the pretext of its not conforming with fire safety regulations. When the believers dug a pond to conform with the fire regulations, the local authorities filled it in again and prohibited church services, despite the fact that permission to hold services had been given by Moscow. Moreover the local authorities tore down the church's cupolas, killing a five-year-old child in the process. Instead of the church the believers have been given a small chapel which does not satisfy fire safety regulations.

THE ORTHODOX

Anatoly Levitin

No one in the Christian wing of the Democratic Movement has been more prominent than the colourful Anatoly Levitin (pen-name Krasnov—see page 279), on whom much documentation is already available. After the police came for him on September 12th, 1969, the Chronicle drew on his extensive autobiographical and other writings to compile this item:

Levitin spent seven years—1949–56—in Stalin's camps. He was later rehabilitated. Levitin's deep religious convictions, and his activities as an Orthodox writer, led [in 1958] to this talented teacher and literary scholar being deprived of the right to teach in schools.

A. Krasnov is the author of a number of articles in the *Journal of the Moscow Patriarchate*. Apart from this, he is the author of a three-volume history of the Living Church.

Since 1959 Krasnov-Levitin has written a large number of works, in which he has spoken out in particular against violations of religious freedom in the Soviet Union: *Struggling for Light and Truth, The Brassy Clatter, The Fiery Chalice, The Drawn Bow-string, On Monasticism, The Free Church*, and others. In recent years he has written two important philosophical works: *Stromati* and *Christ and the Master*, on which the *Chronicle* reported in No. 5. The journal *Science and Religion* has twice written about Levitin-Krasnov (see Vasilev's article 'The Theologian-Inciter', 1966, No. 10, and the section 'A Contemporary "Secular Theologian"' in N. Semenkin's article 'From Anathema to Vocation', 1969, No. 8).

Here we interrupt No. 10 so as to give No. 5's account of the samizdat works just mentioned, and also of two others:

Christ and the Master is an attempt to discuss several basic questions of Christian teaching through a literary and philosophical study of [Mikhail] Bulgakov's novel *The Master and Margarita*. The thread of the argument is provided by the chapters in the novel about Christ. The book is written in a free, discursive manner with frequent digressions into the author's personal reminiscences and reflections.

The Greek word *stromati* literally means "carpet", but in the figurative sense of "miscellany" it was used by various ancient teachers of the Church as the title for their books. Written in the form of observations loosely tied together by the general theme of the part a Christian should play in society, Krasnov's book deals with such questions as the moral responsibility of a Christian to society, the role of the Church in the life of society, and the collaboration of Christians with people of different views in the solution of common moral and political tasks. The author gives a brief survey of the various political trends at the present time and states his attitude towards them. At the end of the book the author gives his political credo, which he defines as "democratic humanism", and calls on people of different persuasions to unite on this basis.

His letter on "The situation of the Russian Orthodox Church" is addressed to the Pope, and it gives an account, based mainly on the author's personal observations, of the attitude of different generations of Russians to religion and the Church, the way in which some young people are turning to the Church, and the relations between different faiths. He raises the need for an inner revival of the Russian Orthodox Church, and examines the difficulties in the way of this. The author speaks of the criticism which he and others have made of the Russian bishops, and contends that such criticism is both justified and necessary. The question of uniting the Western and Eastern Churches is also touched upon in this letter.

The article "A Drop under the Microscope" is about the difficulties which have arisen at the parish level in the Russian Orthodox Church as a result of a change in the parish administration. This change consisted of taking the administration of parish affairs out of the hands of the priest and transferring it to the council of twenty laymen headed by a church elder. The author shows that this reform is in conflict with canonical tradition, and he points out the practical consequences which it entails in conditions of constant interference by the authorities in the life of the church: infringement of the rights of the priest, unchecked power for the elder, who is appointed by the state authorities, etc. As an illustration, the example of the Kikolo-Kuznetskaya church [in Moscow] is described in detail. The author also treats the more general question of the way in which the Russian Orthodox Church has been denied its rights in the Soviet Union, and of the responsibility of the Church hierarchy itself for this state of affairs.

Now No. 10 continues:

During recent years Levitin-Krasnov has also spoken out continually in defence of civil rights, and in defence of people arrested and sentenced on political charges. His signature stands at the foot of numerous collective protests, including the letter to the Budapest meeting [see pp. 86–8]. He is a member of the Action Group for the Defence of Human Rights in the Soviet Union. As a publicist he has commented on the arrest [see p. 327] of B. V. Talantov (*Drama in Vyatka*) and [see p. 136] of P. G. Grigorenko (*Light in the Little Window*).

On September 12th, the Procuracy investigator L. S. Akimova carried out a search in Levitin's flat. During the search, the following works of A. E. Levitin-

Krasnov were confiscated: *A History of the Living Church, On Monasticism, Stromati*, a letter to the Pope, a letter to the Patriarch in support of the letter from [Moscow] priests Gleb Yakunin and Nikolai Eshliman, *Light in the Little Window, Drama in Vyatka, Listening to the Radio, The Brassy Clatter*, and others. Also confiscated were *samizdat* materials and a typewriter.

Just before the search of Levitin's flat, his friends Oleg Vorobyov and Vadim Shavrov had been there. The search began as soon as they had left the house, while they themselves were quickly detained by the police on suspicion of 'stealing suitcases'. Shavrov was released from the police station after the search was over and Levitin-Krasnov had been taken away. Vorobyov was searched at the police station, without a warrant for the search of his person being issued, and the letter 'To the Members of the Politbureau' by V. I. Lenin (about the events in Shuya) was taken from him. He was then sent to the violent patients' section of psychiatric hospital No. 15, from which he was not released until October 20th. Oleg Vorobyov [see plate 63] was among those who signed their names in support of the Action Group's [first] appeal to the United Nations [and later received a six-year sentence in Perm].

For three days A. E. Levitin was held in a preventive detention cell at the police station, and then he was transferred to Butyrka prison. An investigation was begun by the Moscow city Procuracy. (The investigator was Akimova, already well known as chief investigator of the cases of the Pushkin Square demonstration of January 22nd, 1967, of the Red Square demonstration of August 25th, 1968, and of Irina Belogorodskaya.) A charge was brought against Levitin under article 142 of the Russian Criminal Code (violation of the laws on the separation of Church and State) and also under article 190–1. Witnesses are being questioned about Krasnov-Levitin's works, mainly about *Stromati*.

On October 9th Levitin's case was suddenly handed over to the Krasnodar Procuracy, and A. E. Levitin-Krasnov was sent off to Krasnodar [in the north Caucasus].

Soon after Levitin's arrest, a letter began to circulate in *samizdat*, entitled 'To Public Opinion in the Soviet Union and Abroad', signed by thirty-two Soviet citizens, including six former political prisoners (Leonid Vasilev [see p. 120], Zinaida Grigorenko, Alexander Yesenin-Volpin, Victor Krasin, Vadim Shavrov and Pyotr Yakir). The letter says that A. E. Levitin 'was becoming more and more worried by problems of civil freedom, since freedom is indivisible and there can be no religious freedom if basic human rights are being trampled upon. He was the first religious person in our country in the post-Stalin years to affirm this truth and to raise his voice in defence of civil rights and of those who have fallen victims in the fight for civil freedoms.'

A letter by six Christian believers on the subject of A. Levitin-Krasnov's church and religious activities has been sent to the World Council of Churches, with copies to Patriarch Athenagoras, Pope Paul the Sixth and the International Committee for the Defence of Christian Culture. The letter says:

We deeply deplore the fact that the Russian Orthodox Church finds its supporters amongst laymen and ordinary priests, and not among the bishops of the Russian Church, many of whom are barren fig-trees, completely under the control of the Council for Religious Affairs . . . Anatoly Emmanuilovich was doing his duty as a Christian, and none of his activities, which were all in defence of the Christian faith, infringed Soviet laws . . . We, Christian believers and citizens of the Soviet Union, are deeply disturbed by the arrest of the Orthodox writer A. Levitin-Krasnov and [see below] the teacher B. Talantov. We join with them in their protest against the abnormal relations which exist between Church and State, and we demand the opening of the forcibly closed churches, monasteries, seminaries and houses of prayer.

The letter was signed by: J. Vishnevskaya, B. Dubovenko, V. Kokorev, V. Lashkova, E. Stroyeva and Yu. Titov [see plates 40 and 60].

For nearly a year Levitin sat in prison. No. 11 reported that the investigation was "expected to be completed in January 1970". It was. But then the Krasnodar Provincial Court "refused to accept the case and remitted it for further investigation, on the grounds that the charge of libel against Levitin was too vague, and that it was impossible to see exactly what law had been violated as a result of Levitin's incitement and by whom". The Procuracy appealed angrily to the Supreme Court against this unusual show of independence. At the same time it searched Father Yakunin's flat in Moscow, confiscating works by Levitin, and probably inspired the subsequent scurrilous attacks on Levitin, Yakunin, and Eshliman in the paper Trud. Nevertheless, the Supreme Court upheld the Krasnodar court's decision, and on August 11th Levitin was freed.

Undeterred by the continuation of the investigation, he quickly penned a long and vivid essay about his prison experiences before returning to jail with a three-year sentence in May 1971.

THE CASE OF BORIS TALANTOV

Chronicle *readers first learnt of Boris Talantov (see plate 64) from a summary, in the* samizdat *section, of his "Statement to the U.S.S.R. Procurator-General":*

This contains protests against the persecution to which the author, who lives in the city of Kirov [in the western foothills of the Urals], is being subjected for his oppostion to interference by the Soviet authorities in the affairs of the Russian Orthodox Church, and to the acquiescence in this interference by the Church hierarchy.

Talantov's opposition had been vigorous since the early 1960s. Indeed it is from his pen that we have the most remarkable, vivid, detailed and horrifying picture of the effects of Khrushchev's anti-religious campaign on a typical provincial area. He has also written penetratingly on Church history, politics, and Metropolitan Nikodim, and he organized strong support from the Kirov diocese in 1966 for the two Moscow priests' attempt to reduce state control over the Church's life. Through all his writings run a deep love of the Church and its beautiful buildings, and a strong desire to rid Christians of their status as third-class citizens. Time and again he protests against this status, stressing its generally illegal basis. He also shows. with his references to the Baptists, his strong support for Pavel Litvinov and Larissa Daniel, and his condemnation of labour camp conditions, that, like Levitin, he understands the indivisibility of freedom, and that freedom for the Orthodox requires freedom for Baptists and intellectuals as well.

In the light of all this, the Chronicle's *subsequent items about Talantov cause little surprise.*

On June 12th, 1969 Boris Vladimirovich Talantov was arrested in the town of Kirov. He is a 66-year-old teacher of mathematics, who for many years has been exposing the illegal treatment of the Church, and the connivance in this of Church leaders. Talantov has been charged under article 190-1 of the Russian Criminal Code. The inquiry is being conducted by the Kirov Regional Procuracy, under senior investigator Boyarinov.

The *Chronicle* has already reported that the 66-year old B. V. Talantov, a teacher, was sentenced by a court in Kirov to two years in [ordinary-régime] camps. In this issue some details of his trial are given.

The trial opened on September 1st. A group of believers, who sympathized with the accused, tried to get into the courtroom, but the seats had, as usual, been filled in advance.

B. V. Talantov was charged under article 190-1 of the Russian Criminal Code with writing a number of articles of religious content, an article on the nature of the Soviet state, and various draft notes, including comments in the margin of a speech by L. I. Brezhnev. [He pleaded not guilty (No. 9).] Altogether only four witnesses were summoned in court, among them Gleb Talantov, son of the accused, and Nikodim Kamenskikh, a former seminarist. All the witnesses gave evidence in favour of the accused.

Besides the Procurator, a former pupil of Talantov's—who is now a teacher of dialectical materialism—spoke at the trial as a public prosecutor. Talantov's defence was conducted by the lawyer [V. Ya.] Shveisky.

The Procurator agreed with the defence lawyer that the draft notes should not be held against Talantov, but otherwise he upheld completely the charge laid against him, saying that he considered all Talantov's articles, including those of religious content, "deliberately false statements defaming the Soviet political and social system". The Procurator demanded three years in camps for Talantov. The defence completely refuted the charge relating to the articles of religious content. Concerning the article on the nature of the Soviet state, in which there were some sharp criticisms of the Soviet state, the defence lawyer, while he did not agree with the views expressed in the article, maintained that its author sincerely believed in the correctness of his statements, and consequently there was no element of deliberate falsification in the document.

In his final plea, B. V. Talantov reaffirmed his allegiance to his convictions, although he allowed that he might have shown a subjective approach in certain of his judgments. He said farewell to his relatives, since, in view of his age and the state of his health, he had no hopes of regaining his freedom.

On September 3rd the court pronounced him guilty.

A year later, on January 4th, 1971, Boris Talantov died in captivity. The Chronicle *honoured him with a long obituary.*

The Chronicle *has also informed its readers of the man who provided the stimulus to the two Moscow priests by leading a delegation of eight bishops to complain to the Patriarch about Church administration in 1965—Archbishop Ermogen (see plate 62). For doing this he was retired to a monastery. Here, however, he applied himself to writing with the same outstanding success that he had achieved as a pastoral bishop. Thus the* Chronicle *could announce in 1968 the circulation in* samizdat *of two letters and a historical study:*

The first of the letters written by Archibishop Ermogen to the Patriarchate (in which he disputes the legal validity of his dismissal) was written in November 1967, and the second in February 1968. In these letters he not only shows the illegality of his dismissal (brought about under pressure from the authorities as a reprisal for his staunch resistance to actions detrimental to the Church), but also attempts an analysis, from the point of view of both canon and secular law, of the whole question of relations between Church and State in the U.S.S.R.

There is an even more detailed study of this question in his article 'On the fiftieth anniversary of the re-establishment of the office of Patriarch' (December 25th, 1967) which makes numerous references to the decisions of the Ecumenical and National Councils of the Orthodox Church (including the National Council of the Russian Church of 1917–18).

But despite the restrained and dignified style in which Ermogen made his points and discussed the correct historical procedure for the election of a new Patriarch, the Synod proved unable either to accept or to answer his criticisms. Instead, it simply ordered him to shut up.

Another Orthodox writer to emerge into view—from the ancient Russian town of Pskov near the border with Estonia—has been the priest Sergei Zheludkov. Cultivated and intellectual, but also passionately concerned about the Christian's role in society, he is cast in many ways in the Levitin mould. His big samizdat *book* Why I Too Am a Christian *reveals vividly his modern theological thinking. This is how the* Chronicle *comments on two of these letters:*

In a letter to Pavel Litvinov, S. Zheludkov expresses his support for the appeal by Litvinov and Larissa Daniel, 'To world public opinion', and speaks of the aims shared by all 'people of goodwill' irrespectively of how they define their views.

The 'Letter on the Day of St. Nicholas and Victory Day' (May 9th, 1968) is addressed to the heads of various [foreign] churches. It was written after reading Marchenko's book *My Testimony.* Referring to this book, the author of the letter speaks of the grievous situation of political prisoners in the U.S.S.R. and calls on all Christians, and particularly their spiritual leaders, to speak up in their defence.

Before writing the second letter Zheludkov had already protested to his own rulers about the Soviet camps and mental hospitals. He had also generalized to them like his:

Even to me it is clear: the terrible decline of literature and art, the obvious failures in economic life, the mysterious apathy of our young people—all this is the result of the lack of creative freedom. No one is aiming to seize your power—govern, please, but let this be not so much a privilege as a responsibility. It cannot be that the fate of a great people now consists only of the negative results of the absurd phenomena produced by the suppression of freedom and the withering of the spirit.

The Chronicle *also summarizes Zheludkov's* samizdat *essay 'Some Reflections on Intellectual Freedom: a Reply to Academician Sakharov' (see pp. 354–5):*

The author gives his analysis of those absurdities to which society has succumbed as a result of Stalinism: fear, duplicity, apathy. Father Sergei studies the problem of intellectual freedom as a religious problem and states that 'man's freedom does not even belong to God', that 'freedom is man's absolute, holy right and his sacred duty'. But 'today', writes the author, 'all of us Russians, willingly or unwillingly, are involved in a momentous historical experiment on the following subject: What will happen to a great people if it is deprived of its intellectual freedom?'

THE BAPTISTS

More samizdat *documents—over a hundred, in fact—are available in the West from the Baptists than from any other religious group. Many of these have appeared in translation with extensive commentaries. Yet until No. 16 the* Chronicle *had carried only two brief items on this denomination. That said, No. 16 eventually indicated the nature of the problem. The Baptist protests stem from a schism in the Church provoked by the official leadership. In 1960–61 the latter—doubtless under pressure from the authorities—attempted to impose tighter controls on Church life and to reduce evangelism almost to nil. A grass-roots rebellion at once occurred, and the schismatic group began to campaign for greater religious freedom. In 1965 it set up its own organization, which the State has ever since refused to recognize, thus leaving the schismatic communities outside the law. One of the schismatic leaders is the subject of the open letter from the Kiev community summarized here by the* Chronicle:

This letter is the latest in a series of similar ones of 1967 and is in defence of the Baptist preacher G. P. Vins, who was arrested in 1967 [in fact in 1966] and is being subjected to cruel treatment in a camp. The letter is signed by 176 members of the community in the name of 400 Kiev Baptists and Evangelical Christians.

The only other Baptist mentioned in the first eleven Chronicles *is a man already noted (p. 206) as having taken part in a camp strike in 1968 with Yuly Daniel and others. The news in 1969 was:*

Boris Zdorovets, a Baptist from the Donbass, who has spent seven years in a labour camp, has been exiled for five years to Krasnoyarsk Province; at his place of exile the police are carrying out 'educative' work on him, demanding that he publicly renounce his religion.

The Baptists—with perhaps several million adherents—are much less numerous than the Orthodox, with their several tens of millions, yet the volume of Baptist dissent is clearly greater. The poor reflection of this in the Chronicle *doubtless stems from the fact that only a few Baptists come from the intellectual groups which mainly constitute* Chronicle *circles.*

THE UNIATES

An important extra dimension is added to our picture of dissent in the west Ukraine by the following two items. The first is entitled 'New Persecution of Uniate Priests':

In spite of the U.S.S.R. Constitution, which guarantees freedom of conscience, the Greek-Catholic, or Uniate, Church was forcibly liquidated in 1944 [–46] by organs of the M.G.B. [now K.G.B.] in western Ukraine. Priests who did not adopt the Orthodox faith were sent to camps after false charges had been fabricated. The Uniate Church continued to function underground. Its activity has come to life in recent years, and at the same time the number of Uniate priests detained and beaten up by the police has grown. On October 18th, 1968, ten Uniate priests had their homes searched: legally permitted religious objects were confiscated, including even the Holy Sacrament—all this representing a flagrant encroachment into the sphere of religious ritual. At the end of 1968, two Uniate priests were arrested: one in Kolomiya, Ivano-Frankovsk Region, the other in Lvov. In January 1969, an underground bishop of the Greek-Catholic Church, Velychkovsky, was arrested. Velychkovsky is about seventy, he is ill and now in a prison hospital, where his condition is serious. The case is being conducted by the Lvov Procuracy: the charge is unknown. At the beginning of 1969 more searches were carried out in the homes of Uniate priests.

Now the Chronicle *is in a position to give the following clarifications and additional information.*

On October 18th, 1968, searches were carried out at the homes of ten priests of the former Lvov Greek-Catholic metropolianate, including Bishop Vasyl Velychkovsky, the priests Petro Horodetsky, Mykola Ovsyanko, [Ihnaty] Tsehelsky, [Ivan] Lopadchak, [Fylymon] Kurchava, [Mykola] Deyneka, [V.] Sternyuk and others. Ritual objects (chalices, crosses, vestments, Holy Sacraments) as well as religious books, cameras, tape-recorders and money were taken away.

At the same time one of them, Petro Horodetsky, was arrested and charged under articles 187–1 and 138 of the Ukrainian Criminal Code, i.e. propagation of deliberate fabrications which defame the Soviet political and social system, and violation of the laws concerning the separation of Church and State. The investigation of his case was completed in April, and now the trial is awaited.

At the end of 1968 the aged Bishop Vasyl Velychkovsky was arrested in Kolomiya. At present rumours have spread to the effect that he has died in prison, but there is no official confirmation of this.

In the spring of 1969 all over the west Ukraine dozens of searches were carried out among Greek-Catholic priests, also in flats where former nuns were living. Again ritual objects, books, etc., were taken away.

In 1968 in Pochayev there was a meeting of West Ukrainian Orthodox priests—mainly those priests who went over to Orthodoxy under pressure in 1946. Some priests at the meeting complained that they were being interfered with by Greek-Catholic priests who had not accepted Orthodoxy, and that these priests were carrying on their religious activities underground; Metropolitan Filaret gave the Orthodox priests instructions to spy on the Uniates and report on them. He promised to appeal to the party and government, and in person to the First Secretary of the Ukrainian Communist Party, Shelest, and to request him to put an end to the activity of the Greek-Catholic priests.

As the Uniates affirm, referring to information received from Orthodox priests, the court and Procuracy officials have been instructed to put a stop to the activity of the Greek-Catholic Church by all possible means in the course of one year—by the centenary of the birth of V. I. Lenin [in April 1970]. It looks as if precisely this was the reason for the arrests and large-scale searches.

In 1970 the Chronicle *extended its range, reporting for the first time on the persecution of Roman Catholics, Adventists, Jehovah's Witnesses and the sectarian Truly-Orthodox Church.*[65] *All this helps to remind us that despite persecution, some of it built into the law, the U.S.S.R. is a more religious country than many secularized Western societies. Quite apart from private religious observance, perhaps as much as a quarter of the population dares to practise its religion openly, the proportion being higher in the Muslim areas, where Islam is ridden on a relatively light rein, than elsewhere. Part of the reason for this religiosity lies in the failure of the aridly official Marxism-Leninist ideology to satisfy most Soviet citizens as a philosophy for living. While this failure worries the regime, what really alarms it is when the only legally and widely available alternative to Marxism-Leninism—religion, in one or another form—becomes an ideological basis for political opposition. To some extent this has begun to happen. It may well do so increasingly in the future.*

BAPTIST TRIAL IN ODESSA, FEBRUARY 2–7, 1967

["Russian Christians on Trial: Eye Witness Report From a Soviet Courtroom," Published by "Jesus to the Communist World," Diane Books, Glendale, Calif., 1971]

The trial was due to take place at 10 a.m. on 2 February in the club of the mil[1] combine. Its location was altered 24 hours beforehand without any reason being given. Representatives were summoned from a number of places, mainly Party officials and prominent workers, and given leave from work to attend.

By 10 a.m. about 100 believers had assembled, by which time the courtroom was already full of Party workers. Numerous police and the security (KGB) agents were standing outside the building where the trial was to be held. Not only did they prevent the believers from getting into the courtroom, they even stopped them standing outside the building. They chased them some distance away from the clubhouse, round the corner, threatening them with fines and 15 days' imprisonment. Many friends did not go away, but stood at a distance, despite the intense cold.

They let only the defendants' nearest relatives through, claiming that there was no more room in the court.

The defendants N. P. Shevchenko, Ya. N. Krivoi, S. P. Solovyova and V. I. Alexeeva, who had already been in custody for some considerable time, were brought into the courtroom. Then further defendants who had been bound over not to leave the town, G. G. Borushko, V. T. Timchak and V. M. Zaborsky, came in.

The members of the court entered and the trial was officially opened. A representative of the police called out (addressing himself to the rest of the court) "Rise!" The defendants took their places, N. P. Shevchenko and V. Alexeeva knelt down and the former prayed aloud. Everyone present stood speechless with surprise.

Then there was a murmur throughout the room and you could hear people say: "They're praying!" Three policemen went up to them and made Valya get up, but Nikolai went on praying and when he finished, all the defendants and other believers said "Amen". The defendants were taken out of the courtroom straight away and brought back a little while later.

The court noted the following personal details of the defendants:

Shevchenko, Nikolai Pavlovich, born 1913.
Krivoi, Yakov Nikiforovich, born 19__ (date not given in text)
Solovyova, Svetlana Pavlovna, born 1940.
Alexeeva, Valentina Ivanovna, born 1939.
Borushko, Grigori Grigorievich, born 1939.
Zaborsky, Viktor Mikhailovich, born 1936.
Timchak, Vasili Terentievich, born 1929.

Charged under Article 138, Section II, of the Ukrainian Penal Code, Case No. 16827.

The judge defined the defendants' rights.

JUDGE. (to the defendants) What are your requests?

All the defendants asked that their fellow-believers be allowed into the court-room and requested the right to conduct their own defense.

G. Borushko and V. Zaborsky demanded that the prosecution witnesses N. V. Kuzmenko, district superintendent of the Odessa Region, and his deputy F. A. Balaban, and also senior police lieutenant Shamrai, be called.

Solovyova and Krivoi asked permission to use a Bible in their defense.

JUDGE. Alexeeva, why are you refusing to have a defense counsel?

ALEXEEVA. I invited Jesus Christ to be my defense a long time ago (she quotes a Bible text but the judge interrupts her).

JUDGE. For what reasons are you refusing a defense counsel?

KRIVOI. "My witness is in heaven, and my record is on high" (Job 16:19).

SHEVCHENKO. As a believer, I can't be defended by an atheist; God is my defence.

SOLOVYOVA. If a person is mentally balanced (according to Art. 146) he has the right to conduct his own defence.

PROSECUTOR. I consider it admissible to grant the defendants' requests about dispensing with counsel and giving them the right to conduct their own defence. The request for the summoning of additional witnesses is inadmissible. As to the request for believers to be present in court, the door is open and entry is free to all, everyone who wanted to come in is already here. With regard to the request by Solovyova and Krivoi for a Bible to use in the defence, this question will resolve itself in the course of the trial. The opportunity to use a Bible will be given as necessary.

The defence lawyers requested that the defendants' plea for permission to use a Bible and for the calling of additional witnesses be granted, then they left the courtroom.

The judge asked the defendants' opinion on how the trial should be conducted.

Solovyova and Borushko suggested that interrogation begin with the witnesses. The prosecutor suggested that they begin with the defendants. There was an interval while the members of the court left for a consultation. After the interval, none of the believers was admitted into the court. The judge declared that the interrogation would begin with the defendants.

JUDGE (to Shevchenko). What relevant testimony can you give the court?

SHEVCHENKO. I won't give my testimony until all my fellow-believers who are outside are admitted to the courtroom. They are freezing out there, I can imagine what it's like. How can we consider the case calmly here in these circumstances?

The judge demanded that the actual names be given of those whom the defendants wanted to see admitted. They let a few in and said that that was all there were.

N. P. Shevchenko addressed himself to the gallery and asked: "Brothers and sisters, are there some outside who want to come in?"

From the gallery came the reply: "Yes, there are!"

In the gallery, the atheists began to ask: "Who on earth's in charge here, the court or the Baptists?" But just then the believers outside were being chased further away from the courthouse.

JUDGE. Krivoi, give your testimony.

KRIVOI. I won't give my testimony until all those who want to have come in.

The rest of the defendants also refused to testify until all the believers had been admitted.

JUDGE. Defendant Borushko, go out with the police lieutenant-colonel and call everybody to come in.

Borushko went out and gathered all the believers who were in the next street, round the corner, and brought them in.

JUDGE. Shevchenko, what relevant testimony can you give? Tell us your work record. When did you become a Christian? How and in what circumstances did you become an invalid from work?

SHEVCHENKO. I began to work at the age of 16 and became an invalid in 1934 as the result of an accident at work. I became a believer in that same year.

JUDGE. How long have you been a pastor?

SHEVCHENKO. The Church elected me as an elder in 1946 and in 1949 as pastor.

JUDGE. But why were you not elected as a pastor in 1946?

SHEVCHENKO. Because the Church had to test my manner of life. It is only when the Church has ascertained whether a man's life corresponds to the gospel and is convinced that its servant is worthy, that it elects him as a pastor.

JUDGE. What is the difference between the office of pastor and the office of elder?

SHEVCHENKO. An elder can lead a Church meeting, but only a pastor can fulfil spiritual needs.

JUDGE. Was there any break in your activity as pastor?

SHEVCHENKO. A pastor is elected for life.

JUDGE. When you were in places of imprisonment, were you still a pastor?

SHEVCHENKO. Yes, I was still a pastor during those times too.

JUDGE. Tell us why registration was suspended from your congregation, when and for what reasons?

SHEVCHENKO. Registration was suspended in 1958 because an official representative of the Council for Religious Affairs was not invited to the opening of the prayer house and because children were present at services.

JUDGE. Did you continue to meet after the congregation was dissolved?

SHEVCHENKO. Yes we did, but we kept on requesting to be registered the whole time. We applied to Kiev and Moscow for registration several times.

JUDGE. Up to 1958 you accepted the legislation on religious cults?

SHEVCHENKO. It wasn't in operation.

JUDGE. Do you accept the legislation on cults now?

SHEVCHENKO. Yes, I accept it, but I can't agree with certain points.

JUDGE. Name these points.

SHEVCHENKO. We aren't allowed to admit children to services, but it's written in the gospel: "Suffer the little children to come unto me and forbid them not." We weren't allowed to baptize believers under 30 years of age. According to the gospel baptism is carried out on the basis of faith, not age.

We don't agree with the section that forbids freedom to preach outside our own congregation.

Only the Church must elect and dismiss pastors and preachers, but according to the legislation, the official state representative appoints them. The Church is best able to judge who is fit to serve in it, not a secular functionary.

I have already been tried once before and the same charges were brought against me. I served 2 years and 7 months in prison. The Prosecutor-General protested against my sentence, the court reviewed the case and in the absence of proof of criminal action I was rehabilitated, but now the same accusations are being brought again.

JUDGE. At that time there was no such law, but now these activities are countered under the March 1966 decree.

PROSECUTOR. When you were under detention, did you maintain your link with the church?

SHEVCHENKO. We were behind barbed wire fences and you know perfectly well that there's no chance there of maintaining any link.

JUDGE (undoes a parcel and takes out the collection: "Ray of Light"). Look, these aren't just written things, you can tell by the format that they've been done by a specialist. Look at this binding. Where did you get the money for it? Have you any specific funds?

SHEVCHENKO. We don't have any funds. When there's a need, we have a collection. At all our funeral services we get financial help and also believers collect money to buy paper and materials.

JUDGE. Give us the names of those who did the printing.

SHEVCHENKO. I won't answer that question.

JUDGE. Do you know who brought illegal literature to your congregation?

SHEVCHENKO. All believers.

JUDGE. What do you mean, all believers? Who specifically? You say you didn't help to distribute literature. Yannu Shmidt testifies that he got the "Fraternal Leaflet" in your house.

SHEVCHENKO. I didn't consider this as distribution; I was sharing with my brother the Word of God, since the Word of God is the bread of life and spiritual food and our Christian duty is to share.

YA. N. KRIVOI'S TESTIMONY

JUDGE. What have you to say about this case?

KRIVOI. In 1937 I was sentenced to 10 years for my faith in God. I was in prison for 9 years and 6 months. After that my case was reviewed and in the absence of criminal proof I was rehabilitated. Along with me my fellow-believers were sentenced to 25 years' imprisonment and to the supreme punishment—execution. And they were shot. After the review of their cases they were posthumously rehabilitated.

JUDGE (interrupting him). We aren't asking you about that. You were re-habilitated and the previous trial doesn't count. What congregations did you be-long to before? When did you become a member of Peresyp congregation?

KRIVOI. In 1963.

JUDGE. Why did you leave the registered congregation? What were your dis-agreements with them?

KRIVOI. Because a state official was interfering in the internal life of the Church.

JUDGE. You were a member of the illegal all-Ukrainian conference; what docu-ments did you sign there?

KRIVOI. I signed a document, but I don't remember the contents now.

JUDGE. Did you preach at the May-Day celebration?

KRIVOI. No, I wasn't there.

JUDGE. What part did you have in organizing the May-Day meeting?

KRIVOI. I have already answered.

PROSECUTOR. In the pre-trial investigation you said (he quotes): "I stood leaning against a tree. . . ."

KRIVOI. That's false. The investigator wrote that himself, I didn't say it.

PROSECUTOR. The court will check on that (he refers to the report on the affair).

JUDGE. It can't be checked. The defendant hasn't signed it. What were you doing on that day?

KRIVOI. I have proof that I was working on 2nd May.

PROSECUTOR. The court will find out whether you were there or not. Who preached in Gomenyuk's house?

KRIVOI. I was outside and I didn't see the speakers.

JUDGE. Witnesses have testified that you preached.

KRIVOI. I've already answered.

PROSECUTOR. You're obviously avoiding a reply. Who distributed the literature?

KRIVOI. I've nothing to do with that side of things.

JUDGE. You say that in your literature there's nothing but evangelical teaching (he reads an extract from an "appeal" to all believers of registered congregations).

KRIVOI. Read the whole "appeal"—I can't answer from extracts.

PROSECUTOR. I'll read you the exact quotation from this document (he reads it).

KRIVOI. Read on, so that the audience can understand what it's about.

PROSECUTOR. Do you remember what documents you signed?

KRIVOI: Yes, I remember. I don't repudiate those documents that I signed and I'm fully in agreement with their contents.

SVETLANA PAVLOVNA SOLOVYOVA'S TESTIMONY

JUDGE. Defendant Solovyova, do you admit your guilt?

SOLOVYOVA. No. I'm charged with distributing literature. I don't consider that a crime. It's my duty.

JUDGE. What's your profession?

SOLOVYOVA. Painter.

JUDGE. Have you been working as a painter recently too?

SOLOVYOVA. No, I've been on watch duty.

JUDGE. But you also worked in a laundry?

SOLOVYOVA. Yes, I did both.

JUDGE. Tell us, do you enjoy your work?

SOLOVYOVA. Yes, I do.

JUDGE. When did you become a believer?

SOLOVYOVA. Can I start from the beginning?

JUDGE. By all means.

SOLOVYOVA. I came to Odessa as a child. My father had reenlisted and worked at headquarters, and remained there as a painter. I went to evening classes. At home I often heard about God and about believers, but it didn't interest me. I wanted to live like everybody else. My mother was illiterate, she didn't make me go to meetings or believe in God. I grew up with the same aims and the same desires as my fellow-pupils, thinking that only uneducated and old folk believed in God. In school I joined the *Komsomol*. After I had finished school, I was faced with the question of where to go and what to do then. I got a job. I didn't want to stay at home because the conversations about God and my mother's continual prayers and all that religious environment disturbed and haunted me.

I decided to leave home. I told my parents that I was going to enter an institute in Novosibirsk. I said it deliberately, knowing it was a lie. But I couldn't see any other way out and I deceived my relatives and went to Novosibirsk. I took my personal documents with me but I hadn't given in my notice at work, having arranged with my own people that if I didn't pass the exams I'd come back. In Novosibirsk I applied to the institute, but as I hadn't prepared for it and wasn't really keen on it, I didn't get in. But I sent a telegram home: "Passed exams, give notice at work. Staying to study." That's how my life away from home started, a life that began with deception.

Sometimes I used to think: "Does God exist or not?"

JUDGE (interrupting her). This thought stayed with you because they knocked it into you in childhood.

SOLOVYOVA. They didn't knock it into me. If my mother had brought me up in that spirit, I wouldn't have been there, I wouldn't have deceived my parents. I simply knew that believers existed and that they believed in God and sometimes I thought about that, but the cinema, the theatre and all the worldly pursuits didn't leave room for such thoughts and I forgot about them.

After working for a year in Novosibirsk, I came home on leave for 10 days. At home my mother invited me to a meeting, and so as not to grieve her, I went. There I heard about God more fully. This thought stayed in my mind and I began to think about this question more seriously. It didn't leave me in Novosibirsk either, it followed me everywhere. I couldn't stay in those circumstances any longer and I was tortured in my conscience for having deceived my parents. It was a difficult time for me, these were the fruits of the world's education. And then I had the idea of going home. All this happened very quickly. I gave in my notice at work, broke with everything that held me back and came home. At home I straight away began to seek satisfaction and peace for my soul. The world no longer satisfied me. Everything in it revolted me.

Once I went to a meeting at Peresyp. There I heard comforting words. I saw the joyful, happy faces of girls and boys just like me, I saw their goal in life and I understood that here I could find what I had long been seeking—peace for my soul. Here was my happiness, Christ became my goal in life. The Church at Peresyp became my spiritual mother. I found my place in life, I found happiness.

PROSECUTOR. Defendant Solovyova, you have taken up too much time with the story of how you became a believer. It would be better if you would tell us how you distributed illegal literature and whether you consider this a crime.

SOLOVYOVA. I distributed illegal Christian literature and I don't consider this a crime, since it's my duty to give bread to the hungry. I did it with a feeling of compassion, people were interested and I couldn't refuse them. I did distribute literature and I shall go on doing so, if I still have the opportunity, for it's my duty.

JUDGE. You also preached and you don't consider that a crime?

SOLOVYOVA. I haven't preached in the sense that you mean, but all believers are preachers of the Kingdom.

JUDGE. Just imagine what it would be like if everybody in this country began to preach what he liked and wherever he liked, no matter whether people listened to him or not.

SOLOVYOVA. I did no more than speak about Christ—and only where people listened or where they asked me to.

PROSECUTOR. You say you preach only about Christ and that your literature is purely spiritual, but look at this: (he reads an extract from a copy of *Fraternal Leaflet* about the May delegation (1966), where it says that believers were beaten up outside the Central Committee building and remarks indignantly): Is that about Christ? Why, that's slander against Soviet reality.

SOLOVYOVA. It certainly is Soviet reality: I well remember the first blow I got outside the Central Committee building—after that I don't remember the others.

JUDGE. 14 copies of *Fraternal Leaflet* were taken from your flat. Where did you get them? Somebody must have done them and given them to you.

SOLOVYOVA. I'm not going to tell you that. I just got them.

JUDGE. How many did you distribute? 50, 100, 200 copies?

SOLOVYOVA. I don't remember. I tried to give out as many as I could.

JUDGE. Were you there at the May-Day meeting? Do you remember how many people were there?

SOLOVYOVA. I can't tell you. I didn't count them.

JUDGE. But roughly—a hundred, two hundred, five hundred people?

SOLOVYOVA. I don't know, maybe even more. (In the gallery there are astonished exclamations: "You see!")

JUDGE. Do you know the people who were there on May Day?

SOLOVYOVA. I know that they were my brothers and sisters.

JUDGE. Was the defendant Krivoi there?

SOLOVYOVA. No.

JUDGE. How can you tell—could you see all 500 people?

SOLOVYOVA. Yes, I saw them all.

JUDGE. Please tell us what your relations are with the registered congregation.

SOLOVYOVA. What should my relations with them be? They're my brothers and sisters there.

PROSECUTOR. Defendant Solovyova, you said that you were convinced the cinema is a means of agitation—what sort of agitation?

SOLOVYOVA. What do you mean, agitation? It's a means of taking people away from God.

PROSECUTOR. You said that the people in the central congregation are your brothers and sisters?

SOLOVYOVA. Yes, that's right.

PROSECUTOR. Why don't you go there?

SOLOVYOVA. In the first place, as I already said, the church at Peresyp is my spiritual mother. It's my family, that's where I was born.

JUDGE. You mean that in your family you have 'brothers' and 'cousins'?

SOLOVYOVA. Yes, that's right.

JUDGE. What do you consider to be wrong in the central congregation?

SOLOVYOVA. The authorities interfere in the Church there and poison the minds of believers against each other.

JUDGE. Did they do that to you personally?

SOLOVYOVA. Not to me personally. I remember once when I was still going there often—they took a woman out of the meeting; she was a small person and they thought she was a minor.

JUDGE. Who took her out?

SOLOVYOVA (uncertainly). Believers.

JUDGE. What have the authorities to do with that?

SOLOVYOVA. What do you mean, what have they to do with it? It was they who ordered her to be taken out and they had the power to do it.

JUDGE. Do you read books?

SOLOVYOVA. Yes, I used to. Even in prison now I still read.

JUDGE. But there aren't any books about Christ there.

SOLOVYOVA. I can get something precious out of anything.

JUDGE. Very true. Tell us, did you preach at the May-Day meeting?

SOLOVYOVA. I don't remember whether I ever preached at meetings.

JUDGE. Are you a member of the Council of Twenty (Church Council)?

SOLOVYOVA. Yes.

JUDGE. Why did the Church elect you particularly?

SOLOVYOVA. Why do you want to know about me particularly? There are 19 others besides me.

JUDGE. Did you stand out in some way from the rest of the rank and file?

SOLOVYOVA. No, I don't think so. I'm not worthy of that. I'm not worthy to stand before you today, since only the best Christians are brought to trial.

JUDGE. When your flat was searched, they took copies of the Kiev declaration. Why did you keep them?

SOLOVYOVA. To give to others.

JUDGE. Have you already given out a lot?

SOLOVYOVA. I don't remember. I gave them out when necessary.

JUDGE. What would happen if everybody preached his own beliefs and got a crowd of followers around him? Maybe there are some people who don't want to listen to you.

SOLOVYOVA. I'd be very glad if I had the chance and the strength to gather a crowd around me. If some people didn't want to listen, I wouldn't force it on anybody.

JUDGE. Why did you give your boss copies of your pamphlet-letters at work?

SOLOVYOVA. Every day at work a policeman used to come to see me. All the workers began to get curious about why he came. I started to explain and gave them out for people to read.

JUDGE. Did you preach?

SOLOVYOVA. You keep calling me a preacher. In your sense I'm not, but as a Christian I must preach by my life and I spoke about Christ wherever I could, when I had the chance. I speak about Christ on trams and now in this hall and I'll go on doing so.

While their friends were being taken out, all the believers stood in flanking rows and when the defendants passed between them they greeted them with raised hands. Both the defendants and their friends had joyful expressions on their faces. Thus finished the first day of the trial.

On the second day everybody who wanted to came into the courtroom. They brought in the defendants. Valya Alexeeva came first and greeted everybody aloud: "Greetings to all brothers and sisters!" From the audience came the reply, "Greetings to you." The defendants took their places and prayed standing.

The trial was declared open.

JUDGE. Alexeeva, what have you to say about the case?

ALEXEEVA. First of all I want to know whether all my friends have been let in. (They answered that everybody had come in.)

JUDGE. Tell us about yourself. Where did you come from to live in Odessa?

ALEXEEVA. From the Vologda Region.

JUDGE. What was the reason for your coming here?

ALEXEEVA. I was fulfilling the command of Christ: "If they persecute you in one town, flee to the next".

JUDGE. But how were you being oppressed there?

ALEXEEVA. Well, there was only a small group of believers there and atheists and lecturers used to visit me systematically.

JUDGE. So you were frightened?

ALEXEEVA. No, I enjoyed chatting with them. But when they realized that their visits were pointless, then the press started up. They wrote a lot of slanderous articles about me. You know very well how we hold baptisms, but in the paper they wrote a lot of lies—even that my veins were cut and believers drank my blood.

JUDGE. They wrote about you personally in the paper?

ALEXEEVA. Yes, directly about me. Once they did it using a false name, but in such a way that it was obvious it was me. They never left me alone, neither at home nor at work. That was why I left.

JUDGE. Were you invited to come to Odessa?

ALEXEEVA. No, I tried to find out where there was a prayer house and young believers.

JUDGE. Is there a prayer house in Razdelnaya?

ALEXEEVA. No, but there are some not far away.

JUDGE. Did you distribute literature?

ALEXEEVA. Yes I did.

JUDGE. Do you know the Gubanovs?

ALEXEEVA. Yes, they're my good friends.

PROSECUTOR. Did you send letters to them?

ALEXEEVA. Yes.

PROSECUTOR. Did they ask you to send them?

ALEXEEVA. No, but they wanted to meet me personally to have a talk. But I couldn't manage that, and I wrote to them about the life of our family (the Church) and sent them the *Fraternal Leaflet*.

JUDGE. Are you in agreement with the legislation on religion?

ALEXEEVA. Yes, except for some points.

JUDGE. What points do you not agree with?

ALEXEEVA. We're forbidden to help each other. That contradicts the gospel. We can't disobey the commands of Christ. Our faith must be accompanied by works, for faith without works is dead. It says in the gospel: "Add to your faith virtue; and to virtue knowledge; and to knowledge temperance; and to temperance (the judge tries to interrupt) patience; and to patience godliness; and to godliness brotherly kindness; and to brotherly kindness charity."

JUDGE. Were you there on May Day?

ALEXEEVA. I wasn't there on 1st, but I was on 2nd.

JUDGE. Who else was there of the defendants?

ALEXEEVA. I remember Nikolai Pavlovich Shevchenko was, we sat together, away from the crowd and listened.

JUDGE. Who preached? What part did you take?

ALEXEEVA. Guests preached and read poems. I had a poem, but I gave my place up to others who had come from other towns.

JUDGE. Does the literature which was taken from Tikhenko belong to you?

ALEXEEVA. Yes.

GRIGORI GRIGORIEVICH BORUSHKO'S TESTIMONY

JUDGE. Defendant Borushko, what have you to say?

BORUSHKO. Your honour, I request permission first of all to clarify the contents of the charge brought against me. Then I am ready to answer any questions the court wants to put. I am accused of the systematic distribution of illegal literature during 1965–66 on the premises of the prayer house of the Odessa Church. That's a lie. I never distributed any literature on the premises of the Odessa Church.

JUDGE. You said at the pre-trial investigation that at one time this literature used to be at your house.

BORUSHKO. I didn't sign the protocol of the pre-trial investigation—the investigator wrote what he wanted to.

I have been charged with organizing and holding a service on 2nd May in the forest plantation near Shevchenko's farm, which was supposed to have caused a public nuisance by disrupting normal running of road and rail transport in the said district and to have caused material damage to the forest plantation. I've been in Odessa 10 years now and every year I've been at the May-Day service and it's never been brought against me. The court has photographs of the May-Day service in 1965, at which believers from other congregations were also present. That tells you that the May-Day service is something traditional and there's no special organization needed for it.

I personally came to the plantation about 9 a.m. Some fellow-believers were already there. We found our clearing and began to make ready. We hung up a text: "You who remember the Lord, do not be silent!" The meeting began at 11 a.m. I took an active part in conducting the service. Krivoi wasn't there at all, Shevchenko took absolutely no part in it. I preached on the theme of "God the Creator of the universe" on the basis of Romans 1:20.

I spoke of how the world is regulated and develops according to certain laws as revealed by the scientists, but there must also exist the One Who made these laws, that is God. If we look at the world around us, we see many different objects made by the hand of man, but there are things—animals and the plant world—the author of which we have difficulty in identifying. They didn't create themselves. But there wasn't any appeal in my sermon to break the laws on religion. I can't even imagine how that could be associated with such a theme. We played and sang, and generally spent a good day. Then some auxiliary police came up, but they behaved properly. In the end they listened for a bit, stayed a little longer and then gradually dispersed. We picked up all the litter and burned it. What's wrong with that?

PROSECUTOR. Why did you break the law and meet without being registered?

BORUSHKO. I don't consider that we broke the law, according to one basic law, the decree of Lenin, point 5: "Free celebration of religious rites is guaranteed, insofar as they do not disturb public order and do not infringe the rights of citizens of the Soviet republic." Our meetings in flats do not cause a public nuisance and are not connected with any infringement of the rights of other citizens. So the 1929 law contradicts Lenin's decree in this matter.

PROSECUTOR. You aren't interpreting it properly. If you read on, point 6 is: "A citizen's first obligation is the duty to keep Soviet law."

BORUSHKO. I consider my first obligation as a citizen is my duty to work. I work in a factory . . .

PROSECUTOR. What else do you disagree with in the legislation?

BORUSHKO. It violates the principle of the separation of church and state. State officials have the right to remove a pastor.

PROSECUTOR. You appoint another one.

BORUSHKO. He's removed again and a month is given to elect a new one. Otherwise they suspend registration. Shevchenko was removed, Logvinenko was elected, and he was removed by the official, too.

PROSECUTOR. Is there anything else you don't agree with?

BORUSHKO. General meetings for church members can be held only with the permission of the Party district executive committee. For example, if we need to elect a pastor, we have to ask permission from the committee. They may not allow the meeting to take place. That's interference by the state in the internal affairs of the Church.

PROSECUTOR. You signed and duplicated copies of a Declaration on the suspension of Article 124 of the Constitution.*

---

*Guaranteeing the "freedom to hold religious services and the freedom of anti-religious propaganda". Lenin's original constitution had proclaimed the right to "religious propaganda."

BORUSHKO. That was the first such declaration, since we knew that a ne constitution was being worked out and we as citizens placed our request with tl Legal Draft Commission that Article 124 be formulated in such a way as ↑ guarantee complete freedom of conscience. As believers, we did what Christ saic "Ask and it will be given unto you, knock and it will be opened unto you."

JUDGE. In the letter "On unity" you criticize the religious decree which allov believers to participate in cultural life, to go to the cinema and the theatre, an you add: "It's impossible to imagine a more satanic programme."

BORUSHKO. That decree is a document of the official religious body (All-Unio Council) and the state has nothing to do with it. So you're condemning us for no fulfilling that decree?

JUDGE. For what reason did you write that letter?

BORUSHKO. Our whole Church at Peresyp went to the town Church to tall about unity. But when that discussion didn't materialize, we had to address then by letter.

PEOPLE'S ASSESSOR: You said that the legislation was adopted in the period o: the cult of personality. You don't know your history.

BORUSHKO. Let me correct that. In the period of Stalin's activity, when there were significant religious restrictions.

ASSESSOR. The last Baptist congress was in 1926. When did you finish at the institute?

BORUSHKO. They finished me.

ASSESSOR. Why did they expel you from the institute?

BORUSHKO. For my religious convictions. They told me I wouldn't get through in the subject of atheism.

ASSESSOR. Quite right too.

BORUSHKO. You know, this man (pointing to the Assessor) should be tried under the same law.

ASSESSOR. Did you pass in histology?

BORUSHKO. Yes, with the assessment "excellent".

ASSESSOR. So you studied embryology, the science of the development of man. How did you reconcile that with your convictions?

BORUSHKO. In order to speak about the emergence of life, you have to go back to the question of the emergence of the first living cell. There's Oparin's hypothesis, which is still only a hypothesis, that is, a surmise, and unproved.

ASSESSOR. What do you mean? It's been proved by science.

BORUSHKO. It's been proved. When I was at college, Professor Olga Borisnova Lepeshinskaya experimented on a chicken embryo and made a cell out of a non-cellular substance. They gave here the Order of Lenin. Then they checked it and the experiment proved to be false. So the Order of Lenin had to go back. (Laughter in the court, the Judge makes a remark to the People's Assessor.)

PROSECUTOR. Why are children present at your meetings?

BORUSHKO. I'm amazed that our comrade the Prosecutor says children have no right to go to the meetings. I don't know any law that forbids children to attend meetings. The existing law forbids only the organization of meetings specifically for children.

ASSESSOR. You came to Odessa as a young man—were you already a believer?

BORUSHKO. My views were formed during my time as a student.

ASSESSOR. Didn't your elder brother Sergei have any influence on you?

BORUSHKO. Maybe to some extent. But really a man is born again by the Word of God.

ASSESSOR. Is your wife a believer too?

BORUSHKO. She shares my views.

VICTOR MIKHAILOVICH ZABORSKY'S TESTIMONY

ZABORSKY. I plead not guilty to the charge against me.

JUDGE. How long have you been in Odessa?

ZABORSKY. Since 1956.

JUDGE. Where did you come from? In what connection and to whom?

ZABORSKY. I came from Khabarovsk, after being demobilized. I came to relatives.

JUDGE. When did you become a believer?

ZABORSKY. When I was in the Soviet Army.

JUDGE. When did you have a chance to occupy yourself with such matters there?

ZABORSKY. You don't need a long time to become a believer.

JUDGE: What's your job?
ZABORSKY. Stoker.
JUDGE: Did you help to organize the distribution of literature?
ZABORSKY. I'm charged with distributing illegal and slanderous literature. I didn't distribute any such literature.
PROSECUTOR. But witnesses have testified that you did.
ZABORSKY. 1 asked that they should say it to my face.
PROSECUTOR. Did you preach?
ZABORSKY. Yes, I did.
PROSECUTOR. Did you speak in Gomenyuk's house, on May Day?
ZABORSKY. No, I wasn't there at all on 1st May.
PROSECUTOR. Were your children there?
ZABORSKY. Yes, they were.

VASILI TIMCHAK'S TESTIMONY

JUDGE. Tell us about yourself, why did you come to Odessa?
TIMCHAK. I came here from Tarnopol Region in 1956 and I liked Odessa.
JUDGE. Were you already a believer?
TIMCHAK. Yes.
JUDGE. Where did you meet other believers?
TIMCHAK. At the prayer house.
JUDGE. What did you do in Odessa?
TIMCHAK. I worked in a factory, first as a brick-layer, then as a tinsmith.
JUDGE. When you came, was there a prayer house at Percsyp?
TIMCHAK. No, we met in people's houses.
JUDGE. Did you go to conferences in Moscow?
TIMCHAK. Yes I did.
JUDGE. Did you preach?
TIMCHAK. Yes. But you accuse me of calling people to ignore Soviet laws. I never made any such appeal in my sermons.
PROSECUTOR. Were you at the All-Union Conference in Moscow?
TIMCHAK. Yes I was. We adopted a declaration, but there wasn't any appeal in it not to obey Soviet laws.
PROSECUTOR. Were you summoned to the district executive committee?
TIMCHAK. Yes.
PROSECUTOR. You were at the conference—what resolutions did you make there?
TIMCHAK. Yes I was there. We decided Church matters.
PROSECUTOR. Why did you, personally, particularly go to Moscow?
TIMCHAK. The Church elected me.
PROSECUTOR. Why did you all go to Moscow?
TIMCHAK. Because we weren't being allowed to have a congress, to which we had a right:
PROSECUTOR. Do you accept the legislation on religious cults?
TIMCHAK. Yes, but I disagree with certain points.
PROSECUTOR. Which ones?
TIMCHAK. The legislation forbids us to give one another practical assistance. It gives state officials the right to remove a pastor. (He enumerates other points.)
JUDGE. What questions did you decide at the Moscow conference?
TIMCHAK. We wrote a declaration to the government and asked them to recognize our brethren, the Council of Churches. The Council itself was elected.
JUDGE. Where did the regional conference take place?
TIMCHAK. I can't answer that question.
(Here follow the testimonies of the witnesses. First to be called is Nikolaev, a Komsomol official. His testimony against the defendants contradicts what he said at the pre-investigation and reveals, as do later testimonies of other witnesses, the manipulation of the case for the prosecution.
(In the testimony of the witness L. A. Kuprianov there is still further evidence of the difficulties besetting believers on account of the legislation on religion.)
JUDGE. Do you respect Soviet laws?
NIKOLAEV. Why shouldn't we respect them? You ask at work how often I do two shifts in a row; that shows you how I respect them.
JUDGE. All right, but the legislation on religion is also a Soviet law.
NIKOLAEV. The legislation on religion affects believers only. We can't fullfil those points in the legislation which are contrary to the gospel. For example, we

as believers elect a man for spiritual work, then a state official interferes and has the right to remove him. We elect somebody else, and he doesn't like him either

JUDGE. Whom precisely did you elect?

NIKOLAEV. In our congregation we elected Logvinenko, but the state official turned him down.

There's another point I don't agree with. The legislation forbids us to give each other material help. Now I'm in a trade union, and if somebody falls ill or dies, we help towards the funeral wreaths or assist the sick person. Is that wrong?

JUDGE. But what if he's not working?

NIKOLAEV. If he doesn't work then he should be tried as an idler. There's a law about that. But how can we refuse to help if there's an old woman among us who gets 13 rubles pension (£6 a month)—you have to buy her wood and coal.

JUDGE (reads points from the legislation). This giving of financial help is forbidden, but nobody forbids you to give practical help.

NIKOLAEV. What do you mean, nobody forbids it! Some believers once went to the home of an old blind lady to dig her vegetable garden and vineyard—the auxiliary police came along and chased them away. Suppose my house burned down, for example, do you think the believers wouldn't help me? Would you help, brothers and sisters? (He turns to the gallery, answers are heard "Yes, yes!") . . . And another thing, if a man is elected to serve in one congregation, for example in Shevchenkovo, or Peresyp, or in town, then the minister of Peresyp congregation isn't allowed to preach in town and vice versa. But the Lord says, "Go ye into all the world and preach the Gospel to every creature."

(The testimony of several witnesses follows).

JUDGE. Have you seen believers gathering for a meeting?

WITNESS YAKOVCHENKO (an unbeliever). Yes, they come in one way and go out another. They gather in an orderly and quiet way, and by 9 o'clock they're all gone, not a trace of a soul.

JUDGE. What do they do at meetings?

WITNESS. They sing and play, very nicely. They've even got a string orchestra, you can hear it through the whole village

JUDGE. So they cause a public nuisance?

WITNESS. God forbid, they're such quiet folks, they couldn't be a public nuisance.

BORUSKHO. Tell us, witness, was there an appeal in my sermons not to obey the legislation on religion?

WITNESS PARADOVSKAYA (17 years old). Yes there was.

BORUSKHO. What form did it take?

WITNESS. You said, "God is love". (Laughter in court).

S. P. SOLOVYOVA'S DEFENSE SPEECH

Comrade Judges! For 4 months now, while the investigation was going on, they've been trying to prove to me that I'm not accused because I'm a believer, but because I've broken the Soviet legislation on religion.

In 1918 Lenin's decree on the separation of church and state was promulgated, guaranteeing all citizens freedom of conscience.

I'm charged with misinterpreting the concept, "freedom of conscience"—that is, they want to convince me that the legislation on cults doesn't contradict Lenin's decree, but makes it more explicit.

Obviously you can interpret the words "freedom of conscience" differently, but it's a shameful thing for our state, the most democratic in the world, when believers can't meet on May Day and spend it as believers.

The prosecutor was very interested as to whether or not we sang revolutionary songs on May Day. If we'd sung revolutionary songs, we wouldn't have been called up before the authorities.

Isn't that a violation of the Constitution, art. 124, which "guarantees freedom of conscience", and gives us the right to sing religious songs?

A lot's been said about giving material help. The legislation on religion, article 17(b) says: "It is forbidden to render material assistance to other members." I want to tell the court that I don't know of any other state, even the most backward one, where the law demands such a thing—that someone should have the right to control what purposes I can use my honestly-earned money for, and should forbid me to use it to help those in need.

Isn't this point in the legislation a limitation of the freedom of conscience?

In the existing legislation there are points forbidding the activity of circles for children, adolescents, young adults, men and women. But if in our congregation there are young people who want to play instruments, by what international law can you forbid the activity of such circles?

In the legislation there are points limiting the activity of a preacher and of a choir to the area of residence of the congregation in question. This isn't considered a violation of the principle of freedom of conscience. But after all everybody knows that the artists of the Moscow theatre travel not only to different towns, but even to different countries. They aren't restricted in this, let alone called to account for it. If a believer visits another congregation, whether he simply goes as a guest or whether he is in another congregation while on a business trip, or if a choir particularly wants to go to a wedding in some other village, then doesn't the law which forbids this contradict Lenin's decree, article 2?

That point in the legislation where it talks about the right of the official representative to have the presbyter removed, isn't that a violation of Lenin's decree on the separation of church and state? There was a case in our Church: the removal of V. Ye. Logvinenko. Only one reason is known for his removal—the fact that he is a young man; but he's of age, and the Church put its trust in him when they elected him.

Don't all these points, which really restrict freedom of conscience, have one aim in view: to drain all the sap out of believers?

One of the main points of the charge is that according to the existing legislation, any religious society can become active only after registration. Registration is given only on conditions which are contrary to our doctrine. Therefore we as Christians cannot neglect to meet, even though we are deprived of registration.

The charge against us of causing material damage during our celebration of May Day in the plantation is a deliberately-concocted lie. The record of the trees being broken down was put together long after our arrest.

I don't consider the distribution of literature a crime. Instead of giving us freedom to print, you condemn us for this. I did distribute literature and I will continue to do so at the slightest opportunity.

Why are we being tried for breaking the Soviet legislation on religion? The fact that the congregation is unregistered is seen as a crime when Shevchenko and Bondarenko, after being sentenced for precisely the same thing, were rehabilitated while the same legislation was in operation.

The legislation has continued to exist—it's the authorities themselves who are interpreting it differently at different times.

I want to ask the court: when was the mistake made, when they were sentenced, or when they were rehabilitated?

You gave me a great honour when you described me as an organizer. I'm not an organizer, as you accuse me of being. I have friends who are spiritually above me and have worked harder than I. I don't say this because I'm afraid, but because I don't consider myself worthy of such a great honour—to suffer for my Lord.

(Shevchenko asks for postponement of his defence speech, but is deprived of it altogether.)

GRIGORI BORUSHKO'S DEFENCE SPEECH

I consider myself happy to be able to stand before the court, not as a criminal, but as a Christian. I am grateful to you, comrade Judges, for giving those who wanted to be at this trial the opportunity to be convinced of our innocence. And now, dispensing with my legal right to a defence counsel, I shall defend my own case, in the hope that you will graciously hear me out.

Comrade Judges, I am grieved by the fact that the main prosecution witnesses have not been called: Yuleshkin, Shamrai and Kuzmenko. I am beginning to get the impression that the Prosecutor has been absent from court and that our fate has already been decided long ago.

The aim of my defence speech is to demonstrate my innocence of the charges against me, also to show that I am being tried for my religious convictions; to show that the whole indictment did not issue from an actual crime, but was artificially constructed and is the result of an official directive.

The defence is significantly complicated by the fact that witnesses have not been called and therefore the conclusion cannot be a logical one.

Comrade Judges, I was expelled from the medical institute because of my religious convictions. You heard from the witness Moroz's testimony that without having any grievance against me at work, they nevertheless decided at the Party office to dismiss me. And even now in the First Aid section they're threatening me with dismissal. All this is, moreover, a violation of the legislation and if you were to put both our actions in the scales, isn't it obvious that theirs is worse?

And if I'm deprived of freedom, nobody can take away my right to suffer for my Christ.

"Whoever wishes to bear the cross once will be crucified forever . . ."

JUDGE (interrupting). Keep to the point.

The Church lives as long as it suffers. If you look at the history of Christianity, its faithfulness to Christ, Christianity kept its vitality as long as it suffered. And on the other hand, when the Church moved away from the commands of Christ it ceased to suffer.

Comrade Judges, it is in your hands today, in the name of the law, either to justify arbitrary recriminations, or to show all present that there is justice on earth too. Otherwise I say in Lermontov's words: ". . . There remains the judgement of God . . .!" That's all I have to say.

VASILI TIMCHAK'S DEFENCE SPEECH

I consider myself fortunate that I am on the defendants' bench today as a Christian, not as a thief or a murderer or as someone who has violated another's property. And I rejoice in this fate which has befallen me for Christ.

As a Christian, I believe in Christ and I preached about Him and will continue to do so in future.

The Prosecutor *was* present in the courtroom and apparently she didn't hear a thing the witnesses said—she read out something that had been decided on and written down already and didn't make a single extract from the witnesses' testimonies.

I'm charged with being a preacher. Yes, I am a preacher and preaching the Word of God isn't a crime before the law.

I'm charged with participating in activity intended to stir up disobedience to the legislation on religion. This wasn't confirmed by any of the witnesses. Nobody said that I appealed to people not to obey the legislation on religion. We don't preach about state legislation at our divine services, we preach the Word of God which says that all people should repent and accept the Kingdom of God. I preached this Kingdom of God and the witnesses confirmed that. In my sermons I spoke about the love of God, how Christ loved man even to the death on the cross, so that everyone who believes in Him might have eternal life. That's what I preached, what I still preach and will continue to preach.

Everything the Prosecutor says is untrue; we have the right to write to our government; it isn't a crime for us to write a declaration to the government.

In Moscow a declaration was written to Brezhnev to the effect that we had elected the Council of Churches and asked for recognition of it, and that it should not be hindered in the work for which we had elected it. This request of ours had nothing to do with non-recognition of the legislation.

I'm charged with being at a conference of the Odessa, Kherson and Nikolaevsk regions. Yes, I was there, and we were deciding Church matters. We also wrote a declaration to the government, requesting that they recognize our brethren from the Council of Churches. There wasn't any infringement of the rights of citizens in it. As for the congress, we are still asking for it to be allowed under the leadership of its initiators, although we get no reply.

The March law of 1966,* consolidating Art. 138, part II, has no retrospective power over those things which were done before it was promulgated. But you are charging us concerning a conference which took place in 1965.

The prosecutor has said that we completely reject the legislation. That isn't true; I disagree only with a few points. I didn't influence believers against obeying the legislation on cults, this accusation wasn't confirmed by the witnesses and I deny it. I preached Christ crucified.

The prosecutor said that the celebration on 2 May 1966 was organized under my leadership. Not one of the witnesses confirmed this. How could I have organized it when I wasn't there? I went away to the country about that time.

YA. N. KRIVOI'S DEFENCE SPEECH

"The sun of righteousness will arise with healing in his wings," said the prophet, and the folk proverb says, "Truth is like the sun, you can't cover it up with your hand." I believe in truth, but "Faith is the substance of things hoped for."

20 years ago I was sentenced to 10 years' imprisonment for the same crimes for which I am now standing before the court. Along with me, many were sentenced to 25 years, and some to the supreme punishment.

---

*Tightening up on the production of religious literature and public acts of witness, as well as being even more specific than before on the outlawing of Sunday Schools.

During that term I worked hard and built two brickworks, for which they let me out ten months early. During my imprisonment and after it the workers and management agitated for us and, as I learned later, truth triumphed and after 20 years I was rehabilitated. And those who were sentenced to 25 years and those who didn't return from prison were also rehabilitated, the latter posthumously.

And now, too, you know perfectly well that I've done no harm to society or to the state.

You are entrusted, comrade Judges, with the fate of a human being.

I'm charged with organizing activity directed against recognition of the Soviet legislation on religion. Nobody confirmed this. I admit that I disagree with some points of the legislation which deprive believers of freedom of conscience.

We have a law about freedom of conscience, and it's forbidden to intrude on another's conscience according to these laws. Our Council of Twenty, which you call a "guiding body," of which I too was a member, lost all power after we were refused registration.

Yes, I was at the conference in Kiev, but there was nothing illegal in the appeal that we adopted there, it was of a purely religious character. We met for a considerable time, and we didn't write to the government until we were disturbed, but the prosecutor states that you don't interfere in our questions of dogma. The election of a pastor is for us a matter of dogma. Nobody should interfere in this. We aren't against control, that's why we always wrote that we live quietly and meet together, and asked to be registered.

I'm charged with distributing appeals among citizens, but which one of them confirmed this?

As for preaching, it's not only Church leaders who can take part in this, but also ordinary members. I'm a preacher and I don't deny it.

I'm charged with organizing the celebration of 2nd May when I wasn't there, because I was doing some plastering for a Christian brother.

The whole trial has confirmed the falsity of the charges against me.

On the basis of the laws of our state I have committed no crime either against society or against the state. But if I suffer as a Christian, I'm ready to wear handcuffs. I've been a believer for 40 years and you can't re-educate me whatever you do, and you won't break me with any threats.

V. I. ALEXEEVA'S DEFENSE SPEECH

I thank the Lord that on this my spiritual birthday I have been counted worthy to sit on the defendants' bench.

Comrade Judges, if faith in Good has brought me happiness and my heart is overflowing with Him, do you really think I wouldn't tell people? Even the Constitution grants freedom of conscience. So I told everybody who wanted to listen to me that Christ loves every sinner and that the Lord says today: "Do I desire the death of a sinner, and not that he should turn to me and live?"

As for the distribution of literature, I want to say that when this trial is over it will be published in the paper, and we too have the right to write to the government and to our friends in the Church.

For example, I distributed the "Kiev Declaration" which reports certain unjust incidents. If these had not occurred, there wouldn't have been any declaration either.

Secondly, when the article "Prophets and Victims" came out, filled with slander and unjust accusations against the believers Kryuchkov and Vins, the mother of one of them, who was well acquainted with her son's life and had followed it carefully, wrote a declaration to the government in which she refuted the injustice of this article. That was the reason for that letter. Our declarations concern only our Christian life.

I'm charged with going to Moscow, where I was a delegate from the congregation at Peresyp. We're Soviet citizens and every year we cast our votes for those who are to guard our constitutional rights and we have the right to turn to them with our declarations.

For our part we render unto Caesar what is Caesar's and unto God what is God's.

Comrade Judges, you charge me with organizing the distribution of literature and with inciting believers not to obey the legislation on cults. In the course of this trial all these charges have been refuted. The Council and all the congregations that support it, including ours. I consider to be legal, since we have appealed to the authorities many times and still do with requests for registration. But up to now our declarations have been ignored.

Our methods and our actions are open for all to see. The Word of God says: "The way of the just is uprightness" (Is. 26:27).

Pascal said: "Woe to those who do not know their life's aim." Our aim in life is to fulfil the commands of Christ. The first commandment is: "Thou shalt love the Lord thy God" and the second: "Thou shalt love thy neighbour as thyself". If we fulfil these commandments, we don't break state laws in so doing; on the contrary, wherever we can we try to help and give good advice. In the Holy Scriptures it says: "There is no other name under heaven by which men may be saved except the name of Jesus Christ".

N. P. SHEVCHENKO'S FINAL ADDRESS

In 1962 I was sentenced to 4 years imprisonment and 3 years exile for not obeying the "Letter of Instructions" and the Baptist Statutes, for making my home available for prayer meetings, for baptizing believers.

I served 2 years and 7 months in prison, after which I was rehabilitated for lack of criminal evidence. I was re-instated at work and paid a pension for the time in prison.

After my release I worked for 4 months and because I went to Moscow with an appeal to the government I was again suspended from work.

Was anyone responsible for all this?

I stand again before a court, accused of the same thing.

You charge us with slander of the press. I won't touch on the article "Prophets and Victims" in the central paper *Izvestia*—Solovyova has already talked about that; but I want to mention our local paper, *Chernomorskaya Kommuna*, which carried an article saying that believers in the village of Usatovo, Odessa Region, burnt down a house and an old woman in it, as if to say that they made a ritual sacrifice of her. Anyone who wants to look into it can find out for himself that this is a lie, everybody in Usatovo knows the believers.

I was born and brought up in that village, I know everybody there—there isn't even an old woman of that name.

Even now I can't understand how they could pass something like that in a newspaper—to write about something absolutely fictitious. It's just done to arouse popular hatred against believers.

I have no doubt that you're capable of writing a slanderous article about us, too.

JUDGE. That has nothing to do with the case—keep to the point.

SHEVCHENKO. What do you mean, it has nothing to do with the case, when we're accused of slandering the press?—the fact is it's the other way round: you write slanders about believers.

JUDGE. (interrupts) . . .

SHEVCHENKO. I accept this imprisonment with joy, as did the apostle Peter; when they wanted to crucify him he said, I'm not worthy to be crucified like my Teacher, Christ—crucify me upside down" . . .

JUDGE. (interrupts) . . .

SHEVCHENKO. Comrade Judges, I'm not asking you for mercy, but the fate of many people is in your hands, you are expected to judge justly. When King Solomon was entrusted with the judging of the people, he asked the Lord for wisdom.

JUDGE. (interrupting) We're not interested in Solomon.

SHEVCHENKO. "Be wise now therefore, O ye kings; be instructed, ye judges of the earth" (Ps. 2:10).

JUDGE. Sit down, Shevchenko.

G. G. BORUSHKOS' FINAL ADDRESS

I came to Odessa when I was 18. By 1958 I had done two years of higher education and I decided to enter the Medical Institute, but since you had to have three years behind you for this, I decided to try and get into the State University. I went there as a production worker in biological faculty.

And it was there, while I was studying science, that the question of religion came to me in a completely different light. I realised that the greatest scientists, the pillars of science, like Kepler, the discoverer of the laws of planet motion, Newton, discoverer of natural laws relating to the earth, the naturalist Linnaeus, who gave us the classification of the whole animal and plant world, the mathematician Euclid, physician and mathematician Pascal, our first Russian universalist Mikhail Lomonosov, Copernicus, and in our own time, Filatov, Voino-

Yasenetsky and others, had been men of profound religious faith. Therefore I decided to find out myself a definitive answer to the question: does God exist or not—that is, should I be a believer or not? At that time I read the Bible a lot and I came through strong doubts to faith in God. My atheism and unbelief were based on an ignorance of the Bible. I particularly liked the Gospels.

But however strange it may seem, it was just at that time that I went through a most intense inner struggle and uncertainty. I looked at the Bible . . . it was through not knowing it that people didn't believe. I remember during a conversation in the institute, the Vice-Dean said to me: "The Bible says the world stands on three whales". I asked her: "Did you read that yourself?" and she was uncomfortable because she was a scientist but she'd never read the book that so much has been spoken about in every century, the book that people base their lives on, and for which they will give their lives. (The judge interrupts: "Don't start making propaganda").

Well, I liked the Gospels, but I couldn't find in myself the strength to live them out until I realised that to do this you had to be born again, that is, to accept Jesus Christ in your heart—and I turned to Him.

"With His holy freedom
He took the chains from the soul, torments from the heart,
And stains from the guilty conscience" . . .

At that time occurred the first persecutions, but this was according to Christ's words; it ended with my being expelled from the institute, but I had already decided on this path:

Whoever wants to bear the cross once
Will be crucified forever,
And whether there is happiness in life
He will be happy in eternity.

You are appointing us to suffer, but in fact this is preordained by God, for not a hair of our head falls to the ground without His will.

Suffering is Christianity's vital nerve. The Church is alive as long as it suffers, for Christ suffered and called us to do likewise.

I'm an optimist—in other words I believe that if things are bad today, they'll be better tomorrow; if they sentence you today, they'll acquit you tomorrow; if injustices meet you on earth today, tomorrow there'll be justice.

Such a dialectic, if it isn't confirmed on earth, will still triumph in heaven, as it's written: "According to the promise we wait for a new earth and a new heaven in which righteousness dwells."

JUDGE: Borushko, have you any more quotations?

BORUSHKO: Yes I have.

"I want to walk in such a way
That my weary brother
Should hear the rhythm of my steps
And be shaken out of his slumber and inspired
To step out more quickly towards the sacred vision.
That my step should convince the unfaithful
Of the holy, blessed truth,
And that day by day the ranks of warriors
On the way to the goal should be filled with brothers
Whom God's Spirit has awakened to life.
I want to walk so that the children of paradise,
The angels in heaven, should draw men's hearts
And in joyful praise, blessing my path,
Should sing a hymn to the Saviour of the world.
Their praise is poured out at God's throne
Poured out unchanging in sacred harmonies.
In its precious beauty
It has drawn so many sinners to God.
And today the angel choir is not silent . . .
When history's course is run,
To Him who went His way without turning back
Will sound their hundredfold hymn of praise."

V. T. TIMCHAK'S FINAL ADDRESS

I've been a Christian since childhood. My mother brought me up as a Christian from my early childhood, and I am before you today on the defendants' bench as a Christian. Yes, I believe in God, and the Word of God says that it is given to us not only to believe in Him but also to suffer for Christ. I am happy that I have the chance to carry out these words of Christ, one thing I know—He will never leave me. Christ Himself bore sufferings and has never left His followers who have trodden the same path. And I rejoice in this lot—to suffer for Christ. Many of my brothers have been unjustly sentenced and later rehabilitated and I know that you are trying us today, but tomorrow we will be rehabilitated, for lack of criminal proof. Then those who today are asking for these terms of imprisonment will be ashamed.

Many of our brethren have already gone the way of suffering in faithfulness to our Lord, but the Word of God says: "Regarding their end, imitate their faith".

And now today you are separating us from our relatives and loved ones, but I believe that we will meet again on earth, and in eternity we will receive for all our sufferings a joy that will have no end, when we meet our Saviour.

V. M. ZABORSKY'S FINAL ADDRESS

Before I came of age, I decided to leave home so as not to hear about God. I signed up and went to Novosibirsk. They didn't want to take me, but I persuaded the official. They understood my circumstances and did it as a favour.

In a worldly atmosphere I learned to swear like a trooper.

I was soon called up. There among my friends I was the most active composer and teller of dirty stories and I always found a circle of friends to listen. Nobody could beat me at it. I didn't drink wine or vodka there, I only drank some stuff that had a skull and crossbones on the bottle—it's called methylated spirits. I was summoned before a military tribunal to explain my way of life.

It was there, walking on the bank of the Amur, that I remembered the words of my mother: "Son, when you get into trouble, remember God". And then I took off my soldiers' cap and said: "Lord, if you save me from this trial, then from this moment on I'll be your preacher". And it all worked out. There was a complete change in my life. I became a new man, people began to be grateful to me. I was put in charge of a group, but without any rank. Then the men began to get interested in me, when they saw that I no longer joined with them in their former bad ways; I was summoned by the officers, from the lowest to the highest. The commander summoned me and after some inconclusive conversation, he suggested: "If you deny God, we'll give you rank, you'll get more money".

"I've got a rank higher than commander of a regiment".

"What's that?"

"As a Christian," I answered.

Soon they summoned me again and said:

"You know that your faith is a relic of capitalism?"

"You're wrong about that. Our faith existed under Nero and the Roman Empire before capitalism came, it's existed under capitalism, it exists under socialism and, if God wills, it'll exist under communism".

They asked me to go, and when I was summoned again they said:

"You know, Zaborsky, that spies conceal themselves under the mask of your faith?"

"I can't argue about that, because I've never heard such a thing before—but practical experience has shown that spies can get through the Party net, but not through the religious one—Beria for example, and Penkovsky."

A bit later the commanding officer summoned me and said:

"Listen, Zaborsky. We had a soldier once who wore a cross round his neck. We had a talk with him and he took it off, put it on the table and said: 'Give me a Komsomol card'."

I'd do that too, but my God isn't on a crucifix, but in my heart. I can't put Him on the table—to do that I'd have to tear out my heart, in other words stop living, which is impossible. Later I was demoted to be a reservist. The deputy political officer said:

"Well, Zaborsky, off you go now with your God."

"Exactly, comrade major."

"Goodbye, you block-headed Baptist, just go on the way you are doing".

Then I came to Odessa, I was baptized and became a member of the Peresyp Church. I went to the meetings at the prayer house for two years, but after it was closed I and my brothers and sisters met during the cold winter of 1958 outside the wall of the closed prayer house. When our prayer house was given to the poultry farm to use, we tried to meet in flats. That's what we've done up

o now. It was only in the summer of 1966 that I found out about the existence
f the Soviet legislation on religion, which prohibits Gospel teaching and Lenin's
decree. On the basis of this legislation the "Statute" and the "Letter of Instruc-
ions" were issued back in 1960, which led to the great and visible schism in the
Church. Believers were in such a situation that they had to violate something—
either man's or God's iaw.

(The judge interrupts). It is precisely for this reason that I stand before the
court today, as a Christian.

We will not kneel to it".

Judge: (to the police) Please restore order.

(Three policemen quickly go up to Valya and maker her sit down).

SENTENCE

SHEVCHENKO, Nikolai Pavlovich,
BORUSHKO, Grigori Grigorievich,
KRIVOI, Yakov Nikiforovich
SOLOVYOVA, Svetlana Pavlovna,
ALEXEEVA, Valentina Ivanovna
sentenced to 3 years' imprisonment in ordinary regime camps.

TIMCHAK, Vasili Terenticvich
ZABORSKY, Viktor Mikhailovich
sentenced to 1 year's imprisonment in ordinary regime camps.

PERSECUTION OF THE JEWS

REPRESSION OF JEWS IN THE SOVIET UNION

(Edited by Louis Rosenblum, Union of Councils for Soviet Jews)

INTRODUCTION

The Jewish minority in the USSR is subjected to singularly repressive treatment. Special prohibitions are placed upon Jewish education, religious observance, and culture. Discrimination is practiced against Jews in employment and schooling. Anti-Semitism is inflamed by a stream of news articles, books, and cartoons from the government press. As a consequence, an estimated ¼ million Jews have sought permission to leave the Soviet Union. Most desire to reunite with families in Israel.

All but a small number of the applications have been denied, in spite of the fact that the demands to emigrate are legitimate and in keeping with Soviet Constitution, law, practice, and international treaty. The record shows that the Soviet government has allowed the reunion of families and has indeed supported the repatriation of entire ethnic groups living in the USSR, e.g., several thousand Spaniards, 1956–60 and 200,000 Poles, 1957–8. Additionally, the Presidium of the Supreme Soviet on January 22, 1969 ratified the International Convention on the Elimination of Racial Discrimination. Article 5, paragraph d, subsection 2 of the Convention provides that each contracting party to the treaty "guarantees the right of everyone to leave any country, including his own, and to return to his country."

To check the growing 'exodus' movement the Soviet government has resorted to three major stratagems: 'silence' vocal dissidents by letting them leave; discourage application for emigration by intensifying the financial and procedural requirements; and repress Jewish national feeling by arrest of persons possessing Jewish history or Hebrew language books on criminal charges of anti-Soviet activities.

The present wave of repression began with the arrest of Boris Kochubyevsky in Dec. 1968 and his trial in May 1969. Following this came the secret trial in Riazan, Feb. 1970, the infamous Leningrad hi-jacking trial of Dec. 1970, and the recent trials in Riga, Leningrad, Kishinev, Odessa, Sverdlovsk, Kharkov, and Chernovitz. In general, those arrested have been charged with "political crimes" under RSFSR Criminal Code Statute 70 (anti-Soviet propaganda) and Statute 72 (anti-Soviet organization). In addition, defendants in the Leningrad hi-jacking trial were charged with treason and theft of government property. Sentences up to 15 years in *strict* or *special* regime labor camps were meted out.

STRICT REGIME

"they condemn you to an empty belly"

Reproduced below is a brief sketch of the strict regime from *My Testimony*, E. P. Dutton and Co., New York, 1969, pp. 224–7.

"Well, and what about a prisoner's rights? There is his right to correspond (with limitations and censorship). His right to have visits from relatives. His right to buy up to five rubles' worth of food in the camp shop, though only with money earned inside the camp. If he has nothing left after deductions have been made—too bad, he can make do without, even if his relatives are prepared to send money. Not on sale in the camp shop and forbidden because of the regime regulations are: sugar, butter, tinned meat and fish, bread. All you can buy is tinned vegetables or fruit (hardly anybody buys these because they are too dear, they take your whole five rubles), cheap tobacco, toothbrushes, envelopes, notebooks, and you can buy camp clothing if you like—not that anybody does on five rubles a month.

"But these rights are no better than a dream, a mirage. Admin [the camp authorities] has the right to deprive a prisoner of all of them. This is done for violations, and who can say that he commits no violations—if Admin wants to find some? And so they take away your rights—to the shop for instance, for a month, two months, three. And then you have to get by on "basic"—on camp rations that have been worked out on scientific principles to be just enough to keep you from dying off.

"The daily norm is 2,400 calories: 25 ozs. of bread, 3 ozs. of cod, 2 ozs. of meat (the sheepdog guarding the cons gets 1 lb.), 1 lb. of vegetable—potatoes and cabbage, about 1 oz. of meal or noodles, ¾ oz. of fat and ½ oz. of sugar. And that's all. It adds up to one and a half times less than a normal man needs on light work. You will say: what about the shop? But then they deprive you of the shop? Keeping strictly to all the rules and regulations they condemn you to an empty belly!

"But anyway, not even all of this finds its way into the prisoner's bowl. A cart, for instance, comes into the compound carrying meat for the whole camp, 300 lbs. for three thousand men. You look at this meat and you hardly know what to think: is it carrion, or something still worse? All blue, it seems to consist entirely of bone and gristle. Then it goes to be stewed and you're lucky if half an ounce finds its way into your mouth.

You are eating cabbage and you can't make out to begin with what it is: some sort of black, slimy, stinking globs. How much out of the established quota gets thrown on the rubbish heap? And in spring and summer the cookhouse hands can't even bring themselves to throw out the bad potatoes any more, otherwise there would be nothing to put in the soup. And so they throw in the black and rotten ones. If you go near the cookhouse in summer the stench turns you over. Stinking cod, rotten cabbage. The bread is like we had in the war. In number seven we had a bakery in which we baked two kinds of bread, black for camp, white for outside. Sugar, though you would think was foolproof. It won't rot, you don't have to measure it. But then they give it to you damp so that it weighs more. And they give you ten days' ration at a time—5 ozs.—because if they give you your 1 oz. daily, it wouldn't be a question of having nothing to eat as of nothing to see.

"During six years in camp and jail I had bread with butter twice—when I received visits. I also ate two cucumbers—one in 1964 and another in 1966. Not once did I eat a tomato or an apple. All this was forbidden . . .

"And that is what strict regime looks like today. Strict regime, for the most part, is for political prisoners, because among criminals only the persistent offenders get put on strict regime, or those who commit a crime or a violation already in the camps, and even then not for their whole term—they do a stint on strict regime and then go back to normal regime again. For criminals and civil prisoners strict regime is the harshest form of punishment. But for us politicals it is the mildest, our imprisonment begins with this, because it is the minimum awarded by the courts. From strict regime political prisoners can go only to special regime or to the clink. And that is even worse."

PRISONERS OF CONSCIENCE

Presently, more than 40 victims of show trials, staged to repress the growth of Jewish national feeling, are serving sentences in strict and special regime labor camps. Many of these unfortunate people are in need of medical care for serious ailments. All are in physically weak condition as a result of the extended interrogation and imprisonment between the time of their arrest and trial and as a result of the semi-starvation diet in the labor camps.

Brief sketches of several of these prisoners of conscience follow.

[Photographs appear on p. 280.]

PRISONERS OF CONSCIENCE

Name	Born	From	Status	Occupation	Arrested	Trial	Sentence (strict regime unless otherwise noted)
Kochubyevsky, Boris	1936	Kiev	Married (1)	Engineer	December 1968	May 16, 1969	3 years.
Ontman, Liliya	1937	Chernovitz	do.			Jan. 8, 1970	2½ years.
Dzhindzhikhashvili, Avraham	1941	Tbilisi			June 1970		
Dzhanashvili, Beniamin	1923	do.			do.	do.	
Vudka, Yuri [1]	1947	Riazan		Student			
Grilius, Shymeon [1]	1945	Klaipeda		Engineer	August 1969	Feb. 10-19, 1970	7 years.
Vudka, Valeri	1950	Riazan		Student		do.	5 years.
Frolov, Oleg		do.		do.		do.	3 years.
Dymshits, Mark	1927	Leningrad	Married	Pilot	June 15, 1970	Dec. 15, 1970	Death, commuted to 15 years.
Altman, Anatoly	1942	Riga	Bachelor	Engraver	do.	do.	12 years, reduced to 10 years.
Zalmanson, Izia	1949	do.		Student	do.	do.	8 years.
Zalmanson, Wolf [1]	1939	do.		Officer, engineer	do.	Jan. 7, 1971	10 years.
Khnokh, Leib [1]	1944	do.	Married	Student	do.	Dec. 15, 1970	13 years, reduced to 10 years.
Mendelevich, Iosif [1]	1947	do.	Bachelor	Artist	do.	do.	15 years, reduced to 12 years.
Penson, Boris [1]	1946	do.	do.	Artist	do.	do.	10 years.
Zalmanson, Sylva [1]	1944	do.	Married	Engineer	do.	do.	10 years.
Kuznetsov, Eduard [1]	1941	do.	do.	Interpreter	do.	do.	Death, commuted to 15 years, special regime.
Fedorov, Yuri [1]	1944			Worker	do.	do.	15 years, special regime.
Murzhenko, Aleksey [1]	1943			do.	do.	do.	14 years, special regime.
Mogilever, Vladimir	1940	Leningrad	Married (1)	Engineer	do.	Mar. 11, 1971	4 years.
Kaminsky, Lassal	1930	do.	Married (2)	do.	do.	do.	5 years.
Chernoglaz, David	1940	do.	Married (1)	Agronomist	do.	June 21, 1971	5 years.
Butman, Hillel	1933	do.	do.	Engineer	do.	May 11, 1971	Do.
Kornblit, Lev	1922	do.	do.	Mathematician	do.	do.	10 years.
Yagman, Lev	1940	do.	Married (2)	Engineer	do.	do.	3 years.
Drezner, Shlomo	1932	do.	Married (1)	do.	do.	do.	3 years.
Goldfeld, Anatoly	1946	do.	Bachelor	do.	do.	do.	5 years.
Boguslavsky, Viktor	1940	do.	do.	do.	do.	June 21, 1971	4 years.
Bodnya, Mendel	1937	Riga	Married	do.	do.	May 11, 1971	4 years.
Galperin, Aleksander	1946	Kishinev	do.	Worker	do.	Dec. 15, 1970	3 years.
Maftser, Boris	1947	Riga	Married	Engineer	7, 1970	June 21, 1971	4 years.
Shpilberg, Arkady	1938	Leningrad	Married (2)	do.	July 24, 1970	Mar. 24, 1971	2½ years.
Shur, Hillel	1936	Kishinev		Engineer	Aug. 4, 1970		1 year.
Kirshner, Harry	1946	Kishinev			Aug. 5, 1970	June 21, 1971	3 years.
Volashin, Arkady	1946	do.			August 1970	do.	2 years.
Rabinovich, David	1947	do.			do.	do.	Do.
Trakhtenberg, Avraham	1947	do.		Technician	do.	do.	1 year.
Aleksandrovich, Ruth [1]	1947	Riga	Married	Nurse	Oct. 7, 1970	Feb. 21, 1971	2 years.
Shepshelovich, Mikhail	1943	do.	Bachelor	Worker	Oct. 16, 1970	May 24, 1971	1 year.
Shtilbans, Viktor	1947	Leningrad		Physician	November 1970	May 11, 1971	2 years.
Kornblit, Mikhael	1937	do.		Physician	do.	do.	1 year.
Borisov, Igor	1942	do.	Married	Stomatologist	do.	Dec. 23, 1970	7 years.
Levit, Semyon	1947	Kishinev	do.	Physicist	Nov. 17, 1970	June 21, 1971	2 years.
Palatnik, Raiza [1]	1936	Odessa	do.	Librarian	December 1970	June 22, 1971	Do.
Remert, Khaim	1921	Chernovits		Physician	March 1971		5 years.
Kukui, Valeri	1938	Sverdlovsk	Married (1)	Engineer	do.	June 15, 1971	3 years.

[1] Sketch of prisoner presented herein.

ALEXANDROVICH, RUTA ISAACOVNA

Twenty-three years old, born in Latvia, Jewish, student nurse, single. Applied on several occasions with her father, mother, and younger brother for repatriation to Israel. Repeatedly refused. Arrested October 7, 1970, Riga. Charged in accordance with Latvian SSR Statute 65 (RSFSR equivalent—Statute 70) anti-Soviet propaganda. Sentenced May 27, 1971, to one year strict regime. She is due for release in October, 1971. [Now released in Israel]
According to Dr. V. Portnoy, the prisoner's former personal physician presently residing at Ulpan Etsim, Jerusalem, Israel, Miss Alexandrovich suffers from an asthmatic condition and "exacerbation of chronic pyelonephritis."
The latest information on Miss Alexandrovich is as of the last week in July. Her father Isaac Alexandrovich visited Ruth in the camp. He said that Ruth and Sylvia Zalmanson are in the same barracks and both girls work in a factory making canvas gloves with fur lining. But since neither can produce the high production "norm" required, they receive only one-half the food ration. Address: Mordovskaja ASSR, USSR, St. Potma, Posiolok Yavas, Uchrezdenie Ж Х 385.
Relatives: Isaac Alexandrovich, father, Riga, Latvian SSR, USSR Suvorova 16, Kv. 120.
Rivka Alexandrovich, mother, Ein Tzurim 201-3 Talpiot, Jerusalem, Israel.

FEDOROV, YURY PAVLOVICH

Twenty-seven years old, Russian. Convicted and sentenced when he was 17 years old for anti-Soviet views. After his prison sentence his health was poor. He was kept under surveillance by the KGB (secret police) which made him extremely nervous and fearful. Arrested with eleven others in connection with alleged "hi-jacking" attempt in Leningrad, charged in accordance with RSFSR Statutes 64-15 (treason—to flee abroad) and 93-15 (theft of government property). Sentenced to 15 years special regime, without confiscation of property, in absence of such. Address: Mordovskaja ASSR, USSR, St. Potma, Posiolok Yavas, Uchrezdenie Ж Х 385/10.
Relative: N. V. Buzyreva, wife, Moscow, USSR, Serfinisovicha 2, Kv. 167.

GRILLUS, SIMONAS ARONOVICH

Twenty-six years old, Jewish. Engineer, worked on ship repairs in the Lithuanian harbor town of Klaiperdea. He was arrested in August, 1969, after a search of his apartment revealed the possession of books for studying Hebrew and records of Hebrew songs. Charged in accordance with RSFSR Statute 70 (anti-Soviet propaganda) and Statute 72 (anti-Soviet organization). Tried by a secret tribunal. Sentenced February 19, 1970, to five years strict regime.
Earlier this year Grillus was deprived of the right to receive parcels and was put into solitary confinement for 15 days for refusing to take off his *kipa* (skull cap) on Saturdays and other religious holidays. Address: Mordovskaja ASSR, USSR, St. Potma, Posiolok Lesnoy, Uchrezdenie Ж Х 385/19–1.

KHNOKH, LEIB GIRSHEVICH

Born in 1944 in Insar, Mordovskaja ASSR, Jewish. After the war moved to Varaklyany, Latvian SSR. After completing seven years at school, entered the Railway Technical Institute in Daugavpils. Worked as an electrician. In 1965 was called up to the Army but a few months later was declared unfit for military service because of a chronic dislocation of the shoulder. In 1969 he requested permission to leave for Israel but was refused. Married Mary Mendeievich in 1970. Repeatedly signed individual and group appeals to various Soviet and foreign organizations requesting help in leaving for Israel. Arrested with eleven others June 15, 1970, in connection with alleged "hi-jacking" attempt in Leningrad. Charged in accordance with RSFSR Statutes 64-15 (treason—to flee abroad), 93-15 (theft of government property) and Statutes 70 and 72 (anti-Soviet acts). Sentenced on December 25, 1970, to 13 years strict regime without confiscation of property, in absence of such. Reduced on December 30, 1970, by the Supreme Court of the RSFSR to 10 years strict regime. Address: Mordovskaja ASSR, USSR, St. Potma, Posiolok Oziorny, Uchrezdenie Ж Х 385/17.
Relatives: P. B. Khnokh, brother, Daugavpils, Latvian SSR, USSR Virsku 48, Kv. 100.

KUZNETSOV, EDUARD SAMUILOVICH

Twenty-nine years old, born of a Russian mother and a Jewish father, his internal passport states he is Russian but he considers himself to be a Jew. Studied at the philosophy faculty of Moscow University. Spent seven years in prison on charge of anti-Soviet activities. Deprived of right to live in Moscow, Leningrad, and other large cities. Became aware of being a Jew while in prison and talked about his dream to live in a Jewish state. Worked as an English-Russian interpreter in the Riga psychiatric hospital. Married Sylva Zalmanson in 1970. Arrested with eleven others in connection with alleged "hi-jacking" attempt in Leningrad, charged in accordance with RSFSR Statutes 64–15 (treason—to flee abroad) and 93–15 (theft of government property) and Statutes 70 and 72 (anti-Soviet activities). Sentenced to death, without confiscation of property, in the absence of such. Commuted on December 30, 1970, by the Supreme Court of the RSFSR to 12 years strict regime. Address: Mordovskaja ASSR, St. Potma, Posiolok Yavas, Uchrezdenie ЖХ 385/10.

MENDELEVICH, IOSIF MOZUSOVICH

Born in 1947, Jewish. His father sells newspapers. His mother died tragically in 1969[?]. After graduating from school in 1965, entered the Riga Polytechnic. In 1968, applied together with his relatives to leave for Israel, but was refused. In 1969 left the Institute, considering that his being a student there could be an obstacle to the granting of permission to leave for Israel. In 1970, requested permission and was again refused. He has signed various appeals to Soviet and foreign organizations for permission to leave for Israel. In 1970, two weeks after receiving a *Kharakteristika*, a character reference, for the OVIR (Office of Visas and Registration), he was dismissed from work under the pretext of redundancy. Arrested with eleven others June 15, 1970, in connection with alleged "hijacking" attempt in Leningrad, charged in accordance with RSFSR Statutes 64–15 (treason—to flee abroad), 93–15 (theft of government property) and Statutes 70 and 72 (anti-Soviet acts). Sentenced December 25, 1970 to 15 years strict regime, without confiscation of property, in the absence of such. Reduced on December 30, 1970, by the Supreme Court of the RSFSR to 12 years strict regime. Address: Mordovskaja ASSR, USSR, St. Potma, Posiolok Oziorny, Uchrezdenie ЖХ 385/17a.

Relatives: M. A. Mendelevich, father and E. M. Mendelevich, sister Riga, Latvian SSR, USSR, Kirova 18, Kv. 3

MURZHENKO, ALEKSEY

Twenty-eight years old, Ukrainian. Convicted at age 19 for anti-Stalin utterances and served 6 years in a prison camp for political prisoners. Has command of five languages. Twice after he served his term of imprisonment he tried to enter an institute of higher education but both times he was not admitted although he passed a competitive exam. He was told that with his past he 'cannot count on becoming a translator.' Recently Murzhenko worked in a factory at Lozovaya station and was elected chairman of the local trade union committee. Arrested with eleven others in connection with alleged "hi-jacking" attempt in Leningrad, charged in accordance with RSFSR Statutes 64–15 (treason—to flee abroad) and 93–15 (theft of government property). Sentenced to 14 years special regime, without confiscation of property, none being owned. Address: Mordovskaja ASSR, USSR, St. Potma, Posiolok Yavas, Uchrezdenie Ж Х 385/10.

PALATNIK, RAIZA ANATOLYEVNA

Age 35, Jewish, worked in Odessa as a librarian. Shortly after she had written to Israel requesting that her relatives there be located, a search of her apartment was made on October 14, 1970, by the KGB (secret police), and followed by a 4-hour interrogation on October 15. Interrogation and searches continued until her arrest on December 1. Charged under paragraph 187/1 Ukrainian Criminal Code with slandering the Soviet Union. Sentenced June 24, 1971 to two years.

In August 1971, Yekatrina Palatnik, Raiza Palatnik's sister, sent a letter to the International Red Cross and to the Red Cross of Russia describing the deterioration of Raiza's health and asking them to intercede.

"A short while ago when I visited my sister in prison I was shocked that the state of Raiza's health is now worse than it was before her detention. In July

Raiza had a heart attack that left her left hand paralyzed. She had become very thin from undernourishment. It is stifling and hot in her cell and the sanitary conditions are very difficult. Raiza is very ill now as a result of 8 months detention under difficult conditions. Before she was sent to prison she was healthy. Please use your influence on the prison authorities in Odessa to improve the nourishment given to Raiza and her living conditions."

The latest address available is an Odessa prison. Odessa, Ukrainian SSR, USSR, GSP 514 PYA YUG 311/192.

Relative: Sister, Katia Palatnik, Odessa, Ukrainian SSR, USSR, Yakir 23, Kv. 3. [Raiza Palatnik arrived in Israel in December 1972.]

PENSON, BORIS

Aged about 25, Jewish, worked in Riga as an artist in advertising. Did a great deal of painting independently, has a series of works which have never been exhibited because he is not a member of the Union of Artists. In 1969 requested permission to leave for Israel with his relatives (elderly parents) but permission was refused. Arrested with eleven others on June 15, 1970 in connection with alleged "hi-jacking" attempt in Leningrad. Charged in accordance with RSFSR statutes 64–15 (treason—to flee abroad) and 93–15 (theft of government property). Sentenced December 25, 1970 to ten years strict regime with confiscation of property, i.e. his paintings. He is presently in a labor camp for political prisoners in the Potma area. Address: Mordovskaja ASSR, USSR, St. Potma, Posiolok Lesnoy, Uchrezdenie Ж X 385/19–2.

VUDKA, YURY Z.

Twenty-four years old, Jewish. Student at Riazan Institute of Radio Technology. Applied to emigrate to Israel. Arrested in August, 1969. Charged in accordance with RSFSR Statute 70 (anti-Soviet propaganda) and Statute 72 (anti-Soviet organization). Tried by a secret tribunal. Sentenced February 19, 1970, to 7 years strict regime. Address: Mordovskaja ASSR, USSR, St. Potma, Posiolok Lesnoy, Uchrezdenie Ж X 385/19–1.

ZALMANSON, VOLF IOSIFOVICH

Born November 2, 1939 in Riga, Jewish. In 1962 graduated from the Riga Agricultural Academy, becoming a mechanical engineer. Worked as such in Riga up to 1968. Called up into the Army in 1968: this was an obstacle in his application to leave for Israel. Served as a lieutenant in Kaunas, Lithuanian SSR. Arrested with eleven others on June 15, 1970, in connection with alleged "hi-jacking" attempt in Leningrad. Tried separately by a military court under articles of the criminal code covering treason by flight abroad, theft of state property, and military desertion. Sentenced January 8, 1971 to ten years strict regime. Address: Mordovskaja ASSR, USSR, St. Potma, Uchrezdenia Ж X 385.

Relatives: I. V. Zalmanson, father and Z. I. Zalmanson, brother, Riga, Latvian SSR, USSR, Veidenbaum 45, Kv. 22.

ZALMANSON, SYLVIA IOSIFOVNA

Born October 25, 1944 in Siberia, Jewish. In 1968 graduated from the Riga Polytechnical Institute, becoming a mechanical engineer. Worked as a designer at the "Sarkana Zvaigzne" factory in Riga. In 1968 tried in vain to obtain permission to leave for Israel. Appealed to Soviet and foreign organizations. In 1970 married Kuznetsov, Eduard Samuilovitch. In 1970, was deprived of the possibility to appeal again for permission to leave for Israel as the management of her factory refused to give her a personal reference.

Arrested with eleven others on June 15, 1970, in connection with alleged "bi-jacking" attempt in Leningrad. Charged in accordance with RSFSR Statutes 64–15 (treason—to flee abroad), 93–15 (theft of governmet property), 70 (anti-Soviet propaganda), and 72 (anti-Soviet organization). Sentenced December 25, 1970, to ten years strict regime without confiscation of property, in absence of such.

Sylvia has suffered a severe loss of hearing in prison and is likely to go deaf. Her general physical condition is very poor. See letter from her uncle, reproduced below. Address: Mordovskaja ASSR, USSR, St. Potma, Posiolok Yavas, Uchrezdenie Ж X 385.

Relatives: I. V. Zalmanson, father and Z. I. Zalmanson, brother Riga, Latvian SSR, USSR, Veidenbaum 45, Kv. 22.

UNION OF COUNCILS FOR SOVIET JEWS

WESTERN REGION

Bay Area Council for Soviet Jewry, Southern California Council for Soviet Jews, California Students for Soviet Jews, San Diego Council for Soviet Jews.

CENTRAL REGION

Cleveland Council on Soviet Anti-Semitism, Toronto Student Council for Soviet Jews, Pittsburgh Voice for Soviet Jewry, Chicago Council for Soviet Jewry.

EASTERN REGION

South Florida Conference for Soviet Jewry, Zechor-S.E. Virginia Council for Soviet Jews, Washington Committee for Soviet Jewry, Long Island Committee for Soviet Jewry, Montreal Student Struggle for Soviet Jewry, Greater Philadelphia Council for Soviet Jews.

ZALMANSON ABRAHAM,
Bat Yam, Israel, August 25, 1971.

AMERICAN RED CROSS,
Chapter Headquarters,
District of Columbia, U.S.A.

DEAR SIR: My niece Sylva Zalmanson is presently in a Soviet Union labor camp as a result of a court conviction set upon her on Dec. 24, 1970 for her attempt to reach Israel to her freedom.

As her uncle who knows her from birth and saw her grow together with my own daughter, I am also familiar with her past medical history and I am therefore very much concerned for her health.

Sylva has suffered in the past from an open case of tuberculosis, doctors worked hard to save her life from this disease. She was admitted to a special sanatorium for a long period of time to recover from her illness. It is a known fact that persons who suffered from this disease have to be very careful and preserve their health. Under bad living conditions this disease can reappear. Presently Sylva suffers from the disease of peptic ulcer.

I am seeking help through your organization hoping that the American Red Cross will get in touch with the proper channels in the Soviet Union and request to have Sylva's living standards raised by providing her with the proper diet and working conditions.

I would be extremely obliged if you could provide Sylva with permission to receive food packages from either myself or her father in Russia.

I thank you in advance and hope that you will accept my pleas of help for my beloved niece.

Yours truly,

ABRAHAM ZALMANSON.

———

LETTERS FROM POTMA

What follows is a remarkable and shocking document of the daily life and sufferings of the Jewish prisoners of conscience in Potma, the notorious labor camp in Soviet Mordovia. The text, written by a non-Jewish inmate in January 1972, was smuggled to the West. The author's identity must remain a secret for obvious reasons. The degradations of these Asseri Tzion—"Prisoners of Zion"—make it clear that the "Jewish problem" in Russia is far from solved.

[Translated from the Russian.]

I arrived at Mordovia a couple of years ago and here I am in one of the dozens of Mordovian labor camps. I remember well the road from Potma to the place of incarceration. In every direction there were deep woods but on both sides of the road, all around, appeared fences of the camps. It appears that life in these regions occurs only in the immediate neighborhood of the camp. It is possible to see groups of people in prisoner's garb accompanied by guards with automatic weapons and dogs. Next to them are buildings, their existence incomprehensible for us, with slogans atop them.

But basically what stands out are fences, fences and more fences. There are many camps in Mordovia. The prisoners refer to them simply as zones. What are they? Usually, it is an area surrounded by a fence—2 or 3 meters [6½—9¾ feet] in

229

height—a completely closed fence without a single opening. Above it is stretched barbed wire and observation towers are above from which constant surveillance takes place.

ISOLATION

We are isolated from the outside world, awesome, by means of a forbidden zone into which the prisoners are not allowed to enter. It is a plowed area of earth fenced by another row of barbed wire. One finds there an armed detachment which comprises the heavily armed guard. Soldiers observe their shifts in the elevated towers from which automatic orders can be broadcast when any prisoner approaches the forbidden zone.

The zone consists of living quarters and working quarters. We live in barracks which are one to two stories in height. Inside, they are divided into areas of 4–12 persons. Different camps have different arrangements. We sleep on bunks arranged in two levels and at nighttime the light is not turned off, so that we can be watched 24 hours, even while sleeping. This was difficult to get used to.

CLOTHES

All prisoners wear the same clothes. In summertime, cotton pants and shirts; for winter, a thin padded jacket and a hat—all of dark colors, and frequently having been previously worn by other prisoners. Most of our possessions are taken away from us upon arrival, and are not returned until our term of sentence is completed. We are not permitted to wear woolen clothes in spite of temperature as low as 40 degrees below zero centigrade [−40° fahrenheit], a frequently occuring temperature.

Here, one finds prisoners who are being punished for different offenses. One finds murderers, former Nazi criminals and so-called political prisoners. Generally speaking, it is considered that there are no political criminals in the Soviet Union. Therefore, there are no specific laws governing their detentions. Because of that, persons convicted because of their ideas are characterized under Soviet jurisprudence as criminals. For example, in the year 1971, a large group of Jews were sent to Mordovia convicted in several different towns of the Soviet Union for anti-Soviet activity. I have met many of these persons and understand that their sole crime was the desire to emigrate to Israel. And here, all of us are forced to live behind barbed wire.

WORK SHIFTS

The entire life in the camp is dedicated to hard labor. In shops where the majority of the prisoners work, there are two shifts. People work one week in the first shift, in the second week, the second shift. For the first shift, we must get up at 6 a.m., then breakfast, and at 7:30 a.m. is the summons to work. The first shift lasts from 8 a.m.–4:30 p.m., with a 30-minute lunch period from noon–12:30 p.m. At 5 p.m., we leave work, then supper and free time until 10 p.m. The second shift has, in my opinion, the more strenuous work. However, the necessity for rearranging oneself each week is the most unpleasant part.

Here is a schedule for the second shift: 8 a.m. one gets up, breakfasts, and at noon, lunch. At 4 p.m., we arrive for work from 4:30 p.m.–12:30 a.m. We work until 30 minutes after midnight, supper from 7–7:30 p.m. We leave work at 1:15 a.m. We are permitted to sleep at 1:30 a.m. We have only 6½ hours to sleep—from 1:30 a.m.–8 a.m. It is taken for granted that almost everyone working the second shift sleeps from lunch until work (thus, the supposed four hours of free time cannot be used).

In general, it is considered that work is the basis for re-education of criminals and therefore it is assigned the most important and special role in the life of the camp. Both the encouragement and punishment of the prisoner is determined by his attitude toward work. Moreover, work is the only source of existence because from the money earned, with permission of the overseers, the prisoners may utilize up to five rubles per month for purchase of products from the commissary.

The prisoners are utilized in the Mordovian Complex for many types of common labor completely unrelated to their educational and professional backgrounds. The "political" prisoners are used as a rule for the most strenuous and dangerous (healthwise) areas. This I have seen very clearly in the example of convicted Jews, many of whom have received higher education, and prior to arrest held government positions.

THE FACTORY

Zenkovka factory work, to which many are assigned, is the most difficult. One finds there a science associate, Vladimir Mogilever [4 year sentence]; a military engineer, Volf Zalmanson [10 year sentence]; his brother Israel [8 year sentence], a student of the Polytechnical Institute of Riga; Asher Frolov [5 year sentence], a student of the Polytechnical Institute of Ryazan; and Shimon Levit [2 year sentence].

What is Zenkovka? One places into a drill press a *zenker* (reaming tool). It looks like a drill but it has a blunt end. It is not used for drilling, but for widening an opening. One takes an axle, places it into a vise and then turns a valve. Compressed air moves the vise so that the axle is positioned exactly under the reamer. Then it is necessary to move the wheel of the press so that the reamer is lowered into the opening, and widens it. After the opening is traversed, the wheel is rotated in an opposite direction, and the reamer is raised. Then the vise is opened by turning a valve. Without stopping the rotation of the reamer, it is necessary to remove the workpiece and install a new one. Then the entire process is repeated. During a shift, 1200 of these pieces must be processed.

The most dangerous part is to remove the finished piece and install a new one. Switching off the press in this technology was not anticipated, which is a serious infraction of technical safety, completely inadmissable in freedom. The rotating reamer may easily injure the prisoner's hand. Such injuries are fairly common. In addition to the fact that the reamer may injure the hand, sharp, hot chips fly out from under the reamer. To work in gloves is forbidden (it is even forbidden by the rule of technical safety) because if a hand in a glove would be caught under the reamer, then the glove would begin to wind on the reamer with unfortunate consequences—one's hand getting pulled into the reamer.

In addition to the above description, one should add the splashes of emulsion which attack the skin, fumes and horrible noise. The noise is not only from one's particular press, but there is a horrible noise emanating from the workshop itself. Shimon Levit has small cuts all over his hands—a sight hideous to the eyes, and recently he seriously wounded his hand. But this will heal. Volf Zalmanson, without explanation, was transferred here from the technical division where he was involved in engineering work—the only one of the Jewish prisoners. Israel Zalmanson was transferred from the Division of the Chief Mechanic, ostensibly for poor work, although he completed all of his assignments. No one is able to fulfill the work quotas, although Levit is almost able to reach the quotas. The quota load is tremendous and if one does not fulfill it, one is punished.

The loading work is even worse. David Chernoglas [5 year sentence], a former engineer, works in a so-called "emergency brigade". All of us fear assignment to this particular area, the reason being that basically it consists of loading and unloading railroad cars. The work is very difficult and dangerous. Moreover, one may be awakened at any time during the day or night; one does not know ahead of time. Even on a Sunday, one works.

At first glance, sewing of mittens in the camp shop appears to be fairly light work. Canvas mittens sewn in Mordovia are worn by workers far from Mordovia. Such shops exist in almost all the zones. Women confined for political reasons— 14 of them, among whom is the sister of Israel and Volf Zalmanson, Sylva [10 year sentence]. These women are occupied almost exclusively with this work, but even for them, the work is tiring. What can one say about the men: Aryeh Khanokh [10 year sentence], Yosef Mendelevich [12 year sentence], Yuri Fedorov [15 year sentence] Alexis Murzhenko [14 year sentence]—excessive demands must be fulfilled in dimly-lit buildings using machines which continuously, break down. Besides which, the completion of the quota is required under all circumstances, if one is to escape punishment.

Sylva Zalmanson, during work, suffers from constant backache and dizzy spells related to constant eye strain. Because of acute eye strain, Yuri Fedorov was transferred from sewing mittens to turning them inside out—work which is less conducive to strain and acute conjunctivitis in the eyes. In general, he is fortunate because the quota for sewing can be met by few. Even the healthy persons are unable to meet the quota and all suffer consequences.

OUTSIDE WORK

I myself work in construction, as do Tolya (Anatoly) Altman [10 year sentence], Mikhael Shepshelovich [2 year sentence], Boris Penson [10 year sentence], and

Aaron Shpilberg [3 year sentence]. To begin, they were merely assisting pushing wheelbarrows with sand and moving different heavy objects. It was especially difficult for Candidate of Physical Mathematical Sciences Lev Kornblit [3 year sentence], a man of weak health, who has spent all of his life in scientific laboratories and who simply did not have the strength for this type of hard work. Moreover, during transportation to the camp, Lev was so weakened that during the first week he was unable to get up, not to mention the fact that he was still driven to work in such condition and expected to meet his quotas.

The situation is also aggravated by the fact that it is almost impossible to endure the Mordovsky frost in the so-called "special camp clothing." In our existence, various changes occur frequently; at any time, one may expect a transfer to even more difficult and strenuous work. This took place with Tolya Altman and Misha Shepshelovich who work together on a concrete mixer in penetrating winds. And then, one may be sent to work on the press, as happened to the husband of Sylva, Eduard Kuznetsov [15 year sentence]. This work is known as being quite hazardous to prisoners because of virtual absence of fundamental standards of technological safety. In the camp, the press does not have any safety—grill and workpieces have to be replaced without stopping the machine. In freedom, one wouldn't encounter this situation anywhere, but in the camp it is permitted.

The workers here are state criminals. The variety of labor in the camps is united by one single general quality, namely, unreasonably high work quotas, requiring not only experience but also unusual strength. This is possible only with an adequate diet. It is difficult for a newcomer to adjust to camp food.

FOOD

For breakfast: "soup". For those fulfilling the work quotas, additional nutrition is available—cereal with vegetable fats and sugar. Since I do not receive this cereal, I do not go to the mess hall in the morning at all. For lunch, one is given cabbage soup and gruel (either peas or ragu—hardly edible). For dinner, one is given a small piece of fried fish and again gruel. Presently, because of the incidents of an epidemic of influenza, they started to occasionally give one onion to each prisoner. Some onions are also sold in the labor camp commissary, but there were not enough to go around. In general, no fruit or fresh vegetables are ever given or sold. It is interesting to note that in our letters mentioning that we are fed "not badly", this phrase is usually stricken out and the letters are returned by the censor.

In addition to the established camp ration, under the conditions of meeting the work quota and "good behavior", prisoners have the right to buy products in the commissary to the extent of a miserly sum of up to five rubles per month. The assortment of products offered in the commissary is quite meager: margarine, cheese that looks like salami, canned fish of poor quality, candy (hard candy and caramels), grey bread (poor quality white bread), tobacco, fruit jam and also such necessary items as toothpowder, envelopes and stamps. The above assortment has been established officially and has not changed in the course of several decades.

Food in the hospital is substantially better than in the camp according to so-called form 6B. Basic differences: white or grey bread, compote or pudding (thickened with potato starch, not gelatin), milk (250 grams per week), and one piece of meat (50 grams per day) for dinner as the main course. To enter the hospital for treatment and food is the ambition of every prisoner. This is, of course, difficult.

CAMP HOSPITAL

The camp hospital has approximately 120 beds, while the total number of prisoners in the strict and special regime camps serves a population of 1500. The hospital has almost no specialist if one does not count the three therapists, one surgeon and one dental technician, all of whom have just finished medical training and lack experience. The doctors work from 10 a.m.–5 p.m. In evening and night hours, during holidays and relief days, service is not rendered at all since there is no doctor on duty. Instead of a doctor and in place of a nurse and sanitary worker, there is a person—a so-called "paramedic"—who has no medical training. For example, in the hospital of the Seventh Barrack, the paramedic is a former tractor driver.

It is interesting that even in the hospital, in spite of the fact that work is not forced, differences in regime are preserved: for those in the strict regime are in wards, and the specials are usually kept in solitary rooms. In cases of surgical intervention, the sick person is brought on a stretcher directly from the zone by prisoners. Afterwards, following the operation, the patient is carried back to the zone.

The supply of drugs in the medical division is very meager and most of the medicines are kept for a long time beyond the limit of their utility. It is forbidden to receive drugs from relatives. Altman's wife was refused permission to pass on Vikalin to her husband which he needed for stopping cruel pains in his stomach. Federov's wife was forced to leave Sinalar which she brought for her husband Yuri in the guard room. Eventually, the drug was transmitted to the hospital and Yuri has made occasional use of it for curing eczema, which has developed in the camp.

SUFFERING

Vladik Mogilever, who is not able to cope with heavy physical labor (I have already spoken of work in the reaming shop) because of acute nearsightedness, has been transferred to work that has no quotas—into a brigade for producing wooden logs. So he is sawing wood quietly in fresh air. It was possible for him to gain admission into the hospital and obtain from them an appropriate note—which explains the beautiful changes that have taken place for him. For many others, to be admitted to the hospital is like reaching the cup of the holy grail.

Edik Kuznetsov has been suffering with hellish pains in his stomach, suggesting stomach ulcers. He was completely downed by sharp pain following heavy labor and with endless nausea. However, no one believed him and he was driven to work, and was stuffed with some kind of tablet used for dysentery without establishing the diagnosis! There was no mention even of special nutrition, although Edik doesn't even consume one tenth the camp ration.

To attain a diagnosis is a very complex business, which frequently requires several months. Appeals to the camp administration usually brings no results, and despairing prisoners undertake hunger strikes as a protest, which lasts many days and further undermines their health. One pays a high price for any medical service in camp!

Only after a week-long hunger strike was Edik Kuznetsov finally placed into the hospital. As a result of a primitive investigation, the doctor diagnosed gastritis, in spite of obvious symptoms of stomach ulcers. Surprised, Edik requested an x-ray examination, but was "promised" it in a month. No measures were taken except that he was given some tablet to counteract nausea, and now Kuznetsov finds himself back in the zone in the same condition he was before.

His wife, Sylva Zalmanson, is developing a stomach ailment with similar symptoms—sharp pain and nausea. Moreover, her hearing has deteriorated. Sylva needs very badly a thorough medical examination which under the conditions existing in Mordovia is practically impossible to obtain.

Anatoly Altman came into the zone with an ulcer of the duodenum which was diagnosed while he was still free. He began to experience pains almost from the start and was one of the first Jews to gain admission to the hospital. He left the hospital, however, with a diagnosis of gastritis which does not require special nutrition.

Shimon Levit is suffering with inflammation of frontal sinuses. In the course of a long period of time, in view of the absence of a specialist, the only medication he received was headache pills. After a sharp deterioration of his condition, he was relieved of work. He had a high temperature, but due to the fact that the prisoners are conveyed to the hospital on Fridays, even though he was in the same zone as the hospital, all treatment was postponed by almost a week. From the hospital, he was released with temperature, which even now occurs every evening.

Solomon Dreisner experienced for two months severe tooth discomfort and was unable to get an appointment with the doctor. After he was notified that his mother died, he developed an inflammation of the tertiary nerve, this causing him unbearable pain. The head of the medical division, a women, declined to render him emergency medical treatment, threatening him with punitive isolation. He was forced to go to work in his sick condition. Since he was unable to work, he was deprived of a scheduled visit. Solomon wrote several complaints to different departments complaining about lack of medical treatment and his unreasonable punishment. Being led to extreme mental anguish, he has declared a hunger strike for six days. Prison officials have told him to visit a special department in prison and told him he is a troublemaker and is having a bad effect on other prisoners. They have threatened punitive measures.

Jacob Michaelovich Suslensky suffered from heart trouble on Sunday, December 5, 1971. I, myself, was not a witness to his severe pain. Naturally, in the morning he went to the medical division of the prison. He was required to work on the second shift. He requested medication and relief from work at least for one day. Monday, the chief of the medical department, a paramedic Yegenova, told him, "You should spend less time studying the Jewish language." However, she did not release him of his work. When I saw him I was surprised and even more surprised while hearing his account.

Mogilever went after work with the sole purpose of checking out what had happened. The reality has exceeded all expectations. The chief paramedic very quietly repeated all she had told Yacov while Vladik showed a certain amount of confusion. He has reminded the paramedic Yegenova about State 123 of the USSR Constitution, which declares the racial and national equality under law and also State 74 of the Ukrainian Union of the USSR, which punishes those who violate equality under the law. On the question "And where did you learn that Suslensky is studying the Hebrew language?" the chief innocently replied, "Don't you think that the Section G Internal Order has informed us of this?" What is truth is truth. The Section of Internal Order not only informed on us, but it makes the final decision whether a man, for example, would be directed to medical treatment. Let me point out that Yasha (Jacob) already twice has been stricken from the list. He has complained about the poor medical attention to the prosecuting attorney overseeing the Soviet Socialist Republic.

One can easily imagine how such medical service is reflected upon the health of the people, if in order to be medically treated it is necessary to secure from the devil a statement about good behavior—without any verbal dependence on all the rules and regulations of the labor camp. A slight deviation is followed by punishment. The variety of the different punishments in the labor camp is without end, for example, the removal of the right to receive mail and an increase in the duration of sentence.

Prevention of receipt of packages is an example of punishment. By the way, this is the single source of additional food for the inmate, because to receive packages is permitted only after one has served half his sentence, irrespective of his length of confinement. Only one package up to five kilograms [11 pounds] in one year is permitted, and even then provided that your rights have not been rescinded. In a package up to one kilogram [2.2 pounds] which an inmate receives twice a year from the beginning of confinement, one may receive only dry goods. According to the instructions of the camp, these products must involve crackne (a ring-shaped piece of dried mutton) and biscuits. Every other kind of food is forbidden.

Imprisoned Jews have been sent packages of boullion cubes. However, even this was eventually forbidden. The excuse was that while they are dry goods, they are of meat extract and meat is forbidden. Chocolate is also forbidden because "it is a substance that leads to 'excitement'". However, even the lack of this very insignificant addition to the products, makes it more difficult to endure the life in the camp.

VISITS

Even more severe punishment is the removal of visiting rights. For those who are in the camp, the receipt of letters and visits is important as a symbol of human ties. It is understood that the day of the meeting is yearned for with a great deal of excitement which is anxiously anticipated with preparation for several days as if it were possible to live again with one's visiting family, even though the actual duration of the visit is four hours under the watchful eyes of the supervisors. During the personal visit, one is not required to work, according to the desire of the person in charge of the labor camp. However, I have not witnessed even once that a Jewish inmate would have been given visiting rights without requiring him to work an entire working day. In 1971, this was done in the cases of Aaron Shpilberg, David Chernoglas, Victor Boguslavsky [3 year sentence], Lassal Kaminsky, Yuri Fedorov, Anatoly Altman and in general all the imprisoned Jews.

The reduction even with the very brief time for visitation cannot be understood. It is a senseless cruelty if one would consider that the relative may have to travel hundreds of miles to meet this forthcoming difficult blow and others for which they are really not prepared. The supervisors of the visits treat the relatives very harshly and with a deep hatred and this all is allowed to continue without reprisals for these prison officials. In spite of this, none of the relatives enter a complaint, fearing that the duration of the visit will be shortened. Any complaints to the overseer of the labor camp leads to no result. The women's supervisors feel they are in complete authority, even more so. Contrary to the law is the personal search to which relatives are subjected prior to the visit, which, of course, is not sanctioned by any prison regulations. However, it is impossible to say anything; otherwise, visits may be completely forbidden. This is what happened to the wives of Chernoglas and Kaminsky and the relatives of Kuznetsov. It involved actually body contact and turning the pockets inside out and emptying of the pocketbooks. These searches are carried out for the purpose of finding forbidden objects: guns, alcoholic beverages, narcotics, poisons, cigarettes, and food.

Letters and postcards from Israel are criminal objects from the viewpoint of the supervisor. These items are removed after the search. That is about all that one could find on the relatives of confined Jews. However, the degrading process of search is repeated time and again. Frequently the visit is forbidden. The reason given—the work quota had not been fulfilled. Israel Zalmanson has been forbidden his forthcoming visit. At first officials gave a warning. However, he had fulfilled his normal 80% and they punished him. The same thing happened to Alexy Murzhenko. He had not fulfilled his quota for two days and has been denied visitors for all 1972. Alexy declared a 27-day hunger strike. Fedorov and Kuznetsov acted in solidarity with him in a 14-day hunger strike. Alexy is now near death, and has ceased his hunger strike only when the prosecuting attorney promised to change the punishment to something else.

Eduard Kuznetsov is denied all visitors because he does not have any close relations. His mother is bedridden and his wife Sylva Zalmanson is not permitted to visit her husband in the camp compound. Why wouldn't they change a personal visit when he has no relatives, so that he could be visited by friends at least twice per year? However, this has been forbidden. It seems that Edward could have had personal visits with Sylva who is located a few kilometers from him. However, this has been completedly forbidden. At this time the prison officials require the examination of the original marriage certificate, while in spite of the fact in all official documents Sylva and Edward are entered as husband and wife. This difficulty has existed for at least one year, of husband and wife being denied visits.

LETTERS

All the correspondence of the Jewish prisoners is subject to very strict censorship. The doctor is the exception; the rest of the prison officials are censors. The inmates are forbidden to describe the life in the camp—the daily schedule and the quality of food. The correspondence should be strictly personal; otherwise, the letters simply are not transmitted to the people to whom they are addressed or they receive them with many parts stricken out. This is especially sad because political inmates are not able to receive correspondence from their close relatives whose content could not be contested. This is done for the purpose of suppressing the spirit of the inmates and is done to make them feel that since no one writes to them they are completely forgotten. Now it is known that the letters of the wife of David Chernoglas are destroyed before they are delivered. Fedorov and Kuznetsov have not received letters from their relatives during the past two months, while they are being continuously written.

On the other side, the letters from the camp do not reach their relatives while the administration usually claims they are not responsible for the loss. The wife of Murzhenko has not received any news from her husband in three months and this is especially strange because, under normal conditions, the mail works quite efficiently. It was maliciously declared to Boris Penson's mother that the supervisor suggested to her son that he write regularly so that his mother would not worry. When he did write regularly, however, the letters were lost as in many cases.

PROPAGANDA

The "educational work" within the labor camp is well funded, which is incomprehensible. Why should education in the spirit of Soviet morality be given to Jews who forever wish to leave the Soviet Union and live under different conditions? Once a week, political classes take place to which attendance is mandatory while one's absence is punishable. The chief "educator" also works for the "Section of Internal Order." He carefully scrutinizes the attendance and activity at the time of these classes. In the process of education the work does not stop even in view of the opposing national and self-determination and religiousness of the confined Jews. Another sentence, I recall now—Josef Mendelevich—and how they persecuted him for wearing a skullcap, which for a religious Jew is very necessary. Lazar Trachtenberg [2 year sentence] was forbidden to read the annual prayer for his deceased mother, the *Kaddish*, because they have forbidden his receiving from home a *Siddur* (prayerbook) or Bible. This is in order to intercept the possibility of religious agitation in the confines of the labor camp, which is a heinous crime under the conditions of everyday atheist propaganda.

As for the educational objectives of the inmates, it is forbidden to receive books from friends and relatives even through the special "book by mail" organization. The orders for literature are frequently left on the table of the censor. It is difficult to explain why books published in the Soviet Union are forgidden to the inmate. In addition, one can neither receive nor order newspapers of the friendly socialist countries.

HEBREW FORBIDDEN

How strange that there is for the Jews a proscription against studying Hebrew. Captain Patcugan had a discussion with Mogilever on this subject. On the question of why Armenians, Ukrainians, Latvians and other nationalities are permitted to study their native tongues, the chief of operations replied, "They belong to their own nationality whereas you do not," and, "Furthermore, you Russian Jews must speak only in Russian." During the conversation, Captain Patchugan has spoken in angry and offensive terms about the Hebrew language and writing and offended the human and national aspirations of Vladimir Mogilever.

The offensive incident with the illness of Jacob Suslensky was due to his study of the Hebrew language. He was refused entrance to the hospital. I have already described this. For what and due to whom is all this necessary? The prisoners of other nationalities do not have to endure these painful aforementioned experiences. The desire to learn one's language and literature, Major Sorokin from Camp #19 has claimed, is Zionism, which under the conditions of the anti-Zionist campaigns, one can conclude is a direct threat.

But it seems that the Jews are ready to carry through and not be denied their goals.

LETTER FROM PRISON—TRANSLATION

Greetings to you, our brothers and sisters, on Independence Day! This is a holiday for the Jewish People in Israel and in the Diaspora, and also for us, who find ourselves in this camp here in the Soviet Union.

We have not had the opportunity to learn our own language in our schools, and you will therefore excuse our errors in Hebrew.

We have not lived in our own home and you will forgive us that we have not struggled like heroes.

They have not, however, succeeded in taking away from us the Jewish spirit and our hope.

Our people now has its own government, and we therefore believe that we will meet one another in our own land, if not in the next year, then soon.

Привет вам, наши братья
и сестры, в День Независимости!

Это праздник для еврейского
народа в Израиле и диаспоре,
и также для нас, находящихся
в лагере здесь, в Советском
Союзе.

У нас не было возможности
изучать наш язык в школах,
и вы простите нам ошибки
в иврите.

Мы не жили в своем доме,
и вы простите нам, что мы
не боролись, как герои.

Но не смогли отнять у
нас еврейскую душу и
нашу надежду.

Теперь у нашего народа
есть государство, поэтому
мы верим, что встретимся
на нашей земле, и если не
в будущем году, то скоро.

1972 год

/Владимир Могилевер/
/Давид Черноглаз/
/Вульф Залмансон/
/Израиль Залмансон/
/Шимон Левит/
/Соломон Дрейзнер/
/Яков Сусленский/
/Иосиф Менделевич/
/Гилель Шур/

שלום לכם אחינו
ואחיותינו ביום העצמאות.

זה חג לעם יהודי
בארץ ובגולה תפוצה
גם לנו היושבים באחת
רכוז פה בברית המועצות.

לא היו לנו אפשרויות
ללמוד את השפה בבתי ספר
ותסלחו לנו שלא אנו דברית.

לא חיינו בביתנו ותסלחו
לנו שלא נלחמנו כגבורים.

אבל לא יכלו לקחת
ממנו נפש היהודי ותקותנו.

עכשיו יש מדינת
לעמנו, אל כן מאמינים
אנו שנפגש בארצנו
ואם לא בשנה הבאה
אז במהרה.

תשל"ב

Letter Smuggled Out of Potma Camp.

APPEAL OF A GROUP OF FORMER PRISONERS OF ZION TO THE PEOPLE OF ISRAEL, TO THE WORLD JEWISH COMMUNITIES, TO ALL THE PEOPLE OF GOOD WILL!

We, Prisoners of Zion—victims of the anti-Jewish trials in the USSR in recent years—who are now free and in Israel, entreat in behalf of our friends who are still languishing in prisons.

We appeal to all the people of good will, to all the Jewish communities in the world, to the people of Israel—to strengthen the struggle for their release.

We spent only 1–2 years behind barbed wire. But even in this comparatively short period we felt that we were disintegrating physically. Hard work, malnourishment, absence of any elementary medical care, systematic punishments such as transfer to isolation cells or deprivation of food—all these are more than enough to bring a normal, healthy man to a state of total physical exhaustion. And an ill man—to death. A good illustration of this is the death of Yuri Galanskov in one of the Mordovian camps. He was not able to survive the conditions in which he was being held for a period of less than six years, and died only a year before he was due to be released. In the prime of life, only 33 years old, he died because he was not given the elementary medical care he required.

Nevertheless, even the horrible conditions of life, slave labour, brutal punishments do not fully characterise the tragic position of the Jewish political prisoners.

There is another factor, which may seem to be less horrible, but which, in fact, is more dangerous. We refer to the anti-semitic persecution of the imprisoned Jews—humiliation by KGB-men and jailers, beatings and insults from the other prisoners who had once collaborated with the Nazis. This makes the situation of the Prisoners of Zion especially difficult. The imprisoned Jews may complain only to the local administration, but their complaints remain within the confines of the concentration camp and may be transmitted only with the approval of local camp officials. And these officials are inveterate anti-semites who punish the victim of the crime, but not the criminal.

Complete harmony exists between the camp administration and the former collaborators. And it cannot be otherwise, for we are sure that the administrators, as well as the imprisoned collaborators, follow their baser instincts because of the fact that the higher authorities encourage such actions.

The Soviet authorities are now aware that the imprisoned Jews continue to struggle for their right to leave for Israel, even in the concentration camps. So it has been decided to "break these people". For this purpose they have created an unbearable living and working environment. The Soviet authorities and the camp administration do everything possible to hide the truth about the real conditions of the Prisoners of Zion from the public and to keep them in utter isolation.

The dirty work is done behind an iron curtain which they have built.

It has already become an accepted norm that the imprisoned Jews are constantly deprived of the rights to which they are entitled even under Soviet law.

They are unable to receive any information from outside the iron curtain. All this is not at all surprising, this is the very nature of Soviet society. But one cannot but be appalled at the indifference and apathy of world public opinion.

The number of Soviet Jews who are condemned for their desire to leave for Israel is growing daily. In order not to provoke the same reaction as took place after the Leningrad trials, the Soviet authorities are holding spurious trials behind closed doors against individual Jews (Markman, Brindt, Chautzis, Liubarsky, Shkolnik). But the verdicts are not less severe as previously.

We have undergone all the tortures which now await the courageous, innocent people. Now we are in our Homeland. But the thought of the fate of our friends remains with us.

From our own bitter experience we know that any weakening of the world's solidarity with the Prisoners of Zion at present makes their already harsh situation even more horrible.

The 15th of December, 1972, marked 2 years since the first Leningrad trial and on the 24th December 1970 the death sentence verdict for innocent people aroused worldwide indignation.

We, the friends of the victims of these trials, call upon you:

Demand from your governments, parliaments, political parties and public organizations that whenever possible during each and every contact with Soviet representatives they raise the question of the liberation of the Prisoners of Zion; send petitions, letters, telegrams with the same demands to the Soviet authorities;

Organise protest meetings and send the resolutions adopted to the Soviet authorities as well as to the various international organisations;

Write to the Prisoners of Zion, give them moral encouragement!
Freedom for all our brothers, who have been put in concentration camps, their only crime a yearning to remain Jews, a wish to live in their Motherland despite the Soviet policy of forced assimilation!
  Averbuch (Aleksandrovich) Ruth, Voloshin Arkady, Ontman Lily, Palatnik Raiza, Trachtenberg Lazar, Shepshelovich Mikhail, Shor Hilel.

THE CASE OF BORIS PENSON

Boris Penson was born in Tashkent, Uzbekhistan in 1946, his family moved shortly afterwards to Riga. When Boris was only ten years old his father was arrested and sentenced to seven years of hard labor. At fourteen Boris entered the studio of the painter Simon Gelberg. He remained there until the age of seventeen when he himself was arrested and sentenced to hard labor. Released in 1968 after three and one half years in prison, he painted intensively until his second arrest in June 1970. He had become active in the Jewish national movement and had painted posters for Rumbule—the "Babi Yar" of Riga. This short span of activity ended when he was accused and convicted of planning the theft of an airplane to escape from Russia. This time he was sentenced to ten years of forced labor and his personal property was confiscated. He is currently imprisoned in a labor camp, having served two years of the ten year sentence. Boris started a hunger strike on the first of January, 1973, this being the only "legal" form of protest permitted in Soviet labor camps.

Boris Penson's paintings have been secretly brought from Russia by his friends. His work was shown at the Jewish Museum in New York (October and November 1972) and reviewed most favorably. Affected by the squalor and terror of prison, he gropes toward formal means that can evoke the moods of anguish and oblivion, the feelings of being both threatened by and estranged from Soviet society, and the fear of being rendered extinct as a human being.

In his "self portrait" [See p. 282] one senses behind the introverted and restrained expression a confident assertion of the self which is grounded in commitment and defiance. It is an image of a tense young man with great inner resources and strength. The artist shows a genuine inventiveness and potential, Boris Penson, twenty six years old.

Boris Penson writes from a Soviet prison: May 18th, 1972. . . . I am tortured by the vivid experience of an idea that becomes a vision—colors, lines, forms, half-shadows. Often it gets together in a stormy way. This is almost jazz music, an improvisation. One can improvise for a long time. There are variations and more variations, until almost nothing remains of the idea. The outside world can accept or refuse whatever has arisen, there can be empathy, this depends on the force of the work, also much depends on the spectators themselves. . . .

August 12, 1971. It is the same forever, weekdays without end or limit, large round tree trunks, shreds of boiled-out cabbage for lunch. Your letters, even postcards, are feast days. No possibility to paint or draw. I think of paintings. I was always in haste to paint. I have no patience, I want so much to paint. Now I know what I want and how to do it. Everything is clear and lucid, as it never was in that other life. Forgive me for my rare and short letters. There is an unavoidable pair of eyes that poisons the desire to write.

LETTERS FROM BORIS PENSON, SOVIET JEWISH "PRISONER OF CONSCIENCE," MAY 18, 1972

[Translated from Russian]

MOISHE!

You are quite a fellow! Everything's ok. I'm glad you're now forced to take up art. This is not without use. Maybe you'll take up art history seriously? There might be a possibility to study from afar. This is not easy but a worthwhile occupation. I can well imagine how difficult these things are for you now!

Regarding the names for paintings, I can only recommend in difficult cases (maybe this is even better), not to give names but call them "opus no. so-and-so", or "variation, number so-and-so." Often a name is important because it gives a key or a certain superstructure to the painting. And even more to my works, which as you rightly remarked, are specific. This is a difficult task to make you understand, now, in a letter, an idea on the cluster of thoughts that trouble me. But I will try, slightly, to express some of these ideas. These could really form a treatise. I will take just one as an example. But, of course, it is important for you to grasp not an idea but the *very essence* of painting, or rather, of what I want in art.

The idea of civilization appears to me as the antagonism, rendered visible, of the Town and the Steppe. The Town, the City, is the result of civilization, the Steppe is the past. Of course, as you will easily understand, this is quite subjective, a convention, I bring it in a "literary" form, as if it was an essay composed by your friend.

Grey, busy, stifling, the City froze, after becoming empty. Empty, pale, it sailed off into blue space. Now it is violet, under a red sky like clotted blood, and it lights up in a multitude of windows that are small cubbyholes, and then all is black.

In the cubbyholes are people. Everyone has a slit. This is the concrete mass or organized space. At night, many will exist no longer, just like yesterday, just like tomorrow. After giving to the City all their life, they will suddenly leave it, they will disappear, like you will disappear yourself, unavoidably.

Like all women, she came when she was no longer awaited. The dead city all around, silent. She came surprisingly for herself. An empty flat at night. Her bond with the City—black underwear, sophisticated mourning. A stranger, naked, a woman. Lace, dark shadows—a city woman; but still a steppe woman. A Russian Tartar; her body is firm, elongated, her breasts slightly heavy, with hardened nipples; her breasts smell of bitter herbs, of mint. Her legs are strong and smooth.

There is a trembling strip of light on the window, on the floor, on her body.

She is glowing, her underwear is sticky, she is hunted and almost happy. The steppe looks through her eyes.

But these are just words, and it happens even more often that there are not even words, just an unexpressed sensation. This is, for me, a skeleton of "subject matter." This can be a foundation, or be a starting-point. I am tortured by the vivid experience of an idea that becomes a vision—colors, lines, forms, half-shadows. All this finally reaches the cardboard during the process of work. Often it gets together in a stormy way. This is almost jazz music, an improvisation. One can improvise for a long time. There are variations and more variations, until almost nothing remains of the idea. It is covered by pigments, only the experience remains. Work not always gets on. Thus, sometimes, other things happen. That is characteristic of me, maybe.

Existentialism is natural to me in the form of an act, a living through an idea at the very moment it is born, when the process is important in itself. Then the work is finished, it begins to live a life of its own, and already exists for me in another form. (This is like in the old Jewish joke: Chaim, you have so many children, are you so very fond of them?—I am not so much fond of children, as I enjoy this kind of occupation . . .) The outside world can accept or refuse whatever has arisen, there can be empathy, this depends on the force of the work, or one does find something of one's own; then, also, much depends on the spectators themselves . . .

All this, of course, is coarse, superficial. I write like a stormy wave, and in order to formulate all this into a streamlined system, one must touch on many other factors. As you will understand, this is not possible, also I don't like talking about myself, I write it down just for you, I want you to grasp, or rather, to feel the taste of the labor of painting. I do not know how far I succeed to impart this to you.

Your drawing outfit I got. This is all excellent. Thank you! However, there is the fact that just now there have arrived more explicit and more detailed instructions, according to which I can use only simple black pencils and paper. Please send from now on to Mother only pencils of various trademarks (rather soft) and paper.

I embrace you, and await news eagerly.

BORIS.

Shalom MOISHE: I am compelled to write in telegraphic text, hope it will reach you. Your actions are wonderful—everything causes deepest satisfaction. Only the active creation of a situation, where our being here will become a running sore, can bring about success. We react to every persecution by complaining immediately to any authority which might be suitable. It is important that as far as possible, this should receive a broad coverage. However, since all small incidents are dynamic and very quickly lose actuality, there are the things that should receive chief attention:

1. The continuing fact of horrible food (the foodstuffs are only approximately fit for human consumption and the result is 500 calories).

2. We are kept together with war criminals.

3. Since we have renounced Soviet citizenship and on the basis of the above, efforts should be made to have us transferred into a zone for foreigners.

4. The most cruel treatment during hunger strikes (we are forced to work while fasting during the first three days, we are isolated thereupon in the punitive isolator, the doctors treat us worse than dogs, and half an hour after we stop the hunger strike, we are chased out to work.)

You should not get astonished at our frequent hunger strikes—this is the only half-official form of protesting, and according to law, it cannot be a pretext for further persecution.

5. We are continually persecuted because of our nationality (insults, all kinds of administrative pressures, provocations, punishments, the raising of the other inhabitants against us).

Generally speaking, lawlessness, irresponsibility, arbitrary treatment—this of course is no news for you personally. This is about everything I can say on our general situation.

You, of course, feel and know everything. I simply want to stress the justification of your way of acting.

This is everything I can write to you now.

I embrace and kiss you,

Your BORIS.

Do Aliyah—and we are happy.

UKRANIAN NATIONALISM

THE CASE OF YURIY SHUKHEVICH

HIS ONLY CRIME: SON OF GEN. CHUPRYNKA

[From "Revolutionary Voices" 1971, OSB Publishing House, Munich]

To the Chairman of the Presidium of the Supreme Soviet of the Ukrainian Soviet Socialist Republic from the political prisoner Yuriy Shukhevich-Berezynskyi.

28th July, 1967.

STATEMENT

In September, 1963 I was transported under escort through halting places, from the Mordovian concentration camps where I had been imprisoned, to Kyiv into the prison of the KGB (i.e. State Security Committee—Ed.) at the Council of Ministers of the Ukrainian SSR. [See photograph, p. 275.]

I was not notified by anyone about the reason of my transfer into the investigation prison. And only from the fact that from time to time I was taken by officials of the KGB to theatres, museums, factories in Kyiv, and also conducted to Zaporizhia, Kakhivka, Kherson, and Kaniv, I could conclude about the real reasons and demands which I would have to face later.

And this did really happen in July, 1964, when the officials of the KGB, Colonel Kalash, and captains Lytvyn and Merkatanenko put to me a demand that I should write a kind of declaration which could be published in the Soviet press and which would make it evident that I was breaking with the nationalistic ideas. Upon my question whether this should be a declaration that I would abstain from any anti-Soviet activity whatsoever, the answer was that this would not do. I should write something where I would condemn nationalism in general, condemn the activities of the Organization of Ukrainian Nationalists, quote some facts that would compromise Ukrainian nationalists, as well as condemn my father, Roman Shukhevich, who in the years 1944–1950 was the leader of the underground resistance movement in Ukraine.

Upon my refusal to write (or to broadcast any statement of such contents), they proposed to me to describe at least my journey through Ukraine, so that it could be published in the press. When I also rejected this proposal, Col. Kalash stated that I should do it, for then the KGB would initiate proceedings towards obtaining a pardon for me.

But as I do not feel guilty in any way, I could not write such a petition, and this I declared, presenting my motives in a written form. These are as follows:

1. As far back as 1956, the Prosecutor General successfully appealed against the decision of the court at Vladimir (i.e. Vladimir on the Klyazma, east of Moscow—Ed.) by which I was released from imprisonment, on the basis of the decree from 24. 4. 1954, as having been arrested at the age of adolescence, motivating his action by the allegation that I had tried to contact centres of Ukrainian nationalists abroad (without producing any evidence at all) and that my father was the leader of the underground movement of the Organization of Ukrainian Nationalists (which I cannot deny).

2. On the 21st August, 1958, on the day when I should have been released after ten years of imprisonment, on the basis of the decision of the OSO (Osoboye Soveshhaniye—Special Council—Ed.) of the MGB (Ministry of State Security—Ed.) of the USSR I was delivered a new order for my arrest, motivated by the absolutely false accusation of anti-Soviet agitation among the prisoners of the Vladimir prison.

3. The accusations were based on the false testimonies by two agents of the KGB, ordinary criminals, specially prepared by Senior Lieut. Halsky (now colonel Halsky) for that kind of witnessing, for which they were promised special privileges (which they later received).

4. The above-mentioned witnesses (Burkov and Fomchenko) gave false evidence, contradicting one another, or even their previous testimonies.

5. It was put to me as a crime (and as one of the main counts) that I was interested in the details of the death of my father, who was killed on the 5th March, 1950 in the village of Bilohorshcha near Lviv (West Ukraine—Ed.)

6. During my arrest on 21st August, 1958, a few poems by Olha Ilkiv were found among my possessions and confiscated. The poems were purely lyrical. Nevertheless they were enclosed with my case and put to me as a crime on the grounds that Olha Ilkiv had been sentenced for membership in the OUN (Organisation of Ukrainian Nationalists—Ed.) and for illegal activities, and also because her poems had previously been printed in underground publications, about which I learned only during the investigation.

7. The literary expertise (the experts were Lesyn and Kozachuk) was conducted not only in an unsatisfactory, but extraordinarily unscrupulous manner. It qualified the verses found with me and confiscated from me as nationalistic, which bears no relation to reality.

8. Disregarding the fact that "the crime" was committed at Vladimir-on-the-Klyazma (Russian Socialist Federative Soviet Republic) and that, consequently, in accordance with the existing laws, the case should have been heard by the Vladimir Region Court, I was transported to the KGB prison at Lviv where the investigation was continued, and where I was sentenced by the Lviv Region Court.

9. Although the KGB organs camouflage all their activities with the talk about the interests of the people, my trial on 1st December, 1958 was conducted behind closed doors, contrary to the existing laws, and this proves that I was kept hidden from the sight of the people for fear lest the unattractive machinations of the Lviv KGB become known.

10. During the trial the judges did not aim at an unprejudiced consideration of all the details but at executing the instructions of the KGB, to have me sentenced at any price.

11. My appointed defense lawyer (Smirnova) acquainted herself with my case only immediately before the session of the court. Having realised that I could not rely upon any objective defense, I refused to have a lawyer, but the court ignored my request to conduct my defense myself, wishing thus to cover up all the abuses of the juridical norms on their side.

12. The experts of the court literary expertise, during the questioning, allowed themselves very often to transgress the limits of their competence, as defined by law, and put to me provocative questions (with the permission of the court) which referred more to my personal views than to the materials of the case.

13. During the court investigation only the witnesses of the prosecution were heard (Fomchenko and Burkov), while the court did not find it necessary to hear the evidence of twelve witnesses who could have refuted the evidence by Burkov and Fomchenko.

14. Being afraid that even at a trial behind closed doors I would be able by my questions to reveal the falsity of the testimonies by the witnesses for the prosecution, the court did not allow me to put questions to the winesses, which could have unmasked them as the agents of the KGB who were giving evidence according to the instructions received from Halsky.

15. Although it was clear from the first glance that the witnesses were spurious, that their testimonies were false, the court ruled that only they were trustworthy, refusing to accept any other explanations or evidence, declaring that it was the right of the court to give preference to these or other testimonies as deserving trust.

16. When, however, the witnesses proved themselves incapable of fulfilling their tasks, namely to prove logically my guilt, the members of the court and the prosecutor came to their rescue and directly suggested to them what they should answer. Prosecutor Kolyasnikov who supported the accusation proved himself (especially eager in this direction).

17. The members of the court and the prosecutor were more interested in my convictions, as if these were punishable, than in the details of the case, and they persisted in putting a stress on them as well as on whose son I was.

As the result of such irregularities, I was sentenced, according to the wishes of the KGB, to ten years of imprisonment. Although I had previously guessed the reasons for such a sentence, yet shortly afterwards I found out that my premonitions were well founded. Thus, still during the preliminary investigation, in-investigator Vinogradov declared to me that the investigation was only the beginning and that later the officers of the security organs would have to lot to talk about with me.

His words came true shortly after the sentence was passed by the court. Within a few weeks I was called to see Senior Lieut. Halsky and, during the interview, he admitted, without any reservations, that the sentence was passed on the basis of false evidence and that it was without foundations, but—and here I quote his words—"with your views and your convictions we cannot set you free". I should give proofs of my loyalty in the form of a press conference, an article, a pamphlet, or a broadcast in which I would condemn the OUN, my father, etc. "If we were sure that you would talk with us on this sort of subject, we would not have had to resort to such methods as arrest and court trial", Halsky said in conclusion.

It became clear to me that my trial was inspired by the KGB with the intention of blackmail in order to force me to come out with the required public statement, and that it had nothing in common with justice. For an act of this kind I was promised review of the court sentence and release from prison. When however, I refused I was sent to the political concentration camps in Mordovia.

I explained all this in writing to Col. Kalash, and this made further talks on similar themes impossible.

But even afterwards the KGB did not leave me in peace, because already a year later, in July 1965, I was called in the concentration camp to see the local representative of the KGB, Capt. Krut', who declared that I should write a petition for pardon to the Presidium of the Supreme Soviet of the Ukrainian SSR. I refused to write such a thing and agreed to write only a short statement in which I explained that I had been innocently sentenced, and that all my appeals to the judicial and prosecuting organs had been without any results, and therefore I was writing to the Presidium of the Supreme Soviet. The KGB, however, was not satisfied with it and in a categorical form Capt. Krut' demanded from me a petition for pardon, which I refused to write. He then declared that the administration would submit such a petition itself.

As became clear later, no such petition was ever sent, and my statement was not answered. From this I understood that it has not even been sent to the Presidium. And all this comedy was staged only in order that such a petition be attached to my file. For in this way the KGB would have shifted responsibility from itself, because a petition for pardon is tantamount to an admission of guilt. But my "case" was too obviously sown with white threads, as was confirmed by Capt. Lytvyn, who said that the guilt of the Lviv KGB consisted in that it had been unable to prepare the case adequately.

Consequently, they are not troubled by the obvious injustice done, by the violation of legality, but by the incapability to fabricate skillfully the necessary evidence. Therefore this incapability had to be camouflaged by my petition for pardon which then would have wiped out all the traces of the flagrant abuse of the law, the traces of the crime.

Out of my 34 years of life I have spent 19 years in prison. For the first 10 years I was imprisoned on the basis of the decision of the Special Council at the Ministry of State Security of the USSR. And although the 20th Congress of the Communist Party of the Soviet Union declared the Special Council at the MGB an illegal organ, its decisions have not been declared null and void, and therefore many people, myself included, continued to suffer imprisonment, and some still do so. I received the next 10 year sentence on the direct instructions of the KGB on the basis of the evidence fabricated by it. They continue to persecute my mother, Natalia Shukhevich-Berezyns'ka. And all this happens under the resounding declarations about justice, legality, and so on.

No, I have long ago ceased to believe in the declared justice and legality, which I have never seen embodied in practice.

Therefore I turn to you now, when only one year is left before the second term of my imprisonment runs out, not because I have any illusions on your account, not because I hope that you are able to intervene and to vindicate the justice trampled under foot. No!

I turn to you because it may happen that in a few months' time a new crime will be perpetrated against me; they will again fabricate a new case to get me sentenced for the third time.

And, if not, there is no one to warrant that in a few months' time I shall not be killed from behind a street corner by hired assassins as was done with many a political prisoner after their release. I should like to mention just the cases of Lytvyn, Vartsabuik, Bergs, Melnikans and others. Or I shall die a mysterious death.

Or it may happen that a mass crime will be repeated on political prisoners in Mordovia (and everything is ready for that)—that they all will be physically destroyed, and later the executors of that crime will be annihilated.

This was the reason that prompted me to address myself to you, so that you should know these things, and that later, in the future, you would not be able to say that you had not been properly informed, that all this was done without your knowledge, and that you bear no responsibility for similar actions by the KGB.

MORDOVIA—OZERNYI

A LETTER FROM VIACHESLAV CHORNOVIL

["Revolutionary Voices," OSB Publishing House, Munich]

To the Prosecutor; Chairman of the People's Court, Chairman of the State Security Committee at the Council of Ministers of the Ukrainian Soviet Socialist Republic (Ukr.SSR).

I ask nothing from you. Numerous questions, applications, complaints and petitions were shattered against the cold wall of your indifference. With a sullen silence you answered the Lenin Prize Laureate M. Stelmakh, the Shevchenko Prize Laureate A. Malyshko, the world famous aircraft designer O. Antonov, the film director S. Paradzhanov, the composers P. Mayboroda and V. Koreyko, the writers L. Serpilin, L. Kostenko and I. Drach. They did not ask much, just publicity, an open trial of those arrested in Kyiv, Lviv, Ivano-Frankivsk, Ternopil. You were approached with a petition by a large group—over 70 persons—of writers, scientists, students and workers. They also did not want much: to be present at the court trial of their friends, comrades, acquaintances and relations. It was they whom the militiamen later pushed out even from the corridor of the building where, quietly and some distance from the view of human beings, they made short work of the student of the Kyiv Medical Institute, Yaroslav Hevrych. There were many of them surrounded by the militiamen and soldiers in the Lviv Oblast Court and so held, while the court secretly pronounced the verdict on the Horyns. For many a long month the mothers, wives and children longed at least to see their sons, husbands and fathers who were languishing behind the bars. [See photograph, p. 281.]

An orgy of searches and interrogations even now makes the Ukrainian intelligentsia feel sick and prevents many of them from the possibility of continuing their creative activity in peace. You are indifferent to human dramas, to a demoralising influence of fear which, like a repulsive snake, creeps into the midst of many of the Ukrainian families. For you, allegedly, there exists only the law. Let us look, then, at what has now been happening in Ukraine from the point of view of socialist legality. We now have enough material for conclusions. I am not sending my notes because I hope to alleviate the fate of those arrested and condemned. You have already made the people lose the habit of such naive hopes. But not to make known one's attitude to what has been happening would mean becoming a silent accomplice in an act of arbitrariness over socialist legality.

A SLIDE BACK TO TERROR OR JUSTICE?

The Soviet court should not relapse into terror. Its duty is to punish justly for crimes and to re-educate. About the humaneness of the Soviet court a law faculty student learns in his first year. About this the laws say the following: "While applying measures of criminal punishment, the court does not merely punish the criminals, but also has as its aim their guidance and re-education". ("The Law on the Judicial System of the Ukrainian SSR", p. 3).

In recent years there has been a stress made on the widest participation of the public in the re-education of people who infringe on the laws (community courts, probation, people's prosecutors and advocates at a court investigation, etc.). Article 20 of the Criminal Procedural Code of the Ukrainian SSR does not only guarantee the open character of the court investigation (with some insignificant, clearly defined exceptions), but also stresses the necessity, in order to raise the educational role of court trials, to "widely practice the holding of court trials directly at undertakings, building sites, on state and collective farms with the participation in indispensable cases of prosecutors and people's defenders".

The law guarantees all-round, full and objective investigation of the circumstances of cases, envisages punishment of investigators, judges and other persons who try to ensure the conviction of an accused person or a witness by resorting to violence, threats and intimidation. The law clearly defines the norms of legal procedure which safeguard the right of the suspect or accused, guarantee respect of his dignity and give him the possibility of proving his innocence.

245

Finally, and this is particularly important, the law binds the investigating bodies, the office of the prosecutor and the court, "to bring to light the conditions which were conducive to committing the crime, and to take measures through the appropriate bodies to eliminate them . . . making extensive use of the help from the community for the uncovering and elimination of causes and circumstances which are conducive to the commitment of crimes . . ." (Art. 23 of the Criminal Procedural Code of the Ukr.SSR).

Let us say that having noted that the interest in the Ukrainian publications from abroad and in anonymous handwritten literature is connected with acute dissatisfaction with the present-day violations of the Leninist nationalities' policy, and with petty and important discrimination measures regarding the national language, culture, etc.—Themis' servants should of necessity bring to the notice of party and state bodies the problem of that ground which nourishes such feelings and leads to action which the criminal code defines as criminal.

I am basing my notes on the infringement of the elementary requirements of justice on the material, most of which I enclose (in copy from):

1. Enquiry from M. Stelmakh, A. Malyshko and H. Mayboroda to the Central Committee of the Communist Party in Ukraine about arrests;

2. Petitions for public and open court trial procedure sent to the CC of the Communist Party in Ukraine by a group of intellectuals;

3. Petition to the Prosecutor of the Ukr.SSR and Chairman of the KGB (State Security Committee) at the Council of Ministers of the Ukr.SSR on the admission to the trials (78 signatures);

4. Petition from a group of artists to the Supreme Court of the Ukr.SSR in connection with a verdict passed on the teacher Ozernyi;

5. Petition from the writers in Lviv to the Regional Court for parole for V.;

6. Two complaints to the Ukr.SSR Prosecutor from the artist A. Horska at the violation of the norms of legal procedure during the preliminary investigation and trial;

7. Statement from V. Chornovil to the CC of the Communist Party in Ukraine about the spreading of provocative rumours;

8. Warrant on a search of V. Chornovil's dwelling, a record of the search, two complaints to the KGB and one to the court at the unlawful removal of old publications;

9. Letter to the First Secretary of the CC of the Communist Party of Ukraine from the literary worker of the newspaper *Radyanska Ukraina*, P. Skochko, and transcript taken by him of the court proceedings against the teacher Ozernyi in Ivano-Frankivsk;

10. Verdict in the case of the Kyiv University student Ya. Hevrych, taken down in the court;

11. Notes on the first day of the trial of M. Masiutko, taken down outside the court's door;

12. Svitlychna's statement of refusal of services of an advocate;

13. Svitlychna's telegram to the Presidium of the 23rd CPSU Congress;

14. Karavanskyi's case materials: S. Karavanskyi's petition to the Ukr. SSR Prosecutor and the article "About One Political Mistake", the article "Three-faced" (the newspaper *Chornomorska Komuna*, 21. 9. 1965), a copy of a certificate of release from imprisonment (19. 12. 1960), S. Karavanskyi's petition to deputy M. Stelmakh against the illegal 25-year sentence and re-imprisonment without an investigation, Karavanskyi's wife's petition to M. Stelmakh, S. Karavanskyi's appeal to bring to answer the author of the article entitled "Three-faced";

15. Personal impressions from questionings, confrontation with M. Osadchyi, trials of Hevrych, Martyniuk, Rusyn, Kuznetsova, the Horyn brothers, Osadchyi and Zvarychevska;

16. Separate oral reports by eye-witnesses and witnesses (as an exception).

Contradictions between the USSR Constitution and Article 62 of the Ukr.SSR Criminal Code

What the Art. 62 of the Ukr.SSR Criminal Code does not provide punishment for:

"In accordance with the working people's interests and with the aim of strengthening the socialist order of the USSR, the law guarantees: a) freedom of speech; b) freedom of the press; c) freedom of assembly and meetings; d) freedom of processions and demonstrations" (The USSR Constitution, Article 125).

"Agitation or propaganda aiming at subverting or weakening the Soviet authority or the perpetration of defined especially dangerous crimes against the State, the spreading of slanderous inventions for this purpose, discrediting the Soviet State and

social system, and also dissemination or preparation or keeping with this same aim literature of similar content is punishable by loss of freedom for a term from 6 months to 7 years with deportation for a term of five years or without such, or by deportation for a period from two to five years . . . (Art. 62, No. 1, Criminal Code of the Ukr.SSR, chapter entitled "Particularly Dangerous Crimes against the State").

"The Court, prosecutor, interrogator and investigating bodies are duty bound within the limits of their competences to initiate a case in all cases of uncovering of signs of a crime" (Art. 4 of the Criminal Procedural Code of the Ukr.SSR).

"The law is like a pole, it sticks out no matter how you turn it" (a Ukrainian folk saying). The artist of great talent P. Zalyvakha, the art critic B. Horyn, the Lutsk Teachers' Institute lecturers Moroz and Ivashchenko, teacher Ozernyi from Ivano-Frankivsk region, the Kyiv Medical Institute student Ya. Hevrych, the Kyiv scientists Rusyn and Martynenko, the Kyiv University laboratory assistant Kuznetsova, the pensioner from Feodosiya Masiutko and others were tried and convicted according to Art. 62 of the Ukr.SSR Criminal Code.

However, the Art. 62, very "popular" at present, is unconstitutional. The Supreme Soviet should either annul it, or make it more definite.

In the present version this article completely strikes out those forms of freedom which the USSR Constitution guarantees to the citizens. When somebody criticises today's nationality policy for its deviation from the Leninist norms, then he is fully entitled to it under the Constitution (even if he is mistaken). But according to the Ukr.SSR Criminal Code, this person may be sent to a strict regime camp by interpreting the criticism as "propaganda aiming at subverting or weakening the Soviet authority" (although the point at issue was only the moral soundness of this authority).

Had anybody in the day of Stalin's rule thought of criticising the cult of his person and in Khrushchev's day his itch for reorganisation, could not this have been interpreted (and it was!) as "spreading slanderous inventions denigrating the Soviet State and social system"? It seems that every argument which does not conform with the directives could be described as such "slanderous inventions".

These thoughts have been supported by practice over the past few months. The judges stretch the elastic article of the code like a concertina. Everybody interprets the term "anti-Soviet" as he likes. (In Ivano-Frankivsk old-time aphorisms, the word "campfire" and Shevchenko's poems have become anti-Soviet.) Yaroslav Hevrych has been condemned to five years of strict regime imprisonment for several photographic copies of books. From the teacher Ozernyi they confiscate and name at the trial "History of Ukraine" by Arkas, passed by Tsarist censorship, the periodical Zhinocha Dolya (Woman's Fate) and the non-political book "The Ukrainian Bohemia" by the modernist Pachovskyi (these books are available at libraries). On the other hand, they release the engineer Sadovskyi and teacher Ivanyshyn "on parole" and tell their colleagues that this man or that woman "distributed slanderous materials" (i.e. they did the same as Hevrych). They condemn M. Horyn to six years, P. Zalyvakha to five years in strict regime camps, and release Svitlychnyi and Kosiv without a trial, although all were accused of the same offense. Where is the logic, then?

The law must be formulated clearly and, according to Art. 4 of the Ukr.SSR Criminal Procedural Code, not a crime must be left unpunished. But if the present-day trials are held not to frighten the public, but with sincere desire to adhere to the letter and the spirit of the law, then, having said "a", it is necessary to say also "b". It is necessary immediately to imprison also those who gave the book to Hevrych, Martyniuk or to Ozernyi. After 6 or 7 months in the care of KGB they would tell in their turn where they got the book and would get the deserved "legal" 5 or 6 years of hard regime and so forth. This would lead to the inconsiderate scholar who showed these special stock notes to somebody, or to a poor chap who out of idle curiosity took some book from a tourist or a relation who came from abroad. It is also necessary to deal with anecdotes. For many of them are purest "slanderous fabrications" which "discredit the State and social order". The bringing to trial for anecdotes so popular among townsfolk would help radically to solve the housing shortage in big towns.

Article 62 of the Ukr.SSR Criminal Code, if applied honestly, enables the population of camps to be expanded to, or even to surpass Stalinist limits. The great possibilities of this article which can be applied without exception to anyone who repeats after Mayakovskyi's hero: "We, comrades, need not think if the leaders think"—is also illustrated by this fact:

Refusal to Give Evidence in Court

... After I refused, on 16th April, to give evidence at a closed trial in Lviv, it was announced to me that I was being brought to trial in accordance with Art. 172 of the Ukr.SSR Criminal Code (refusing to testify). The decision was in itself unlawful, for I refused to give evidence only at a secret trial. But even this decision was not enough for the enraged prosecutor Antonenko and judge Rudyk. They annulled their own decision and on 19th April decided to make me answer in accordance with Art. 62 of the Ukr.SSR Criminal Code. These dispensers of justice were not in the least perturbed at the lack of factual support as to my "anti-Soviet" activity (with the exception of petty statements by Osadchyi not supported by witnesses or myself), they knew very well what Art. 62 was ... True, the Ukr.SSR Supreme Court annulled this illegal decision on 17th May. Perhaps for the mere reason that a signal was not given yet from "above" to imprison another group of "anti-Soviet agitators and propagandists" ...

Even Stalin Was Not Afraid of Anti-Soviet Literature

V. I. Lenin was not an all-forgiving humanist. But even in that tense period when there were the exploiting classes in the country and when enemies pressed from all sides, Lenin was able to agree in 1920 to the abolition of the death penalty. In his day Chekists (ChK men) tracked down those who with arms in their hands came out against the Soviet rule or prepared themselves for an armed sally, but they did not hunt convictions. Lenin did not order imprisonment of a certain Sukhanov for an anti-Marxist book, but entered into a polemic with the author. Even Stalin, when he still did not dare to break the Leninist norms of social life, was not afraid of anti-Soviet literature.

In 1928 the Leningrad workers' publishing house "Priboy" published a large edition of a book by a White emigrant, V. Shulgin "The Year 1919" which over-spilled with gall as regards the revolution, and expressed the hope of degeneration of the Soviet system. The book was reprinted from a foreign edition complete and unabridged. A short preface stated that Shulgin "is an extreme rightwing nationalist and monarchist", "brazen Jew hater", that he propagated "zoological policy of nationalism" (and we shall add that he was not only an instigator of pogroms of Jews, but also an inveterate enemy of the Ukrainians). It was said that the book would be useful to the reader at large, for it would help him to see the enemy at a short distance and to struggle against chauvinism.

From then on the floor was taken by Shulgin himself, and there were no warnings and no explanations:

"As a rule, chrezvychayka (extraordinary commission; ChK—translator) must kill somebody. For the authority which exists on blood only it is dangerous not to have people who commit murders constantly; otherwise they might lose the habit . . ." (p. 95)

"This is the headquarters, i.e. the place where they work out methods of how to force the 150 million people to labour without rest in order that 150 thousand layabouts who call themselves "proletariat" could do nothing. This system, as it is known, is called "the dictatorship of the proletariat." (p. 107)

"The Bolsheviks' love of parades is no less than in the era of Paul I." (p. 107)

"It has been said that chrezvychayka received from Moscow 400 absolutely trustworthy and splendidly trained people. Whether or not is was true. I do not know, but their external appearance indeed affected the imagination, if it did not terrify it . . . These people had a well fed and satisfied appearance. Of course, chrezvychaykas petted and nursed these trustworthy dogs . . ." (pp. 118–119)

"When a small handful of people of Kornilov, Alekseyev and Denikin thrashed their hordes it did so only because it was organised on a correct basis—without any "committees" and "conscientious discipline", i.e. it was organised "in the manner of the Whites",—then they understood . . . and they re-established the army . . . Of course, they think they have created the Socialist army which has been fighting "in the name of the International"—but it is nonsense . . . In actual fact they have re-established the Russian army . . ." (p. 108)

"Our main and our real slogan is United Russia . . . When Denikin went we did not actually lose him, but hid him somewhere for a time . . . We have rolled up the banner . . . And who raised it, who unfurled the banner? Strange as it may seem, this is really so . . . The banner of united Russia was in fact raised by the Bolsheviks. Of course, they do not say this . . . Of course. Lenin and Trotsky continue to trumpet the International. Allegedly, it was the Communist army that fought for the planting of the "Soviet republics". But this is only outwardly so . . ." (p. 108)

"Socialism-will disappear, but the frontiers will remain . . . In any case, one can see that the Russian language for the glory of the International has occupied one sixth of dry land . . . And it has become apparent that no matter who sits in Moscow, be it Ulyanov or Romanov (forgive this vulgar contrasting), he is compelled, he "must," as khakhly (derogatory term for the Ukrainians—trans.) say, do the work of Ivan Kalita". (p. 198)

"The Reds think they have been fighting for the glory of the International . . . In fact, without knowing it, they shed their blood in order to re-establish the God-protected Russian State only . . . With their red armies "formed whitewise" they move in all directions until they reach the hard limits, where there begins strong resistance by other State bodies . . . those will be the real frontiers of the future Russia. The International will disappear, but the frontiers will remain . . ." (p. 207)

When I wrote down quotations from this book, I put "Leningrad, 1926" after each quotation. I was afraid of the appearance of comrades from the KGB for yet another search and of being accused, after tearing out the quotations—in accordance with Article 62 of the Criminal Code of the Ukr.SSR—of malicious slander of the Soviet regime, of Lenin, and even of the great power chauvinism. The fear was not completely groundless. Somewhere in Kyiv Oblast KGB my exercise book is kept safe with various quotations from the works of writers and with the bibliography of Ukrainiana published abroad. There is not a single sentence of my own authorship. Making marginal notes, I did not know when and in what context I would use those materials (if at all), but in the KGB they know well that all that was for the "anti-Soviet propaganda and agitation", for "subversion", "weakening" and "spreading of slanderous fabrications". Otherwise, they would not have kept the exercise book half a year together with 35 books of old issue, among which is even a set of a Ukrainian journal of 1900.

In 1926 Stalin was not afraid that all who read Shulgin's book would become inveterate monarchists and would bring down the Soviet authority. Ten years later he was already suspicious of treason and shot his closest comrades-at-arms, and 20 years later this was called the personality cult. Decades have passed by since, and suddenly in the speeches of some of the leaders the old notes have sounded.

What Did the KGB Deputy Tell Scientists From the Ukr.SSR Academy of Sciences?

Wittily the Deputy Head of the State Security Committee (KGB) at the Ukr. SSR Council of Ministers, comrade Shulzhenko, told scientists from the Ukr.SSR Academy of Sciences about the foreign intelligence services—until he came to the "ideological subversions". According to his arguments, all oppositional feelings and activities inside our country are exclusively the result of the bourgeois propaganda and intelligence service influence. Thus, should the bourgeois world suddenly cease to exist at the wave of a magic wand, everything would be lovely in the garden. In the country all would delight in the fate of the passportless serf, bound for life to his collective farm. In the towns the Ukrainians would be proud of the fact that they had become renegades without their kin or nation. Nobody would be ashamed for democracy, dropping into a ballot box unread papers with the name determined at the oblast or rayon level Party committee. The noted literary critic I. Svitlychnyi would not spend eight months in prison, the art critic B. Horyn and the artist Zalyvakha would not find themselves behind barbed wire but would with impunity have called the Russification an act of internationalism and would placidly have rejoiced at the success of such "internationalism".

The Deputy Head of the KGB made one more discovery for the Kyiv scientists. It seems that it would suffice for a person with a still unstable world outlook to read a book with a "subtext" which in a veiled manner criticises our system, as in this person there emerge anti-Soviet feelings. Hence it is not far to the conclusion: fence people off from the undesirable book by all means, even with the help of prison and severe regime camps. But where is then the Marxist thesis that social existence (not hostile books) determines consciousness?

For ten years I was educated in a Soviet school. In the concluding sentence of a school essay I tried unfailingly to mention the Party and Stalin, even if it happened that I was writing about the "Song of Prince Igor". For five years I studied assiduously Marxism-Leninism at the university. All other disciplines were based unshakably on the Marxist principles. Finally I passed an examination for the degree of candidate of Marxist-Leninist philosophy. And suddenly by accident there fell into my hands some Ukrainian book, published abroad, and, hey presto,

249

I have become bourgeois nationalist (without the bourgeoisie!). Later I read a Peking brochure about the "opportunism of the CPSU" and changed into a Maoist. Later still I listened to the speech by the Pope of Rome on the radio (as a matter of fact, it figured in the accusation of the teacher Ozernyi), and became a Jesuit.

Is it not for the purpose of isolating the Soviet citizens from such kaleidoscopic changes of world outlook that Art. 62 of the Ukr.SSR Criminal Code was thought out? Marxism-Leninism, without doubt, is stronger than bourgeois ideologies. Meanwhile here they put people on trial for reading a book published in the West, while our books and newspapers full of sharp criticism of capitalism, bourgeois nationalism and the current policy of the capitalist countries, can be easily acquired (even by post) in the USA, Canada and in a number of other foreign countries. There is published in Kyiv specially for the Ukrainian emigrants the newspaper *Visti z Ukrainy* which it is impossible to read here, in Ukraine, because it contains a specialised truth, just for export. Could it be that non-Marxists learned better than our leaders the Marxist-Leninist thesis that revolutions and social and economic tranformations are not for export, that an idea will take root on a new ground only when the social, economic and political conditions are ripe for this purpose, that to forbid spreading of ideas means contributing to their strength and attractiveness. For the latter reason, of course, the inspirers and executors of these arrests and trials which have been rolling across Ukraine in a sinister wave should be also liable for punishment according to Art. 62 of the Ukr.SSR Criminal Code.

What does Art. 62 of the Ukr.SSR Criminal Code teach the citizens? It teaches them blindly and accurately to follow in the footsteps of the latest newspaper norms; it teaches them the bureaucratic morals of philistinism—to fear and to look over their shoulders.

How Are "The Particularly Dangerous Anti-State Criminals Unmasked?"
"The sanctity of citizens' homes and secrecy of correspondence are protected by law". (USSR Constitution, Art. 128)
"Unlawful search, unlawful eviction or other acts that violate the sanctity of citizens' homes committed by official persons are punishable by imprisonment . . ." (Art. 130 of the Ukr.SSR Criminal Code)
"Violation of the secrecy of correspondence by official persons is punishable by corrective labour . . ." (Art. 131 of the Ukr.SSR Criminal Code)
The Party considers that the moral code of a builder of Communism includes these moral precepts:
". . . humane relations and mutual respect among people; one human being is to another human being a friend, comrade and brother . . ." (CPSU Programme)
"In an age when the whistling of rockets have awaked Mars' inhabitants, who could have thought that in the town shadows were following someone"... (M. Kholodnyi)
It is easier to work for the KGB men than for the militia men. A hooligan or a murderer takes to a hiding place, but a "particularly dangerous anti-state criminal" takes the rostrum at a jubilee soiree (for example, devoted to Shevchenko) and speaks. Afterwards he goes down the street, accompanied by his friends, quietly, without looking back over his shoulder. A "secsot" (secret agent) may walk almost alongside and listen to everything. If at a KGB signal "the particularly dangerous man" is sacked at work, he does not complain, for he knows that the KGB embodies the supreme, final justice. If he does not weep or repent and continues "dangerous talk", he must be dealt with in a more serious manner. The most modern technology comes *to our aid*. It is not difficult to make an agreement with the post office, telegraph and telephone exchange. Ask the employees of the post office and telephone operators and someone will tell you in secrecy how correspondence is censored and conversation checked. They even have a name "*podslushka*" (listening in—this is the name for a floor, most probably in Khreshchatyk Street, where they put to use Art. 128 of the USSR Constitution). If an "especially dangerous person" lives on a higher floor (and this is very often the case), then he suddenly notices that the loft, open until now, is tightly closed and he is not permitted to enter it for his own possessions which are stored there. Or else, he is given another flat and, at night behind the wall where nobody lives, he hears a sort of noise. Or he discovers under the bed in a students' boarding house strange metal "antennae" with concealed leads through a window and down (something like this was found under the window of the student of the Kyiv Medical Institute, M. Plakhotniuk).

Thus a new inmate has appeared in your flat. He hears everything: with whom and about what you talk, what you whisper into your wife's ear . . . If you are conscious of this "unregistered lodger" then your life becomes a hell. You weigh every word, you become uncommunicative and nervous. You become used to speaking in whispers and look around, and give the fico to a person who tries impudently to photograph you and your friends . . . Occasionally you make a mistake and offend an honest person, having taken him for a secret agent (secsot). In the meantime a dossier started on you grows thicker . . . Would you say that this is fabrication, that there is some purpose for Art. 128 of the USSR Constitution and the relevant articles of the Criminal Code? That, ultimately, the, degrading, spying, listening in and peeping through the keyholes of Soviet citizens whose crime consists perhaps in that they try to think differently, should be alien to the spirit of our system?

The Affair Concerning the Writer Kontsevych and the Horyn Brothers

In the summer of 1965, some two or three months before the arrests were made, friends from Kyiv came to the writer Yevhen Kontsevych. They came to Zhytomyr, not to commit "particularly dangerous crimes", but to congratulate a friend bed-ridden with paralysis on the occasion of his birthday. Following them there gate-crashed the uninvited local "poet" Oksentiy Melnychuk, barely familiar to Kontsevych. Incidentally, Zhytomyr KGB men had not even informed their envoy that it was Kontsevych's birthday. Therefore the newly emerged Sherlock Holmes had to talk nonsense; he came to ask after your health (this at eleven o'clock at night, in the rain, to a suburb?), and brought a little album of exotic pictures . . . Later, when Yevhen had looked through them all he would take the little album back . . .

After this he sat at the table, chewed and swallowed jokes about his second occupation, and strained his ears.

The next day, late in the evening, the hosts remembered the "gift" from Melnychuk. Inside the cover of the album they found a minute transistor device, either a magnetic tape recorder, or a radio transmitter. They were stunned . . . they did not expect such a present. Melnychuk came for the small album in the morning. Having been told all he deserved and given a push in the right place, he went to his chiefs at the double. A little while later a group of KGB men, led by a Colonel, arrived by a motor vehicle. They started to apologize and beg weepingly for the birthday present. Kontsevych took pity on them and gave it back. But unwisely, for he would have had something with which to illustrate his talk to scholars at the Ukrainian Academy of Sciences.

How is one to explain the Zhytomyr incident? What did the KGB men wish to hear at a birthday party table, where there were gathered some people, some even unacquainted one with the other? How is one to reconcile with the lofty principles of the moral code of a builder of Communism the detestable fact of planting of devices and eavesdropping at a very sick man's bed? Of the man who writes brilliant and courageous stories, who has given no reason for suspicion for any criminal activities, and whom the press has compared to Korchagin?

Of course, the secret agents (secsots) do not operate everywhere in such a crude way as in Zhytomyr. Melnychuk should have taken a course of lectures from the Lviv based sleuth, Yaroslav Korotnytskyi, (also a "poet"). Having appeared in Feodosiya, where the Horyns were on holiday, he quite accidentally met his fellow countrymen on a beach and, inter alia, told them the sad story of his life. It seems that he had suffered in Stalin's camps, and there wrote verses about Ukraine. He apparently felt lonesome, the poor man, for he hardly heard a word in his mother tongue. Later, visting his fellow countrymen with a bottle of good wine, he initiated conversation about the unfortunate Ukraine. . . When the Horyns were departing, it was, of course, Korotnytskyi who saw them off at the station. When it happened that the ticket office ran out of tickets, he somehow secretly moved by entreaties the stern looking train conductress to accept another two passengers. He had convinced her, so that at Dzhankoy Station she ran herself to get tickets. And at last but one station before Lviv the Horyn brothers were arrested. Even before this happened the "poet" took a plane to Lviv to continue his provocations. . .

One could quote such facts again and again. The metamorphoses in the loft of the Lviv based scientest, Mykhailo Horyn, about which he used to talk with bitter irony before his arrest. . . Something similar in the home of the critic Ivan Svitlychnyi. . . The same "ghosts" which appear at a literary soiree, or "play" under the windows of Ivan Franko's son or grand-children, or follow in the street one of the young poets or critics . . . and give a reason to a poet to joke sadly: "And I rejoice, having wiped off perspiration with my hand, white as a sheet . . . In my life, this "ghost" is the first whom I have fled."

PRELIMINARY INVESTIGATION OR PROOF OF A "CRIME"

(a) Search and arrest.

"When issuing an arrest warrant the public prosecutor is duty bound to get acquainted with the material of the case himself, and if necessary to question the accused (suspect) on the matter of the submitted charge and on the circumstances connected with the application of the preventive measure". (*Art. 157, Ukr.SSR Criminal Procedural Code*)

"Of the arrest of a suspect or accused and of his whereabouts the investigator must inform his wife or other next of kin, and also inform his employer". (*Art. 181, Ukr. SSR Criminal Procedural Code*)

"During a search or confiscation only articles and documents which are relevant to the case *may be removed . . ." (Art. 186, Ukr. SSR Criminal Procedural Code*)

"The acts and decisions of the investigating bodies may be made subject to an appeal to the prosecutor who is duty bound to examine the appeal within three days. The prosecutor's decision on the appeal is communicated to the plaintiff." (*Art. 110, Ukr.SSR Criminal Procedural Code*)

One raven will not take another raven's eye out (a Ukrainian proverb). Finally, the dossier is completed. The person in question speaks about the Russification, criticises those in authority, defends human dignity and the human being's right to independent thinking. There is no doubt, this is a "particularly dangerous anti-State criminal". He must be given such a lesson that others should lose the itch. But for the sake of form, give the appearance of legality, get a prosecutor's warrant for search and arrest. Secret agents (secsots) observe closely when some Ukrainian book or manuscript article on the situation in Ukraine produced abroad would fall into the hands of the "particularly dangerous" person. In accordance with the thoroughly unconstitutional Art. 62 of the Ukr.SSR Criminal Code, this is very "material evidence".

Then there appear in the flat defenders of the state security and carry out a search. Like a prisoner-of-war, with your hands up, you wait while your "friend, comrade and brother" goes through your pockets. Sometimes, in order to frighten your wife or neighbours completely, he would propose to you also to surrender your weapon (KGB demanded a weapon from the Kyiv electrician, Peredenko, whom they found in bed.) Then they will show an order. This states that the search is being made "in order to expose and remove the documents of any anti-Soviet content circulated by him" (see enclosures Nos . . . and . . .) [Transl. note: the quotation from the order is in Russian]. But, when after 7 or 9 hours, having taken the owner with them, the custodians of security lock the flat, they take with them complete stacks of old books (some which were "circulated" 70 years ago in the days of the Emperor Franz Joseph), letters, diaries, notes for a scientific paper.

Do not think of writing a protest, refer to the Art. 186 and bring in arguments that letters to your beloved one you wrote not for the purposes of anti-Soviet propaganda, that some authors of anti-Soviet books removed from you died before the revolution. You won't get an answer either from the investigator, or the public prosecutor. The same will happen later, when you complain about the falsification of the record of the investigation, about threats, etc. (although the Ukr.SSR Criminal Procedural Code contains Articles 110, 129, 189, 234 and 236 which institute defined terms for replies to complaints and petitions). Sometimes KGB men just forget the boring formalities. In this way they removed from Masiutko's brother, a Lviv artist, without any warrant for a search and removal, three books deadly dangerous for the Soviet system: a collection of verses by Bohdan Lepkyi, a first form reading book of an old issue, and a torn "geography" text book (in Russian). If during a search the custodians of security's eye caught sight of a book or photographic copy of a so-called "anti-Soviet" book, published abroad, the prison doors are closed behind you for many months. A preliminary investigation then begins.

The scheme outlined above is not a dogma. Sometimes they make arrests on a train, on the way back from a vacation (student Hevrych), or on a holiday (critic Svitlychnyi, the Horyn brothers and teacher Ozernyi). At the same time at your flat they turn everything upside-down, take away "Notes of the Shevchenko Scientific Society", "Geography of Ukraine", the book "Kobza and Kobza Players" (kobza is a lutelike string instrument), and other "anti-Soviet" literature (search of Svitlychnyi), but say not a word to the wife about the arrest of the husband. They do not say this on the next and the third day either. Only later, having taken pity, they reply finally that the husband did not fall under a train, was not drowned in the sea, but is completing his holiday in the gaol of the Kyiv KGB. There was even less fuss with Ya. Hevrych's father. For two weeks he imporuned the militia, and then the KGB in Kosiv, Ivano-Frankivsk and Kyiv before he discovered the fate of his son. The prosecutors, it seems were not very considerate when they issued a warrant for a search and the arrest. They had no need "personally to examine the case documents", and to question the suspect "on the merits of the submitted charge" (see Art. 157 of the Ukr.SSR Criminal Procedural Code). Otherwise the watchful prosecutor's eye would have immediately noticed the falsity of the charge. The arrests, undoubtedly, were carried out on a centralised instruction "from above". This is borne out convincingly by the fact that a large group of people, the majority of whom were not acquainted among themselves and were not even connected, were arrested simultaneously in various regions of Ukraine. (They have now been tried separately or in groups of 2 or 3 persons).

(b) The questioning of accused and witnesses, and confrontation.

"... The court, prosecutor, investigator and the person conducting the investigation have no right to put the responsibility of substantiating the evidence on the acccused. It is forbidden to demand evidence form an accused by force, intimidation and other unlawful measures". (Art.22 of the Ukr.SSR Criminal Procedural Code)

"The questioning of the accused, except in extraordinary case, should take place during the day". (Art. 143, Ukr.SSR Criminal Procedural Code)

"The accused, in the event of his request, is accorded the possibility of writing down his evidence by himself ... " (Art. 146, Ukr.SSR Criminal Procedural Code)

The same applies to witnesses (Art. 170, Ukr.SSR Criminal Procedural Code):

"At the request from the next of kin and near ones of the arrested the investigator or the prosecutor can permit them a visit to the arrested... " (Art. 162, Ukr.SSR Criminal Procedural Code)

The publication of evidence given by the participants in a confrontation during the preliminary investigation is permissible only after the submission of evidence by them during the confrontation and their inclusion in the record . . . Those questioned have the right to demand supplements and corrections to be entered in the record. These supplements or corrections must without fail be entered in the record". (Art. 178, Ukr.SSR Criminal Procedural Code)

"To force to give evidence during the questioning by way of unlawful acts on the part of the person who conducts an investigation or preliminary investigation is punishable by imprisonment for a term of up to three years. The same act linked with the use of force or with cruel treatment of the person under questioning is punishable by imprisonment for a term of from 2 to 8 years. (Art. 175, Ukr.SSR Criminal Code)

"Why do you look for guilt in me, a common man, and when you find it not, then you are angry with me?" (S. Zalygin). It is not necessary to jam somebody's fingers in the door, to drive needles under the finger nails, to hit in the face in order to force a man to look on his acts as on a terrible crime, and even to admit that which is needed by the investigator for the completion of a preconceived scheme. It suffices merely to lock a person for several months in a stone bag with bars, excrement bin and other attributes of prison life, to forbid visits from any relatives for six months, to hammer into his head day after day and several hours daily a feeling of tremendous guilt, and finally to reduce the man to such a state that he cannot immediately recognize his own wife. As a result of moral terror, threats and promises (which are conveniently forgotten at the trial), the necessary evidence is squeezed out of a person. During a confrontation with Y. Hevrych at the begining of last December the witness Horska asked: "Say, Yaroslav, what made you lie against me?"—and heard the characteristic answer: "Here they can teach one during one hundred and five days to tell lies". Understandably, they did not enter this phrase in the record of the confrontation in spite of Horska's request.

Here is the dialogue between the judge and the teacher Ozernyi at the trial . . .

"You told the witness that you had read it [concerns a manuscript article on the occasion of the setting on fire of the library of the Ukrainian SSR Academy of Sciences at Kyiv,—V. Ch.]. During the investigation you said that you took the article out of a briefcase and handed it to the witness. Did you hand it over or did you mention it? Which statement is correct?"

"This made here in the court".

"Why then didn't you say this during the investigation?"

"During the questioning I was so tired that sometimes I also signed things with which I was not in agreement. I was questioned for 11 hours, later for 10 hours."

"Did they allow a break?"

"For lunch." (Eleven hours, plus 10 hours, plus lunch time and it is one day already. And what about Art. 143 of the Ukr.SSR Criminal Procedural Code?)

"Were you tired?" (A naive question . . . Had the judge been questioned without any sleep and rest, perhaps also he would admit that the trial he was conducting was anti-Soviet . . .)

"Yes. I told the investigator that I did not give Malyarchyn the documents. I got tired and signed what was written down. I was called for questioning 46 times. On that particular occasion I was questioned for 6 hours 48 minutes. The testimony I make here is correct. I told this also to the investigator. He wore me out so much that I said: 'Write down what you like'. I signed.

At the same trial witness A. Matviyenko stated that in accordance with Article 234 of the Ukr.SSR Criminal Procedural Code she was now announcing a protest against terrorist methods of questioning employed by Captain Rudyi. Then this conversation took place:

Prosecutor: "What terrorist method did Rudyi permit himself against you?"

"It was terror of moral nature. I cannot use unprintable words here . . ."

"How did he threaten you?"

"He said that he would rob me of absolutely everything I have. What is this?"

"It is enough. You spoke about the womanly pride?"

"Yes, it was abused."

"You said during the first investigation . . ."

"During the first investigation you sucked at my letters."

"Why didn't you tell the truth?"

"They frightened me . . ."

"How many times did Rudyi question you?"

"Four days. From 9 in the morning till 7 in the evening."

A. Matviyenko's protest was concealed; Captain Rudyi is questioning another victim somewhere, while candidate of philosophy A. Matviyenko, according to the court verdict, has joined the company of the unemployed intelligentsia.

We do not know by which unprintable words Capt. Rudyi insulted the candidate of philosophy A. Matviyenko, but Captains Klymenko and Rybalchenko and Colonel Sergadeyev in Lviv swooped down openly on the witness Liuba Maksymiv with foul language. Seeing that their eloquence made quite an impression on the frightened girl, they stepped up the pressure: "You, dirty scum, we shall make your and your family's life a hell here in Lviv and in Drohobych."

Do you think that Sergadeev, Klymenko and Rybalchenko were tried under the provisions of Art. 175 of the Ukr.SSR Criminal Procedural Code and sent to develop the national economy of Mordovia or some other autonomous republic? Nonsense! Colonel Sergadeyev will send many a fellow there yet; he is not the head of the investigation department of the KGB in Lviv for nothing.

The legal procedure code contains an article envisaging permission for accused to write down their own testimony themselves. Why, then, was nobody accorded the possibility of availing himself of this right? The investigators sometimes presented the evidence so craftily that everything was turned upside-down. I. Svitlychny's sister when she read the record taken during a questioning in Donetsk, refused point blank to sign "her own" testimony, because it was written in such a way. "The investigator did not always write down what I wished him to", complains Ozernyi at the trial. During a confrontation between the accused Osadchyi and witness Chornovil in Lviv, Captain Klymenko, infringing on Art. 173, told how everything "had happened", while Osadchyi repeated it after him. When Osadchyi said that after all he most probably did not take down Eisenhower's speech delivered at the unveiling of the Shevchenko's monument in Washington (a frightening anti-Soviet document) from the witness, Klymenko jumped at him: "Why did you say then earlier during the questioning that you had taken it?" Osadchyi's doubts disappeared immediately.

The witness nevertheless asked for the expression of doubt to be recorded, but received the answer that it was not his business to interfere with Osadchyi's testimony, that he should read through and sign his own testimony only.

Article 15 of the Ukr.SSR Criminal Procedural Code states that until the court's verdict is passed "nobody may be declared guilty of the crime committed". But during a visit to him by his pregnant wife the same Osadchyi spoke even about the place of his future imprisonment, the camps for political prisoners in the Mordovian ASSR. I know very well that before his arrest Lviv University lecturer M. Osadchyi knew nothing of the Mordovian camps . . . Bogdan Horyn also received similar information as to his future from his investigator and long before his trial told this to his fiancee. And the investigator Malykhin made a mistake of one year only when already in December of last year he told Olha Horyn how many years her husband would get . . .

If the fate of those imprisoned is decided in the KGB why then is there any need for that farcical comedy with trials (and closed trials at that)? Is it not easier to make up a list of "particularly dangerous" and to place against every name: for this one—seven years; for this one—five; for that one—four years . . .

Incidentally, the KGB men who "guarded" the closed court trial of Hevrych were more forthright when they told the fans expelled from the corridor: "You will all finish there" . . . While the plainclothes "guardians" of the court trial of Hevrych, pointing to a "Black Maria", informed with an air of epic calm: "We have many such vehicles. There are enough for all of you" . . .

In addition an investigator also makes use of a carrot—admit that you have committed a terrible crime, also disclose all who read the books too—and you will be pardoned for a sincere admission. The teacher Ozernyi came to his trial with such confidence. He was the more confident because of his meeting with the Chairman of the KGB at the Council of Ministers of the Ukrainian SSR, about which Ozernyi said at the trial: "On 20th November 1965 in the premises of Ivano-Frankivsk KGB I had a meeting with the Chairman of the State Security Committee, Nikitchenko. After the talk next day I learned that Nikitchenko at a KGB counsel took account of my admission". Therefore Ozernyi conducted himself with dignity at the trial, rejected groundless accusations from the prosecutor and absurd evidence from such witnesses as the illiterate teachers Melnychenko and Khatsko. He even joked with the arrested Gereta who, as a witness, was brought from Ternopil: "Is your case finished? I shall soon come to you as a guest" . . . To which the judge interjected ominously: "Do laugh, Ozernyi. It is not known who will have the last laugh". The last to laugh was the judge.

The State charge presented by the prosecutor Paraskevych and the inhumanly severe demand of a six-year imprisonment were to Ozernyi as a bolt from the blue sky. Shattered and completely lost, he repented, cried, begged and referred to "the great justice "of the Soviet court in his concluding remarks. It seems that this was exactly what was needed to be extracted from him. Logically, the punishment should have been reduced in order that all the others caught reading books should admit the guilt not five or six months after the imprisonment, but immediately, hoping for pardon. Nothing doing. And the court met the savage demand of the prosecutor. Maybe because it was already too late to depart from the instruction received earlier "from above" (where they did not take into account a possibility that Ozernyi might confess). The Supreme Court, when the farce of Ivano-Frankivsk became known to the public, did not free Ozernyi, but reduced his punishment to three years.

Even specially selected people were not admitted to all the trials that followed. And, most likely, further facts of moral terror (maybe not only moral terror? How is one to know with trials?), of perfidy and deceit were brought to light. It is not without reason that during a meeting with his brother after the trial Y. Hevrych complained bitterly about the savage KGB investigator Koval who deceived him, having first promised golden mountains for a "clean heart" admission of a "crime". The golden mountains have turned into five years in camps under severe conditions . . .

The following facts also throw some light on the methods of conducting the preliminary investigation: evidence acquired by unlawful, inhuman ways of evesdropping with the help of apparatus installed in flats were used during investigation. On this basis Mykhailo Horyn said to one of the witnesses during a confrontation: "Do not be obstinate, they know everything. My flat was bugged". The incident at Kontsevych's birthday party was already mentioned. After, all, investigators did not try very hard to conceal this. At one interrogation, when M. Kosiv could not remember a piece of conversation, they made this offer to him: "If you wish, we shall make it [a recording—translator] spin for you".

In order to cause a moral shock and extract the required confession, the interrogators do not fail to dig into the intimate life of the defendants and witnesses, although it has no connection with the case. This happened during an interrogation in Ozernyi's case. Sticky hints at some sort of allegedly existing intimate relations between the witness and the defendant filtered through even into the court room:

"So, you know Ozernyi well?"

"I met him twice. During this time I convinced myself of his honesty."

"This you did during the outing on a boat and in a restaurant?"

"This has no connection with the case."

The interrogators Rybalchenko and Rapota assured L. Horbach that she had been kissing Osadchyi under the doorways, although Horbach is barely acquainted with Osadchyi. This trick of the KGB interrogators is not a Ukrainian national achievement. As is evident from the petition to the USSR Prosecutor General from Yu. Daniel's wife, Moscow interrogators also blackmailed the witnesses in this way.

Searches

Olga Vorbut, a Kyiv University student arrested for several days at the beginning of September, was submitted to a degrading procedure of personal search and stripping. Nothing was found, for, of course, they did not expect to find anything, but they forced out a "confession" and incurably injured the person's soul. The same procedure was carried out periodically in the cell with every prisoner.

Notes

M. Zvarychevska through a "good" watchman and a "commiserating" cellmate received three notes form M. Horyn, and one even from outside, from Olha Horyn. The notes were not very different from each other: "Myhailo is telling everything. The witnesses tell everything. You too must tell everything and extricate yourself (!)". Later it became clear that neither Mykhailo nor Olha Horyns sent any note to Zvarychevska; they were drawn by some handwriting specialist in one of the KGB laboratories.

Threats

I personally, as a witness in Osadchyi's case, had to listen to threats and insults, beginning from a pitiful "sympathy" from Captain Koval in Kyiv: "Think about your children . . . You will finish in prison", to a cynical rudeness from Captain Klymenko in Lviv: "Why do you lie and try to wiggle out? We can make it so that you will never be released from here . . ."

Similar facts can be quoted indefinitely. And as a result of such acts and prolonged imprisonment it happens that people of a weak will lose control over themselves. I do not wish to believe rumours that the imprisoned are given medical preparations with their meals which weaken the will and make a person indifferent and agreeable to anything. As a matter of fact, closed trials provide ground for such rumours. Even Horyn's advocate made helpless gestures: his client repented for everything, confessed against himself about what there was and was not; he even refused the private meeting with the advocate guaranteed by law. As if to say, there are no secrets between me and the interrogator . . . You see what a friendship has sprung up after spending seven months behind bars.

In Makiyivka, Donetsk oblast, the teacher Petlyak, frightened by sudden interrogations "with passion" wrote down his confession on several dozen pages. Because there was no evidence of "crime", Petlyak on those few dozen pages analysed the thoughts and feelings of his acquaintances, friends and his own. He even reached the point when he began to look for dubious "subtexts" in his own collection of short stories. The "Donbas" publishers were in trouble after this and argued that "subtexts" should be sought in the short stories themselves and not in the confession of the frightened Petlyak. The tragi-comedy ended with the fact that Petlyak's acquaintances were frightened by court proceedings and sacked from their jobs.

(c) Imprisonment and time-limits of preliminary investigation.

"*A preliminary investigation in criminal cases should be completed within* two months . . . In particularly complicated cases *a regional prosecutor can, at a reasonable decision of the investigator, extend the period of investigation by* one month *more. The Ukr.SSR Prosecutor or the chief military prosecutor alone may in* exceptional cases only *prolong further the period of the preliminary investigation.*" (Art. 120, Criminal Procedural Code of the Ukr.SSR).

"*When there is sufficient evidence to think that the accused, if set free, will evade the interrogation and court trial or prevent the establishment of the truth in the criminal case, or will resort to crime . . . the investigator and prosecutor have the right to apply to the accused one of the preventive measures . . .*" (Art. 148, Criminal Procedural Code of the Ukr.SSR)

"The keeping in custody during the investigation of the case may not last more than two months. *This term may be extended only because of* a special difficulty *of the case* by the regional prosecutor or by *military prosecutor of a district or fleet to* three months, *and by the Ukr.SSR Prosecutor and chief military prosecutor to* six months *from the day of taking into custody. The USSR Prosecutor General may in exceptional cases extend the period of keeping in custody by additional term of* not more than three months." *(Art. 156, Criminal Procedural Code of the Ukr.SSR)*

Let us assume that the person who read a book himself and gave the book to another person is indeed such a dangerous criminal that the so-called preventive measures must be used against him during an investigation. But why prison and complete isolation from people, as a rule? If a written statement not to leave the place were taken from Hevrych who photographed several books, or if he were let out on bail, this surely would not have prevented anyone from finding out that Hevrych took his photographs in the house of his acquaintance, Morhun, and told his fiancée, Sendurska and her brother about them. The law says that detention in prison for more than three months may be permitted "because of special complication of the case", and longer than six months in "exceptional cases" only. Does photocopying a book and reprinting an anonymous article constitute such a "special complication" and an "exceptional case"? And how is one then to qualify rape, murder and embezzlement of public property? Are we truly returning to the Stalinist times when a murderer was called a "socially akin element", while a writer or a painter was considered a dangerous enemy?

Every effort is made to break the will of the arrested and to force him to use in the court words learnt by heart. The longer a man stays behind bars and the more he has, in place of his former intellectual friends, the KGB interrogator with his one-track song about the terrible crime and repentance as the only interlocutor, the longer will the cell lock click and the watchful guard look through the peep-hole, the greater the guarantee that the man would be transformed into clay from which it would be possible to make anything at will. What we have here is a malicious delaying of investigation with the aim of complete levelling down of human dignity and social impulses. They regularly suppress in the man all that is human and revive animal instincts of fear and self-preservation.

Let us take the case of Osadchyi, which I know best, as a witness. He was arrested on 28th August 1965. In the first few days Osadchyi completely satisfied the inquisitiveness of the Lviv KGB men. The claims against him were so insignificant that the investigation could have been completed in one week. But only one month later, on 30th September, a search was made at my place, as one of the few witnesses in Osadchyi's case, and they began to interrogate me in Kyiv. One month later again I was called to Lviv for interrogation and confrontation. I repeated what I had said on 21st September, and Osadchyi repeated his evidence from the end of August. Then again a calm of several months. . . .

Having had enough behind the bars, Osadchyi, at the time of the last visit from his wife, spoke sincerely of the wish to part with the prison cell and to get into a camp. Osadchyi's crime (as I learnt during the interrogation and from other witnesses) had been so insignificant, while repentance and obedience so unlimited and the past so bright (as a TV studio editor, instructor of the ideological department of a regional party committee, and lecturer at Lviv University) that one week after the arrest he could have been released on parole, taking into consideration that "the crime and the person who committed it" presented no "great social threat" and that "the actions of the defendant did not cause serious consequences, and the defendant himself repented sincerely" (Art. 10 of the Ukr.SSR Criminal Procedural Code). Osadchyi spent almost eight months without trial, dreaming now not about the title of candidate of sciences (not long before his arrest he defended a dissertation) but about a camp. . . .

In our time it is appropriate for dreams to become reality: on 19th April 1966 Lviv regional court for no reason at all condemned Osadchyi to two years in camps with severe regime. However, the year 1966 is not 1930, and it is not so easy to fabricate another SVU (Union for the Liberation of Ukraine). Two attempts to hold "open" trials of the arrested ended in complete defeat for those who conducted the trial.

Moroz in Lutsk spoke about the Russification, unequal position of our "sovereign" republic, and stated that he was no bourgeois nationalist, that he did not desire either the return of bourgeoisie, or nationalism, but wanted Ukraine to have the same rights as have her Socialist sisters Russia, Poland and Czecho-Slovakia. Ozernyi in Ivano-Frankivsk, although he "admitted his guilt" came out morally and intellectually head above the judges and some of the witnesses.

The students of Lutsk teachers institute also spoke with enthusiasm about their lecturers. Having suffered a fiasco, the dispensers of justice have resorted to such an ultra-lawful and superhumane measure, as the closed court trial . . .

MOROZ REPORT FROM THE BERIA RESERVATION

An appeal by the Ukrainian historian Valentyn Moroz

[From "Revolutionary Voices", 1971, OSB Publishing House, Munich]

To the Deputies of the Supreme Soviet of the Ukrainian SSR
From political prisoner unlawfully sentenced at Lutsk on January 20, 1966

The search has ended. The fugitive comes out of the bushes. "I surrender, don't shoot! I have no weapons!" The pursuer comes closer, capably unbolts the submachine gun and puts three bullets one after the other into the living target. Two more rounds are heard: two other fugitives who have also surrendered are shot. The bodies are carried onto the road. Police dogs lick the blood. As always, the victims are brought in, thrown down by the camp gates to frighten others. But suddenly the corpses stir: two are alive. But it is impossible to shoot anymore; people are everywhere. [See photograph, p. 281.]

This is not the beginning of a detective novel. This is not a story about escapees from Buchenwald or Kolyma. This took place in September 1956, after the 20th Congress had condemned the personality cult, and the criticism of Stalinist crimes was in full swing. Everything written here can be verified by Algidas Petrusiavicus, incarcerated in camp No. 11 in Mordovia... He survived. Two others—Lorentas and Yursha—perished. Such incidents were everyday occurrences.

Green Mordovia stretches in a narrow strip from west to east. Green on the map, green in reality. In the Slavic sea—an island of melodic Mordovian names: Vindrey, Yavas, Potma, Lyambir. In its northwest corner there is a Mordovian state forest reservation. Here law reigns—hunting is strictly prohibited. But there is another reservation, not to be found on any map, where hunting is permitted all the year round. If an accurate map of Mordovia were to be drawn, its south-west corner would have to be divided into squares, separated by barbed wire and dotted with watch towers. These are the Mordovian political camps—the land of barbed wire, police dogs and man-hunts. Here, the children grow up amidst barbed wire. Their parents cut grass and dig potatoes after work. "Dad was there a search? And what did you find?" Then they will grow up and learn the philosophy of these lands: "Camp means bread". You get a pood of flour (about 36 lbs.) for catching a fugitive. It was even simpler in the Aldan camps: a Yakut brought a head and received gun-powder, salt, whisky. Just like the Dayaks in Borneo, only the head was not brought to the chief who was adorned with necklaces of human teeth, but to a major or a captain, who had taken a correspondence course at the university and gave lectures on legality. In Mordovia it was necessary to do away with such tradition: too close to Moscow. Such a trophy could fall into the hands of a foreign correspondent—then try to prove that it's a forgery, invented by the yellow press.

Three Lithuanians were shot even though they had not been sentenced to be executed. Art 183 of the Criminal Code allows three years' imprisonment as punishment for an escape, and Art. 22 CC Ukr.SSR even prohibits "the infliction of physical suffering or the degradation of human dignity" of the prisoners. The court of the Lithuanian SSR (a sovereign state, according to the constitution of the said country) gave permission to the KGB men to keep the prisoners in isolation—nothing more. According to the constitution, Ukraine is also a sovereign state, and is even represented at the UN. The courts try thousands of Ukrainian citizens and ... send them abroad. A precedent unheard of in history: a state sends its prisoners abroad. Perhaps Ukraine has no room for camps, as is the case in the principality of Monaco? However, room was found for seven million Russians—but, it seems, there is no room for political prisoners, Ukrainians, on their native soil. Thousands of Ukrainians were transported to the East—and there were engulfed by grey obscurity. They were swallowed up by the dungeons of Solovki, by the sands of Mangyshlak, later by Stalinist construction projects—the pyramids of the 20th century which have devoured millions of slaves. They were transported not only in groups of prisoners—those "voluntarily" resettled are also devoured by the Russification meat-grinder in the boundless expanses of Siberia and Kazakhstan, and they are lost forever to the Ukrainian nation. The ancient peoples considered the place where the sun sets to be the Land of the Dead. In the future Ukrainian legends such a country will be found in the East.

The civilizational level of a society is measured by the degree of its concern for the well-being of its citizens. An accident in a Belgian mine buried over ten Italian emigrants. Italy exploded with protests, official notes abounded, questions in parliament resulted. Ukraine also has a parliament—the Supreme Soviet of the Ukr.SSR. I do not know whether there are people there who remember their right to question the government. I do not know whether these people remember any of their rights as deputies, except the right to raise their hand while voting. But I know that the Supreme Soviet of the Ukr.SSR is the highest authority in Ukraine according to the constitution. It authorized one of its subordinate institutions—KGB—to arrest, to try and to do what it pleased concerning the future fate of the people accused of "anti-Soviet activities". Honourable deputies of the Ukrainian Parliament, let's chase away drowsiness for once; let's set aside debates on sows, cement mixers and the effects the use of super-phosphates has on national economy. Let these problems be resolved by experts. Let's forget about the Land of Sweet Yawns for once and transfer ourselves to Mordovia and find out: a) who these people uprooted from normal life are who have been placed at the complete disposal of the KGB men; b) to whom the fate of these people was transferred.

THE TRIAL OF THOUGHT

In 1958, Makhmed Kulmagambetov, a lecturer in philosophy at Frunze medical institute (now an inmate in camp No. 11) brought a statement to the dean's office: please settle my account. The reason?—Disagreement with the programme of instruction. This decision caused a sensation. The herd of career men, who have been outrunning each other in the attempt to reach the trough, trampling conscience, dignity and convictions under foot in order to climb higher and to profit at their neighbour's expense, could not understand how a person could refuse 120 roubles merely because his views have changed! Kulmagambetov became a blue collar worker. But in 1962 he was arrested. The court at Kustanay sentenced him to 7 years' imprisonment and to 3 years' exile for "anti-Soviet activity". How did it manifest itself? The chief prosecution witness was the head of the staff of "Sokolovrudstroy" (ore mine construction) Trust, Makhmudov. The only thing which he could say in court was to repeat Kulmagambetov's words: "I do not want to teach what I do not believe in." This was the latter's reply to the question: "Why aren't you working in your branch of specialization?" Other accusations were the same. The investigator also admitted: "In reality there is no reason for trying you, but you have a dangerous way of thinking." A typical example, almost an everyday occurrence in the practice of the KGB, but unique for its sheer arbitrariness. As a rule the KGB men try to fabricate at least the appearance of "anti-Soviet" activity. But here, in the far off province, they did not deem even this formality necessary and admitted that Kulmagambetov was being condemned for his opinions. Thousands upon thousands of people have been tried according to this system, even though their cases may have been more cleverly "presented". Article 126 of the Constitution of the USSR proclaims freedom of speech, press, manifestations and organizations. Art. 19 of the UN Declaration of Human Rights speaks about "freedom to seek, receive and impart information and ideas through any media and regardless of frontiers". Therefore Art. 62 CC Ukr.SSR is nothing more than a violation of the above-mentioned documents, a Stalinist survival. The formulation "agitation or propaganda conducted with the aim to undermine or weaken the Soviet regime" under conditions when the KGB men themselves are determining the degree of "subversiveness" of the material, fosters unlimited arbitrariness. In Moscow every year tens of books by foreign authors are published, filled with sharp criticism of the Soviet regime and Communist ideology. If Art. 62 CC is really a law, then the publication of these books is a criminal act. A law is a law only when it is applied to all. Where is the logic: I can freely propagate the views of Hitler, published in the periodical *Voprosy istorii* (Questions of History), yet I will be tried for my own typing of Hitler's memoirs! Thus, Art. 62 is nothing but a tool of arbitrariness in the hands of the KGB, which makes it possible for them to put an inconvenient person behind bars for keeping any book not published in the Soviet Union.

I and my friends are condemned for "propaganda directed at the separation of Ukraine from the USSR". But Art. 17 of the USSR Constitution speaks clearly about the right of every republic to secede from the USSR. The right of every nation to separation was laid down in the pact on the civil and political rights of men adopted at the 21st session of the UN General Assembly.

. . . It seems that there are enough facts. A conclusion can be reached: people condemned for "anti-Soviet agitation and propaganda"—are those who think differently, or those who think, period; those whose spiritual world did not fit the Procrustean bed of the Stalinist standards which are diligently guarded by the KGBists. They are those who dared to use the rights proclaimed in the constitution, who raised their voice against the shameful oppression of the KGB, against the violation of the constitution. They are those who do not want to learn the slavish, double-bottomed wisdom which interprets the words of the constitution "Ukraine's right to secede from the USSR" as "keep quiet if you value your life."

DESCENDANTS OF YEZHOV AND BERIA

A characteristic of a man or an environment can always be subjective. Therefore it is best to deal with *autocharacteristics*. And it is very good that the author of these lines has a fancy bouquet of autocharacteristics provided by the KGBists of themselves and their system. The KGBists were not mean with words and in general were unceremonious in their talks with prisoners, strongly convinced that their words would not go beyond the sound-proof doors of their offices, that the icy terror of silence on which they constructed their Golgotha would never thaw. But all ice thaws at one time or another, and words, which were growled into our faces at the inquiry and in camp, as if spoken through a gigantic megaphone, were echoed with a thousand voices throughout the whole world.

Where are the roots of the KGB? If we retrace those paths by which the KGBists came down to our reality, we will find ourselves in the horrible thickets of Stalinist jungles. General Shulzhenko, assistant head of the KGB at the Council of Ministers of the Ukr.SSR, was elected a deputy to the Ukrainian Parliament from the Khartsyzk district. Where did this parliamentarian pursue his career? In order to become a general of the KGB in 1967, it was necessary to start as a Beria lieutenant or captain in 1937. What did the KGB captains do in 1937? They killed people for not performing a norm (or merely for sport) in Kolyma. This is not a secret to anyone anymore: Moscow journals are writing about it. In Ukraine they shot innocent people three days after they had been arrested. Their arguments are familiar: it was all Beria's fault; they were only carrying out orders. The same argumentation was used by the defence at the Nuremberg trials. It would seem that only Hitler was responsible. But the trick did not work. Even a new concept: "Murder behind a desk" has appeared in the German language. I have no doubts that sooner or later it will find a place in the Ukrainian language as well.

Perhaps the KGBists have changed, have become different? No, they themselves proudly consider themselves to be Stalin's descendants. A representative of the Ukrainian KGB in the Mordovian camps, Capt. Krut, told me: "And what have you got against Stalin? Of course, he had some shortcomings, but on the whole he deserved a high grade"; and in a conversation with Mykhailo Horyn, Krut frankly said: "Too bad that we are in Mordovia and not in the North" The head of the department of investigation of the Georgian KGB, Nadiradze, told poet Zauri Kobalia (confined to camp No. 11) in 1963 during an investigation: "Did you know that I was here in 1937? Remember that!"

Now they do not wear Stalin' tunics any more and "take correspondence courses" at universities. It is a correspondence course in the full meaning of the word. A student's book is brought to the institute and the "faculty", hypnotized from the cradle on with the word KGB, records a grade without ever seeing the student. A representative of the Ivano-Frankivsk KGB, Kazakov, admitted to me: "Here you spoke about totalitarianism. But I'm no *totalizator*." And the representative of the Ukrainian KGB in camp No. 11, Harashchenko, made short work of all Masiutko's arguments on the unresolved national question in Ukraine: "You speak about a national question. But when a widow turns to the Kolkhoz head for straw—do you think he will refuse?" And these intellectuals are entrusted to decide categorically the questions which even in specialized journals are considered to be moot points. Kazakov, Krut and a Kyiv KGBist, Lytvyn, "cross examined" me together. "What else did you need? You had a good job, an apartment . . ." And for several hours tried to prove that an individual has nothing but a stomach and several yards of intestines. An idea? Protection of Ukraine from the threat of Russification? Here for my interlocutors the discussion clearly left the familiar ground and became part of the sphere of children's tales. They did not hide the fact that they did not really comprehend it.

An idea . . . Naturally, a great deal is said about it in books, and it is generally unacceptable to say that you have no ideas. But for an idea to be a motive for human activity—that they have never encountered in their midst. Mykhailo Horyn heard the following at the Lviv KGB: "Today is the day of the Chekist.— What day of the Chekist?—Payday." When one speaks seriously about it, it is a myth, with which someone has intoxicated the people and which drags a person away from normal existence based on three major concepts: money, the love of power, women. But an idea—it is a kind of psychological disorder, not always comprehensible, it is true; but one must reckon with it, as with a factor, on the same level with the three others, normal and understandable. Captain Kozlov (Iv.-Frankivsk) lectured me as follows: "One is bought for money, another by women, but some are hooked by an ideal." For an idea to be born independently in a human head—that is unsurmisable.

It would be naive to consider this state of affairs an accidental "infringement" on the social development of the society. A system in which a poet receives a catalogue of permitted images, an artist—a list of permitted and prohibited colours, has its roots in the past, and is a continuation of certain forces and conditions. Before our very eyes these forces are gradually thawing, and the conditions stop being the norm of intercourse among people. KGBists sense this and place all the blame on Khrushchev, who supposedly toppled the idols, which at one time were honoured thoughtlessly. With the same success it is possible to consider a cock, an author of dawn, but this is too great a truism to be placed into the skulls of generals and majors with sky-blue loops.

When Levko Lukianenko asked Capt. Denisov, an investigator of the Lviv KGB: "What is the purpose of Art. 17, which gives every republic the right to secede from the USSR?"—the latter answered: "For abroad" (!). This is what it is! It seems that the KGBists realize very well that they are not defending "socialist legality", but the right to violate it without being punished. They have no illusions whatsoever about their institution and look at it simply as a place where the pay is the highest and it is possible to get apartments without waiting.

KGBist Kazakov brought a letter to me from the rector of Ivano-Frankivsk Pedagogic Institute, where I had worked earlier. I said: "When somebody wants to write me—let him do it through the mail." To this Kazakov replied: "It would be too great an honour." Thus, he feels that the KGB in no case can pretend to receive such respect as is accorded the post office. Why then do the KGBists dislike people showing disrespect towards them?

KGB representative from Kyiv, Lytvyn, declared to me: "We arrested you upon demands from the community. Otherwise the people would tear you to pieces." That's funny! Why then are political prisoners tried at closed court sessions and why doesn't a word appear about them in the papers?—The KGBists realize very well the illegality of their acts and therefore hide political trials from human eyes, at the same time as the trials of German policemen-murderers are being widely publicized.

AT THE RESERVATION

Here—is the only place where the KGBists can completely ignore all laws and norms. Here—is a place where they continue to forge fear. The main efforts are directed at killing everything human in a human being—only then does it become dough, from which almost anything can be shaped. A prisoner can in no way violate the regulations of the regime, but as soon as the KGBists feel that he had not given up, has not acknowledged evil to be a normal condition, kept his dignity—all sorts of pressure are applied to him. And only when they can convince themselves that a human being has sunk to the level of a mere consumer of food—only then are they reassured.

An Osset, Fedir Byazrov, was a thief. Then he became a Jehovah's Witness and stopped stealing. It would seem that the "instructors" should have been content. Byazrov thought so too. "What do you want from me? I no longer steal and do nothing wrong. And nobody is forbidden to believe in God."—"It would be better if you stole." This is no accident. Pointing to criminals they told many political prisoners: "They are thieves, but they are our people. But you—are enemies." This is whom the KGBists are protecting. Morally degenerate people—are the element in which they feel at home, like a fish in water. A bandit is their man. A KGBist knows how to talk to him. He is a ready informer for a dose of narcotics. In him it is not necessary to kill such an incomprehensible but strong force as dignity.

Agents are used not only in the role of eavesdroppers. Prisoner Lashchuk was known to be a KGB agent. All knew about it: in the Taishet camp No. 11 in 1958 a denunciation written by him was taken away from him. In April 1964 he wounded Stepan Virun (from a group of jurists sentenced in Lviv in 1961) with a knife in camp No.7. When Virun, after leaving the hospital, talked about it with Capt. Krut, the latter unceremoniously declared: "They will take off your head, if you don't get wise." (Virun did not acknowledge his sentence as legal and wrote complaints.)

Art. 22 of the Criminal Code of the Ukr. SSR proclaims: "Punishment does not have as its aim inflicting physical sufferings or degrading human dignity." There-fore, all methods of pressure on the prisoners applied by the KGB are violations of the law. But where are those who were called to see that the laws were enforced, i.e. the procurator's office? There is a procurator's office in Mordovia. And it would be a lie to say that it closes its eyes to arbitrariness or washes its hand of it. On the contrary, the local procurators, rolling up their sleeves, are helping the KGBists to do their dirty work at full speed. In a talk with an assistant prosecutor of the Dubravnoye camp administration I called his attention to the fact that people suffering with an acute stomach ulcer are given starvation diets, contrary to the law. And he answered me very calmly: "This is the point of the punish-ment—to hit the stomach." What right do these sadists have to call themselves the defenders of the law?

Compulsory work for political prisoners is a violation of the UN convention on the prohibition of forced labour. Moreover, the KGBists themselves admit that work is looked upon as a method of pressure. Many are told: "We do not need your work; we want you to reform." A prisoner, who should have been sent to a lock-up room, is transferred to hard labour, where it is impossible to perform the norm and where he is punished for failure to fulfil the norm. All rights due to prisoners are treated as privileges which can be taken away. Lukianenko and Mykhailo Horyn, for instance, were deprived of the right to see their families in 1967, even though it is their right (not a privilege) which nobody can take away from them, just as nobody can take away the right to nourishment. Can they take away the one occasion in the year that you can see your relatives? In com-parison it suffices to mention that in England a prisoner has a right to see his family every week!

A system of education through hunger is also without precedent. Everywhere, political prisoners have always received food parcels in unlimited quantities. We have a right to receive only two parcels a year after completing half the term "under conditions of good behavior"—is there a need to comment on these words? The bare minimum of nourishment, stipulated by the FAO (an organ of UNES-CO), is 2,700 calories, the brink of starvation—2,400. Beyond that a deteriora-tion of physical and mental capabilities of a human being begins. In the lock-up room to which I am confined the "raised" norm consists of 2,090 calories. There is an even lower one—only 1,324 calories. Therefore a crime is continually per-petrated for decades. All should remember that in Nuremberg they tried for mur-der by iron as well as for murder by starvation. It is interesting to note whether the Ukrainian Red Cross will be interested in the crimes perpetrated in Mor-dovia, even to the same degree as in the crimes in Africa? Camp food made half of the people sick. Here a new method of pressure—medicine—comes into play. Anyway, in order to be a doctor or a nurse in camp, it is not mandatory to have any knowledge of medicine. A former German policeman, Malykhin, a murderer of many people (now in camp No. 11) was a nurse in camp No. 7. He lacks not only medical training, but education in general. However, he has merits in the eyes of the KGB. Of course, it doesn't happen like this all the time, Now we are treated by an Estonian, Braun, who used to be a driver of an ambulance. No matter how you look at it, but it is impossible to call him a stranger to medicine

The regulations state that prisoners who are confined to a lock-up room are not to be deprived of medical help. But what do these regulations mean when camp doctors frankly declare: "We are first Chekists, then medics." Mykhailo Masiutko, suffering with a stomach ulcer, is in a very serious condition. But all attempts to have him sent to a hospital or at least to give him dietetic food have proved useless. The KGBists in white coats said: "Of course, we should send you, but we would be punished for it. It is not permitted to give you injections", and some unceremoniously say: "You should not have let yourself be caught." Of course, the arsenal of camp medicine is far from being exhausted. Is it an accident that there is such a high percentage of mentally ill in camps? The research into the role played by camp medicine is still waiting for the author . . .

Octopus' tentacles have a firm grip on the prisoner even after he leaves the camp's gates. Yarema Tkachuk, convicted in 1958 in Stanyslaviv was told by Capt. Krut: "You will have no life, if you won't get wise. We will fix it so that you will neither have a family, nor a roof over your head." And Kazakov promised me that I "will be sorry."

And this was not just intimidation. In 1957 Danyol Shumuk (now at camp No. 11) was arrested in Dnipropetrovsk for "anti-Soviet agitation". Major Sverdlov of the republican KGB unceremoniously admitted that the accusation is false. But this is beside the point. A choice was given to Shumuk, a man just released from prison: either you will be placed behind bars again, or you will become an informer, as a man who is greatly respected in the circles of former prisoners, and who will not arouse suspicion. For two days Shumuk was held illegally at KGB headquarters without an arrest warrant being presented and was persuaded. Major Sverdlov declared: "If you will agree to cooperate with us—I will tear up the arrest warrant and the protocols of the inquiry right before your eyes." Art. 173 of the Criminal Code of the Ukr.SSR says that "criminal prosecution of a person who is known to be innocent . . . together with the accusation in committing of a particularly dangerous state crime"—"is punishable by the deprivation of freedom for the term of 8 years." Nobody sentenced Sverdlov to 8 years, not even to 8 months,—he had the right to violate all laws without being punished. This is why he is a KGBist. Shumuk, on the other hand, went to Siberia again to serve a 10-year term for remaining an honest man. And now, before his release, a sick man who began his prison career when arrested by the Polish secret police and spent 27 years behind bars, is called out by Capt. Krut and promised: "You will have no life." Shumuk is in a lock-up room for "the preparation of anti-Soviet manuscripts". This is what the KGBists have called his memoirs: five arrests under Poland, a German camp for prisoners of war and his escape from it, and his crossing of the entire Ukraine on foot, from the Poltava region to Volyn, avoiding the roads and German policemen.

When it is necessary to place somebody in a lock-up room—they will place him there not only because he "expressed himself in an anti-Soviet way" but also for "keeping still in an anti-Soviet way".

Prisoner Vovchanskyi was placed there because "he is angry with the Soviet authorities"—this is how it was written in the decision! In order to go to camp it is nonetheless necessary to have a "dangerous way of thinking". But from the camp to a lock-up room the road is much easier: here, as we have seen, people are placed not only for thoughts, but also for attitudes. Masiutko, Lukianenko, Shumuk and I were incarcerated for writing complaints, which were treated as "anti-Soviet manuscripts". Mykhailo Horyn did not write any "manuscripts"—but he was nevertheless imprisoned with us. What for? Capt. Krut says that he found Ivan Dzyuba's memorandum addressed to the CC CPU in his possession. Bogdan Horyn, in a talk with Lytvyn and Marusenko, asked: "Is Dzyuba's memorandum an anti-Soviet document?"—"No, it is not."—"Why then was my brother imprisoned?" To this question Marusenko replied: "An error occurred." There was no error. Horyn, as well as the others, are kept in a lock-up room because they brought with them to the camp the truth about the events in Ukraine and have no intention of keeping it quiet.

The camp routine is completely and in full transferred from the times of Tsar Nicholas I. A portrait of the Latvian poet, Knut Skuinek, painted by the artist Zalyvakha was taken away from him and the painter himself (!) was forced to cut up his work! Does such a society have the right to criticize the Chinese "Red Guards"? The robots in uniforms destroyed all Zalyvakha's paintings they could find and confiscated the paints. Upon demands to show the law which permits this, the artist received the following reply: "I am the law for you!" The corporal told the truth. He—is the incarnation of the law which was made during Shevchenko's times, who also had no right to write or paint.

These are the methods of "re-education" employed by the KGBists. And what are the results? What do the "reformed", who are held up as an example to us, who receive parcels and narcotics from the KGBists, look like? They can be seen together at holiday concerts before May 1st or November 7th. On the stage—an unusual collection of faces, ploughed by all possible vices, a bouquet of criminals of all colors, who it seems have come right out of the pages of a criminology textbook. Here—are all the wartime criminals, those who killed thousands upon thousands of Jewish children, representatives of all sexual perversions, narcotic addicts who inject cat's blood into their veins if they have nothing else handy. This is—a choir. "The party is our leader", "Lenin—is always alive." If at least one KGBist believed in these ideals, the defenders of which he is proclaiming himself to be—would he permit this? The "reformed" walk about camp with emblems on their sleeves which say SVP (Sektsiya vnutrennego poryadka—Internal Police Section). The prisoners interpret these letters to mean "Soyuz voennykh prestupnikov" (Association of War Criminals).

After all this, is it still possible to say seriously that the KGBists are protecting the Soviet government? On the contrary: all their activity undermines and discredits it, pushes the people to the road of opposition.

A Finn, Vilho Forsel (now in the Vladimir jail), graduated with honours from Petrozavodsk University and worked on a Karelian state farm. As an interpreter he accompanied the Canadian Communist delegation throughout Karelia. After the trip the KGBists demanded that Forsel disclose the contents of conversations which the Canadians had with people who approached them. Forsel refused declaring that the law does not give anyone the right to treat him in this way. Then he was told: "Good, you will beg to cooperate with us." Several days later he was thrown out of work and no other place would hire him. If this is a crime, then there is no one to blame but KGB.

Churchill said: "Not one anti-Communist brought so much harm as Khrushchev."—No one else, but the KGBists, in their turn, took over his shoe and are pounding with it at all rostrums both in the UN and outside it, successfully compromising the state, whilst proclaiming themselves to be its defenders. Whilst searching us, they regularly confiscate the "UN Declaration of Human Rights". On my demand to have it returned Krut answered: "It is not allowed to keep the Declaration." An assistant of the prosecutor with whom I spoke admitted that he never read it. At "political classes", which are conducted by semi-literate corporals for artists and writers, the prisoners at one time entered into a discussion with Senior Lieut. Lyubayev (camp No. 11) supporting the Declaration with arguments. To this he indulgently answered: "Listen, but it is only intended for Negroes."

Anyway, there is no need to prove which particular actions are compromising Communism. Poltoratskyi, who recently has been specializing on the Chinese "Red Guards", clearly indicated that it is necessary to consider this phenomenon "as capricious caricature, as an attempt to discredit a just socialist society that has been dreamed about for centuries". This, first of all, is Mao's order "to send actors, poets, scholars . . . to the villages for retraining, that is those same people's communes. It is not hard to imagine what will happen to an elderly scholar or writer, when he is harnessed to a plough for several days to plough the fields." (*Lit. Ukraina*, 24. 2. 1967). Of course, it is not hard to imagine. Let Poltoratskyi come to Mordovia and see how an artist, Zalyvakha, sent for retraining, is throwing coal into the furnace. He was given the post of a fireman with the deliberate intention of killing all desires in him—except to sleep.

Further, the forced dressing of people in caps is considered a disgrace to Communism. "The fact that workers in factories wear caps of different colours was noticed immediately. Apprentices and those who did not perform a norm were without caps. Those who performed the norm—wore yellow caps. And only those who over-performed could put on a red cap." (*Nauka i religiya* (Science and Religion) No. 3, 1967, p. 7). Had this happened in Tientsin or Wuhan, Poltoratskyi would immediately speak about the mockery of a human being. But I have to disappoint you: such a rule was put into effect in the Osh sewing factory in Kirghizia. And if this is the case, then there can be no talk of mockery. This is simply a method of emancipating a woman in Central Asia.

The newspaper *Izvestia* (No. 78, 1967) wrote that "the Maoists openly challenged Marxism-Leninism . . . declared the assimilation of non-Chinese peoples as their aim". If this is a "challenge" to Marxism-Leninism, then such learned men as Agayev and Kravtsev should also be considered Maoists. Their "works" are regularly published in Moscow and Kyiv. The former thinks that all languages of the USSR, except Lithuanian, Latvian, Estonian, Georgian and Armenian, have no prospects—that is, they should be Russified. The latter tries to convince Ukrainians that to keep up with the times—means replacing their native language by Russian.

As we see, Mao is not the only author of "capricious caricatures and attempts to discredit the socialist society dreamed about for centuries".

— When a person is tried for a "dangerous way of thinking";
— when dissidents are re-educated through hunger in lock-up rooms;

— when an artist is told what colour paint to use,
— when the UN Declaration of Human Rights is considered a disruptive document, even though it has been ratified by the government;
— when the Ukrainian language is called with impunity the "Banderist* tongue" by official persons;
— when people who are struggling against chauvinistic oppression in Ukraine are put behind bars, at a time when the world is living through an epoch of national revivals—
— all this—is a disgrace to the state that permits such phenomena.
And its peak—is the rule of the descendants of Beria over the spiritual life of society. It is a pitiful society, where problems of philosophy are solved by punitive organs behind barbed wire.
A crime is a crime, and it is inevitably followed by reckoning. Someone will have to answer for those shot and killed by starvation, to answer in accordance with the constitution which sometime will nonetheless become law. And for the robot who can calmly pierce a person with a spear, it will also be necessary to answer— by the one who stole his soul, who sucked a human being out of him.
The truth has long arms!

April 15, 1967.

VOICE OF DESPAIR AND PROTEST

["Revolutionary Voices," OSB Publishing House, Munich 1971]

Editor's note:
Ukrainian newspapers in Western Europe have published a letter from Ukrainian prisoners incarcerated in Camp No. 17 of the Dubravnoye regional administration of the slave labour camps of the Mordovian Autonomous Soviet Socialist Republic. The letter reached the free world in a clandestine manner.
Among the prisoners in the Mordovian camps there are some of the 70 Ukrainian intellectuals arrested and sentenced in Ukraine in 1966, as well as the two other writers, Daniel and Siniavsky.
The letter proves once again that concentration camps continue to exist in the USSR and their inmates are often political prisoners serving long term sentences, people who were made invalids and cripples by long and hard imprisonment. Even if people serve short sentences, the conditions are so severe that they become physically broken after a comparatively short time. The letter proves the continuance of persecution of religion and its adherents. It also proves that the spirit of resistance among Ukrainian patriots remains unbroken.
Below is the full text of the letter.

LETTER FROM UKRAINIAN POLITICAL PRISONERS FROM A SOVIET CONCENTRATION CAMP

"The No. 17 camp of the Dubravnoye Camp Administation is situated in the village of Ozernoye in the Zubova Polyana district of the Mordovian Autonomous Soviet Socialist Republic. It is divided into two zones: in the first, the main one, there are about 700 women convicted for "ordinary" crimes, and in the other there are 276 male political prisoners. Captain Novikov is camp commadant; Captain Annenkov is commandant of the No. 17–A camp section, i.e. of the male zone; Senior-Lieutenant Zabaykin is head of the health department; Captain Ivan Romanovich Krut' is plenipotentiary of the State Security Committee (KGB) for No. 17 camp.
The majority of the male prisoners are invalids. There are 208 second category and 51 third category invalids. There are only two cold and overcrowded barracks in the male zone, with poor ventilation. Food is brought from the female zone and though a prisoner's ration is poor to start with, he does not even receive this meager ration fully. Bread is sour, poorly baked, inedible even for a healthy person, not to speak of sick people who make up a majority of the camp inmates. Medical assistance is in fact absent, which can be seen from the following example: On January 7th, 1967, prisoner Mykhailo Soroka who spent 31 years in Polish and Russian jails (24 of them in Soviet prisons) fell seriously ill. As became evident, he had a heart attack. In such cases qualified medical assistance is urgently necessary. However, a free medical assistant appeared only after 4 days had passed. Only on the seventh day the sick man was taken to the sick bay (until then he

---

*Stepan Bandera was a Ukranian nationalist leader, murdered in Munich by Soviet terror apparatus.

was in the barrack). All this time he (Soroka) was under the care of medical assistant Mykola Yevdokimov, a fellow prisoner, experienced but powerless in these circumstances when there are no medicaments or instruments.

In the sick bay there are only 7 beds (for 225 invalids, a majority of whom are aged and seriously ill). There are no medicines and the prisoners have no right to receive them from their relatives (even vitamins, though food is so miserably poor). A dentist is unheard of. Theoretically, those seriously ill should be sent to the central hospital of the Dubravnoye camp administration (No. 3 camp in the village of Barashevo). But this is not always possible, as in Soroka's case, when the sick person cannot be transported (particularly on the terrible roads).

Often, too, dispatch to the central hospital is useless. Thus there have been several cases when doctors sent a prisoner to the central hospital having diagnosed a cancer disease, and doctors from the central hospital instead of freeing the prisoner on the grounds of ill-health (which they are entitled to do), sent him back to the camp with the diagnosis—acute gastritis. And only death and dissection of the body of the deceased confirmed the correctness of the former diagnosis. People are released only in such cases when death comes a few days after release. What better can be expected of people who do not make one step without the instructions of the KGB and the Operations Department.

The decisive voice in the central hospital belongs to the head of the regime, Captain Kitsayev, who discharged Dr. Horboviy from the hospital and sent him back to the camp, although his treatment was far from completed. Similar cases are not rare. The head of the health department Yeremeyeva stated in No. 11 camp, during Karavanskyi's hunger strike, that she knew about the hunger strike, but was unable to do anything because there had been no instructions from the Operations Department. The prisoner Ivan Maksym applied for medical treatment to the surgeon in No. 11 camp, but the latter refused even to talk to him, calling him a simulator. This resulted in the prisoner's death. Medical personnel from among the prisoners are not much better. Only people who are in the service of the KGB and Operations Department are taken there. Neither medical education nor knowledge play any role whatsoever. For example, the following medical students, prisoners Yaroslav Hevrych and Dmytro Verkholiak, were dismissed from work in the health department and transferred to general work in a workshop, although there is a shortage of medical workers. At the same time individuals who never had anything to do with medicine, as for example Malykhin and others who are in good books of the KGB and Management Department are working as medical orderlies. If there is an experienced and conscientious senior medical assistant in the No. 17 camp, this is so only because, while working at the central hospital, he was disliked by some of those who have no relation to medicine, and they sent him here to the No. 17 camp.

Altogether No. 17 camp has been created as a punitive camp. Administration does not try to cover it up in conversations, although officially it is not regarded as such. Apart from invalids, people who have not the slightest intention to submit to the so-called educational work among the prisoners and with their example can negatively influence the mass of the prisoners in this direction, have been gathered here. Therefore, a policy of reprisals with regard to the prisoners, is forcefully carried out here. Its aim is to undermine the health of the prisoners and to suppress the slightest symptom of the spirit of insubmission and protest. With this purpose in view the organised production (the sewing of gloves and construction) is based on a system of compulsion, arbitrary punishment and reprisals. Prisoners who work in construction have not been issued with warm special clothing (felt boots and padded clothing). The average temperature in the shop usually stays within the limits between $+5°$ and $+9°$ centigrade. And on the floor the temperature is usually below the freezing point. Thus there cannot be any talk about normal work in conditions when one has to handle metallic parts of the machine. Nonetheless they demand fulfilment of work quotas from the prisoner, although these cannot be fulfilled even under normal conditions, not to speak of the present situation when equipment is broken, when the premises where the prisoners have to spend nine hours each day (given the 8-hour working day for the prisoners), are not heated.

One hour is allowed for the so-called lunch break and rest, but it is not only no rest, but additional punishment, because people are forced to spend an additional hour in a cold building. Lunch and supper are given in unsanitary conditions, on generally dirty premises, without tables, so that a prisoner is forced to eat at the place of work, i.e. by his machine. There are no facilities for washing one's hands, because one small wash-basin cannot provide enough water for everyone, and there is no water in the work zone, neither are there any towels. Smoking in the workshop and in the passage is forbidden. And as there is no place provided where one could smoke, prisoners are compelled to smoke in a small corridor leading to the street, where doors are constantly opened and there is constant draught (with 30° centigrade of frost.)

The administration constantly threatens with reprisals against those who fail to fulfil the norms (and at present no one is able to fulfil the norm), and will carry out these threats as soon as the period of training ends (at the beginning of February 1967). As there is a shortage of manpower, because second category invalids are entitled to stay off work, the administration openly declares that it will set up a local medical committee with the purpose of taking away the rights of invalids from the disabled persons and forcing them to work. Camp commandant, Capt. Annenkov, has said it openly.

The point is that up to now this was a camp for female political prisoners (until 29th December, 1966, i.e. to the date of our arrival) most of whom were women sentenced for their religious convictions, that is people who less than anyone else had been able to put up resistance to the arbitrariness of the camp administration, or even to protest against the oppression. It must also be added that—in an overwhelming majority—these were elderly women. As the overlookers say, they were exhausted beings, clad in rags, who were forced to work in cold premises where temperature rarely rose to 2–3 degrees above the freezing point, and often fell below the freezing point even. As the system of oppression has become a tradition here, the administration has the intention to continue it in the future, too. No wonder that the overlookers are frankly saying that the more we complain against the infringement of our unlawful rights by them, the more they are praised by their superiors and vice versa.

Have the prisoners tried to complain against these numerous infringements, reprisals and injustice? They have, and have done so many a time, but without any effect. The camp commandant, Capt. Annenkov, replied with shouts that things would remain as they were. Chief engineer replied to the complaint that we are compelled to consume our food in cold premises, in unhygieneic conditions, that this was none of his concern and advises us to address similar questions to "Ivan the Wind". After many complaints a medical inspector came from the health department of the Dubravnoye Camp Administration, who, in the first place, did not believe that temperature in the shop was too low (he did not agree to its being measured on the spot), stating that "norms had always been fulfilled and overfulfilled here". After we mentioned that we had recently sent a number of complaints signed by the shift master (a free man), dealing with the temperature in the workshop, he merely enquired to whom these complaints were addressed, and was dissatisfied that they were addressed to the Attorney General's Office and not the Camp Administration.

As regards the complaint by the writer Daniel about the outrageous case of the sick man, M. Soroka, this medical inspector stated that this was no longer a topical question (the sick man did not die when he did not receive medical treatment) and tried to make Daniel recognise that everything in the camp was in order (which he needed for formally dismissing the matter), to which the latter did not agree. No wonder that when the prisoners demand what is due to them according to the law, representatives of the administration do not bother to do anything and simply reply: "You may complain," because they know that no one will pay the slightest attention to our complaints. To whom is one to complain when our former "educators" sit in the offices of higher authority? The following fact may bear witness to their standards of behaviour. For two or three years the former operations manager from camp No. 19 was acting as a doctor at the No. 7 camp. He was dismissed from his job in camp No. 19 for an attempt to violate a nurse. At present he is employed as duty officer at the prison in the town of Ruzayevka in Mordovia. At present, Senior Lieutenant Nekrasov is in charge of the guard detachment at camp No. 1. Previously he was a medical assistant in the same camp. Supervision by attorneys is the same as that by doctors (attorneys very often change their seats from those of law officers to camp commandants, officials of the administration, and vice versa, as happened with our present deputy head of the Dubravnoye Camp Administration, Nekachan).

Mention was made already of correspondence and parcels. I wish to add that permission to receive packets with printed matter which we are lawfully permitted to receive—depends (just as letters) on the will of the KGB functionary (in the given case, Capt. Krut'), which makes our right illusory.

Representatives of various nations of the Soviet Union are held in the camp. There are Latvians, Lithuanians, Estonians, Russians. As could well have been expected, there are a great many Ukrainians.

Who are they?

(There follows a list of Ukrainian prisoners whom the author (or authors) of the letter segregate into the following groups: "participants in the national liberation struggle 1942–1954, as well as various clandestine groups of a similar character"; "those sentenced for their religious convictions (Catholics, Baptists, Jehovah's Witnesses, etc.)"; "those sentenced for the so-called anti-Soviet agitation, for an attempt to cross the frontier and similar crimes"; "for crimes committed during the war". The list gives: the prisoner's surname and name, region, year of birth, when arrested, sentence in years. There are altogether 114 names. Obviously this list does not contain all the Ukrainian prisoners of No. 17–A camp, because at the end of some groups there is "and others".)

Although all the listed Ukrainians have been sentenced by the courts of the Ukrainian Soviet Socialist Republic, they are held (and have always been held) in the camps of Russia. This is another superfluous proof of the abdication of the Ukrainian Soviet Socialist Republic from its sovereignty—the carrying out of the sentence of its courts.

There are only 17 people of the working category, i.e. people able to work, in the camp.

The head of the Dubravnoye Camp Administration is Colonel Gromov, notorious for his arbitrariness in the 40's and 50's in Kamyshlag (Kemerovo region) (West Siberia—Ed.).

The head of the KGB Department at the Dubravnoye Camp Administration is Lieut.-Col. Blinov.

THE CASE OF THE BALTIC FLEET OFFICERS

["Uncensored Russia," Peter Reddaway. American Heritage Press, New York, 1972]

The time has come for the party to look people in the eye and revise its ways. If, however, all our methods of struggle give no positive result, then time will present the task of creating a new party, which, after a prolonged ideological struggle, will lead a socialist society to the triumph of Reason, Justice and Humanism, and enable Intellectual Freedom to flourish in our country... Russia is waiting for new people.

GENNADY GAVRILOV,
September 1968.

Without doubt this chapter contains some of the most dramatic material in the Chronicle. *The material is also of the greatest importance for gaining a clear view of some of the Democratic Movement's more radical components. But, tantalizingly, there is not yet enough of it. While it conjures up vivid images, their edges are blurred and they have yet to come fully into focus.*

One thing, however, is clear: Grigorenko and Altunyan are not isolated cases of military involvement in the Democratic Movement. Baltic Fleet Officers, linked with civilians and apparently operating mainly from Tallinn, the capital of Estonia, have injected a vigorous strain of their own constructive thought into the movement. Whether this will lead eventually to a top-level military involvement in politics, possibly one day a take-over, is too early to say. Such traditions are weak in Russia: the Decembrist officers were an exception in 1825. Nevertheless, the general phenomenon of army take-overs has spread through so much of the last two decades that the eventual infection of the Soviet military can by no means be ruled out. Who knows, indeed, whether Lieutenant Ilin, who apparently tried to assassinate the top party leaders in January 1969, represented only himself? Or did he come, as rumour had it, from some army group prepared—unlike the naval officers—to use terrorism in the tradition of the People's Will, the group which killed Alexander II in 1881?

The first indication that things were brewing in Tallinn came when two documents reached the West at the end of 1968. The first concerned the well-known essay by Academician Sakharov [not printed here], which he had circulated in final form in the summer. It was signed 'Numerous representatives of the technical intelligentsia of Estonia', a formula which left open the possibility—a likely one—that both Estonians and non-Estonians, both civilians and military people, were involved. The Chronicle *reported:*

Sakharov's study has evoked a response from representatives of the technical intelligentsia of Estonia. In an article entitled 'To Hope or to Act?' they maintain that Sakharov 'puts too much faith in scientific and technical means, in economic measures, in the goodwill of those who control society, and in people's common sense', and that 'the root causes he sees and the remedies he advocates are external, material ones, while the inner, spiritual, political and organic ones are ignored'. The article says that what we need most of all is a moral revival of society, since, 'having destroyed Christian values, the materialist ideology has not created new ones'. This has given rise to a society in which solidarity is an external, mechanical thing, and one which is actually based on socially alienated individuals who are fearful of their neighbours and feel insignificant and lonely before the state machine. New moral values are essential. The authors of the article demand not only intellectual freedom, but also political freedom, real democracy and a renunciation of the doctrine of militant, aggressive communism in foreign policy. The authors of the article conclude that the 'leading minds of our society' should apply themselves to working out new social, political and economic ideals.

This was a call for a political programme. The document had, moreover, put forward ideas somewhat more radical than the Chronicle's summary would suggest. Written soon after the Czechoslovak occupation, it warned: 'For twelve years already, since the 20th party congress, we have waited and asked our leadership for liberating reforms. We are prepared to ask and wait for a certain time longer. But eventually we will demand and act! And then tank divisions will have to be sent not into Prague and Bratislava, but rather into Moscow and Leningrad!'

As for foreign policy, "was it not our country which 'joined' to itself, in the period 1939–49, 700,000 square kilometers of territory . . . ? We must give up the senseless accumulation of territory, the expansion of our great-power might, and our aggressive policies . . . Since not just half but the greater part of the responsibility for the tension in the world lies with us, it is we who must make the first and biggest moves towards reconciliation.'

The second document—an 'Open Letter to the Citizens of the Soviet Union' dated September 1968 and signed 'Gennady Alekseyev, communist'—made various similar points from a more Marxist position, and provides the epigraph to this chapter.

Then, in October 1969, the Chronicle reported the appearance in samizdat of the 'Programme of the Democrats of Russia, the Ukraine, and the Baltic Lands':

This document gives an exhaustive analysis of the world revolutionary movement, the world national liberation movement, and the ideological state of the world. The positive programme set out in this document is extremely interesting.

Now written on this document is a second title: "Programme of the Democratic Movement of the Soviet Union". Maybe, therefore, in order to distance itself from this programme, and perhaps also to discourage particular groups from writing in the name of the movement as a whole, the Chronicle quickly added this note:

The tenth issue of the *Chronicle* gave a brief account of the "Programme [of the Democrats of Russia, the Ukraine and the Baltic Lands]". This account must be considered unsatisfactory. The analysis of the contemporary international situation and the socio-political picture of the world presented in the programme cannot of course be considered "exhaustive", as the tenth issue of the *Chronicle* rashly stated. The words "exhaustive analysis" smack of dogmatism. The problems of the modern world are *inexhaustible* in their variety and complexity, and they certainly cannot be exhausted by any one programme. The programme expresses the views only of a certain group of people.

Mostly likely, we may conclude, this perhaps small group wanted to circulate its programme under a rather presumptuous title precisely in order to stimulate debate and find out how acceptable it was to wider circles.

But which people made up this anonymous group, the only effectively underground one linked with the Democratic Movement? It seems likely that they were connected, either directly or indirectly, with the authors of the two earlier documents. For the programme—a long, 20,000-word work—develops in detail, often using similar terminology, the ideas of those documents. The mention of "the Baltic lands" is also suggestive. It was, in any case, the asked-for programme.

The latter is, unfortunately, too long to analyse here. But let us just note a few points: first, its militancy. One example of this is its epigraph, an unusual quotation from Alexander Herzen. It reads: 'Socialism will give rise in all its phases to extreme consequences, to stupidities. Then once again a cry of renunciation will burst forth from the titanic breast of the revolutionary minority, and once again a deadly struggle will begin, in which socialism will occupy the place of today's conservatism and will be conquered by an advancing revolution of which we do not know.' Secondly we should note the Programme's tendency to praise Western democracy, sometimes to the point of idealization. The authors—it appears to be the joint work of people who have specially researched different parts of it—come out clearly for a mixed economy not all that different in nature from the capitalist economies of Western Europe. This marks them off from almost all the other tendencies in the Democratic Movement, which in the rare cases when they discuss economics in depth, usually prefer various forms of market socialism. What also mark the group off are its evident exaggeration of the Movement's strength and its advocacy of underground as well as legal methods of struggle. In reviewing its two substantial documents of 1970 the Chronicle criticized it severely on these points, waiving its usual ban on value judgments.

Now, while bearing in mind that the Programme's authors quite possibly had no direct links with the Baltic Fleet officers arrested in 1969, we can pass to the Chronicle's coverage of their case. Despite the apparent inaccuracy of this coverage in one or two places, it is all presented here in the original sequences:

According to unconfirmed rumours, a number of officers of the Baltic Fleet have been arrested in Tallinn, Leningrad and Kaliningrad. Rumours suggest that the arrests were made in connection with the distribution of a letter by Alekseyev, addressed to the citizens of the Soviet Union, about the invasion of Czechoslovakia.

The report that the arrests of officers of the Baltic Fleet were connected with the letter by Alekseyev has been confirmed. The letter was a protest against the sending of troops into Czechoslovakia. According to information received, thirty-one people have been arrested in Estonia, not all of them officers. For example, in Tallinn an engineer, Sergei Soldatov, was arrested.* About a quarter of those arrested are Estonians. Although rumours, possibly spread by official circles, say that those arrested are members of a nationalist movement, materials circulating at present in Russian and Estonian *samizdat* are convincing proof that the opinions of the arrested people are generally democratic and anti-Stalinist, and that their demand for equal national rights is a logical part of their general system of thought. One of the arrested is a coastguard officer of the Baltic Fleet, Alekseyev.

ARRESTS OF OFFICERS OF THE BALTIC FLEET

Following inexact and partially contradictory reports of arrests of Baltic Fleet officers, the *Chronicle* is now publishing accurate information.

In May 1969 the naval officers Gavrilov, Kosyrev and Paramonov were arrested in Paldiski, a town near Tallinn, and in Kaliningrad [on the Baltic coast near Poland]. They are accused of founding a 'Union to Struggle for Political Rights', the aim of which was the realization in the U.S.S.R. of the democratic rights and freedoms guaranteed by the Universal Declaration of Human Rights. It is reported that during searches K.G.B. officials found a printing press intended for the publication of uncensored literature.

The investigation is being conducted by the K.G.B. organs of the Baltic Fleet. The investigators—Captain Bodunov, Major Drach and Colonel Denisenko—are officials of the K.G.B. and the Baltic Fleet Military Procuracy. The Procurator supervising the investigation is Kolesnikov.

The K.G.B. investigation organs are attributing the leading role and the 'Open Letter to the Citizens of the Soviet Union', signed by G. Alekseyev, a pseudonym, to Gavrilov. As far as can be ascertained, Gavrilov is holding firmly to his principles during investigation. Thanks to the testimony of Kosyrev, the K.G.B. have evidently reached the conclusion that the arrested men have connections with Leningrad, Moscow, Tallinn, Riga, Baku, Perm and Khabarovsk. It appears that Paramonov too is giving the investigators helpful testimony. The investigators are intent on discovering whether the arrested men had any connection with Ilya Gabai, who was arrested in Moscow in May 1969, and also with those citizens who have signed protests against violations of human rights in the U.S.S.R. The arrested officers are at present in the K.G.B. prison in Tallinn.

The unique documents in the next item presumably reached the Chronicle *through either a leak or a blunder in the K.G.B.:*

THE INVESTIGATION INTO THE CASE OF NAVAL OFFICER G. V. GAVRILOV AND OTHERS CONTINUES

On June 20th, 1969, a K.G.B. detective squad searched the flat of S. I. Soldatov in Tallinn. The search warrant, signed by Captain Bodunov, a senior investigator, indicated that citizen Olga Bondarenko had testified that Soldatov had been meeting a stranger in her flat. Confiscated during the search were personal correspondence with the Soviet writer V. M. Pomerantsev, the Declaration of Human Rights, poems called "Dream of Freedom" and "On the Death of Kennedy", extracts copied from *Confessions* of J. Rousseau, and a *samizdat* philosophical manuscript, *Man and the World.*

First interrogation. June 24th, 1969. In the Estonian K.G.B. headquarters, Pagari Street 2 [Tallinn], senior investigator A. Nikitin.

INVESTIGATOR. We should like to question you . . . *for the moment* as a witness.

SOLDATOV. In connection with which case am I being questioned?

INVESTIGATOR. You are being questioned in connection with the case of Gennady Vladimirovich Gavrilov and a group of Baltic Fleet officers charged with anti-Soviet activities. Are you often in Moscow?

SOLDATOV. That is irrelevant to the case under investigation.

INVESTIGATOR. Are you acquainted with Yakir?

SOLDATOV. I wish to state that I am not prepared to give you any information about my acquaintances or my spiritual life.

(There follows a lengthy explanation about how refusal to testify can be a criminal offence.)

SOLDATOV. If you have any material evidence against me, lock me up without my collaboration.

*Modification in No. 10: "It turns out that Soldatov has been forcibly interned in a psychiatric hospital."

INVESTIGATOR. We have a lot of evidence against you. You have had connections with these officers. We know that for certain.

SOLDATOV. Then draw up an indictment on the basis of that evidence.

(Soldatov is taken into another office.)

COLONEL BARKOV. You aren't an enemy of Soviet power?

SOLDATOV. I am an enemy of lawlessness.

BARKOV. Then why don't you assist the investigation, and confirm what is obvious? We know for sure that the accused Gavrilov got your address from Yakir and has been meeting you. Your obstinate refusal only increases our suspicions. Evidently you have some anti-Soviet peccadillos on your conscience and feel uncomfortable . . .

SOLDATOV. I've already said 'Lock me up without my help.'

BARKOV. We once interrogated and released a young man who had written an anti-Soviet poem. Later he started asking us to lock him up, if only for a year. Your vanity evidently makes you, too, aspire to appear a martyr.

SOLDATOV. I simply want to live my life as an honest man.

BARKOV. Then how are we to understand your attitude to Soviet law?

SOLDATOV. These laws are themselves imperfect and frequently conflict with human rights.

BARKOV. But Solon said: 'If laws are imperfect, then let the lawgiver's error be forgiven.' Think what sort of position you will put the worthy Captain Bondarenko in. After all, his daughter confirms that you have met the officers in her flat.

SOLDATOV. That's a matter for her conscience. I know what I myself am talking about.

BARKOV. Think of the fate of these young officers. One of them is already completely beyond your help, but you could ease the position of another of them . . .

SOLDATOV. I can't ease anyone's fate by going against my conscience.

BARKOV. Now that's simply cruel. How can you talk about human rights and struggle for them after saying that . . .

SOLDATOV. Well, then, I will confirm just the evidence of Bondarenko's daughter and the officers—if that will save someone.

(Soldatov confirms that he had met someone; he cannot remember the time, place, appearance or names; the conversation was on general topics and he had noticed nothing illegal.)

BARKOV. Why didn't you invite this person to your home?

SOLDATOV. My wife doesn't like having strangers in.

BARKOV. Did they give you any documents? Did they discuss with you the foundation of a 'Union of Fighters for Political Freedom' and the publication of a newspaper called the *Democrat*? Did you promise to get hold of type-metal? Do you know a document called 'To Hope or to Act?'?

(Soldatov answers each question in the negative.)

BARKOV. What is your political credo?

SOLDATOV. The government is obliged to listen to the opinions of dissenters, for the democratic intelligentsia, and to implement democratic freedoms, which it is not doing. (Signs record of interrogation.)

BARKOV. Whether you like it or not, the question of your relations with Yakir will inevitably be brought into the open.

SOLDATOV. That won't change my position.

BARKOV. You're evidently dissatisfied with our policy in Czechoslovakia?

SOLDATOV. I'm not thrilled to bits by it.

BARKOV. You'd like West Germany to send its troops there?

SOLDATOV. I would prefer not to have this sort of argument in a K.G.B. office. Goodbye.

Second interrogation. June 28th, 1969. In the Estonian K.G.B. headquaters, senior investigator A. Nikitin.

NIKITIN. What can you say about the letter to the party Central Committee signed by you and your comrades at the Leningrad Polytechnic Institute?

SOLDATOV. Only that the answer we got to it didn't satisfy us.

NIKITIN. Where did you get the exercise-book containing political notes?

SOLDATOV. I found it in a lecture-hall and kept it.

NIKITIN. Where did you get the *samizdat* philosophical manuscript?

SOLDATOV. I don't remember.

NIKITIN. Where did you get the poems 'Dread of Freedom' and 'On the Death of Kennedy'?

SOLDATOV. I refuse to answer.

NIKITIN. How did your correspondence with the writer Pomerantsev begin? Is he your friend?

SOLDATOV. Just an acquaintance. It was on my initiative. I have no other information to give. I protest against the illegal confiscation from me of materials not relevant to the case, including the Declaration of Human Rights.

NIKITIN. Address your protest to the Special Department of the Baltic Fleet. It's their instructions we're carrying out.

SOLDATOV. I am a civilian. My documents are irrelevant to the case of these officers.

NIKITIN. We decide whether they are relevant or not.

SOLDATOV. That's where the arbitrariness starts. Article 140 of the Russian Code of Criminal Procedure has been violated.

NIKITIN. But that sort of thing happened in the past. Things are different now.

SOLDATOV. What about the arrest of people for their beliefs, the confinement of healthy people in psychiatric hospitals?

NIKITIN. That question is decided by medical experts, not by us. We even help ex-political prisoners to find work.

SOLDATOV. Your charitable activities stare us in the face.

NIKITIN. We sent a couple of b——s to prison, and you're up in arms, kicking up a fuss for all the world to hear. What about the country's prestige? (A reference to Daniel and Sinyavsky.)

SOLDATOV. It's a question not of the nation but of principle. It's a matter of freedom of speech and artistic expression. Besides, one person who fights boldly for freedom is worth more than a million cowardly nonentities.

NIKITIN. Well that's as may be. It's all very abstract. But I still hope that you'll change your negative attitude to the K.G.B.

SOLDATOV. Even if you managed to convince me that you are observing legality at the moment, who will give a guarantee for the future?

NIKITIN. Of course, if the international situation becomes tenser, we will take steps against those who have been shooting at us(??).

(SOLDATOV signs an order forbidding him to leave Tallinn.)

Third interrogation. September 3rd, 1969. In the Special Department of the K.G.B. for the Baltic Fleet, Toompea Street 8, senior investigator Captain Bodunov.

BODUNOV. We are not satisfied with your evidence to the Estonian K.G.B. I hope you've seen sense.

(The records of the interrogation of the accused A. V. Kosyrev are now quoted: 'I asked him (Soldatov) to assist in the establishment of a "Union of Fighters for Political Freedom" and in the publication of a paper, the *Democrat*, to which he very willingly agreed . . . He also agreed to get hold of type-metal . . . His telephone number was obtained from Yakir . . .')

BODUNOV. What have you to say about that?

SOLDATOV. I can't remember any such conversation. We talked about general subjects.

BODUNOV. Have you known Yakir long?

SOLDATOV. Why are you so persistently interested in Yakir? As far as I know, he is a universally respected citizen who in legal ways defends human rights.

BODUNOV. But his personal friend I. Gabai has been arrested. I had a word with the investigator who interrogated him.* So he's not involved only in legal affairs.

SOLDATOV. I have nothing to say on that score. It's not clear why Kosyrev needed to meet me.

BODUNOV. He saw in you a fighter.

SOLDATOV. I hadn't deserved that.

BODUNOV. Right, wait in the next room.

(There follows a confrontation and an identification procedure, in the course of which Kosyrev identifies Soldatov and confirms his evidence about their conversation.)

BODUNOV (to Soldatov). What have you to say to that?

SOLDATOV. I consider the base and cowardly conduct of Kosyrev unworthy of an officer.

BODUNOV (slapping his hand on the table). I will not stand for any insinuations. You are sitting on a powder-keg which may explode at any moment.

* The investigation of Gabai's case was carried out by senior investigator B. I. Berezowsky of the Uzbek Procuracy [*Chronicle*'s note—pp. 136-40].

SOLDATOV (to Kosyrev). There exists the K.G.B.'s court, and also the court of your comrades and of history. To *that* court you will have to answer your whole life long.

BODUNOV. There's no 'K.G.B. court', only the Soviet People's Court.

SOLDATOV. There's also the court of conscience. It is important to remain honest in all circumstances.

BODUNOV. You and your honest conduct won't be strolling around freely much longer.

SOLDATOV. Experience shows that honest people have frequently lost their freedom and become political prisoners. Then they have been rehabilitated. I'd rather be rehabilitated than a swine and free . . . I request the opportunity to speak at the trial.

BODUNOV. Why?

SOLDATOV. In order to express my opinion about this case.

BODUNOV. In whose name? Who has authorized you? A Komsomol or trade union organization?

SOLDATOV. In the name of the democratic intelligentsia.

Fourth interrogation. In the Special Department of the Baltic Fleet. September 4th, 1969. Senior investigator Bodunov. (Confrontation with G. V. Gavrilov, the chief accused. Gavrilov does not recognize Soldatov.)

SOLDATOV. I demand to be allowed to take part in the coming trial.

BODUNOV. There is nothing for you to do there. You aren't helping in the search for the truth.

SOLDATOV (to Gavrilov). My name is . . . (gives his names). Remember that I shall always be glad to meet you. How can I help?

GAVRILOV. Perhaps we *will* meet. There's nothing I need.

Fifth interrogation. September 23rd, 1969. (Soldatov has been summoned to the Special Department of the Baltic Fleet, where he is awaited by K.G.B. Major Tikhonov and three men in white coats, headed by military doctor Petrenko. They turn out to be doctors from the Republic Psychiatric Hospital. The examination proceeds as follows:

'Were your parents ever sick?'—'No.'
Are you an only child?'—'Yes.'
'Did you start school at the normal age?'—'Yes.'
'What were you keen on at school?'—'Mathematics and sports.'
'Did you aspire to be a leader?'—'No.'
'Why did you leave secondary school at the age of eighteen instead of nineteen?'—'The war.'
'Why did you choose mechanical engineering?'—'I liked it.'
'Did you do well in your examinations?'—'Yes.'
'How did you choose your friends?'—'For their honesty and intelligence.'
'Why did you move to a different factory?'—'I changed my line.'
'Don't your work-mates envy you?'—'No.'
'What are your relations with your work-group?'—'Perfectly correct.'
'Ah, only "correct". Why not warm?'—'One can't make friends to order.'
'Don't you think you could make a technical breakthrough?'—'No.'
'Are your parents hard-hearted towards you?'—'No.'
'What made you marry your wife?'—'I liked her.'
'Have you ever had experience of unrequited love?'—'Yes.'
'Do you confide your views to your wife?'—'She judges me by what I do.'
'Is your wife content with you?'—'Ask her. Pick your questions more carefully.'
'Do you feel that life is hard and people are hard on you?'—'No.'
'Do you believe in the supernatural? In the hereafter?'—'Those are controversial questions.'
'Your favorite authors are . . . ?'—'Zweig, Dickens, Tolstoy.'
'Have you ever been to church?'—'I have.'
'When did you become interested in religious and moral problems?'—'When I learned to think.'
'Why are you interested in them?'—'Not everything in life is as it should be.'
'Why do you like Tolstoy?'—'He explores problems of human existence.'
'Your attitude to military service?'—'I haven't yet adopted a definite attitude to it, because it's peacetime.'
'What do you think of *Man and the World*, the manuscript found at your flat?'—'There's a lot I can't understand.'
'Where did you get it from?'—'From acquaintances.'
'What is your attitude to the sending of troops into Czechoslovakia?'—'Negative.'

'How should the question be settled?'—'Peacefully.'

'You wouldn't like to head a delegation at negotiations?'—'I'm not qualified in politics.'

'What do you think of Soviet policy?'—'To make an analysis you need information from both sides. I haven't got that.'

'Don't you consider yourself able to change the Soviet political system?'—'History is made by the masses.'

'Why have we gathered here for this conversation?'—'The K.G.B. is worried about my health.'

'Why is the K.G.B. interested in you?'—'Because of my inconvenient views and undesirable acquaintanceships.'

'Don't summonses to the K.G.B. embitter you?'—'I've got used to them.'

'Does the present situation embitter you?'—'At the moment I feel ashamed for the medical profession.'

'Have you ever had bumps on your head?'—'Yes, lots.'

'Why do you have that ironic smile all the time?'—'I'm enjoying this solemn ritual. It reveals your powerlessness.'

In early 1970 Soldatov was, despite his attempted self-defence through the courts, dismissed from his job, and two unnamed officers were arrested in Poland in connection with the Gavrilov case. In June Gavrilov, aged thirty-one was sentenced by a Leningrad military tribunal to six years in strict-régime camps, and Aleksei Vasilevich Kosyrev, twenty-eight, to two years. Georgy Konstantinovich Paramonov was consigned to the Chernyakhovsk prison hospital. The charges, under articles 70 and 72, concerned the formation by these naval engineer officers of a 'Union to Struggle for Political Rights'.

Twenty Years for the "Sins" of Their Fathers

Yury Shukhevich, the son of a general in the Ukrainian resistance, was sentenced to indefinite imprisonment at age fourteen, not because of anything he himself had done but simply because he was the son of his father. The same fate befell Pyotr Yakir, the son of a Jewish general executed by Stalin. Both men were released after serving twenty years in the camps. Both men are now back in the camp because of their continuing opposition to the Communist dictatorship.

Yury Shukhevich

Pyotr Yakir

THE CASE OF YURI GALANSKOV

The pathetic appeal addressed to the United Nations by Yuri Galanskov prior to his death in the camps in January 1973 appears on page 120 of the hearing. At the left top is a photo of Galanskov taken prior to his arrest. At the right top is another photo taken in prison. The photograph below shows Galanskov's injured wife, Olga, being carried from the trial of her husband by Pavel Litvinov (left) and Alexander Daniel (right), January 12th, 1968.

Yuri Galanskov   Yuri Galanskov

Wife, Olga Galanskov

Anatoly Marchenko
Author of "My Testimony"

Vladimir Bukovsky
Now serving twelve years for smuggling out documents on the
abuse of psychiatry for political terror

LEADERS OF THE SOVIET RESISTANCE

General Pyotr Grigorenko
Now fraudulently confined to a mental
institution

Dr. Alexander Trusnnovich
NTS leader kidnapped from Berlin by
Soviet agents

Ilya Bokshtein
See story on page 150

Natalya Gorbanevskaya
Russian poetess and resistance leader,
released from fraudulent mental
confinement last year—with a
chemically altered personality

Imprisoned Leaders of the Social Christian Resistance

Igor Igurtsov

Boris Talantov

Leonid Borodin

Levitin-Krasnov

Vyacheslav Platonov

Mikhail Sado

Imprisoned Jewish Resistance Leaders

Volf Zalmanson   Silva Zalmanson   Israel Zalmanson

Leib Khnokh   Vladimir Kukui   Aleksandr Galperin

IMPRISONED UKRAINIAN RESISTANCE LEADERS

Svyatoslav Karavansky

Valentyn Moroz

Vyacheslav Chornovil

Ivan Dzyuba

Boris Penson: "Self-Portrait"

ABOUT THE AUTHOR

The author, **Avraham Shifrin,** who was born in Minsk in 1923, lived in Moscow until 1941. There he was inducted into the Soviet Army and into active service in World War II. His father, Isaak Shifrin, had already been arrested for having told an anti-Stalin joke. He died after ten years imprisonment in a forced labor camp.

As the son, of a camp convict, Shifrin was assigned to a delinquint battalion. Wounded twice at the front, he was released from service as an officer. After the war, he studied law and became a legal advisor and attorney. He was arrested in 1953 and sentenced to death for anti-Soviet activities. His sentence was later commuted to 25 years camp imprisonment. Released after ten years' camp internment and four years' exile, Shifrin became an advocate of Soviet Jews wishing to emigrate to Israel. He was also active in the distribution of Leon Uris' novel, *Exodus,* in the Soviet Union. In 1970, he was permitted to emigrate to Israel, where he now lives. In his books, *The Fourth Dimension,* and *U.S.S.R. Labor Camps* (The Interrogation; Shifrin's testimony before a U.S. Senate committee), he describes his experiences in Soviet prison camps. He produced an 80-minute documentary film, *Prisonland* (Prison Country), on the persecution of non-conformist Soviet citizens. He has written numerous articles for newspapers and periodicals on the same subject.

Today, he is director of "The Research Center for Prisons, Psych-prisons, and Forced Labor Concentration Camps of the U.S.S.R."

The author welcomes correspondence.
Enquiries and gifts for the Underground Church may be sent to

CHRISTIAN MISSION TO THE COMMUNIST WORLD

IN USA:

P.O. Box 443
Bartlesville, OK 74005
U.S.A.